"Linguistic Symposium on Romance Languages".

Studies in

ROMANCE
LINGUISTICS

Proceedings of the Fifth Linguistic Symposium on Romance Languages

MICHIO PETER HAGIWARA

Department of Romance Languages
University of Michigan

NEWBURY HOUSE PUBLISHERS / ROWLEY / MASSACHUSETTS

Library of Congress Cataloging in Publication Data

Linguistic Symposium on Romance Languages, 5th,
    University of Michigan, 1975.
    Studies in romance linguistics.

    Bibliography: p.
    1. Romance languages—Congresses.   I. Hagiwara,
Michio P.   II. Title.
PC11.L53   1975   440   77-764
ISBN 0-88377-071-7

Cover design by Gillian P. Ingram

NEWBURY HOUSE PUBLISHERS, Inc.

 Language Science
Language Teaching
Language Learning

ROWLEY, MASSACHUSETTS 01969

Printed in the U.S.A.   First printing: April 1977
                                               5   4   3   2   1

FOREWORD

This book is a result of the Fifth Linguistic Symposium on
Romance Languages, held at The University of Michigan on
March 20-22, 1975. The conference was a continuation of the
tradition begun by the First Symposium held at the University
of Florida in 1971 and other symposia sponsored in subsequent
years by the University of Illinois, Indiana University, and
the University of Texas at Austin. Those who attended the
conference ranged from linguists of international reputation to
graduate students and language teachers studying or interested
in Romance languages and linguistics. The research papers
presented covered a wide spectrum of topics in synchronic,
diachronic, and comparative studies from structural as well as
generative-transformational points of view.
  The Symposium consisted of nine sessions, each with two to
four papers and a short time allotted for questions and
discussion after each presentation. In order to give as much
variety as possible, we did not adopt a central theme or group
the papers according to any set categories. Moreover, we
invited four scholars from among the best-known Romance
linguists to present lecture-length papers in two afternoon
sessions. The response to our announcement and call for papers
was enthusiastic and overwhelming. We received inquiries from
many colleges and universities throughout the country and from
abroad. A total of sixty-two abstracts were submitted to us,
and the task of the Selection Committee was indeed an arduous
one. Fifteen papers were eventually selected for presentation.

In order to encourage active audience participation in the discussions, individual papers were made available through preregistration to those who were interested in a particular linguistic area. This book represents all the papers given at the Symposium, some with a few editorial changes. The discussions following the papers were not recorded and therefore do not appear in the book. However, the written comments submitted by the panel members and audience after the evening session on contrastive analysis and applied linguistics have been included. It is hoped that the book will be a valuable resource for those interested in research in Romance linguistics.

As Coordinator for the Symposium, I am deeply indebted to Professor Allan F. Smith, Vice President for Academic Affairs, Professor Billy E. Frye, Dean of the College of Literature, Science and the Arts, and Professor Frank P. Casa, Chairman of the Department of Romance Languages and Literatures, who made the conference possible with their generous financial support. I also wish to thank Professors Servio T. Becerra, Lawrence B. Kiddle, Clifford S. Leonard, Raleigh Morgan, Ernst Pulgram, David L. Wolfe, and Mr. Jean-Jacques Thomas, the members of the Romance Linguistics Section of the Department of Romance Languages and Literatures, who also helped make it so successful. I am further grateful to Professor Mark G. Goldin of Indiana University, whose experience with previous conferences was a valuable resource in the preliminary planning of the Symposium. I express appreciation not only to Larry L. Dishman, Eugene A. Fong, Gladys Saunders, and Yves M. Verret who served as chairpersons for some of the morning sessions, but also to the following members of the Selection Committee who were responsible for the high quality of the papers presented: Professors Clifford S. Leonard, Lawrence B. Kiddle, and David L. Wolfe of The University of Michigan, Professor Jean Casagrande of the University of Florida, Professor William Cressey of Georgetown University, and Professor Mark Goldin of Indiana University.

This book was made possible by financial support from the Office of the Dean, College of Literature, Science and the Arts, the Horace H. Rackham School of Graduate Studies, and the Department of Romance Languages of The University of Michigan. I also wish to express my gratitude particularly to Professor Ernst Pulgram and Professor Lawrence B. Kiddle for their constant encouragement in the preparation of the Symposium and for the publication of its proceedings. Last but not least, thanks are also due to Judie Birdsall and Susan Morris who prepared the final camera-ready copy of the manuscript and Jeannette M. Ludwig and Arlene C. Malinowski for their careful and patient work in proofreading it.

Ann Arbor, Michigan   M.P.H.

November 1976

CONTENTS

viii Contents

studies in

ROMANCE LINGUISTICS

THE HEURISTICS OF SUBSTRATUM

DIETER WANNER

University of Illinois

1. Substratum as an historical explanation

As a special case of 'languages in contact', the hypothesis
of relevant substratum influence on the evolution of a
particular aspect of a language basically has the function
of explaining a change which appears *extraordinary* within
a theoretical framework embodying explanatory hypotheses
about the manner and causes of language change. The acceptance
of possible substratum influence represents a case of postulating an auxiliary hypothesis designed to save the core of a
theory (here the theory of 'normal' linguistic change).[1]
However, this substratum hypothesis presupposes the (implicit
or explicit) adoption of a framework specifying the conditions
and restrictions under which interlanguage penetration can take
place. The present paper will attempt to integrate the
substratum hypothesis into linguistic theory in such a way
that the hypothesis might come close to being testable on an
empirical level. The result will have mainly heuristic
significance in facilitating a separation of the meaningful
from the empty and/or spurious alleged substratum cases. This

1

differentiation is not unimportant, especially within Romance linguistics where a large number of characteristic sound changes[2] in the evolution of the various languages have been attributed to varied substratum causes. On a general level, there is a conspicuous absence of arguments which could crucially falsify the substratum hypothesis as well as of arguments which could yield convincing support to this same hypothesis. Thus, either historical linguists close their eyes to the whole problem complex, or they take a dogmatic stance on the issue. I would like to propose an alternative in the form of a reasoned answer.[3]

2. The substratum situation

For present purposes a substratum situation shall be characterized by a language shift away from the substratum language L(s) towards the target language L(t); L(s) and L(t) must coexist in effective bilingualism within the same community and within (at least some) individual speakers. Over a period of time L(t) will develop into the only means of communication and concomitantly L(s) will become extinct in that speech community. But during the period of bilingualism L(s) can exert such an influence on L(t) that a certain grammatical property X of L(s) (definable in terms of its grammar G(s)) is transferred to L(t) which in turn is thereby changed into L(t'), i.e. the target language as modified through the addition of property X.[4]

   The postulated period of bilingualism between L(s) and L(t) provides the factual (although not necessarily causal) link between the two languages, thus ruling out any achronological claims based on 'biological predispositions' or 'hereditary factors' responsible for the distortion of L(t) into L(t'). From cases of bilingualism described in the literature (cf. especially Weinreich 1953) it is clear that interference may take place in a natural way. This is evidenced by the phenomenon of second-language 'accent' where some properties of the native language are carried over into the target language; and also from the existence of pidgin and creolized languages which show a much more radical amalgamation of distinct languages. In the same way, regionalisms in the rendition of a standard language may be understood as interference problems on the basis of a non-identical dialect of the standard language. Thus the incipience of the substratum influence, namely the transfer of property X from L(s) to L(t), must be due to the same interference principle observable in modern bilingualism. The point which it leaves unanswered is the perpetuation of the interference product L(t') after the extinction of L(s): If L(s) is no longer used in the speech community, the original motivation for introducing the distorting property X into L(t) has ceased to exist. The answer must be provided on the basis of a framework which allows for ordered heterogeneity within a speech community (cf. Weinreich 1953 and Weinreich et al. 1968) in such a way that L(t') emerges as the relevant means of communication in the later stages of bilingualism and in the ensuing period of

renewed monolingualism after the language shift. But this
type of situation has never been monitored successfully to
my knowledge; thus it will not be possible to derive any
substantiation from this point of view. More importantly
for what concerns the Romance languages, the precise sociolinguistic conditions prevailing during and after the period
of postulated bilingualism are all but unrecorded. The
impossibility of this type of argumentation in trying to
support alleged substratum cases is well documented by the
unresolved cases (cf. Jungemann 1955 for an impressive list
of such cases). As a consequence I will concentrate on some
purely formal implications of the substratum hypothesis.
I will assume, for the sake of the argument, that from the
sociolinguistic point of view there exists the possibility
of substratum influence as described in this section.

3. Delimiting the linguistic characteristics of substratum

In order to give to the substratum hypothesis as much specificity as possible it is crucial to integrate it with the
main body of the theory of linguistic change. On this basis,
I will argue successively for four important characteristics
of any substratum situation: (a) the change which is claimed
to be due to substratum influence is equivalent to a (chain
of) change(s) which must be regarded as conceivable within
the framework of linguistic change *not* incorporating the
substratum hypothesis; (b) there must be a level of *compatibility* between G(s) and G(t) in terms of which it is possible
to talk about the transfer of a grammatical property X;
(c) the *grammatical material* susceptible to substratum
transfer is heavily limited in its nature; and (d) the *mode
of implementation* of a substratum-induced change is radically
different from any 'naturally' implemented change.

3.1. Evolutionary vs. mediated sociolinguistic change

For the first contention--any substratum-conditioned change
is equivalent to a purely evolutionary shift--it is important
to keep in mind that all three languages involved in a substratum situation, L(s), L(t), and their product L(t'), are
natural human languages. Thus the change from L(t) to L(t')
must also fall into the class of changes which is predicted
as conceivable by our theory of linguistic change.[5] This
means in turn that the change from L(t) to L(t') could have
occurred even in the absence of the particular alleged
substratum influence: the assumption of relevant substratum
in the explanation of this change is not crucial, but merely
incidental. The postulate that the addition of the property X
to L(t), resulting in L(t'), is due in principle to a conceivable evolutionary change is a heuristic move: if the
substratum hypothesis is complementary to the theory of normal
evolutionary change in such a way that the two classes of
envisaged changes do not overlap, it will follow that the
observation of any change not included under evolutionary
change must lead to the postulation of substratum influence

in such a case regardless of whether there is any independent evidence for this or not; i.e. we are forced to postdict the existence of a substratum language. This is untenable since it amounts to making the theory of evolutionary change unfalsifiable and thus useless.[6] If on the other hand substratum-induced and normal evolutionary changes are (partially or fully) overlapping, then the substratum hypothesis loses its relevance altogether as an explanatory principle of linguistic change: a given change could be due to substratum influence, but nothing crucial hinges on this hypothesis since the same change is also interpretable as a normal evolutionary change.[7] Thus it seems preferable at least on the heuristic level to equate the possible effects of substratum influence with conceivable evolutionary change and to deny any generalized function to the substratum hypothesis. The initially mentioned apparent motivation for postulating substratum, the extraordinary character of a sound change, cannot be regarded as valid since the superficially extraordinary has now been recognized as another form of the ordinary, i.e. evolutionary change.

As an illustration of this point consider the case of Castilian $f > h$.[8] The elimination of phrase-internal intervocalic f has been attributed to a Proto-Basque substratum for what concerns its occurrence in Castilian and Gascon. The fact that a strikingly similar change $f > h$ is also documented (although less well studied) for some dialects of Northern Italy, Calabria (Southern Italy), and Sardinia would make it mandatory under an explanatory interpretation of the substratum hypothesis to postulate substratum influence for all three new cases in addition to the Proto-Basque assumption for Castilian and Gascon. Yet there is no foundation for a claim to this effect. By not attributing any explanatory function to the substratum hypothesis, on the other hand, this problem does not arise: a change $f > h$ under the relevant environmental conditions (possibly as a metachronic correspondence) is subsumed under evolutionary change; the only task is to evaluate the relevance of the alleged Proto-Basque influence for Castilian and Gascon, as debated recently by Naro vs. Rivarola (1972).

3.2. Level of compatibility

There is presumably general agreement on the contention that evolutionary linguistic change is not simply a change in the surface forms of a language, but rather a change in the principles accounting for these surface forms, i.e. in the grammar. Thus the grammars of L(t) and L(t') are compatible with each other through the mediation of the theory of conceivable historical change. This means that G(t) is constituted in such a way that it presents structures at some point in the derivation which are affected directly by the change consisting in the formal equivalent of what I call here 'property X'; as a consequence the corresponding output structures in L(t') are observably different from those in L(t). Since in the claimed substratum case

property X is defined in terms of the grammar of the substratum
language L(s), it follows (in conjunction with the first
argument) that there must be a level of compatibility not
only between G(t) and G(t'), but also between G(s) and G(t').
Only in this way can property X be transferred from L(s) to
L(t). The implication of this argument is that only a
restricted class of grammatical properties can possibly be
transferred; substratum change cannot just be the transmission
of *any* aspect of L(s); it is necessarily constrained by the
articulation of language into different kinds of principles
and elements accounting for the surface forms in the language.

   Looking again at the *f* ⪼ *h* case for an illustration, it
is possible to describe property X as a Proto-Basque language-
specific grammatical principle which states that all [+anter-
ior, -coronal] segments are either [-continuant] if L(s)
had no [f] or [Φ], or [-strident] if it had no [f] but did
have [Φ]. This phonetic redundancy statement could equally
well be implanted in L(t), thereby eliminating [f] and
substituting for it the available most closely associated
surface segment ([p] or [pʰ] or [Φ]). In another case, Izzo
(1972, esp. 173-5) has shown that the *gorgia toscana* (the
change of phrase-internal intervocalic voiceless stops to
fricatives, *p, t, k* → *Φ, θ, h*) cannot be due to alleged
Etruscan substratum. This specific substratum claim is
vitiated by many other flaws, but it also offers an example
of the violation of the compatibility condition. First, the
phonetic property of fricativization (in intervocalic or any
other position) is not what is found in Etruscan: here it
is rather aspiration of stops, if the Etruscan symbols
resembling Greek aspirate letters mean anything. Second,
these 'aspirates' are definitely not restricted (in their
orthographic distribution) to the environments demanded by
the Tuscan result. In other words, there is no grammatical
compatibility between the two phenomena.

3.3. Type of material transferred

Due to the requirement of a level of compatibility between the
two languages L(s) and L(t) there arises the need to specify the
range of phonological properties which can be (or conversely,
cannot be) transmitted. The property X must be observable as a
transparent surface effect, whether the property X ultimately
depends on some more elaborate phonological principle or exhausts
itself in a mere surface formulation (e.g. blocking of a specific
phonetic segment or the like). It is possible to be more specific:
assuming a standard framework (cf. Chomsky and Halle 1968, ch.8)
the phonological component consists of: (a) phonological rules,
(b) allophonic distribution statements (unless they are subsumed under (a)[9]), (c) ordering statements of some of these
rules, (d) possible underlying forms (in terms of their
segments in isolation and their sequencing), (e) possible
surface segments (again in terms of isolated sounds and
their cooccurrence restrictions), and (f) the lexicon as the
basis of repository of all these principles. There is a
qualitative difference between the principles (b) and (e) on

the one hand vs. (a), (c), and (d) on the other: whereas
the first group encompasses those principles making statements
about the phonological forms which must be inherently true
in all cases (they act as filtering devices to assure well-
formedness), the second group can be contradicted by exceptions
of all types at different levels of the derivation. The
always-true principles have an independent status for the
language in question, they define its phonetic level in the
form of generalizations about all the strings of the language;
the not-always-true principles on the other hand depend on the
content and the structure of the lexicon of this language: the
phonological rules and their ordering interaction (if any) are
basically the expression of the relationship between alternating forms of specific lexical items. Since in the normal
historical substratum case the two languages in contact are
for all practical purposes genetically unrelated, this implies
that in the transition from L(s) to L(t) the lexicon pertaining
to L(s) is given up and replaced with the unrelated lexicon
of L(t). The transferrable material in substratum situations
cannot belong to the class of lexicon-based phonological
properties, but only to the more restricted set of always-true
statements. Therefore, only allophonic distribution statements, surface restrictions on allowable segments, and surface
restrictions on allowable segment sequences (= syllable structure conditions) may partake in the interference between L(s)
and L(t).

An interesting case of the transfer of an allophonic
distribution statement from G(s) to G(t) is Celtic Lenition
= Romance Intervocalic Voicing (Martinet 1952). The compatibility condition is met at the shallow level of phonological
derivation in the form of a process which basically weakens
any phrase-internal intervocalic consonant by one degree on
a strength parameter. Later restructurings, due to different
subsequent changes in Celtic and Proto-Romance, produce the
distribution patterns now found (or reconstructible) in the
two language groups. Property X in this case would be a
principle which can only be stated in non-orthogonal features
as a single process. Both Celtic and Proto-Romance would
have presented the relevant cases for an automatic/allophonic
application of such a rule.

In substratum cases where genetically closely related
languages L(s) and L(t) are involved, e.g. dialects of one
language, it should also be the case that some lexically
based phonological properties may be transferred (as long as
the level of compatibility is met). This can be seen e.g. in
the Swiss rendition of Standard German: both Swiss German
and Standard German utilize umlaut to mark some nominal
plurals. Its occurrence is not predictable on purely phonological grounds in either dialect. Whereas Standard German
has sg. [hunt] vs. pl. [hundə] 'dog', Swiss German dialects
show umlaut: sg. [hund] vs. pl. [hünd]. Now in regional
Swiss Standard German the item frequently appears as sg.
[hund] vs. pl. [hündə]; and similarly for a number of diverg-
ing items. Property X here is identifiable with a specification of the range of applicability of the umlaut rule in

nominal plural formation, a property which is clearly based
on the lexicon. But it might be more appropriate to term this
type of interference lexical borrowing rather than a transfer
of phonological property.

Overall, the restrictions on the possible grammatical
content of property X define a set of changes which is either
a proper subset of the historical changes conceivable within
the theory of language change or at the most coextensive
with the evolutionary changes, depending on how restrictively
the theory is formulated.

3.4. Mode of implementation

Recent investigations into the mode of implementation of a
sound change have brought to light the fact that the notion
of abrupt change is inadequate to describe the trajectory of
closely monitored changes in progress (cf. the lexical
diffusion hypothesis of Wang 1969, Cheng and Wang 1970, Chen
1972; and the studies done by Labov 1972:ch.2, 7 with
heterogeneous speech communities). According to these findings sound change spreads gradually through the susceptible
lexical items in such a way that categorical phonological
delimitation of the class of items which have undergone the
change vs. the class which has not undergone it (yet) is
not exhaustively feasible at any point in the evolution.
Changes induced by substratum are different in this respect
since they are implemented in globo at one point in the
history of L(t). Thus it must be impossible to observe in
any substratum case a period of variant application of a
phonological principle; the change from L(t) to L(t') in
the bilingual setting with L(s) must be a qualitative leap.

Due to the crucial extralinguistic setting of bilingualism,
L(t') springs into existence as a result of imperfect learning
of L(t) by speakers of L(s). The retention of property X
in the rendition of L(t) is comprehensible if property X
represents a defining characteristic of L(s) belonging to the
class of always-true phonological principles as pointed out
above. These phonological principles constitute a relative
standard of unavoidability applicable to phonetic surface
manifestations; whatever the property X may be in specific
terms, it is an automatic aspect of the phonetic level of L(s).
The imperfection of the learning process is motivated in terms
of the properties of L(s), and the imperfect learning process
is in a certain sense the extension of the situation of the
native language learning process according to Stampe where
a speaker may fail to unlearn a natural process: here, the
natural process on the universal level is replaced by the
automatic process natural in relation to the basis of experience, i.e. to L(s). In this way the production difficulty
associated with L(t) which is characterized by the absence of
property X is attributed (wrongly) also to L(t). The goal
in this imperfect learning is however only achieved if the
automatic status of property X is preserved in L(t): if
there were only a variable implementation of this principle,
the situation would have been complicated since the residual

class of items which do not conform to it must be defined,
and the original problem (absence of property X in surface
forms of L(t)) still subsists. In other terms, substratum
changes are substitution changes, a characteristic which has
always been well known.[10]

The substitution change interpretation cannot be maintained
for the *gorgia toscana* since there is sufficient documentation
to see the change setting in gradually, affecting first only
k sometimes, later generalizing to all cases of *k* and spreading
to *p* and *t* in some dialects over a few centuries (from XVI
on; cf. Izzo 1972:173-4). The situation for *f >h* is almost
unreconstructible since its period of implementation antedates
the documentary tradition of Castilian or Gascon (before IX).
And even when the documents set in they show a highly blurred
picture due to the cultist pressures of the literary tradition
which could at least partially restore orthographic *f* for the
etymologically unquestionably recognizable items containing
f in Latin. In Gascon the modern dialects show a somewhat
more consistent absence of *f*, but the documentary tradition
is less rich than in Castilian. In a similar way, in practically all accessible alleged substratum claims in Romance
languages the conditions of implementation of the change are
beyond observation or reconstruction. Negatively, this condition on the mode of implementation of a change is able to
exclude at least some claims: the irregular appearance of
intervocalic voicing in Tuscan dialects (Lt. *LACU >*It. *lago*,
but Lt. *FOCU >*It. *fuoco*) can only mean that here Celtic
Lenition was not directly taken over from a substratum population, but at best that the voicing process was imported on
a sporadic basis.

The importance of this qualitative difference between
substratum and normal evolutionary change lies in the fact
that it yields a means of distinguishing through observation
between the two types of change by focusing on the available
evidence for their implementation through time. Unfortunately,
this demarcation criterion is not applicable to most of the
alleged substratum cases in Romance due to the lack of pertinent direct or indirect testimony about the period of bilingual contact between native speakers of Latin and native
speakers of a substratum language.

4.   The function of the substratum hypothesis

The initial impression that it is the function of the substratum hypothesis to (help) explain extraordinary cases of
language change must be revised: the changes in relation to
which this hypothesis could possibly be relevant are a subset
of the conceivable evolutionary changes; also, the substratum
hypothesis cannot explain any change in its own right. If
the substratum hypothesis is to have function at all it must
be in connection with the actuation problem of change:
although a certain change is implemented only at time *t*(x),
it would have been linguistically possible that it appeared
in the language from time *t*(x-n) on (i.e. the structures
defining the necessary predisposition for the particular

change existed since an earlier time). Can the substratum
hypothesis be regarded as a possible answer to the question of
what circumstances set some sound changes in motion? This
seems to be logically possible, always under the condition
that the relevant requirements on the linguistic situation of
the substratum interference are fulfilled. But in order to
prevent this revised substratum actuation hypothesis from
degenerating into an all-inclusive form--postulating an
unidentified substratum influence for each case of unexplained
actuation (cf. above the strong version of the substratum
hypothesis providing a mechanism for postdicting substratum
influence)--it must be the case that such a claim always be
regarded as exceptional: it is made possible in any given
instance due to some fortunate circumstance of historical
documentation, and it cannot assume a logical status different
from that of a coincidence of historical events. On the
theoretical level, the substratum (actuation) hypothesis
belongs to the realm of historical investigation; this field
is bound, by the nature of its data, to the *elucidation of
specific situations* of the social sphere. On the other hand,
diachronic linguistics as part of the effort to explain the
domain of the non-trivially restricted and species-constant
human linguistic capacity must operate within a *theoretical*
(=general) framework; thus only hypotheses which allow
coherent and meaningful generalizations can play a part in it.
The substratum hypothesis can only be relevant in the case of
singular statements; its effect is to dissolve a potentially
interesting problem for the theory of linguistic change into
an historical accident, shifting the problem away from L(t)
and L(t'), throwing it back to L(s), and not solving it for
what concerns the appearance of property X in L(s). A well-
supported substratum case amounts to not more than an incidental correction of the historical picture for a given
language L(t). That this is not an explanation can be appre-
ciated by considering the fact that the explanation for this
change on the linguistic level must be given in terms of the
notion of compatibility, i.e. by describing what the
influence of L(s) on L(t) was and how it could be transmitted.

5. Heuristic considerations

As must have been expected from the beginning, the result is
mainly negative. Although substratum influence appears to
be a phenomenon which has a theoretically deduced place in
historical linguistics. On a heuristic level, I would nevertheless see two positive contributions which the foregoing
considerations can make. First, if these speculations are
not invalidated by some basic flaws, they offer a means of
distinguishing between those cases where the invocation of the
substratum hypothesis can be regarded as meaningful vs. those
where one or more of its tenets are violated. This is not an
overwhelming contribution, but for those of us who run into
the problem of deciding between entering into arguments with
respect to some alleged case of substratum influence, or

rather not, it might provide some guidance. Secondly, and more importantly, if this picture drawn of substratum interference is in any way approaching reality, it must be possible to find cases where the prediction of the sudden implementation of a substratum-conditioned change can be observed. In the case of a positive result in connection with a number of well-monitored cases it would amount to the confirmation of an interesting bipartition on the typology of linguistic change, and to a reliable diagnostic test for any instance of meaningful substratum influence.

NOTES

[1]Cf. Lakatos 1970 for these terms and their function in constructing theories. Obviously, the alternative is to modify the core of the theory. The neogrammarian 'sound laws' plus 'analogy' are another case of saving the core through the introduction of an auxiliary hypothesis. In both cases, substratum and analogy, the problem set degenerated rapidly, however, without eliminating the responsible hypotheses altogether.

[2]I will restrict myself to a specification of the mechanism for phonological substratum influence which is by far the most widely researched and discussed field of investigation. Specifically, I am not interested in this context in the instances of lexical substratum traces; lexical borrowing cannot be disputed in any diachronic framework. On the other hand, syntactic substratum influence is not sufficiently sharply formulable to warrant discussion here.

[3]The lack of conclusive arguments establishing a specific substratum claim as valid on the one hand, and on the other the existence of a number of conclusive rejections of interpretations invoking substratum influence (cf. Izzo 1972), does not invalidate the hypothesis as a whole. Rather, this asymmetry is due to the logical impossibility of conclusive proof (either of a theory or of any specific hypothesis) as opposed to the sufficiency of one falsifying argument to destroy any specific claim.

[4]Property X will be regarded here as a variable ranging over positive and negative values, i.e. the addition of property X to $G(t)$, for instance, can refer to the elimination of a surface segment from $L(t)$ under the influence of its absence from $L(s)$; or it could be used for the addition of an allophonic distribution principle present in $G(s)$ but absent from $G(t)$.

[5]I am not making any specific claims about the naturalness of the conceivable changes delimited by the theory of linguistic change. A theory of conceivable change, including changes which in deeper analysis are metachronic correspondences, is

admittedly weak. But a stronger version of the theory,
one which distinguishes between 'natural' and 'unnatural'
changes, does not seem feasible to me at this point.
Ultimately, even the theory of conceivable changes must be
reducible to naturalness restrictions.

[6] Such a framework has been described in an unpublished
earlier version of a paper by Vennemann (1969) where he
applied it to the first consonant shift of Germanic.
Although he rejected it before its appearance, it is interesting to note that this position has been proposed in the
generative transformational framework. I do not wish to
attribute this view to V.; rather I take the responsibility
for resuscitating it here on myself.

[7] There are two forms of this assumption: in a weak
version, it is claimed that any alleged substratum case has
a correspondence in a chain of evolutionary changes where it
may be necessary to interpolate crucial intermediate steps;
its stronger version, that to each substratum change there is
a corresponding evolutionary change in one step, is probably
false. Even in well-controlled evolutionary changes, due to
specific situations of documentation, it is frequently
necessary to postulate unattested intermediate stages. The
present studies on sound changes in progress (e.g. Labov 1972,
ch.2) illustrate the causes for the need, and provide the
justification for the postulation of such interpolations.

[8] For a collection of opinions about the relevance of
substratum influence in this evolution, cf. Jungemann 1955;
some of the more important sources and discussions are found
in Menéndez Pidal 1950:198-233; Doman 1969; Penny 1972;
Naro 1972; Rivarola 1972. The inadequate representation of
this change as $f > h$ is kept here only for its commonly
understood referential value, but it is not intended to state
the change accurately.

[9] The difference between (a) phonological rules, and (b)
allophonic distribution statements is not clearly made in
the standard framework on a qualitative level; however in
certain developments based on the standard framework, i.e.
'natural' versions of it, this distinction is central. For
NGG e.g. it is the opposition between 'via-rules' and phonological process (cf. Stampe 1969). In the SPE framework,
the difference is secondary and relies on the fact that the
phonological rules (here = (a)) may have exceptions of
different type and tend to be much more heavily ordered with
respect to other rules than the more shallow, transparent
allophonic rules.

[10] Variable rules of G(s) present a different problem: if
they can be transferred as property X to G(t) they would
superficially contradict the hypothesis postulated here since
as variable rules their surface effect in L(t) would necessarily be identical to that of a gradually implemented phonological rule. On a second level of analysis, however, the
sudden implementation of property X would still be true: the
variable rule could only be implemented in L(t') by the

native speaker of L(s) with the same applicability conditions
which characterize the rule in L(s). The qualitative leap
would be less abrupt (not from zero to 100 percent but from
zero to any intermediary degree according to the situation in
L(s) in all applicable cases in L(t)), but it would still rule
out the slow emergence of this alternation process from an
idiosyncracy of a few items through larger and larger sets
until it reached completion. Moreover, a variable rule of
highly reduced applicability, one which is still in its
inception in L(s), could not constitute a phonetic principle
defining an important surface aspect of L(s) such that it
could fall under the teleological motivation for the transfer
of material from G(s) to G(t): the production difficulty
due to the regular presence of A in context X - Y and of ·B
in W - Z (but not vice versa) simply does not exist for the
(still) variable allophonic rules.

REFERENCES

Chen, Matthew. 1972. The time dimension: contribution
     toward a theory of sound change. Foundations of language
     8:4.457-98.
Cheng, C.C. and W.S.-Y. Wang. 1971. Tone change in Chaozhou
     Chinese: A study in lexical diffusion. POLA 12, CW 1-21.
Chomsky, Noam and Morris Halle. 1968. The sound pattern of
     English. New York: Harper and Row.
Doman, Mary G. 1969. *H* aspirada y *F* moderna en el español
     americano. Thesaurus 24.426-58.
Izzo, Herbert J. 1972. Tuscan and Etruscan. Toronto:
     University of Toronto Press.
Jungemann, Frederick H. 1955. La teoría del sustrato y los
     dialectos hispano-romances y gascones. Madrid: Gredos.
Labov, William. 1972. Sociolinguistic patterns. Philadel-
     phia: University of Pennsylvania Press.
Lakatos, Imre. 1970. Falsification and the methodology of
     scientific research programmes. Criticism and the growth
     of knowledge, ed. by I. Lakatos and A. Musgrave, 91-196.
     Cambridge: University Press.
Martinet, André. 1952. Celtic lenition and Western Romance
     consonants. Language 28.192-217.
Menéndez Pidal, Ramón. 1950. Orígenes del español. 3rd ed.
     Madrid: Espasa-Calpe.
Naro, Anthony J. 1972. On '*f>h*' in Castilian and Western
     Romance. Zeitschrift für romanische Philologie 88.435-47,
     459-62.
Penny, Ralph J. 1972. The re-emergence of /f/ as a phoneme of
     Castilian. Zeitschrift für romanische Philologie 88.463-82.
Rivarola, José Luis. 1972. Sobre *F>H* en español. Zeitschrift
     für romanische Philologie 88.448-58.

Stampe, David. 1969. The acquisition of phonetic representation.
    Papers from the Fifth Regional Meeting of the Chicago
    Linguistic Society, ed. by R. I. Binnick et al., 433-44.
Vennemann, Theo. 1969. Historical Germanic phonology and the
    theory of marking. Unpublished mimeo. University of
    California, Los Angeles.
_____. 1973. Phonological concreteness in natural generative
    grammar. Towards tomorrow's linguistics, ed. by C. J. Bailey
    and R. Shuy. Washington, D.C.: Georgetown University Press.
Wang, S. S.-Y. 1969. Competing changes as a cause of residue.
    Language 45.9-25.
Weinreich, Uriel. 1953. Languages in contact. The Hague:
    Mouton.
_____, W. Labov and M.I. Herzog. 1968. Empirical foundations
    for a theory of language change. Directions for historical
    linguistics, ed. by W. P. Lehmann and Y. Malkiel, 95-195.
    Austin: University of Texas Press.

THE AUXILIARY IN ROMANCE

FREDERICK B. AGARD

Cornell University

Not long ago, while endeavoring to develop a formal basis for
contrastive Romance morphosyntax, I came upon a paper by the
late Professor José Pedro Rona, entitled 'Tiempo y aspecto:
análisis binario de la conjugación española.'[1] Although this
hoary taxonomic problem of tense and aspect might bear more
detailed reviewing, I will spare the reader and will limit
preliminaries to outlining the notions brought from my
training in structural linguistics and my brief ventures
into generative grammar (e.g. Agard 1969), and to summarizing
those of Rona.

   The structuralist in me had rejected the traditional grammarian's inclusion of 'have' + participle periphrases among
the fourteen-odd Romance 'tenses'.[2] For the structuralist the
so-called 'perfect tenses' were not only phrasal structures
but they repeated the self-same battery of tense-inflections
on the auxiliary verb. Moreover, tense was held to be a
morphological, i.e. inflectional, category; had not tradition
also made the blunder of calling English *shall/will* + verb
the future 'tense'? In Classical Latin, not only tense but
also aspect and mood and voice were all inflectional, in a

14

symmetrical network of oppositions;[3] and although there was
no way to claim that voice was inflectional in Romance, mood
clearly enough was and it seemed as though aspect must be
too, at least residually, underlying as it surely did the
preterite-imperfect contrast seen in Spanish (Sp) *cantó* ≠
cantaba. If that contrast was indeed aspectual, then that
between the simple tense and the perfective phrase with 'have'
(Sp *cantó* ≠ *ha cantado*) could not also be aspectual; and
whatever it was called, there was the equivalent of 'be'
+ gerund (*está cantado*) also to be put in the same category.
Pedagogically I was content to label these periphrases as
'completive' and 'progressive' phrases or (later on) 'cores'.[4]
However, as for the inflectional system proper, it seemed
unfeasible to separate aspect from tense from mood morphemi-
cally--in *cantara*, for instance, what segment signals past
tense and what segment signals subjunctive mood?--and hence
to avoid a single inflectional system with seven mutually
exclusive 'tense/mood' morphemes, relegating the 'aspectual'
difference between the imperfect (indicative) and the preterite to the realm of semantics. During a subsequent struggle to adapt that rather uninteresting seven-tense/mood
system into a generative framework embodying the notion of
an auxiliary (AUX) as one immediate constituent of a sentence,
and at the same time to establish a common base for a
contrastive study of any two or more of the Romance languages,
an adverse reaction to Rona's thesis furnished me with a
needed impetus. Rona was flaunting tradition by claiming
that Spanish, uniquely among the Romance languages, instead
of expressing tense inflectionally and aspect periphrastically,
does just the opposite. The error of the old way, he asserts,
was the opposing of *ha cantado* 'has sung' to *cantó* 'sang'
instead of to *canta* 'sings', and of *va a cantar* 'is going to
sing' to *cantará* 'will sing' instead of to *canta* 'sings'. Thus
he offers us the paradigm seen in 1, with tense on the horizontal axis and aspect on the vertical.[5]

(1)   TIEMPO

	Atemporal	Retrospectivo		Simultáneo		Prospectivo	
A	canta	ha		está		va	
S	cantaba	había		estaba		iba	
P	cantó	hubo		estuvo		fue	
E	cantara	hubiera	cantado	estuviera	cantando	fuera	a cantar
C	cantará	habrá		estará		irá	
T	cantaría	habría		estaría		iría	
O	cante	haya		esté		vaya	
	cantase	hubiese		estuviese		fuese	

Rona fails to label his tense-oppositions any more simply
than we see. His positing of the first column as 'atemporal'
--i.e. 'timeless' or, in a more contemporary sense, 'unmarked
as to time', is valid enough for a start--certainly all but

the item *cantó* express variable correlations between the 'now'
of the utterance and that of the verbal act or state.   But
his horizontal analysis seems to lose cogency when we take
into account two other realities:
    a.   the perfectly viable co-occurrence of Retrospective
and Simultaneous, as in *ha estado cantando* 'has been singing',[6]
or of Retrospective and Prospective as in *ha ido a cantar* 'has
gone to sing';[7] in other words the embarrassing co-occurrence
of two implicitly mutually exclusive tenses;
    b.   the non-admissibility of all but the first two items
in the Prospective column, for the reasons made clear in (2),
which demonstrates that underlying the surface use of *ir* +
a + infinitive are two different verbal structures: one
is semantically equivalent to English 'go (to)...', involving
the feature [locomotion], and the other to English 'be going
to (=/gónə/)...', involving the feature [expectation], and
negatively specified for [locomotion].[8]

(2)	a.	Yo voy a cantar.	j.	Yo voy a venir.
	b.	Yo iba a cantar.	k.	Yo iba a venir.
	c.	Yo fui a cantar.	l.	*Yo fui a venir.
	d.	Yo iré a cantar.	m.	*Yo iré a venir.
	e.	Yo iría a cantar.	n.	*Yo iría a venir.
	f.	Yo he ido a cantar.	o.	*Yo he ido a venir.
	g.	...para ir a cantar	p.	*...para ir a venir
	h.	...yendo a cantar	q.	*...yendo a venir
	i.	¡Vé a cantar!	r.	*¡Vé a venir!

In other words 2a, b are perfectly ambiguous out of context,
meaning either 'I go (and) sing', i.e. [+locomotion -expecta-
tion], or 'I am going to sing', i.e. [-locomotion +expecta-
tion]; while in 2c-i the *ir* part can only be interpreted as
[+locomotion].   On the other hand the *ir* of 2j, k can be read
only as [+expectation] whenever the following verb itself
involves either [locomotion] in the opposite direction
(*venir, entrar, salir*...) or [state] (*amar, pensar,
existir*...).   And finally 2 l-r are anomalous because the *ir*
which has to be read as [+locomotion] and the following verb
which specifies either [+locomotion] in a different direction
or else [+state -locomotion] simply make an infelicitous
collocation.[9]
    Once Rona's horizontal axis is bent, there is perhaps not
much point in scrutinizing the further two-dimensional aspect
matrix which he provides for any one of the vertical columns.
Let us glance at it nonetheless, in 3:

(3)   ASPECTO

                    Real   Virtual

        Imperfectivo Perfectivo Hipotético Dubitativo

Permansivo   canta   cantó   cantará   cante
Impermansivo   cantaba   cantara   cantaría   cantase

Again the Perfectivo/Impermansivo *cantara* 'had sung' seems
simply dragged in to make the matrix symmetrical; the form
cantara as the semantic equivalent of *había cantado* is definitely archaizing not to say obsolete in present-day standard
Spanish, and is vigorously competing with, not to say
encroaching on, *cantase*.

Be that as it may, Rona's conclusions are two.

First conclusion: Aspects can be neutralized, but tenses
cannot--in other words neutralizations can occur in the
vertical (e.g. between *cantara* and *cantase* or between *canta*
and *cantará* or *cantaba* and *cantaría*) but never in the horizontal as between *cantó* and *ha cantado*. Says he: 'No podemos
en ningún contexto sustituir una forma simple por su corres-
pondiente compuesta, ni una forma compuesta por otra, sin
provocar alteración del significado.' But as I understand
this, it is simply not true because in certain contexts
there is perfectly viable neutralization of *canta* and *va a
cantar* or of *cantaba* and *iba a cantar*, of *canta* and *está
cantando* or of *cantaba* and *estaba cantando*.

Second conclusion: A tense can constitute a subclass of an
aspect, or vice versa. Although this second conclusion fails
to strike me as particularly useful, Rona's entire thesis
and its evident shortcomings have nevertheless caused me to
try once again rethinking the tense/aspect question for
Spanish and indeed for all the Romance languages. The
results of this rethinking are, for the moment, the following.

We may start from the premise that all languages have an
element that is essential to every Sentence. This indispensable prime constituent, which alone makes a Sentence a
Sentence, has been seen by traditional grammar as a 'finite
verb'; by transformational-generative (T-G) grammar as a
smaller unit which it designates as the AUX. Abiding by this
latter concept, we may ask what form-classes, in Spanish,
fill this AUX function. The verb in a Sentence always carries
a P(erson)/N(umber) suffix, but this is merely the sign of
syntactic linkage between an NP functioning as Subject and a
VP functioning as Predicate--that is to say, a mere agreement-
copying of nominal features onto the verb, by a late surface
rule. But hidden below that there lurks the very *sine qua non*,
the element privileged to receive copied P/N suffixes, namely
the closed class of suffixes which are none other than the
structuralist's old tense/mood morphemes, or Rona's aspect
markers.

Before analyzing these formatives further, we must pause
to ask if all seven[10] of them are truly in contrast. It is
possible to argue either that they are or that they are not.

In other words, one linguist will insist that indicative
and subjunctive are at best in partial complementation,
therefore inherently contrastive, while another will claim
that *mood* is a syntactically generated feature of tense.
Without attempting to decide which position is the 'right'
one, we shall do well to adopt the latter for heuristic
purposes. The solution proposed in this paper to the AUX
problem will prove adaptable to either analysis of mood.

Still before we do proceed, however, we must also inquire
whether there exist in Sp whole 'auxiliary' or 'modal' verbs
which, along with our affixes, are exclusively in the domain
of the AUX by virtue of never occurring *without* one of the
five affixes. First, what about the initial constituents
of *ha cantado* and of *está cantando*: are they in this sense
dominated by the AUX? They are not, because we can elicit
para haber cantado or *para estar cantando* or *habiendo
cantado*, with instead one or another of the 'non-finite'
suffixes that adapt VP's to embeddings or nominalizations
but are in fact excluded from the AUX. Second, what of the
so-called 'modal' item in *quiere cantar* or *puede cantar* or
debe cantar: is it dominated by the AUX? Again the answer
is no, for these *soi-disant* modals too can occur in non-
finite structures. So can quantities of other verbs like
tener que, empezar a, tratar de, dejar de, seguir and verbs
of [locomotion] like *ir* or *venir* in the meaning of 'go
(to)...' or 'come (to)...', etc.

We cannot deal here with the analysis of the VP as Verbal
Core ± Complement, nor defend the claim that *ha cantado* and
puede cantar and *tiene que cantar* are unified verbal cores
while *está cantando* and *sigue cantando* and *viene a cantar*
are verbal cores + complements. That is a separate descriptive problem. Here and now we are still on the trail of
AUX-dominated verbal items and we shall find one for certain:
the item *ir a*, which Rona attempts to make into his 'Prospective' Tense, but which as pointed out in 2 and reiterated
herewith in 4 *cannot* occur in non-finite structures.

   (4)   a.   va a venir
         b.   iba a venir
         c.   *(para) ir a venir
         d.   *yendo a venir

In other words, the verbal item in view here co-occurs
exclusively with the AUX affixes. However--and here we pick
up the clue to the completion of our analysis--this crucial item
co-occurs with only two of our five morphemes, namely, those
of the 'present (indicative or subjunctive)' and the 'imperfect
(indicative or subjunctive)', thus yielding a skewed matrix
looking like 5:

   (5)   0   canta   cantaba   cantó cantará cantaría
         1   va a cantar   iba a cantar

with tentative 'tenses' on the horizontal and something other
than 'tenses', (so call them 'aspects'), on the vertical.
This skewing can be quite effortlessly corrected on the basis
of the analogy shown in 6 to yield a new matrix 7:

(6) a.   Juan dice que canta   /...va a cantar   /...cantará

     b.   Juan$\begin{Bmatrix}\text{decía}\\\text{dijo}\end{Bmatrix}$que cantaba /...iba a cantar /...cantaría

(7) 0   canta   cantaba   cantó
     1   cantará   cantaría
     2   va a cantar   iba a cantar

In other terms, the 'conditional' being to the 'future' as the
'imperfect' is to the 'present', and there being no general
metarule constraining the members of a given morpheme class
(say that of aspect) to be all non-affixal or all affixal in
form, what emerges looks more and more like an AUX with a
two-tense system: Past and Non-Past, together with two
optional, mutually exclusive[11] aspects. Yet 'preterite'
cantó, which combines with neither of the two, emerges looking
like something of a sore thumb. How then to handle it?
   One possible source for a lead is the doctoral dissertation
of David Nasjleti entitled 'The Spanish Preterite: its
Aspectual Features' (1971). Nasjleti labors at length to
pin down the elusive and loosely-used term 'aspect' to
exclusive application to the syntactic and semantic characteristics which distinguish the present and past, the perfective present and past, and the preterite from each other.[12]
He then proposes the feature assignment seen in 8:

(8)	Present Imperfect	Present Perfect Pluperfect	Preterite
[fulfilled]	−	−	+
[accomplished]	−	+	+
[terminated]	−	±	+

Does this arrangement afford us a clue? Nasjleti's [fulfilled]
means to him 'that the results of the action are effective
immediately upon the occurrence of the action (105)'; later
he states that the preterite 'signals the fulfillment of the
total span of the predication... [and] in doing so...imposes
closure on the predication, which, in this way, expresses the
potential for actualization of the process as completely
exhausted, either by becoming real as in *Juan vino*, or by
failing to become real, as in *Juan no vino* (108)'.
   Within our present framework, one solution might be to
reduce the tenses to just two--Past and Non-Past--and to add
a third aspect which could co-occur only with Past Tense in
a portmanteau morph at the surface; the objection is that this

aspect would have no overt form of its own and therefore
its independent existence would be impossible to motivate.
An alternative and seemingly more attractive solution would
be to posit three tenses, feature-specified as in 9:

(9)	Present	Imperfect	Preterite
[past]	-	+	+
[fulfilled]	-	-	+

and to further stipulate that the 'plus-plus' Preterite blocks
aspect because it is semantically incompatible with the
feature of [expectation] which inheres in both of the aspects.
If an action (or state) is fulfilled in the absolute past, it
cannot at the same time be expected in the present or future.
There is one bit of independent motivation elsewhere in
the grammar for the blocking of aspect in the AUX. It
involves syntactic selection of the Subjunctive Mood. If
the dominant core (of wanting, expecting, ordering, permitting
or the like) contains the feature [affective], and selection
of the Subjunctive Mood is therefore obligatory in the AUX
of the embedded Sentence, then aspect is blocked. There is
not even a morphological way for 'Aspect One' (-rá, -ría) to
combine with the Subjunctive, and while 'Aspect Two' in the
Subjunctive is morphologically possible and indeed occurs
in sentences like 10a; nevertheless sentences like 10b get
starred:

(10)   a.   Yo dudo que Juan vaya a venir.
       b.   *Yo quiero que Juan vaya a venir.
       c.   Yo no quiero que Juan vaya a venir.

Then how do we account for the acceptability of 10c?[13] Assuming that the negative particle is 'raised' to the dominant
core on transforming the basic structure of 11:

(11)   Yo quiero + Juan no vaya a venir

we may say that *no ir*, even when clearly [-locomotion], can
be representing a semantically specialized case of verbal core
plus complement--an idiom so to speak, exactly parallel to
English 'not go and ...' or 'not go...-ing'--and not our
Aspect Two at all. This interpretation seems confirmed in
imperative constructions, which can be viewed as non-finite,
having no AUX and therefore no aspect,[14] as in 12:

(12)   a.   ¡No vayas tú a venir aquí!   'Don't you go coming
                                                        here!'

       b.   *¡Vé tú a venir aquí!

One question remaining to be disposed of is: can the two
aspects co-occur, with Aspect One affixed to Aspect Two?   We
may note that *irá a cantar* actually is ambiguous: it can
mean 'will go (to) sing' or 'must be (=probably is) going
to sing'.   One semantic feature of Aspect One (Non-Past *-rá*,
Past *-ría*) is conjecture or speculation on the speaker's part
as to the reality of a present act or state, as in 13:

(13)   Juan cantará muy bien.   'John must sing (probably
                                  sings) very well.'

Another semantic feature of Aspect One, mutually exclusive
with the first, is prediction of a future act or state, as
in 14:

(14)   Juan cantará mañana.   'John will sing tomorrow.'

Since Aspect Two (*ir a*) is also predictive, and always
predictive, it is possible to achieve a combination of the
two features in view by using both aspects at once, as in 15:

(15)   Juan irá a cantar   'John must be going to sing
              pronto.   soon.'

   One verbal item we have deliberately not touched on yet is
haber de.   Is *ha de cantar* just another verbal core analogous
to, say, *tiene que cantar* or *debe cantar*, or could the *ha de*
part be functioning as an aspect in the same way as *-rá* in
cantará or as *va a* in *va a cantar*?   Its semantics proves
nothing about its syntax, for while it closely resembles *-rá*
as to both prediction and conjecture, it also shares the
meaning range of being to, or being supposed to, with *deber*.
The test question is whether *haber de* is solely in the domain
of the AUX, and it is a question which cannot be answered
with finality.   Let us consider the examples in 16:

(16)   a.   Yo he de cantar.   e. ? habiendo de cantar
       b.   Yo había de cantar.   f. *Yo he habido de cantar.
       c. ? Yo hube de cantar.   g. *(para) haber de cantar.
       d. ? Yo habré de cantar.

All speakers will agree in accepting 16a, b and in rejecting
16f, g; but 16c-e will elicit varied reactions.   In the
language as a whole they do exist, but in one or another
dialect, regional or social, they may be felt as stilted,
old-fashioned, or somehow non-viable.   Our conclusion could
be that in those dialects where only 16a, b are well-formed,
haber de constitutes in fact an Aspect Three in the AUX, and

that the whole language may indeed be moving, diachronically
speaking, in that direction--in the direction, that is, of
expanding its aspectual category.[15]

We may now conclude by broadening our horizon in the
interest of ascertaining whether all five standard Romance
languages have or do not have the same basic AUX structure.
It seems that the rewrite rule AUX → Tense (Aspect)[16] is
indeed fully valid as shared by four of the five--Spanish,
Portuguese, French and Italian. Tense in all four will
rewrite as Present, Imperfect, Preterite. Portuguese *cantara*
'had sung' need not represent a separate tense, but merely
an archaizing variant of the existing phrasal core *tinha
cantado*.

Aspect will expand exactly the same in Portuguese as in
Spanish,[17] with some varieties innovating to include *haver de*,
and with the possibility of combining the two Aspects to
form *irá cantar*, etc.

French has an Aspect Three in the form of *venir de*, neatly
balancing the *aller* of Aspect Two: *venir de* locates an act
or state in the immediate past, just as *aller* locates it in
the immediate future--or at least tends to, in opposition
to the less-marked predictive/conjectural Aspect One -*ra*.

Italian has only one filler for the Aspect slot: semantically predictive/conjectural, with the forms Present -*rá*,
Imperfect -*rebbe*.[18]

As for Rumanian, the basic formula which rewrites AUX as
obligatory Tense plus optional Aspect does not appear workable
because the existing forms resist arrangement in the two-
dimensional matrix. There are six relevant forms, as illustrated in 17:[19]

(17) cîntǎ   'sings'   va cînta   'will sing'
      cîntǎ   'sang'   ar cînta   'would sing'
      cîntá   'was singing'   cîntase   'had sung'

We may take the 'subjunctive' *cînte* as a syntactic alternant
occurring only after the subordinator *sǎ*, and both *are sǎ
cînte* and *o sǎ cînte* as mere stylistic variants of *va cînta*.
In addition there is the perfective core *a cîntat* 'has sung'.
The 'pluperfect' *cîntase* cannot comfortably be relegated to
the position of imperfect-tense correlate of *a cîntat* despite
the non-existence of *avea cîntat* for 'had sung'; nor can
'conditional' *ar cînta* reasonably be called the imperfect-
tense correlate of 'future' *va cînta*, not only because the
first elements are lexically unrelated but also because they
bear no tense relationship to each other as do Spanish *cantará*
and *cantaría*[20] or French *chantera* and *chanterait*. Nor is
either free variant of *va cînta* capable of adding tense
variation. Thus in Rumanian, instead of Tense (Aspect), we
seem to have an AUX consisting of just Tense: indeed the
traditional Present, Imperfect, Preterite, Pluperfect, Future
and Conditional.

One of the Rumanian tenses positively specified for [past]

is the Preterite, cognate of all the Western Preterites, and this leads us to conclude with a question. Why is it that the Preterite Tense, which we earlier characterized figuratively as a 'sore thumb', is slowly but surely atrophying in Rumanian, Italian and French? I hope that an answer may be implicit in the foregoing analysis. The unhealthy Preterite manages to remain operational in some registers in all of those languages, including regional spoken standards in Rumania and Italy; but within each language as a whole it is recessive, and is being steadily replaced by the Present Tense of the Perfective Core, thus reducing the Tenses to two (Non-past and Past) and eliminating the opposition of the features labeled by Nasjleti for Spanish (see above, p.19) as [fulfilled] vs. [accomplished]. Morphophonemic recalcitrance would be at most a contributory factor in the reduction, I believe; it is true that Spanish and Portuguese have ironed out some of that complication from their still fully viable Preterites. Portuguese, at the other extreme, has exercised the Preterite back to robust health by assigning it much of the work of the Present Tense of the Perfective Core, i.e. by transferring some of the semantic load of *tem cantado* onto *cantou*, while at the same time *cantara* too lingers on as a register variant of *tinha cantado* or *havia cantado*. The perfective, i.e. [accomplished] nuance still inherent in the Portuguese Preterite may, in point of fact, represent the persistence of a trait inherited from Latin that survived two major shake-ups in the AUX system: the first already in Common Romance ('Vulgar Latin'), when the symmetrical network of tense-aspect-mood-voice contrasts was decimated; the second in Italo-Western Romance, when the foundation for a new Tense (Aspect) pattern was laid. But that is another story.

NOTES

[1] Read at the 18th Congress of the International Linguistic Association (Arequipa, Peru, March 1973).

[2] Refer for example to Ramsey 1956 (revised by R.K. Spaulding).

[3] As described for example in Hill (1958:464-73).

[4] The former in *Speaking and Writing Spanish* (1949) and the latter in *Modern Approach to Spanish* (1963, revised 1968).

[5] I modify Rona's table here by (1) substituting *cantar* for *tomar*; (2) supplying the row beginning with *cantaría*, which he must have omitted inadvertently; (3) adding his own labels; (4) removing the first-singular P/N suffix as superfluous. (I am prepared to claim that the 'third singular' forms

illustrated carry no P/N suffix at all.)

[6] Though not, of course, also *está habiendo cantado '*is having sung'.

[7] Though not also *va a haber cantado 'is going to have sung'.

[8] One negativized variant equates with English 'not go and..., not go...-ing', likewise [-locomotion]. See p.20.

[9] It is to be noted, by way of refinements, that I can say Fui a entrar allí, (with two compatible [+locomotion]'s,) whenever I am not actually '(in) there', but cannot say Fui a entrar aquí if I am actually '(in) here', except if the latter implies that at some earlier point I 'went to' in the sense of 'started to, made to' (but didn't dare, couldn't, or what not) come in here. Likewise, while *¡Vé a venir! '*Go (to) come!' is ill-formed, ¡No vayas a venir! or (No quiero que) vayas a venir, both containing the negative particle, are well-formed and again we note the clearly [-locomotion] interpretation of the ir. Again, see p.20.

[10] We shall insist on seven rather than Rona's eight by reason of ruling out -ara as a separate ('pluperfect') morpheme and collapsing it with 'imperfect subjunctive' -ase; see above, p.15.

[11] But see note 15 below.

[12] His labels are different, but I take the liberty of translating them into the present more conventional terminology.

[13] Cf. note 10 above.

[14] This statement is of course controversial; one can argue that imperatives derive from transformations which delete the dominant [+affective] core (e.g. Yo...que tú no vayas → No vayas tú.), or that negative ones do while positive ones are basic (e.g. Vé tú); but I would defend the claim that all imperatives are not only basic, but lack the AUX.

[15] Although soler 'be in the habit of' might be yet another candidate for aspectual status, since only suele cantar and solía cantar are usual, its failure to occur in other forms is perhaps too easily explained away on grounds of semantic incompatibility.

[16] This formula represents the underlying constituent order; in the surface output, 'affix-hopping' takes place. All three tense morphemes, being suffixes, attach themselves to the first verbal constituent in the core, be it the lexical verb itself, or perfective haber (plus participle of the lexical verb), or modal poder, deber, etc. (plus infinitive of the lexical verb), in the absence of Aspect; to either of the Aspect morphemes, in their presence. Aspect One being suffixal also, a double 'hop' occurs whenever it is present, e.g. -ía + -rá + canta → -ría + canta (or -ía + cantará either way) → cantaría.

[17] Except, of course, that Aspect Two ir does not contain

the function word *a*.

[18]It matters not at all, synchronically, that -*rebbe* comes historically from the Preterite rather than the Imperfect of *avere*.

[19]See Agard 1958.

[20]See note 6 above.

REFERENCES

Agard, Frederick B. 1949. Speaking and writing Spanish. New York: Henry Holt and Co.

_____. 1958. Structural sketch of Romanian. Language 34:3 Supplement [Language Monograph 26].

_____. 1963 [rev. 1968]. Modern approach to Spanish. New York: Holt, Rinehart and Winston.

_____. 1967. Stress in four Romance languages. Glossa 1:2.

Hill, A.A. 1958. Introduction to linguistic structures. New York: Harcourt, Brace and Co.

Nasjleti, David. 1971. The Spanish preterite: its aspectual features. Ithaca: Cornell University dissertation.

Ramsey, M.M. 1956. A textbook of modern Spanish, revised by R.K. Spaulding. New York: Holt, Rinehart and Winston.

Rona, José Pedro. 1973. Tiempo y aspecto: análisis binario de la conjugación española. Paper read at the 18th Congress of the International Linguistic Association, Arequipa, Peru.

LUSITANIAN PORTUGUESE [ɐ] IS [+ATR] AND [+CP]

WAYNE J. REDENBARGER

Boston University

1. Traditional phonetic description of [ɐ]

The vocalic systems of both Brazilian and Lusitanian Portuguese contain a distinctive vowel usually transcribed with an upside-down 'a', and pronounced [ɐ]. Traditionally it has been classed as a central vowel substantially higher than phonetic [a]. Gonçalves Viana (1892:10) places it like this (omitting dozens of his other symbols):

Figure 1   i   u

                    e   o
                              ɐ
                         ɛ   ɔ
                         a

26

It has been described impressionistically by scholars such as
Mattoso Câmara (1953:70) as *abafado* which is to say 'hollow
or choking'. Barbosa (1965:59) says it is 'a central vowel
which rather reminds one of the French [œ] of *peur*, yet
different from it since the Portuguese is not rounded.' It is
notorious among Portuguese teachers as the most difficult
sound to teach American students to perceive and produce
correctly.

As a phonological problem, a vowel higher than [a] and
yet neither so front as [ɛ] nor as back as [ɔ] is difficult to
handle in a binary distinctive feature framework. M.E. Mateus
in her 1973 dissertation assigns the distinctive feature
specification [-high, -low, +back, -round] to the segment [ɐ]
(10). She does not explain her choice of these particular
features, nor does she offer any supporting data of an impressionistic, acoustic, or phonological nature. Since, on the
contrary, the acoustic data we shall analyze below clearly
indicate that [ɐ] is a *front* vowel, and moreover since the
several phoneticians who established the International Phonetic
Alphabet concur in hearing a distinct impressionistic contrast
between [ɐ] and [ʌ] (IPA 1949:9), we are forced to discard
Mateus' analysis of this segment as well as her rules in which
it is utilized.

The purpose of this paper is to present both phonetic and
phonological arguments to establish a more plausible feature
specification for the segment [ɐ], basing our analysis on its
phonological behavior in both Portuguese and Old French, and
on recent phonetic measurements of [ɐ] in the Portuguese of
Lisbon. Since this analysis employs recently formulated
distinctive features dealing with the position of the tongue
root, a brief explanation of these features is in order.

2.   The tongue root distinctive features

The formulation of the 'tongue-root features' is surely one
of the most significant improvements on the system proposed by
Chomsky and Halle (1968), who recognized (306) a basic flaw
with the distinctive feature [±low] because it made incorrect
predictions regarding secondary articulations. Moreover,
Michael Brame's work on the emphatic consonants in Arabic
(Brame 1970:22-3) showed that the distinctive pharyngealization
of the emphatics is best codified not by the features [low] and
[back] but by a new feature signifying a backing of the tongue
root to create a constricted pharyngeal passage. Since that
same backing of the tongue root has long been observed in low
vowels like [a] and [ɑ] (for example, Delattre 1969) these two
formerly separate phenomena--pharyngealized consonants and
low vowels--are now united under the single feature [+CP] (for
Constricted Pharynx).

Analogous to the feature [+CP], which is accomplished by
moving the tongue root from a neutral position backwards, is
the other new tongue root feature [ATR] (for Advanced Tongue
Root). Note in Figure 2 (x-ray data from Perkell 1969) first
the middle position of the tongue root for the vowel [ɛ],
second its backness for [a], and third its advanced position or

frontness for [i]:

Figure 2

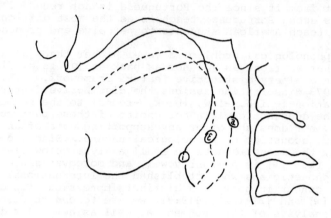

Thus the tenseness one feels just above his larynx when articu-
lating tense vowels is now seen to be the tenseness of those
muscles contracting to pull the tongue root forward (Halle and
Stevens 1969:211). The feature [ATR] supercedes both the feature
'covered' and the feature 'tense' of Chomsky and Halle 1968,
since both are accomplished by the same mechanism: advancing
the tongue root.

   In summary, the slight difference in the tongue body height
in tense-lax pairs like [i]~[I], [e]~ [ɛ], etc. which had traditionally been their defining difference (Smally 1963:363) is
now seen to be but a secondary upward bunching effect caused
by the backing of the tongue root. What was thought to be
cause is now seen as effect--and not surprisingly so since the
movement of the tongue root has until recently been almost
impossible to observe. Using these tongue root features, a
basic binary schema such as Figure 3 is possible (English vowels
are shown in order to avoid clutter, slanted bars indicating
that they are underlying segments):

Figure 3

	[+ATR,-CP]		[-ATR,-CP]		[-ATR,+CP]	
	[-back]	[+back]	[-back]	[+back]	[-back]	[+back]
[+hi]	/i/	/u/	/I/	/U/		
[-hi]	/e/	/o/	/ɛ/	/ɔ/		/a/

We may think of the three charts as corresponding, from left to right, to the tongue root when advanced, neutral, and backed, i.e. in the same physical plane as the x-ray data in Figure 2. Notice that there is no chart for the fourth mathematically possible feature combination, namely [+ATR,+CP], since those muscles which advance the tongue root are in opposition to those which back it to constrict the pharynx. If both sets of muscles contract simultaneously there will be a neutralization of forces and therefore no movement from the neutral position. As Ladefoged (1971:75) puts it, the vowel [a] 'can be produced only by contracting the muscles which oppose those that pull the tongue root forward; consequently such a vowel cannot be TENSE in the technical sense'. (here Ladefoged is defining *tension* as 'the degree to which the tongue root is pulled forward,' i.e. [+ATR], to use Halle and Stevens' label).

I should now like to present two phonological arguments which indicate that the Portuguese segment [ɐ] is [+CP] and [+ATR], representing the fourth mathematical possibility in Figure 3, where that combination was not thought possible.

3.   Portuguese [ɐ]--the phonological arguments

Of the following surface vowels of Lusitanian Portuguese--all of which appear as simple oral vowels--the four 'walled in' by the lines, [ə], [ɛ], [a], and [ɔ], are the only ones which are never nasal vowels as well:

Figure 4

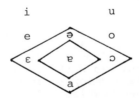

This distribution is produced by the rule of 'Pre-Nasal Advancing' which in a distinctive-feature framework using tongue root features would be codified as assigning [+ATR] to all vowels which precede a nasal consonant:

$$V \rightarrow [+ATR] \ / \ \underline{} \ \begin{matrix} C \\ [+nas] \end{matrix}$$

Referring back to Figure 3, this means that sound shifts /ɛ/ → /e/, /ɔ/ → /o/, and most importantly for our purposes here, /a/ → /ɐ/ as well, do occur.

For example, all 3sg. Present Indicative verbs in Portuguese have [-ATR] vowels for their stressed vowel, whether they come from an underlying [+ATR] or [-ATR] vowel:

in -a- themes:	m[ɔ́]ra	'he resides'
in -e- themes:	m[ɔ́]ve	'he moves'
in -i- themes:	s[ɔ́]be	'it rises'

But before a nasal, however, one sees instead [+ATR] vowels, and *only* [+ATR] in the stressed vowels in the same 3sg. Present Indicative forms:

-a-	c[ṍ]nta	'he counts'
-e-	c[ó]me	'he eats'
-i-	m[é̃]nte	'he lies'

And analogously, where there used to be only oral [a]:

-a-	f[á]la	'he speaks'
-e-	b[á]te	'he beats'
-i-	p[á]rte	'he leaves'

there is now only [ɐ] when underlying /a/ is followed by a nasal:

-a-	c[ɐ́̃]nta	'he sings'
-e-	l[ɐ́̃]mbe	'he licks'
-i-	b[ɐ́̃]ne	'he forbids'

Note first that /a/ is [+CP] by definition, as shown in Figure 2; second, under such a rule as Pre-Nasal Advancing whose sole operation consists of marking vowels [+ATR], we find /a/ → [ɐ]. It cannot have given up its [+CP] value, or it would have become [-high,-round,+ATR,-CP], i.e. [e], which it obviously is not. It would seem to have become [+ATR] while retaining its [+CP] value.

We are not forced to rely on the evidence of this single rule to show that the /a/ → [ɐ] change is accomplished by adding only [+ATR], even given the rule's straightforwardness. There exists another rule in Portuguese which does precisely the same thing--'Unstressed Vowel Advancing' has the effect of making all unstressed vowels [+ATR]:

/ɔ/ → [o]	m[o]vémos	'we move'	(cf. m[ɔ́]viɭ)
/ɛ/ → [e]	progr[e]dímos	'we progress'	(cf. progr[ɛ́]sso)
/o/ →	d[o]émos	'we ache'	(cf. d[ó]r)
/e/ →	p[e]rdémos	'we lose'	(cf. p[é]rda)
/a/ → [ɐ]	f[ɐ]lámos	'we speak'	(cf. f[á]la)

Thus we find a second unambiguous phonological rule changing only one distinctive feature and in which [ɐ] again patterns as a vowel with the value [+ATR].

The rule is also easily shown to be independently legitimate and correctly formulated in this framework. Some might argue, for instance, that the Unstressed Vowel Advancing rule does not exist at all but rather the stress/laxing rule which causes the stressed vowel of verb forms to take on the value [-ATR] (see above) in some cases does not operate, thus leaving underlying vowels 'unlaxed', that is, [+ATR]. There are two

reasons why it is not circular to say that alternations such
as *d[ɔ́]rme* ∼ *d[o]rmímos* and *m[ɔ́]ve* ∼ *m[o]vémos* are produced
by 'laxing' an /o/ in the case of *dorm-*, and by 'advancing'
an /ɔ/ in the case of *mɔv-*. First, the underlying vowel cannot
be predicted by rule (cf. Harris 1974:67). Second, it can be
shown that Stress/laxing and Unstressed Vowel Advancing are
not true reverses of one another. In the Stress/laxing rule

$$\begin{array}{l} V \\ [+str] \end{array} \rightarrow [-ATR]$$

/a/ is unaffected since it is already [-ATR]: /fala/ → [fála]
'he speaks'. But in the case of Unstressed Vowel Advancing
an entirely new vowel is created, namely [ɐ]. Thus it is clear
that two changes through Laxing, /e/ → [ɛ], and /o/ → [ɔ],
cannot fully 'undo' three changes brought upon by Unstressed
Advancing /ɛ/ → [e], /ɔ/ → [o], and /a/ → [ɐ]. We also
know this is not just legerdemain with the underlying forms
since in Brazilian speech it is only through the operation of
Pre-Nasal Advancing or Unstressed Advancing that one can
generate an [ɐ]. With absolutely no surface examples of a
stressed oral [ɐ], and thus with the only occurrences of [ɐ]
coming in either pre-nasal position or in an unstressed
syllable (where our independently motivated rules derive them
from /a/), it cannot be seriously maintained that [ɐ] is an
underlying vowel.

   To summarize the import of Pre-Nasal Advancing and Unstressed Advancing, it has been shown that these two separate rules
both add the single feature [+ATR] to vowels, and in both
cases underlying /a/ [+CP] changes to [ɐ]. It would seem on
the weight of this phonological evidence that the underlying
segment [ɐ] with [+CP] is [+ATR] as well.

4. The acoustic phonetic evidence

The original rationale for having ruled out segments marked
'plus' for both of the tongue root features was the assumption
that such an opposing of muscular forces would leave the tongue
root in its neutral position, i.e. [+ATR,+CP] ≡ [-ATR,-CP].
Consider however the data shown in Figure 5 (based on M.R.D.
Martins' recent study of Lusitanian Portuguese vowels):

Figure 5:   First formant frequencies plotted against second
            formant frequences. English data (in parentheses)
            is Peterson and Barney (1952:183). Portuguese
            data [in brackets] is M.R.D. Martins (1973:311).

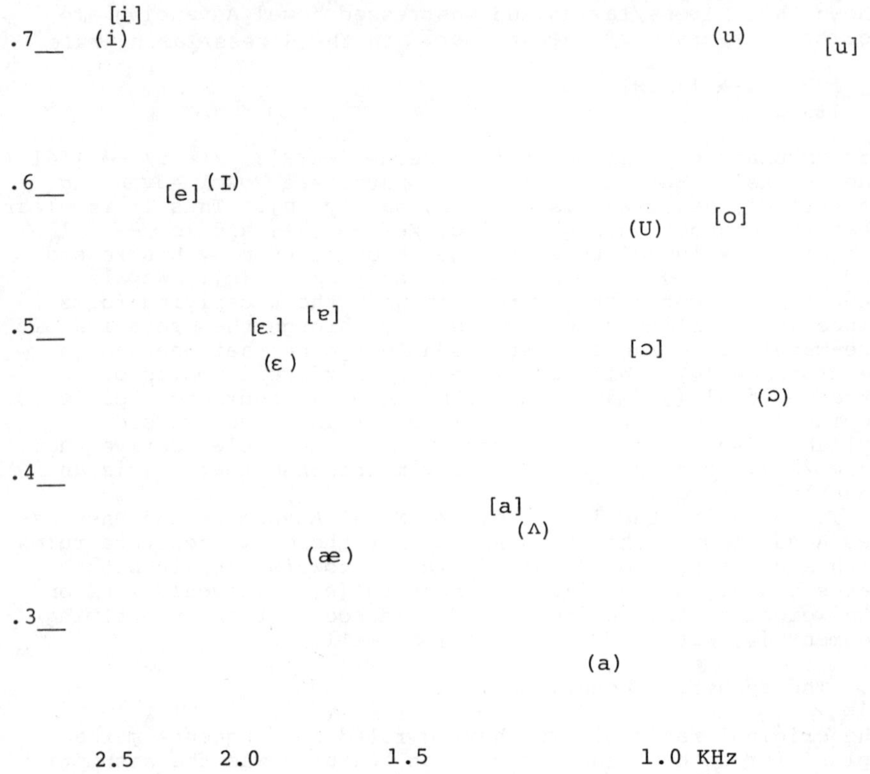

```
      [i]
.7__  (i)                                           (u)      [u]




.6__          [e] (I)
                                              (U)    [o]


.5__              [ɛ ] [ɐ]
                   (ɛ )                          [ɔ]
                                                        (ɔ)

.4__
                              [a]
                              (ʌ)
                  (æ )

.3__
                                     (a)


      2.5      2.0        1.5              1.0 KHz
```

Note that in comparison to the rest of the Portuguese
phonetic segments there is several times less 'phonetic space'
between [ɐ] and [ɛ] than there is between any two other
segments. The F_3 values for these two vowels are also virtually identical; [ɛ] at 2.57 KHz versus 2.56 KHz for [ɐ]
(Martins 1973:311). The similarity to [ɛ] is significant
since [ɛ] is the [-high,-round] vowel produced with the tongue
root in neutral position, i.e. [-ATR,-CP] (cf. Figure 3).
    My reason for employing these data from acoustic phonetics
is based on Gunnar Fant's statement (1973:5) that 'each position of the articulatory organs has its specific F-pattern',
and that whatever ambiguities do exist 'are not very important
in normal speech'. Applying his principle, I infer therefore
that the virtual identity of formant pattern between Portuguese [ɐ] and Portuguese [ɛ] is due to both vowels being
produced with identical articulatory configurations. It was

our prediction based on phonological considerations that
[+ATR,+CP] vowels would have the same tongue root position as
[-ATR,-CP] vowels. We now see that the acoustic phonetic
facts agree exactly with that prediction, thus furnishing
strong, independent evidence for the accuracy of this analysis.

5. A third Portuguese rule--/e/ dissimilation

We have already seen two phonological rules which generate [ɐ]
from an underlying /a/. If indeed [ɐ] is as close to /e/ as
it is to /a/, that is, distinct from each by a difference in
only one tongue root feature, we would predict on grounds of
phonological proximity that it would also be natural for the
shift /e/ → [ɐ]. In the Lisbon dialect there exists just
such a rule:

/e/ Dissimilation:

$$
\begin{bmatrix} /e/ \\ +syl \\ -high \\ -rnd \\ +ATR \\ -CP \\ +str \end{bmatrix} \rightarrow \quad [+CP] \quad / \underline{\quad} \begin{bmatrix} +high \\ -back \end{bmatrix}
$$

In this dialect, when a stressed underlying /e/ is followed by
a palatal segment, the /e/ dissimilates by acquiring the
feature [+CP] thus giving it 'glidability' in both the tongue
root and tongue body as well. To clarify the notion 'glidability', consider the maximal diphthong [aj] where there is
gliding distance in both tongue root and tongue body:

$$
\begin{array}{cc} /a/ & /j/ \\ \begin{bmatrix} -ATR \\ +CP \\ -high \end{bmatrix} & \begin{bmatrix} +ATR \\ -CP \\ +high \end{bmatrix} \end{array}
$$

It would be an assimilation for the nucleus [a] of the diphthong to acquire the same tongue root specification as its
following glide, thus becoming [ej]; in the case of our Lisbon
Portuguese we find the reverse--[ej] → [ɐj] where /e/ dissimilates its [CP] feature from underlying minus to plus,
hence:

ceio	['sɐju]	'I eat dinner'
passeio	[pɐ'sɐju]	'a walk'

Note that the change takes place not just before [+high,-back]
glides but before all high front segments:

vejo	[vɐžu]	'I see'
mexo	[mɐšu]	'I stir', etc.

The rule of /e/ dissimilation, then, is important for

showing that [ɐ] can be derived equally well from an /e/
as well as from an /a/, not just in theory but in fact. It
is further evidence that my proposed analysis of [ɐ] as 'half
/a/ and half /e/' in the sense that it is both [+ATR] and
[+CP] is a reasonable one.

6.   Theoretical conclusions

Outside the immediate implications for Portuguese phonology,
our demonstration that Portuguese [ɐ] is [+ATR] and [+CP]
has shown that the redundancy principle [+CP] → [-ATR] and
its corollary that [+ATR] → [-CP] are not universal principles
of phonology. The relation is a very common one which holds
for many natural languages, but it is merely common--not
universal. It is, in that respect, similar to the often-seen
relation [+round] → [+back], also a very common feature of
markedness, but not one that holds for every language since
a certain percentage (especially of Asian languages) do
violate it. Thus it seems appropriate to label [ɐ] as a
very highly marked segment for violating the relation [+ATR]
→ [-CP], but, like back unrounded vowels, [ɐ] is not an
impossible segment. If [+ATR,+CP] is possible in vowels, we
would expect to find it in consonants as well; indeed Kiparsky
1974 has indicated that there may be evidence for it. If
that can be shown, it will further strengthen my argument
that Portuguese [ɐ] is [+ATR,+CP].

7.   An example from Old French

Having offered three phonological arguments as well as concur-
ring acoustic phonetic evidence from Portuguese in support
of my analysis of [ɐ], I should like to briefly examine a
well-known problem in historical French phonology and propose
a solution employing [ɐ], paralleling the analysis for Portuguese.
      In Old French, underlying /e/ before a nasal underwent a
phonological change. We know this to be the case since at
the time of the writing of the *Chanson de Roland* all nasalized
vowels (/__[+nas]) assonated freely with their oral counterparts except for /e/ /__[+nas]. A few writers allowed this
new vowel to assonate with [a] and [ã], but it was clearly
kept apart from oral [e].
      The clue to the identity of this nasalized vowel lies in
its behavior when French later reanalyzes *nasalized* vowels as
underlying *nasal* vowels. The result is a rule

$$V \qquad \rightarrow \qquad [-ATR]$$
$$[+nas]$$

corresponding to the oft-noted behavior of nasal vowels which
once having 'raised' (→ [+ATR]) tend later to 'lower'
(→ [-ATR]) (see Freeman 1970:8 for a list of references).
Since there is a redundancy rule in French saying

$$\begin{array}{c} V \\ [\text{-ATR}] \end{array} \longrightarrow [\text{-high}]$$

this nasal rule which creates [-ATR] vowels feeds that redundancy rule causing the following shift so that we end up with
only four nasal vowels [ã], [ẽ], [õ], and [õẽ]:

(a)   underlying [-ATR] vowels are not affected,
(b)   [+ATR,-high] vowels → [-ATR],
(c)   [+ATR,+high] vowels → [-ATR] and lower to [-high]

(a) (b) (c)

/ẽ/   ◇ [ẽ]
   /ẽ/ → [ẽ]
      /ĩ/ → [ẽ]
/õ/   ◇ [õ]
   /õ/ → [õ]
      /ũ/ → [õ]
/õẽ/   ◇ [õẽ]
   /ø̃/ → [õẽ]
      /ỹ/ → [õẽ]
/ã/   ◇ [ã]

Now, most significantly, when this new vowel created from
underlying /e/ /__[+nas] undergoes the single feature change
to [-ATR] it becomes an [ã] also. The question then is 'what
vowel, when changed from [+ATR] → [-ATR], will then become
an [ã]?' The answer is of course [ẽ]:

$$\begin{bmatrix} \text{/ẽ/} \\ \text{-high} \\ \text{-rnd} \\ \text{+ATR} \\ \text{+CP} \end{bmatrix} \begin{bmatrix} \text{/ã/} \\ \text{-high} \\ \text{-rnd} \\ \text{-ATR} \\ \text{+CP} \end{bmatrix}$$

We then hypothesize that the early change of /e/ /__[+nas]
was a shift from /e/ to [ɐ]. Note that this change is
exactly parallel to the [e] → [ɐ] change already shown to
occur in Lisbon Portuguese. The fact that a few writers
allowed what I reconstruct as [ẽ] to assonate with [ã] is
also explained since the [ẽ] ~ [ã] confusion is an easy one--
as any beginning Portuguese student will attest. This solution to the problem of how /ẽ/ became /ã/, which I have
outlined here, thus requires absolutely no modification of
the general Old French rule V̄ → [-ATR]; it explains all the
facts concerning assonance, and needs only one feature change
to get from /e/ to [ɐ]. I submit that the economy of this
phonological relation, especially considered in conjunction
with the acoustic and phonological arguments for Portuguese
presented earlier, furnishes support to my analysis that the
phonological segment [ɐ] is both [+ATR] and [+CP].

REFERENCES

Barbosa, Jorge M. Marais. 1965. Études de phonologie
   portugaise. Lisbon: Bertrand.
Brame, Michael. 1970. Arabic phonology. Cambridge, Mass.:
   M.I.T. dissertation.
Chomsky, Noam and Morris Halle. 1968. The sound pattern of
   English. New York: Harper and Row.
Delattre, Pierre. 1969. L'/R/ parisien et autres sons du
   pharynx. The French Review 43.5-22.
Fant, Gunnar. 1973. Speech sounds and features. Cambridge,
   Mass.: MIT Press.
Freeman, Michael. 1970. The pronunciation of the tonic vowels
   from early Old French through pre-modern French. University
   of California dissertation.
Gonçalves Viana, Aniceto dos Reis. 1892. Exposição da pronuncia
   normal portuguesa para uso de nacionaes e estrangeiros.
   Lisbon: Imprensa Nacional.
Halle, Morris and K. N. Stevens. 1969. On the feature 'Advanced
   Tongue Root'. RLE QPR 94.209-15.
Harris, James W. 1974. Evidence from Portuguese for the
   'Elsewhere Condition' in phonology. Linguistic Inquiry
   5.61-80.
International Phonetic Association. 1949. The principles of
   the International Phonetic Association. London.
Kiparsky, Paul. 1974. The vowel features. To appear in Papers
   from the Northeastern Linguistic Society, Fifth Meeting.
Ladefoged, Peter. 1971. Preliminaries to linguistic phonetics.
   Chicago: University of Chicago Press.
Martins, Maria Raquel Delgado. 1973. Análysis acústica das
   vogais tónicas em português. Boletim de Filologia 22.303-14.
Mateus, Maria Elena Mira. 1973. Aspectos da fonologia
   portuguêsa. Lisbon: University of Lisbon dissertation.
Mattoso Câmara, Joaquim Jr. 1953. Para o estudo da fonêmica
   portuguêsa. Rio de Janeiro: Organização Simões.
Perkell, Joseph. 1969. Physiology of speech production:
   results and implications of a quantitative cineradiographic
   study. Cambridge, Mass.: MIT Press.
Peterson, Gordon E. and Harold L. Barney. 1952. Control methods
   used in a study of the vowels. Journal of the Acoustical
   Society of America 24.175-84.
Smalley, William A. 1963. Manual of articulatory phonetics.
   Tarrytown, N.Y.: Practical Anthropology.

PARADIGMATIC EVOLUTION OF DIPHTHONGS:
MARSIAN ITALIAN AND CHICANO SPANISH

MARIO SALTARELLI

University of Illinois

1. Purpose

This paper shows (a) that the ongoing evolution of two
geographically separated varieties of Romance, Marsian Italian
and Chicano Spanish, indicate that grammatically equivalent
changes result under equivalent sociolinguistic conditions;
(b) furthermore, that two radically opposed types of diphthongs
or vowel breaking phenomena, namely the Marsian alternation
[I] vs. [ay] and [U] vs. [aw] as well as Chicano [o] vs.
[we], receive equivalent treatment in the morphological
system (i.e. the alternation is eliminated in both
languages), but with opposite phonetic results (i.e. the
undiphthongized form [I,U] remains in Marsian, whereas the
diphthongized [we] is kept in Chicano); (c) moreover, that
the evolution of these diphthongs, observed in the course of
this century through three generations of speakers and the
documentation of grammarians, does not proceed gradually
through intermediate phonetic stages; (d) finally, that the
evolution of these diphthongs, although phonetically abrupt,
proceeds gradually through the morphological paradigms of the

language. That is, morphemic alternations are abruptly
leveled at one point in time, but only within the confines
of morphological categories like the verb paradigm or the
gender paradigm. Furthermore, this paper maintains (e) that
a synchronic rule-account of diphthongization/monophthongiza-
tion phenomena must be 'justified' within the paradigmatic
system of the language in question; (f) and that the discovery
of the system of paradigms in a given language at any one stage
in time is evidenced, at least in part, by its contiguous stages.
Accordingly, an extremist Saussurian separation between the
synchronic and the diachronic aspects of language would be
questioned on empirical as well as theoretical grounds.

2. Marsian diphthongs: [I] vs. [ay] and [U] vs. [aw]

The Marsian Italian dialect which I am describing is that of
Pescasseroli (Province of Aquila, Region of Abruzzi) high in
the Apennines where the river Sangro has its source. Because
of its remote geographical location, the vernacular of Pescasseroli (Pesculum Seroli) has evolved free from external
linguistic influence at least since the eleventh century
(Croce, 1924), in a sociolinguistic condition of 'strong
internal monitoring' (Saltarelli, 1974). Even the rich
tradition of Italian dialect studies has left this speech
community practically untouched. The closest community
covered by the linguistic atlas is Scanno (Province of Sulmona,
AIS 656), six hours away by high mountain trail over Monte
Palombo. In the last three generations, however, a sociolinguistic condition of 'weak internal monitoring' has gradually prevailed, particularly in the last generation. During
the 1960's the community experienced a total change from an
efficient income-in-kind economy to a booming year-round
hotel industry.
   In general, I am reporting the effect which a sociolinguistic condition of 'weak monitoring' has had on this dialect.
In particular, I concentrate on a most salient feature in the
evolution of its morphology: the diphthongs [ay] and [aw]
exemplified in 5. Before discussing these data on diphthongs,
it will suffice to make the following remarks about the
vocalism of this dialect and its distributional system:

(1) a. stressed/closed syllable: a ɛ e ɔ o i u
     b. stressed/open syllable: a ɛ e ɔ o I U
     c. unstressed syllable: a ə

where the alternation between 1c and 1a,b, based on the feature stress, and the alternation between 1b and 1a, based on
the syllable structure, allows us the capture of two fundamental phonetic generalizations:

(2) a. *Vowel Reduction:* In unstressed position vowels
         other than /a/ reduce to schwa.
     b. *Vowel Laxing:* High vowels are lax in open
         syllables.

Two additional phenomena are observed in the vowel distribution of the speech of Pescasseroli:

(3) *Vowel Raising:* Vowels other than /a/ are raised to the next higher level when in the next syllable a vowel other than /a/ follows.

(4) *Vowel Breaking:* Stressed mid-vowels diphthongize when they occur in an open syllable and the next syllable contains the vowel /a/.

Viewed within a generative framework, the four rules in 2 and 3 above presuppose that stress has been determined. The only consideration of rule interaction is that *Raising* feeds *Laxing*. The total effect of these four distributional principles accounts for the considerable deviation that we find between the phonetics of Pescasseroli and that of Standard Italian.. Observe, for example, the derivation of the adjectives 'narrow' (It. *stretto/a*), 'good' (It. *buono/a*), 'black' (It. *nero/a*):

(4) masc.   fem.   masc.   fem.   masc.   fem.

stréttV	strétta	bónV	bóna	nérV	néra	
stríttV		búnV		nírV		Raising
					náyra	Breaking
		bŰnV		nɪ́rV		Laxing
strítta		bŰnə	búnə	nɪ́rə		Reduction

In 4 above, the underlying segment V stands for incompletely specified vowel in unstressed position. In fact, on the basis of earlier observations (cf. 1) there are no grounds for identifying completely any vowel other than /a/ in morphemes which never receive stress. Moreover, in 4, the segments *I* and *U* stand for the lax counterparts of front and back high vowels, respectively.

Laxing and *Reduction* are purely phonetic rules. *Raising* is also phonologically defined here (in another paper, Saltarelli, forthcoming, I have considered the theoretical implications of a morphological alternative). But *Breaking*, which accounts for the diphthongization phenomena under consideration, differs in that it is partially lexicalized for items which do not exhibit a masculine/feminine alternation, i.e. one must know the subset of lexical items which diphthongize. I have observed that more 'conservative' speakers (mostly people over 60) use this paradigm-conditioned rule as an almost entirely phonetic phenomenon, 'liberal' speakers (mostly people over 30) have a lexicalized form of the rule, and 'radical' speakers (mostly under 30) have eliminated the phenomenon altogether. There is evidence, furthermore, for gradual elimination of nonparadigmatic diphthongs but on a much slower item-by-item basis.

Let us now consider the sample list 5 where under Marsian the diphthongized/nondiphthongized forms are entered in a generation order from the older to the younger generation, showing thus the effects of the ongoing evolutionary process (the Marsian entries are in phonetic transcription):

(5) Standard Italian   Marsian

peperone	pəparáwlə, pəparÚlə	'pepper'
fagiolo	fašáwlə, fašÚlə	'bean'
fuoco	fáwkə	'fire'
piena	kYáyna	'flashflood'
uovo	áwə	'egg'
Opi	áwpYə	'Opi' (place name)
dispensa	máysa	'pie safe'
legna	láyna	'firewood'
fieno	fYáynə	'hay'
rena	ráynə	'gravel'
sera	sáyra	'evening'
mela	máyla, mÍlə	'apple'
pantaloni	pandaláwnə, pandalÚnə	'trousers'
oro	ą́wrə	'gold'
ora	Úra	'hour'
padella	frəssáwra, frəssÚra	'frying pan'
tela	táyla	'cloth'
pera	páyra, pÍrə	'pear'
cenere	čáynə	'ashes'
sete	sáytə	'thirst'
seta	sáyta	'silk'
sposa	spáwsa, spÚsa	'betrothed (f.)'
vuoi	báwə, bÚ	'you want'
mena	máyna, mÍna	'he hits'
no	náwnə	'no'
quella	kʷáyla, kʷÍla	'that one (f.)'
piena	kYáyna, kYÍna	'full (f.)'
nera	náyra, nÍra .	'black (f.)'

To summarize the data, in 5 we observe that the alternations
[I] vs. [ay] and [U] vs. [aw] are unstable. In the last three
generations one can observe a definite tendency toward the
elimination of such alternations, the leveling being in favor
of the nondiphthongized [I] and [U] form. People over 60 say
[pəparáwlə], whereas those under 30 say [pəparÚlə]. The
population between 30 and 60 is divided between the diphthongized and the nondiphthongized forms.

We notice also three distinct patterns of evolution
squarely based on morphological paradigms: the verb paradigm,
masculine/feminine paradigm, and the noun paradigm. Only
rarely does one hear diphthongized forms in verbs, even from
very old people. The few remaining forms I found were [báwə]
now replaced by [bÚ] (It. *vuoi* 'you want'), and [máyna] now
replaced by [mÍna] (It. *mena* 'he hits'). Diphthongs are
absent in the verb paradigm of middle-aged and young people.
In the masculine/feminine paradigm, where the diphthong is
strictly governed by the presence of /a/ in the next syllable,
only young people are rapidly abandoning the alternation
[náyra/nÍrə] (It. *nera/nero* 'black') for [nÍra/nÍrə]. Nouns
not exhibiting a masculine/feminine alternation are gradually
losing the diphthong as time goes by, but generally only if

the item ends in schwa: [pəparáwlə] changes to [pəparÚlə],
but the evolution is very slow in this last case.

In conclusion, it seems clear that the ongoing evolution
of diphthongs in Marsian proceeds strictly according to the
morphological structure of the language, with the verb going
first.

3. Evolution of diphthongs in Chicano

The recent evolution of Spanish in communities of northern
Mexico and their migrant movements in the United States also
exhibits leveling of diphthongs as a salient characteristic.
Marsian and Chicano as two distinct varieties of Romance show
an interesting correlation. Like Marsian, Chicano is in a
sociolinguistic condition of 'weak internal monitoring',
overwhelmed by integrative and other pressures. Like Marsian,
Chicano Spanish is eliminating morphemic alternations between
diphthongized and nondiphthongized forms. Strikingly, the
ongoing change in Chicano seems to be another example of
paradigmatic evolution of diphthongs.

Briefly, in its recent evolution, this language has
eliminated the [o] vs. [we] alternation but only in first
conjugation (i.e. -ar) verbs, with the result that [we]
appears in all forms regardless of stress:

(6)   Chicano   Standard Spanish

        vuélar   'to fly'   volár

        vuélo   vuelámos   vuélo   volámos
        vuélas   vuélas
        vuéla   vuélan   vuéla   vuélan

        vueládo   voládo
        vuelándo   volándo
        vuelé   volé
        vuelába   volába
        vuelára   volára

Unlike in the case of Marsian, the Chicano material came
to my attention through published works. We can be thankful
for the monumental work by Espinosa 1930 for the early recording of this evolutionary phenomenon. The theoretical implications of this phenomenon for generative phonology were
discussed by Harris 1973, 1974.

I have found evidence that leveling occurs not only with
regular alternations [o] vs. [we] but also with exceptional
alternations of the type [u] vs. [we]. Standard Spanish 'to
play' *jugar, juego, jugando,* etc., is Chicano (Chicago)
juegar, juego, juegando, etc. It is also well known that the
phenomenon of leveling started with first conjugation *o-ue*
verbs but spread gradually through the lexical set of verbs
which belong to this conjugation. It seems that at present
the phenomenon is beginning to spread to other conjugations:
muerir 'to die'. Unlike Marsian, Chicano maintains the

undiphthongized form unchanged in all other paradigms, although
the forms may have been originally derived from a verbal root:
voladór 'flier', *volánte* 'flywheel', *volandéra* 'washer',
voladúra 'blasting', etc.

As in the case of Marsian, the conclusion is that Chicano
shows that the evolution of its diphthongs occurs not across-
the-board. Rather, the paradigmatic structure of the language
in question determines the stages of its evolutionary process.
In comparing the Marsian and the Chicano evolution of diphthongs, one notices that Marsian has undergone an evolutionary
process whereby diphthongs have been leveled according to a
hierarchy of paradigms which went as follows: verb $>$ gender
$>$ other. The developments in Chicano so far appear to confirm
the primacy of the verb within the paradigm hierarchy.

4. Excursus on *a*-diphthongs

On the basis of the internal workings of the phonological
system in the dialect of Pescasseroli, it seems quite clear
that the diphthongs [ay] and [aw] should be derived from an
underlying mid-vowel, respectively /e/ and /o/. We have seen
that an independently motivated rule of *Raising* or umlaut
would account for the fact that the undiphthongized form is
a high rather than a mid-vowel. Moreover, the rule of *Laxing*,
also independently motivated, accounts for the fact that the
undiphthongized form is high and lax, rather than mid and
tense (cf. 2b). The conditioning factor appears to be clear
only in the case of the gender alternations. We shall, therefore, define two rules, one for the gender paradigm a, and
one for the other cases.

(7)   a.   [   ] → [a]   /___$[\begin{smallmatrix}mid\\V\end{smallmatrix}]$ C_o^1 [a]   gender

      b.   [   ] → [a]   /___$[\begin{smallmatrix}mid\\V\end{smallmatrix}]$ C_o^1 [V]   lex-B

Whether the rule is morphologically or lexically conditioned,
the phonetic result is the same, a low vowel is inserted before
the mid-vowel which, in turn, becomes a glide.

This type of *a*-diphthong is a relatively rare occurrence in
Romance, and its geographical distribution does not appear
to indicate any discernible substratum pattern. For example,
searching the Italian linguistic atlas (*AIS*, VIII, 1574) for
the adjective 'black' (It. *nero/nera*) I did not find alternations of exactly the same type as Marsian has. However, the
diphthongized form [ay] is found in the Engadine, the Castel-
nuovo D'Asti (Piemonte), Crecchio (Foggia), Faeto (Benevento),
and San Fratello (Messina). Vegliote (Dalmatia) also appears
to have this very same type of diphthong for front as well
as back mid-vowels (Hadlich, 1965), but without the typical
alternation found in Pescasseroli. It would appear that
these diphthongs in Marsian are the reflexes of Latin long
mid-vowels, as has been proposed for Dalmatian. But the
correspondences are not always quite precise as we find
[áwə] (<ŏ) 'egg', [náyra] (<ī) 'black', [áwrə] (<aw) 'gold'.

REFERENCES

Croce, B. 1924. Pescasseroli. A chapter in Storia del regno
    di Napoli. Bari: Laterza.
Espinosa, A. 1930. Estudios sobre el español de Neuvo Méjico.
    Buenos Aires.
Hadlich. R. 1965. The phonological history of Vegliote.
    Chapel Hill: University of North Carolina Press.
Harris, J. W. 1973. On the order of certain phonological rules
    in Spanish. A Festschrift for Morris Halle, ed. by Anderson,
    R. and P. Kiparsky. New York: Holt, Rinehart, and Winston.
_____. 1974. Morphologization of phonological rules: an
    example from Chicano Spanish. Linguistic studies in Romance
    languages, ed. by Campbell, R., M. Goldin, and M. Wang.
    Washington, D.C.: Georgetown University Press.
Jaberg, K. and J. Jud. 1928. Atlante linguistico-etnografico
    dell'Italia et della Svizzera. Zofingen.
Saltarelli, M. 1974. Leveling of paradigms in Chicano Spanish.
    Proceedings of the Colloquium on Hispanic Linguistics,
    Amherst, Mass., July, 1974.
_____. 1975. Remarks on the acquisition, development and
    death of emigrant languages in the U.S.A. Studies in
    language learning.
_____. Forthcoming. The Marsian verb paradigm. Festschrift
    for Robert A. Hall, Jr., ed. by Pulgram, E., R. Di Pietro,
    S. Cartledge, and D. Feldman.

ASPECTS OF SPANISH VERB MORPHOLOGY

JAMES W. HARRIS

Massachusetts Institute of Technology

1. Introduction

Previous studies of Spanish generative morphophonology (for
example, Foley 1965, Harris 1969, Brame and Bordelois 1973),
like those of other languages, have arrived at 'underlying'
or 'systematic phonemic' representations by a process of
triangulation back from the 'surface' or 'systematic phonetic'
representations of sets of forms sharing morphemes. Only
rarely have questions been raised concerning the principles
of word formation that control these concatenations of morphemes. Consider, for example, the forms in 1, which are
typical of the data studied in Chapter Five of Harris 1969:[1]

(1)	Verb stem	Nominalization	Agentive	Adjective	Misc.
a.	/adapt+a-/ *adapta-*	/adapt+a+t+ion/ *adaptación*			
b.	/adopt+a-/ *adopta-*	/adopt+ion/ *adopción*	/adopt+a+t+or/ *adoptador*	/adopt+iv+o/ *adoptivo*	
c.	/abort+a-/ *aborta-*			/abort+iv+o/ *abortivo*	/abort+o/ *aborto*
d.	/suc+t+ion+a-/ *succiona-*	/suc+t+ion/ *succión*			
e.	/un+i-/ *uni-*	/un+ion/ *unión*	/un+i+t+or/ *unidor*	/un+i+t+iv+o/ *unitivo*	
f.		/pun+i+t+ion/ *punición*		/pun+i+t+iv+o/ *punitivo*	

In Harris 1969, interest is focused on the relationship between
'underlying' and 'surface' forms and on the rules that mediate
this relationship. Little attention is directed to facts
like the following:

i.   the nominalization *adaptación* (1a) contains a 'theme
        vowel' while *adopción* (1b) is athematic although
        adoptador is not;
ii.   there is no nominalization **abortación* or **aborción*
        with the root *abort-* (1c);
iii.   the verb stem *succiona-* (1d) contains the nominal
        succión, and there is no nominalization **succionación*
        or **succioncíón* of this verb stem;
iv.   the nominalization *unión* (1e) not only is athematic
        but also lacks the augment /t/ found in the agentive
        unidor and the adjective *unitivo*;
v.   there is no verb stem **puni-* 'punish' (1f) correspond-
        ing to the nominalization *punición* 'punishment' and
        the adjective *punitivo* 'punitive.'

In spite of this catalog of idiosyncracies, it is hardly
open to question that Spanish has principles of word formation,
which could be called morphological rules. We will mention
only one of several illustrated in 1: although it is an
idiosyncratic property of individual forms with a given root
whether or not they contain a 'theme vowel' (*adaptación* versus
athematic *adopción*), all forms with a given root that do have
a theme vowel have the same one, according to the conjugational
class of the root. Thus *adaptación* rather than **adaptición*;
punición/punitivo rather than *punición/*punativo* or **punación/
punitivo*, and so on.[2]
Few generative grammarians doubt that a grammar has a component that accounts for the form and composition of words, or
that morphological rules exist. There is at present, however,
no explicit general theory of morphology in generative grammar.
A few preliminary investigations have appeared,[3] but as yet
little crucial empirical evidence has been brought to bear
on the details of the content and organization of the 'morphological component' of a generative grammar.
Recognition that there exists such a subject matter as
morphology is not new among generative grammarians. For
example, in Harris 1969 derivations of the sort illustrated in
2 are proposed:

(2) 1st conjugation 2nd conjugation 3rd conjugation

pas+á+ba	com+í+ba	viv+í+ba	
-	$\emptyset$	$\emptyset$	b→$\emptyset$/i+__
pasába	*comía*	*vivía*	

The 'underlying' or 'systematic phonemic' representation of
the imperfective aspectual morpheme in past tense verb forms
is /ba/, in all three conjugational classes. The initial *b*
of this representation is deleted in second and third conjuga-

tion forms by the rule shown in 2. Now, the author fully
recognized in 1969 that this rule is a morphological rule, a
rule of allomorphy. More specifically, it applies to no form
other than the aspectual morpheme illustrated in 1; its sole
function is to control the shape of this one morpheme. Still,
the rule in question is not explicitly labeled in Harris 1969
as a 'morphological' or 'allomorphic' rule, nor is it formally
distinguished in any other way from the rules that surround it.

From the earliest formative period[4] to the present, generative transformational grammatical theory has eschewed certain
methodological restrictions ('discovery procedures') and other
assumptions that might have led to a clear 'separation of
levels' between morphology and phonology. A theory has
evolved in which in general no formal distinction is drawn
between morphological rules and phonological rules. This
theory is thus literally 'morphophonological'. Such a line of
development was natural, if not inevitable, and, it is widely
agreed, has contributed significantly to our understanding of
the nature of morphophonological systems of natural languages.
On the other hand, it is also widely agreed that generative
morphophonological theory, in its better-known versions,[5] is
excessively powerful. That is, it allows too much latitude
in the choice of phonological descriptions. To the extent
that this is correct, generative phonological theory fails
to achieve the goal of explanatory adequacy.

Evidence has begun to accumulate that the study of morphology may provide an empirically supported basis for limiting
the class of linguistic descriptions permitted by generative
theory. Stated programmatically, the strategy is this: we
seek to replace the current theory T, which says essentially
'there are morphophonological rules', by a more restrictive
theory T', which says essentially 'there are morphological
rules with certain properties and there are phonological rules
with different properties'. It is crucial that T' permit only
a proper subset of the grammars permitted by T. It might be
noted, incidentally, that it is hardly a matter of controversy
that a domain of morphology exists as a subject for serious
investigation. What is at issue is whether or not there
exists a linguistically significant level of representation
that is intermediate in degree of articulation between that of
the 'word' and that of phonological representation. In other
words, are linguistically significant generalizations found
whose expression depends crucially on the existence of a
level of morphological representation? The traditional answer
to this question is of course that such generalizations are
found in abundance, and I know of no evidence from current
work that challenges this view.

In this study we will not attempt to make a major contribution to the nascent general theory of morphology in generative grammar, nor will we attempt a general outline of Spanish
morphology within the framework of generative grammar.
Instead, we will investigate one particular area that has been
treated inadequately thus far, namely, vowel alternations in
verb forms. In nouns and adjectives, the vowels of roots
obey certain constraints and may participate in certain

alternations. In verbs, the constraints are heavier, the
alternations are slightly different, and both depend in part
on arbitrary conjugation-class affiliations, among other
morphological properties. It thus seems natural to look to
a theory of morphology for elucidation of these matters.

2. Verb stems of the second conjugation (*e*-themes)

The roots of most second conjugation verbs in Spanish show
no vocalic alternations at all in inflectional paradigms, and
a relatively small number exhibit only the common stress-
controlled vowel ~ diphthong alternations *e* ~ *ié* and *o* ~ *ué*,
as illustrated in 3:

(3)   *tendémos*   *tiéndo*   'We/I tend'

       podémos   *puédo*   'We/I can'

There are, however, two morphological peculiarities of this
conjugational class; (a) the existence of a number of morphologically complex stems like *obscurece-* 'darken' and (b) the
fact that the high vowels *i* and *u* are systematically excluded
from phonetic representations of second conjugation roots.
Consider the examples in 4:

(4)   Adjective/noun   Verb stem

      obscur+o   'dark'   obscur+ec-   'darken'

      tard+e   'evening'   a+tard+ec-   'become evening'

      dur+o   'hard'   en+dur+ec-   'harden'

      loc+o   'crazy'   en+lo[k]+ec-   'go crazy'

      nobl+e   'noble'   en+nobl+ec-   'ennoble'

The roots in 4 may occur in other forms as well, for example
obscur*idad* 'darkness', nobl*eza* 'nobility', and loc*ura* 'crazi-
ness'. The composition of verb stems like those illustrated
in 4 is determined, in part, by a morphological rule whose
effect can be stated roughly as in 5:

(5) $\begin{bmatrix} X \\ \begin{Bmatrix} \text{Adj} \\ \text{Noun} \end{Bmatrix} \\ \vdots \end{bmatrix}_{\text{Root}} \Rightarrow \begin{bmatrix} \begin{bmatrix} \begin{Bmatrix} \emptyset \\ a \\ én \end{Bmatrix} \end{bmatrix}_{\text{Pfx}} + \begin{bmatrix} X \\ \vdots \end{bmatrix}_{\text{Root}} + \begin{bmatrix} /ec/ \\ \text{Verb} \\ \text{2conj} \\ \vdots \end{bmatrix}_{\text{Sfx}} \end{bmatrix}_{\text{Stem}}$

The prefixes associated with 4 and 5 have no independent
meaning, and the choice of *a-*, *en-*, or no prefix is an arbitrary property of particular roots. The suffix *-ec-* often, but
not always, has the meaning roughly of 'inchoative,[6] and it is
patently of the second conjugation, as shown by the relevant

inflected forms, for example *obscurecer*, *obscurecemos*. The
roots x in 5, on the other hand, have no inherent conjugational
class affiliation. If the affix -*ec*- is marked as belonging
to the second conjugation, there is no need for the roots in
question also to be so marked. More importantly, we will see
directly below that these roots must not be so marked. Subsequent remarks will also give a clearer picture of the system
in which rules like 5 operate.

Let us turn now to the second peculiarity mentioned above.
With the exception of vowels in the class of stems illustrated
in 4, all vowels in second conjugation verb roots must be from
the set of phonemes /a,e,o/; the high vowels /i/ and /u/
are excluded. This is clearly a morphological restriction
peculiar to the second conjugation, rather than a general
phonological restriction, since there are nouns like *alquiler*,
bachiller, *mujer*, and so on, that have the form of second
conjugation infinitives, aside from the high vowel. These
observations have been pointed out in the literature, in
greater or lesser detail.[7] So far as I know, however, it has
not hitherto been pointed out that the absence of high vowels
in second conjugation verb roots not only reflects a constraint
on verb forms but also is involved in actual morphophonological
alternations. Consider the examples in 6:

(6) Verbs   Non-verbs

a. *absten-* 'abstain'   *abstinente*   'abstinent'
                             abstinencia 'abstinence'

b. *comet-*   'commit'   *comitente*   'committing'
                                            (adjective)
                             comisión   'act of committing'

c. *convenc-* 'convince'   *convincente* 'convincing,
                                            persuasive'
                             convicción   'conviction,
                                            persuasion'

d. *corromp-* 'corrupt'   *corrupto*   'corrupt'
                                            (adjective)
                             corruptor   'corrupter'
                             corrumpente 'corruptive'

e. *encend-* 'light, set   *incendio*   'fire' (noun)--also
              fire to'   *incendiar* 'to
                                            burn' (first
                                            conjugation)

f. *llov-*   'rain'   *lluvia*   'rain' (noun)

g. *prend-*   'seize, capture' *prisión*   'act of seizing'

h. *prove-*   'supply,   *provisión*   'act of supplying,
              provide with'   providing
                             provisto   'supplied with'

			provisor	'supplier'
i.	*romp-*	'break'	*ruptura*	'break, breaking' (noun)
j.	*somet-*	'submit'	*sumisión*	'submission'
			sumiso	'submissive'
k.	*venc-*	'overcome, be victorious'	*victoria*	'victory'
			victorioso	'victorious'
			invicto	'undefeated'

How are we to explicate the principles that determine the allomorphy observed in the surface forms of 6? Let us take 6b *comet-/comitente/comisión* as a specific case. These three words obviously contain one and the same root, which we can represent neutrally as COMET (which should perhaps be segmented into the prefix CO plus the root MET, but this is irrelevant in the present context). It is not sufficient to say only that COMET is manifested as /komet/ in verb forms, as /komit/ before the theme vowel plus the adjectival suffix -*nt+e*, and as /komis/ before the nominalizing suffix -*ión*. To say no more than this is to merely restate the data without reference to any language-particular generalizations or general principles that might underly the data. It is equivalent, in fact, to treating the allomorphy of COMET as though it were an instance of the worst possible case, namely, suppletion (e.g. like *ser*, *era*, *fui*, etc.).

At least one language-particular generalization concerning COMET and the other roots in 6 is obvious: in verb forms of the second conjugation, high root vowels are disallowed. It is clear that no comparable generalization can be made about second conjugation roots in non-verb forms. In particular, it is not the case that mid root vowels in second conjugation verb forms always alternate with high vowels in non-verbs, as can be seen from the small sample of forms in 7:

(7) Verbs   Non-verbs

    corro- 'corrode'   *corrosión* (*corrusión) 'corrosion'
                      corrosivo (*corrusivo) 'corrosive'

    envolv-'wrap (up)'   *envoltura* (*envultura) 'wrapping'

Examples such as 6e *encend-/incendio/incendiar* and 6j *somet-/sumisión/sumiso* suggest that more than one vowel, in fact all vowels, of a given second conjugation root are subject to the constraint that they cannot be high in verb forms. Prefixes, however, are not subject to this constraint, as is shown by examples like *dis+pon-* 'dispose' and *im+pon-* 'impose'. The root of *somet-/sumisión/sumiso* of course derives historically from *sub+mitt-*, but the feeling of composition has been lost. Compare *submarino* 'submarine' and other similar examples, where prefixation is perceived as such, and the cluster -*bm-* is retained. There is also no feeling of

prefixation in *encend-/incend-* and indeed historically there is
none.

Formalism is not the issue at this point, but all the observations just made can be consolidated into the rule shown in 8,
which will serve as a basis for further discussion:

(8)   V → [-high]/... [2conj] ...⌉
$$ \qquad \qquad \qquad \qquad \qquad \qquad \rfloor_{\text{Verb stem}} $$

Rule 8 is a morphological rule, not a phonological rule: it
does not express a strictly phonological generalization;
rather, it refers only to morphemes idiosyncratically marked
[2conj], and to these in strictly verb forms only. Prefixes
are not marked with conjugation-class features--there is no
prefix associated exclusively with any particular conjugation--
and accordingly rule 8 does not apply to them. Also, roots
preceding the suffix *-ec-* are not marked for conjugation class;
thus they escape rule 8 and are free to have high vowels in
verb forms. The following derivations, to be commented on
below, will perhaps be useful in clarifying the discussion
so far, although they are obviously incomplete and only
suggestive:

(9)   Inherent (lexical) properties of morphemes:

[/obskur/, +Root, ±Adjective, ±___idad, ±___ec, ...]

[/sumit/, +Root, 2conj, ±Verb, ±___ión, ...]

[/ec/,[8] +Affix, 2conj, +Verb, +k-insertion, ...]

[/yon/, +Affix, +Noun, +Feminine, ...]

Morphological representations (=output of 5 and other
rules of word formation:

[obskur+o]$_{Adj}$ [[obskur+ec+e]$_{St}$+s]$_{Vb}$

$$\qquad \qquad \qquad \qquad \qquad \qquad \qquad \text{Rule 8}$$
$$\qquad \qquad \qquad \qquad \qquad \qquad \qquad \text{Other rules}$$

[sumit+yon]$_N$ [[sumit+e]$_{St}$+mos]$_{Vb}$
$$\qquad \qquad \qquad \quad \text{somet+e} \qquad \qquad \qquad \text{Rule 8}$$
$$\quad \text{sumis+yon} \qquad \qquad \qquad \qquad \qquad \text{Other rules}$$

Phonological (dictionary) representations:

/obskur+o/	/obskur+ec+e+s/	
oβskur+o	oβskur+ec+e+s	Spirantization
[oβskúro]	[oβskuréces]	Output of all rules

/sumis+yon/	/somet+e+mos/	
[sumisyón]	[sometémos]	Spirantization Output of all rules

Although the derivations in 9 omit many details,[9] they
do allow us to relate the data at hand to the proposals of
Halle 1973, which we will accept here as a first approximation
to a general theory of generative morphology. Following Halle,
we will say that the grammar of a language L contains a list
of the morphemes of L together with information about the
idiosyncratic semantic, syntactic, morphological, and phonological properties of each morpheme. The dictionary of L is
a list of all the words that occur in L together with information about the idiosyncratic properties of each word. The
morphological component of the grammar of L is a set of statements concerning the form of words in L, that is, the set of
conditions that an item must satisfy in order to be admitted
to membership in the dictionary. The phonological component
has access only to the dictionary; the dictionary representation of a word serves as input to the phonological rules.
   Relating this sketch to the derivations in 9, we see that
the lexical entry of the root contained in the noun *sumisión,*
the adjective *sumiso,* and the verb stem *somete-* contains, along
with other information including the feature [2conj], the
underlying phonological representation /sumit/. Rule 8, as a
morphological rule, states a condition that items must satisfy
in order to be admitted to membership in the dictionary of
Spanish. Thus 8 specifies that in dictionary representations
(the input to phonological rules), the root in question must
have the shape /somet/--with non-high vowels--in verb forms.

3. Verb stems of the third conjugation (*i*-themes)

The dictionary representations of all third conjugation verb
stems are of the form (Prefix)+Root+(V). That is, there are no
affixes in the third conjugation analogous to second conjugation
-ec-. In the third conjugation, any of the vowels /a,e,i,o,u/
may appear in the most abstract representations of roots, but
the distribution of vowels in surface representations is tightly
constrained. Consider the examples in 10:

(10) Verbs   Non-verbs

   a. *cubr-*   'cover'   *cobertura*   'covering' (noun)
                           cobertor   'bed cover'
                           cobertizo   'covered shelter'

   b. *dirig-*   'direct' *dirección*   'direction'
                           director   'director'
                           directo   'direct' (adjective)

   c. *exim-*   'exempt' *exención*   'exemption'
                           exento   'exempt' (adjective)

   d. *mull-*   'soften' *muelle*   'soft'
                           molicie   'softness'
                           molitivo   'softening' (adjective)

                           also
                           molificar   'to soften' (1st conj)

e.	*oprim-*	'oppress'	*opresión*[10]	'oppression'
			opresor	'oppressor'
			opresivo	'oppressive'
f.	*recib-*	'receive'	*recepción*	'reception'
			receptor	'receiver'
			receptivo	'receptive'
g.	*redim-*	'redeem'	*redención*	'redemption'
			redentor	'redeemer'
h.	*sirv-/*			
	serv-	'serve'	*servicio*	'service'
			servidumbre	'servitude'
			servil	'servile'
i.	*concib-/*			
	conceb-	'conceive'	*concepción*	'conception'
			concepto	'concept'
j.	*pid-/*	'request,	*petición*	'request,
	ped-	petition'		petition'
k.	*rind-/*		*rendición*	'rendition,
	rend-	'render'		rendering'
l.	*repit-/*			
	repet-	'repeat'	*repetición*	'repetition'

We see from 10 that although mid vowels can occur in third
conjugation roots, these roots are constrained in verb forms
so that in the vast majority of cases mid vowels are disallowed
altogether, and in a minority of cases (e.g. 10h-l) are permitted
under certain circumstances (see below). Furthermore, it is
not the case that high root vowels in third conjugation verb
forms always alternate with mid vowels in non-verb forms, as
can be seen from the small sample of forms in 11:

(11) Verbs   Non-verbs

    aflig-   'afflict'   *aflicción*
                          (**aflección*)   'affliction'

    bull-   'stir about, *bullicio*   'uproar,
            be noisy' (**bollicio*) noise'

    describ- 'describe' *descripción*   'description'
                      (**descrepción*)
                      descriptivo   'descriptive'
                      (**descreptivo*)

In short, for the vast majority of third conjugation roots,
vowels in non-verb forms are not predictable but those in
verb forms are predictable as to whether they are high or
mid: verb forms may have only high root vowels. This fact

leads us immediately to propose the morphological rule 12, which states a condition on the admission of third conjugation verb stems to the dictionary:

(12) $\begin{bmatrix} V \\ -low \end{bmatrix} \rightarrow$ [+high] / ... [$\overline{3conj}$] ...]$_{Verb\ stem}$

In order to illustrate more clearly the role of 12, we show in 13 relevant steps in the derivation of the noun *cobertura* (10a) and the verb form *cubrimos* (first person plural present indicative and preterit):

(13) Inherent properties of morphemes:

[/kobr/, +Root, 3conj, ±Verb, ±___*tur*, ...]

[/tur/, +Affix, +Noun, +Feminine, ...]

Morphological representations:

[kobr+tur+a]$_N$ [[kobr+i]$_{St}$+mos]$_V$

kubr+i   Rule 12

kober $\emptyset \rightarrow$ e /C___rC

Phonological (dictionary) representations:

/kober+tur+a/   /kubr+i+mos/

[koβertúra]   [kuβrímos]   Output of all rules

   I am unable to find in the third conjugation a clear case, like second conjugation *somet-/sumiso*, etc., of a root with more than one vowel affected by 12. As far as I can see, all third conjugation stems consist of a monosyllabic root with or without a prefix, or of a polysyllabic root only the last vowel of which could possibly be affected by 12. There are two types of the latter. One can be illustrated with *sacud-* 'shake', whose *a* is not affected by 12.[11] The other type can be illustrated with *escup-* 'spit', *esculp-* 'sculpt', and *esgrim-* 'fence, wield (a sword, etc.)'. In such forms the initial *e* cannot be affected by 12 since it is not present in lexical representations, but is instead inserted in the environment #___s[+consonantal] by a well-known late rule of epenthesis (cf. *checo₊slovaco* but *eslovaco*, *ali₊scaf₊o* but *escaf₊andra*, etc.).
   In Harris (to appear) it is argued that rule 12 applies to all third conjugation verb stems--including those like 10h-1 and others with allomorphs containing surface mid vowels--the only exceptions being a few irregular and/or defective verbs like *concernir*. All of the evidence supporting such a position cannot be reviewed here, nor is it really necessary to do so. The data in 10a-h are sufficient to establish the point for the vast majority of third conjugation roots.

4. Forms in -*Vmiento*

The masculine-noun-forming suffix -*mient+o* is highly productive, being roughly equivalent to English -*ment* as in *development, abandonment, elopement,* and so on. A rough count in a rhyming dictionary (Peñalver 1940) shows some 250 such forms with second and third conjugation roots (with -*imiento*) and many hundreds of them with first conjugation roots (with -*amiento*). Not all of the +*V+mient+o* forms found in a rhyming dictionary are also found in standard dictionaries such as the *Vox*; for example *destruimiento* 'destruction', *escribimiento* 'writing'. Nevertheless, native speakers can identify and produce them without the slightest hesitation. As far as I know, there is no way of predicting which roots have -*Vmiento* forms and which do not.

Although -*Vmiento* forms are clearly syntactic nouns, native speakers without training in linguistics feel strongly that they are very much like verbs, that they are based on or derived from verbs in some way. This strong intuitive judgment finds support in a number of morphological facts.

i.   All -*imiento* forms are thematic. Contrast other non-verb forms with verbal roots, which are idiosyncratically thematic or athematic, as illustrated in 1.

ii.   All -*Vmiento* forms have corresponding strictly verb forms actually in use (unlike *punición, punitivo* in 1f and other examples). Thus, from the non-existence of a verb **pun-* 'punish' we can predict the non-existence of *punimiento 'punishment' (despite the existence of *punición, punitivo, punible*), and so on.

iii. -*Vmiento* forms invariably share all idiosyncratic peculiarities of the corresponding verb stems if these are different from non-verb forms. For example, second conjugation *obed+ec+i+mient+o* (**obed+i+mient+o*) 'act of obeying' contains the suffix -*ec*- as does the verb stem *obed+ec-* 'obey', unlike the adjective *obed+iente* (**obed+ec+iente*) 'obedient' and the noun *obed+iencia* (**obed+ec+iencia*) 'obedience'. For another example, both nouns *aper+tur+a* 'opening' with *p* and *aber+tur+a* with *b* exist in more or less free variation; but from the verb stem *abr-* (**apr-*) 'open' it is predictable that *abr+i+mient+o* 'opening' has *b* rather than *p*. Examples of this sort could be multiplied easily.

iv.   All -*Vmiento* forms have at least one meaning that is fully predictable from that of the corresponding verb stem, namely, 'act or effect of [root]'. As is well known, this sort of predictability is not always possible in other cases of 'derivational morphology'.

The native-speaker judgments under discussion can be reconstructed formally, and the morphological facts just listed, and others, can be derived as deductive consequences if the word-formation rules of the morphological component of the grammar include a rule that can be stated approximately as in 14:

(14) $[x]_{Stem_V} \implies [[x]_{Stem_V} + mient + o]_N$

Stated informally, 14 makes the claim that -*Vmiento* nouns
have incorporated within them intact verb stems, whatever
the peculiarities of the latter may be. Let us illustrate
14 with a few specific examples.

Second conjugation *obed+ec+i+mient+o* must have -*ec*-
according to 14 since the verb stem *obed*+ec- has this suffix.
Relevant stages of derivation are shown in 15:

(15) $[obed]_{Root}$
       $[obed+ec]_{Stem}$ Rule 5
       $[obed+ec+i]_{Stem}$ Other rules[12]
       $[[obed+ec+i]_{St} +mient+o]_N$ Rule 14   (morphology)

       /obed+ec+i+mient+o/   Dictionary representation
       [oβeđecimyénto]   Output of all rules
                                                           (phonology)

Second conjugation *sometimiento* 'act of submitting' has
mid root vowels, unlike the noun *sumisión* 'submission' and the
adjective *sumiso* 'submissive' according to 14 because roots of
second conjugation verb stems may not have high vowels in
dictionary representations 8. A partial derivation follows:

(16) $[sumit]_{Root}$
       $[sumit+i]_{Stem}$ Stem formation[12]
       $[somet+i]_{Stem}$ Rule 8
       $[[somet+i]_{St} +mient+o]_N$ Rule 14 (Dictionary
                                                    representation)

The derivations of all existing -*miento* nouns containing roots
like those illustrated in 6 are analogous to 16.

Third conjugation *recibimiento* 'act of receiving' has a
high root vowel, unlike the nouns *recepción*, *receptor* and
the adjective *receptivo*, according to 14 because roots of
third conjugation verb stems may not have mid vowels in
dictionary representations 12. A partial derivation is given
in 17:

(17) $[re+ceb+i]_{Stem}$
       $[re+cib+i]_{Stem}$ Rule 12
       $[[re+cib+i]_{St} +mient+o]_N$ Rule 14 (Dictionary
                                                    representation)

The derivations of all existing -*miento* forms containing
roots like those illustrated in 10 are essentially analogous
to 17.

In short, the incorporation into the morphological compo-

nent of rule 14, which is a reasonable reconstruction of
native-speaker judgments concerning the relationship of
-*miento* nouns to verb stems, permits the surface representations
of all -*miento* forms to be accounted for without recourse to
any descriptive machinery that does not have independent
motivation elsewhere in the language.

It should also be noted that the device embodied in 14
of embedding a verb stem into a noun is itself not unique to
the specific set of forms generated by 14. Consider the sizable
set of feminine nouns like *nevada* 'snow fall', *comida* 'food,
meal', *salida* 'departure, exit', etc., whose stems have
precisely the form of the past participle (minus the final
vowel) of the corresponding verb: first conjugation *nev-*
'snow', past participle *nevado*; second conjugation *com-* 'eat',
past participle *comido*; third conjugation *sal-* 'go out,
depart', past participle *salido*. Strikingly, the nouns under
discussion share any and all idiosyncratic properties of the
corresponding past participles. A small sample of examples
follows. The root *volv-/vuélv-* '(re)turn' has the athematic
past participle *vuelto*; the corresponding feminine noun is
also athematic: *vuelta* '(re)turn'. The root *pon-* 'set (said
of the sun)' has a peculiar athematic past participle *puesto*;
the corresponding feminine noun is *puesta (del sol)* '(sun-)
set'. The root *i-/va-/fu-* 'go' has suppletive allomorphs; the
past participle is *ido* and the corresponding feminine noun is
ida 'going'. All of these peculiarities can be, and in fact
apparently must be, accounted for by positing a morphological
rule whose effect is to embed past participles intact (except
for the final vowel) into the stems of the nouns of the type
under discussion.[13]

NOTES

[1]Throughout the present study, Spanish examples are usually
given in conventional orthography. Where greater explicitness
is needed, the customary // and [] are used, and an acute
accent sometimes marks the position of primary stress where
standard orthography does not.

[2]I am aware of only one exception to this generalization:
given the verb stem *responde-* 'accept responsibility' we would
expect **responsible* 'responsible' and **responsibilidad*
'responsibility' instead of the actually occurring forms
responsable and *responsabilidad*. (There is no stem **responda-*
or **responsa-* with the appropriate meaning.) Forms like
brama- (verb stem)/*bramido* (noun) 'roar', *ronca/ronquido*
'snore', *estalla/estallido* 'burst', etc., are not exceptions
to the morphological generalization in question, since the *i*
is part of the noun-forming suffix -*ido* meaning 'noise of
[root]'.

[3]For example, Dell 1970, Matthews 1972, Halle 1973, Harris 1973, Aronoff 1974, Anderson 1975, Harris (to appear), Jackendoff 1974.

[4]For example, Chomsky 1951, Halle 1959 and 1962.

[5]For example, Chomsky and Halle's *The Sound Pattern of English* (1968).

[6]Among other idiosyncratic properties of this suffix is the fact that it has an epenthetic *k* in certain environments, e.g. first person singular present indicative *endurezco*, present subjunctive *endurezca*, etc. For discussion see Harris 1972. The set of verbs with -*ec*- is closed. That is, it is not the case that all noun and adjective roots can appear in such verb stems; for example, *mal+o* 'bad' but *(a/en+)mal+ec-*, *diccionari+o* 'dictionary' but *(a/en+)diccionari+ec-*, etc. If there is any basis for predicting which roots can appear in such stems, I do not know what it is.

[7]For example, in Togeby 1972:262-4, Brame and Bordelois 1973:124-5.

[8]For convenience, *c* can be taken to represent [s] or [θ].

[9]For example, the *t/s* alternation in *somet-/sumisión/sumiso* and other forms. This alternation is treated in some detail in Harris 1969:143-53, but I would now handle it rather differently. In any event, the evidence presented there shows convincingly that this alternation is not strictly phonological but is instead controlled by a morphological rule.

[10]The root *prim* occurs also in *deprim-* 'depress', *reprim-* 'repress', *imprim-* 'impress, print', and *suprim-* 'suppress', all of which have non-verb forms analogous to *opresión*, *opresor*, *opresivo*. As far as I know, the alternation *m/s* is unique to these stems, although it may be connected with the *n/s* alternation in *pon-/pues+to* 'put', etc.

[11]Perhaps *sa-* is a prefix anyway; compare *a+cud-*, *re+cud-*, *per+cud-*. In any event, there seems to be one puzzling exception to the generalization that 12 does not affect *a*. Consider *exacción* 'act of demanding, exacting' but *exig-* 'demand, exact' (verb), *exigente* 'demanding, exacting' (adjective), *exigencia* 'demand, exigency'. If the lexical representation of the root is /eksag/ then it is not clear how to account for the *i* in *exig-*, etc.

[12]See Harris (to appear) for fuller discussion.

[13]I have gone into considerable detail in this section in order to show clearly that -*miento* forms can be accounted for in a principled way in an analysis quite different from that of Brame and Bordelois 1973. These authors consider the surface root vowels in -*miento* forms, like those of infinitives, to be also the underlying root vowels, in all cases. They give no supporting argument, however, for the assumption that infinitives and -*miento* nouns are decisive in this respect,

rather than non-verb forms like all of those in the right-hand
columns of 6 and 10.

REFERENCES

Anderson, S.R. Forthcoming. On the interaction of phonologi-
  cal rules of various types. Journal of Linguistics.
Aronoff, M. 1974. Word-structure. Cambridge, Massachusetts:
  M.I.T. dissertation.
Brame, M.K. and I. Bordelois. 1973. Vocalic alternations in
  Spanish. Linguistic Inquiry 4.111-68.
Chomsky, N. 1951. Morphophonemics of Modern Hebrew. Phila-
  delphia: University of Pennsylvania M.A. thesis.
Chomsky, N. and M. Halle. 1968. The sound pattern of English.
  New York: Harper and Row.
Dell, F. 1970. Les règles phonologiques tardives et la
  morphologie dérivationnelle du français. Cambridge,
  Massachusetts: M.I.T. dissertation.
Foley, J.A. 1965. Spanish morphology. Cambridge, Massachu-
  setts: M.I.T. dissertation.
Halle, M. 1959. The sound pattern of Russian. The Hague:
  Mouton.
_____. 1962. Phonology in a generative grammar. Word 18.54-
  72.
_____. 1973. Prolegomena to a theory of word formation.
  Linguistic Inquiry 4.3-16.
Harris, J.W. 1969. Spanish phonology. Cambridge, Massachusetts: The MIT Press.
_____. 1971. Aspectos del consonantismo español. Los
  fundamentos de la gramática transformacional, ed. by H.
  Contreras. México: Siglo XXI.
_____. 1972. Five classes of irregular verbs in Spanish.
  Generative studies in Romance languages, ed. by J. Casagrande and B. Saciuk. Rowley, Massachusetts: Newbury House.
_____. 1973. Las formas verbales de segunda persona plural
  y otras cuestiones de fonología y morfología. Revista de
  lingüística teórica y aplicada 11.31-60.
_____. Forthcoming. La morfología en una gramática
  generativa: alternancias vocálicas en las formas verbales
  del español. El español y la lingüística generativo-
  transformacional, ed. by J. Guitart and J. Roy. Barcelona:
  Ediciones 62--Península.
Jackendoff, R. Forthcoming. Morphological and semantic
  regularities in the lexicon. Language.
Matthews, P.H. 1972. Inflectional morphology. Cambridge:
  Cambridge University Press.
Peñalver, J. de. 1940. Diccionario de la rima. Buenos
  Aires: Sopena Argentina.
Togeby, K. 1972. L'Apophonie des verbes espagnols et
  portugais en -ir. Romance Philology 26.256-64.

Vox: Diccionario general ilustrado de la lengua española.
   (1964) Barcelona: Biblograf.

SUPERFICIALLY ILLOGICAL "NON": NEGATIVES IN COMPARATIVES*

DONNA JO NAPOLI AND MARINA NESPOR

University of North Carolina

1. Introduction

In Italian the word *non* is used as a negative element similar
to *not* in English. Thus 1b and 2b are the negative counterparts
of 1a and 2a, showing VP negation and NP negation respectively:

(1)   a.   Maria viene
         b.   Maria non viene.
            'Mary comes/does not come.'
(2)   a.   Tutti gli uomini ti guardano.
         b.   Non tutti gli uomini ti guardano.
            'All the men/Not all the men are looking at you.'

There are other uses of *non* that do not correspond to English
not: for example, the well-known cases of 'double negation',
illustrated in 3 with *nessuno* 'no one'.

(3)   Non viene nessuno.
       'No one is coming.'

In this paper we consider a use of *non* that is frequently found in comparatives and that has no English counterpart in these structures:[1]

(4) a. Maria è più intelligente di quanto è Carlo.
     b. Maria è più intelligente di quanto non sia Carlo.
         'Mary is more intelligent than Carlo is (not).'
(5) a. Maria è più intelligente di quanto tu credi.
     b. Maria è più intelligente di quanto tu non creda.
         'Maria is more intelligent than you believe (not).'

This use of *non* is frequently cited as an example of a 'pleonastic element' and is said to be optional in comparatives. We will present an analysis of 4 and 5 accounting for many differences between a and b, both semantic and syntactic. We will show that this *non* is not limited to comparatives, but occurs in various structures, many of which have counterparts with *not* in English. While we have not done a detailed study of languages other than Italian, we expect our analysis to be helpful in understanding similar uses of negative elements in other languages.

2. Pragmatics

The semantic difference between a and b in 4 and 5 lies in what is presupposed by the speaker, rather than in what is asserted. In the literature on presupposition there is reference to logical and pragmatic presuppositions. S' is a logical presupposition of a sentence S if from S we can conclude S' and at the same time from -S (to be read 'not S') we can conclude S' (see Horn 1969). It is also often mentioned that logical presuppositions remain unchanged under questioning (see Kiparsky and Kiparsky 1970). One way to find a logical presupposition of an S is to replace the intonation center in surface structure by a variable (see Chomsky 1971). Pragmatic presuppositions, on the other hand, are the conditions under which an S is appropriate (see Lakoff 1971). They involve the speaker and, often, the listener, while logical presuppositions follow from sentences themselves without regard to speaker, listener, or context (see Keenan 1971 and Karttunen 1973).

  Our *non* is used when certain pragmatic presuppositions are present. In fact, questioning or negating a comparative drastically affects the possibility of having *non* (see 2.1 and 2.2 below). *Non* appears when the speaker is assuming, but has not been told explicitly and therefore is not entirely sure, that the assertion of the comparative is contradictory to some previously held belief--most often the belief of the listener, but not always. In order to see this, consider the following contexts:

Context 1 (for 4a)

Dario: Dimmi cosa pensi di Maria e Carlo
          'Tell me what you think of Mary and Carlo.'
Paolo: Maria è più intelligente di quanto e/??non sia
Carlo, ma lui è molto più simpatico.

'Mary is more intelligent than Carlo is, but he is much nicer.'

Since Dario has in no way revealed his opinion of Maria and Carlo, it would be very strange for Paolo to assume that Dario holds opposite beliefs from his own. Thus *non* does not appear in Paolo's response.

Context 2 (for 4b)

Dario: Carlo è così intelligente che dubito che Maria possa vincerlo a scacchi.
    'Carlo is so intelligent that I doubt that Mary can beat him at chess.'
Paolo: Ma ti sbagli! Maria è più intelligente di quanto non sia/è Carlo e potrebbe vincerlo senza molti sforzi.
    'But you're wrong! Mary is more intelligent than Carlo is(n't) and she could beat him with little effort.'

Here Dario has explicitly said that Maria probably cannot beat Carlo at chess. However, he has only implied that Carlo is more intelligent than Maria. Paolo may, accordingly, assume that Dario thinks she is less intelligent, and thus use *non*. But if Paolo is more assertive, he may take Dario's remark as equivalent to an explicit evaluation of Maria's intelligence. In such a case, he would not use *non*. Thus there are two possible responses here, with differing amounts of intensity on the part of the speaker's attitude toward his contradiction of the listener's evaluation of Maria and Carlo.

Context 3 (for 5a)

Dario: Maria ha continuato a dire sciocchezze. È proprio cretina, sai?
    'Mary continued to say stupid things. She's really an idiot, you know?'
Paolo: Ma ti sbagli! Conosco Maria molto bene ed è più intelligente di quanto tu credi/??non creda.
    'But you're wrong! I know Mary very well and she's more intelligent than you think.'

Here Dario explicitly states his evaluation of Maria. Therefore Paolo responds most naturally without *non*.

Context 4 (for 5b)

Dario: Non ho capito per niente quest'ultima lezione, comunque non credo che valga la pena di chiedere aiuto a Maria.
    'I didn't understand at all this last lesson, but I don't believe it's worth the trouble to ask Mary for help.'
Paolo: Secondo me fai male, dovresti chiederglielo. Maria è più intelligente di quanto tu non creda/(?) credi.
    'As I see it, you're making a mistake, you should ask her. Mary is more intelligent than you (wouldn't) believe.'

Here Dario is not explicit as to his evaluation of Maria's intellect. Thus Paolo assumes that she is more intelligent than Dario thinks, and uses *non* accordingly. However, if Paolo takes Dario's remark as a strong indication of his evaluation of her intellect, then he need not use *non*.

In these four contexts we see that *non* appears when there is a bit of uncertainty or indefiniteness about the speaker's assumption. But it cannot appear if there is absolutely no justification for the speaker's assumption (context 1) or if the speaker need not assume anything since explicit statements of the listener's opinions have been made (context 3). The comparative without *non* can appear in all contexts, but it is a second choice in contexts 2 and 4, where a suitable assumption for having *non* on the part of the speaker seems appropriate to the context. Thus, *non* is not possible in all comparatives of inequality (contrary to the analyses of Seuren 1969 and Antinucci & Puglielli 1971); rather, *non* is present in some comparatives and not in others.

Also, the *non* of comparatives is similar to *only* in English (see Horn 1969) in that, like *only*, it expresses an expectation. So in 6 (Horn's example),

(6)   Only Muriel voted for Hubert.

the speaker is revealing that he expected someone other than Muriel to vote for Hubert. Our *non* reveals that the speaker expects his statement to contradict someone's previously held belief. Various constraints on the distribution of *non* in comparatives can be explained by this presuppositional analysis.

2.1. Questions

Non does not appear in questioned comparatives of the type seen in 4:

(7)   a.   È più intelligente di quanto è Carlo?
      b. *È più intelligente di quanto non sia Carlo?
         'Is she more intelligent than Carlo is?'

Since in 7 the speaker is asking the listener whether a comparison of inequality is true or not, the speaker cannot simultaneously contradict the beliefs of the listener (nonrhetorical questions do not contradict, but only ask for information). Thus *non* does not appear in questioned comparatives like 7 because a proper context is not present. If 7a and 7b are negated, yielding a question conducive to an affirmative response from the listener, the comparative with *non* is still out:

(7)   c.   Non è più intelligente di quanto è Carlo?
      d. *Non è più intelligente di quanto non sia Carlo?
         'Isn't she more intelligent than Carlo is?'

Again 7d is rejected on semantic grounds: one does not simultaneously expect the listener to agree (the expectation revealed by the matrix *non*) and to contradict him (the expectation revealed by the embedded *non*).

Non, likewise, cannot appear in many questioned comparatives of the type seen in 5:

> (8) a. *È più intelligente di quanto tu credi?
>   b. *È più intelligente di quanto tu non creda?
>   'Is she more intelligent than you think?

8a is out because one does not normally ask someone for a confirmation of something they do not believe; 8b is out because the speaker will not ask the listener to confirm the opposite of what he expects him to believe. However, if the belief of the listener is a past belief which he may or may not still hold, the speaker can question the comparatives both with and without *non*:

> (8) c. È più intelligente di quanto tu credevi?
>   d. È più intelligente di quanto tu non credessi?
>   'Is she more intelligent than you thought?'

8c is good because it is perfectly natural to ask the listener to confirm whether or not a past belief was correct; 8d is good because it is also natural to ask him now to confirm the opposite of what we expect he used to believe. Likewise, 9 is natural:

> (9) a. È più intelligente di quanto lui crede?
>   b. È più intelligente di quanto lui non creda?
>   'Is she more intelligent than he believes?'

To ask information about whether someone is more intelligent than a third person believes or than you expect a third person to believe, is semantically fine. Thus a context for 9b with *non* can be found. If the distribution of *non* were determined by factors other than semantic ones, it would be very difficult to explain the acceptability of 8d and 9b in contrast with that of 7b and 8b. But with semantic criteria, one can explain the distribution above in a simple way.

2.2. Negation

It is common to find inequalities in which the matrix verb is negated, as in 10:

> (10) a. Maria non è più intelligente di quanto è Carlo.
>   b. Maria non è più intelligente di quanto tu credi.
>   c. Maria non è più intelligente di quanto crede Dario.
>   'Mary is not more intelligent than Carlo is/you think/Dario thinks.'

It is also possible to find inequalities in which the verb in the lower clause is negated with the normal sense of a negation. Thus in 11 we have an example of the lower verb being negated by the *non* seen in 1b, while in 12 we have an example of the *non* of 4b:

> (11)   Io sono stata all'estero più giorni di quanti Maria
>   non è andata a lavorare.
>   'I've been abroad more days than Mary has not gone to
>   work.'   (e.g. Mary hasn't gone to work for 10 days
>   and I've been abroad for 11 days.)
> (12)   Io sono stata all'estero più giorni di quanti Maria
>   non sia andata a lavorare.
>   'I've been abroad more days than Mary's gone to work.'
>   (e.g. Mary has gone to work for 10 days and I've been
>   abroad 11 days.)

However, when the matrix verb is negated, it is not possible
to have our special *non* although it is possible to have a
regular *non* (of the type seen in 1b).   Thus corresponding to
10-12 we have 13-15:

> (13)   a.   *Maria non è più intelligente di quanto non sia
>   Carlo.
>   b.   *Maria non è più intelligente di quanto tu non
>   creda.
>   c.   *Maria non è più intelligente di quanto non creda
>   Dario.
> (14)   Io non sono stata all'estero più giorni di quanti
>   Maria non è andata a lavorare.
>   'I haven't been abroad more days than Mary hasn't
>   gone to work.'   (e.g. Mary hasn't worked for 10 days
>   and I've been abroad for fewer than 10 days.)
> (15)   *Io non sono stata all'estero più giorni di quanti
>   Maria non sia andata a lavorare.

We must account for the unacceptability of 13a, 13b, 13c and
15.   Consider first 13b.   By saying Maria is not more intelligent than the listener believes, the speaker is agreeing with
the listener.   Thus there is no expectation of contradicting
the listener, and, on semantic grounds, *non* is excluded.
Likewise in 13c, the speaker is saying Maria is not more
intelligent than Dario believes.   Thus he cannot simultaneously
expect to contradict Dario, and *non* is out.   In order to
understand why 13a is out, consider 4b again.   The presupposition of the speaker in 4b is that someone does not expect
Maria to be more intelligent than Carlo.   In 13a, if the
presupposition were that someone expected Carlo to be more
intelligent than Maria and that the assertion of the inequality
would contradict this belief or expectation, then *non* could
be used.   But here the assertion is that Maria, in fact, is
not more intelligent than Carlo.   Thus, rather than contradicting the belief (presupposed to be held by someone) which
non would reveal, the assertion agrees with it.   So in 13a the
semantic environment for *non* is not met, and it cannot (and
does not) appear.   15 is out for reasons entirely parallel
to those presented for the exclusion of 13a.
   If we tried to account for such facts on the distribution
of our *non* without reference to semantics, we might propose

a constraint which says that our *non* cannot appear if the
matrix verb is negated. Such a constraint cannot apply at the
surface level for three reasons. First, at the surface level
the difference between the *non* of 14 and that of 15 is not
apparent. It is true that the verb in 14 is indicative while
that in 15 is subjunctive. Thus one might propose that the
constraint can look at the surface mood of the verb and determine which kind of *non* is involved. However, we claim in 3.2.2
below that there may be some speakers who use the indicative
mood with our *non*. For such speakers we do not see how our
non could be distinguished at the surface level. Second, we
argue in 3.2.2 below that subjunctive comparatives without *non*
are derived from subjunctive comparatives with *non*, by a rule
deleting it. If there were a surface constraint against the
appearance of our *non* after a matrix *non*, we would expect the
comparatives from which our *non* has been deleted to be fine
after a matrix *non*. This is not the case. Thus, if we delete
the *non* out of 13, all the sentences are still unacceptable:

(13')   a. *Maria non è più intelligente di quanto sia Carlo.
        b. *Maria non è più intelligente di quanto tu creda.
        c. *Maria non è più intelligente di quanto creda
           Dario.
           'Mary isn't more intelligent than Carlo is/you
           think/Dario thinks.'

From 13' we see that the constraint at hand cannot be operating
at the surface level, since there is no appearance of our *non*
at the surface level. And, finally, our *non* appears in constructions other than comparatives: in section 4, it may follow
a matrix *non* in some cases. Therefore, a surface constraint
cannot account for the distribution of *non*. Thus, our *non*
does not appear in the examples in this section because it is
out at some underlying level. If we are correct in claiming
that the examples in section 4 contain our *non*, then the fact
that it can appear there after negated matrix verbs means that
there cannot be a syntactic constraint operating on an underlying level throwing it out after a matrix *non*.
    For these reasons, such a constraint cannot easily describe
the distributional facts on *non* shown here. However, with
semantic criteria, the exclusion of *non* from these sentences
is accounted for.[2]

2.3. Equality

It has often been noted that the *non* of 4b and 5b cannot appear
in comparisons of equality:[3]

(16)   a. Maria è tanto intelligente quanto è Carlo.
        b. *Maria è tanto intelligente quanto non sia Carlo.
           'Mary is as intelligent as Carlo is.'
(17)   a. Maria è tanto intelligente quanto tu credi.
        b. *Maria è tanto intelligente quanto tu non creda.
           'Mary is as intelligent as you think.'

Both Seuren 1969 and Antinucci & Puglielli 1971 attribute the
lack of *non* here to the fact that comparisons of equalities
link two similar things while inequalities (in which *non* can
appear) link two dissimilar things.[4] However, if this were the
correct explanation, one would expect our *non* to appear in
negated comparisons of equality such as 18a. But in fact, *non*
cannot appear (18b):

> (18) a. Maria non è tanto intelligente quanto tu credi.
>   'Mary isn't as intelligent as you think.'
>   b. *Maria non è tanto intelligente quanto tu non creda.
>   'Mary isn't as intelligent as you don't think.'

Since the semantics of 18a are very similar to 19a, and
since our *non* can appear in an S such as 19b:

> (19) a. Maria è meno intelligente di quanto tu credi.
>   'Mary is less intelligent than you think.'
>   b. Maria è meno intelligente di quanto tu non creda.
>   'Mary is less intelligent than you think.'

we conclude that our *non* is excluded from comparisons of
equality for reasons other than the fact that equalities link
two similar things.
  Saltarelli 1974a does not mention our *non*. But we assume
from his analysis of the subjunctive mood that he would
attribute the absence of our *non* in comparisons of equality
to the lack of the subjunctive mood. *Non* appears only when
the verb is subjunctive, as shown below (and as discussed in
3.2.2). Contrast 20ab (indicative) and 20cd (subjunctive):

> (20) a.?*Maria è più intelligente di quanto non è Carlo.
>   b.?*Maria è più intelligente di quanto tu non credi.
>   'Mary is more intelligent than Carlo is/you think.'
>   c. Maria è più intelligente di quanto non sia Carlo.
>   (=4b)
>   d. Maria è più intelligente di quanto tu non creda.
>   (=5b)

Since equalities cannot have the subjunctive, *non* cannot appear:

> (21) a. *Maria è tanto intelligente quanto (non) sia Carlo.
>   b. *Maria è tanto intelligente quanto tu (non) creda.

  Saltarelli attributes the absence of the subjunctive in
equalities and its presence in inequalities to the notion of
'identified reference': if a proposition has identified
reference, it is in the indicative mood; if it has unidentified
reference, it is in the subjunctive mood. Exactly what constitutes identified reference is not clear, especially in the
light of examples like 22 (which are not mentioned by Saltarelli):

> (22)   Benchè tu l'abbia già fatto, voglio che tu lo faccia
>   di nuovo.

'Although you have already done it, I want you to do
it again.'

Here *abbia fatto* is subjunctive, yet the proposition it appears
in relates an event that has already taken place.   If an event
that has taken place does not have identified reference,
what does?   Furthermore, Saltarelli fails to note the presence
of the indicative in inequalities such as 4a and 5a, and thus
does not account for the fact that in his analysis some inequalities have identified reference while others do not.[5]   Finally,
if the comparative clause in 19b has unidentified reference,
why doesn't the comparative clause in 18 have unidentified
reference?   The problems with this analysis seem insurmountable
to us.

In order to see why our *non* cannot appear in comparatives of
equality, whether negated or not, one must first understand
that comparatives of equality using *tanto...quanto* occur only
when the speaker is comparing with precision.   One cannot use
tanto...quanto if one has only a vague presumed knowledge of
the comparison.   Thus, consider the following two contexts:

Context 5 (in which tanto...quanto *can appear)*

Dario: Maria è bravissima!   È forse la più intelligente
ragazza che conosco.
       'Mary is really smart!   She's possibly the smartest
girl I know.'
Paolo: Hai ragione.   Ho notato le sue risposte nella
lezione di matematica oggi--ed è tanto intelligente quanto
tu credi.
       'You're right.   I noticed her answers in math class
today--and she's just as intelligent as you think.'

Context 6 (in which tanto...quanto *cannot appear)*

Dario: Maria ha fatto bene oggi a scuola per la quarta
volta.
       'Mary did well at school today for the fourth time.'
Paolo: *Sì, è tanto intelligente quanto tu credi.
       'Yes, she's as intelligent as you think.'

In context 5 Paolo knows precisely how intelligent Dario
considers Maria to be.   Thus *tanto...quanto* can be used.   In
context 6 Paolo infers from Dario's comment that he considers
Maria intelligent, but there is no precision here as to how
intelligent Dario considers her to be, making *tanto...quanto*
inappropriate in Paolo's response.

We have stated that our *non* occurs when the speaker
presupposes a certain evaluation of Maria's intelligence, but
not when an explicit evaluation has been made (context 3 in
section 2).   Since *tanto...quanto* requires explicit and precise
knowledge while *non* requires inferred and imprecise knowledge,
non is excluded from comparisons of equality on semantic
grounds (i.e. *non* and *tanto...quanto* are semantically mutually
exclusive).

In support of this explanation, we note the following facts.
In sentences in which a precise knowledge of the degree of
inequality is known, *non* cannot appear (23a-d). Likewise,
if there is an element requiring precise knowledge of another
person's belief, *non* cannot appear (23e):[6]

(23)   a. *Maria è molto più intelligente di quanto non
            sia Carlo.
        b. *Maria è molto più intelligente di quanto tu non
            creda.
            'Mary is much more intelligent than Carlo is/you
            think.
        c. *Maria è due metri più alta di quanto non sia
            Carlo.
        d. *Maria è due metri più alta di quanto tu non creda.
            'Mary is two meters taller than Carlo is/you think.'
        e. *Maria è più intelligente di quanto tu non creda
            con assoluta certezza.
            'Mary is more intelligent than you believe with
            certainty.'

All the examples of 23 are fine without *non* and with the
indicative mood, as we would expect.

3.   Underlying structure

4a and 5a differ from 4b and 5b by the contexts in which they
may appear and by the presence or lack of *non*. Since *non*
reveals a certain presupposition of the speaker, there is a
question as to whether or not there need be a syntactic
difference between a and b of 4 and 5. Kiparsky and Kiparsky
1970 offer a syntactic difference to parallel the presuppositional difference between factive and nonfactive complements.
On the other hand, Lakoff 1971 claims that presupposition-free
syntax is not possible, pointing to several syntactic processes
that seem to be conditioned by presuppositions.[7] Since a
syntax that is presupposition-free is much less powerful than
one that can make reference to it, we would hope to be able to
offer a syntactic difference to parallel the presuppositional
one in these sentences. And, indeed, proposing a syntactic
difference sheds light on the facts given in 3.2.
The underlying structures we propose for 4 and 5 are given
in 24 and 25. All details not directly relevant to this study
have been omitted:[8]

(24) a. (underlying 4a)

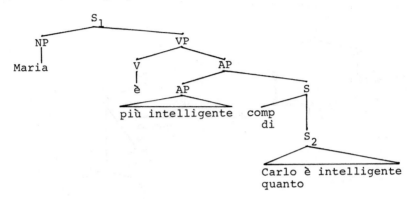

b. (underlying 4b)

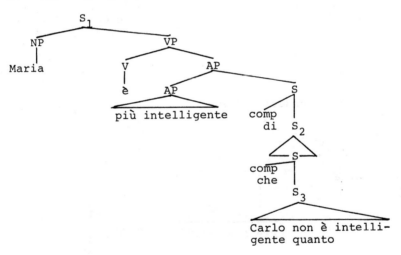

(25)   a.   (underlying 5a)

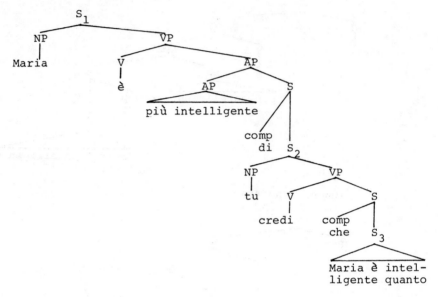

b.   (underlying 5b)

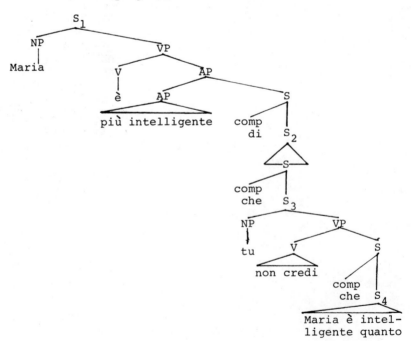

In the comparatives with *non* there is one more clause in the
underlying structure than in the structure of the corresponding
comparatives without *non*. In 24b and 25b this extra clause
is labeled S_2. We have not attached any lexical item to S_2, nor
have we indicated what kind of complement (subject, object) S_3
is in S_2. This is because S_2 represents an *abstract* sentence
in that it is never lexically realized and has varying meanings.
In 24b, S_2 means roughly 'someone is surprised that' and in
25b, it means 'I expect that'.

3.1. Defense of the abstract S.

The proposal of an abstract S such as S_2 in 24b and 25b is
not new. Lakoff 1968 argues for abstract higher Ss to dominate
subjunctive clauses that appear unembedded in surface structure
in Latin and modern Spanish.[9] Morgan 1969 proposes that in
underlying structure presuppositions are conjoined to the left
of performatives. These presuppositions have abstract verbs
of supposition with many characteristics of performatives.
While we have proposed an abstract S for semantic reasons,
there is syntactic evidence that this S does appear in underlying structure. In fact, a lexically-realized S may occur
in the same position as our abstract S_2:

(24')   Maria è più intelligente di quanto ci si aspetta
        che non sia Carlo.
        'Mary is more intelligent than one expects that
        Carlo is(n't).'
(25')   Maria è più intelligente di quanto io mi aspetto
        che tu non creda.
        'Mary is more intelligent than I expect that you
        (don't) believe.'

Thus an S-node clearly can intervene between the main and
the comparative clauses. Furthermore, an argument in support
of our abstract S is supplied by the behavior of gerunds.
Consider the following sentences:

(26)   a.   Ho visto Maria guidando per la strada.
             'I saw Mary while I was driving down the street.'
        b.   Ho incontrato quella ragazza lavorando nella
             fabbrica.
             'I met that girl while I was working in the
             factory.'
        c.   Ho scoperto Gianni giocando nella soffitta.
             'I discovered Johnny while I was playing in the
             attic.'
        d.   Parlavo alla ragazza facendo smorfie.
             'I was talking to the girl while I was making
             faces.'

Gerunds (the *-ndo* forms) can have their subject deleted only
under identity with the higher subject,[10] and not with an
object, as seen in 26.
   Now consider 27, which gives comparatives of the type seen
in 5:

(27) a. Tua moglie è meno fedele di quanto, rendendomi
         conto dell'importanza della fedeltà nel matrimonio
         per te, tu non sia pronto a immaginare.
     b. *Tua moglie è meno fedele di quanto, rendendomi
         conto dell'importanza della fedeltà nel matrimonio
         per te, tu sei pronto a immaginare.
         'Your wife is less faithful than, realizing the
         importance of fidelity in marriage for you, you
         are ready to imagine.'
     c. Tua moglie è meno fedele di quanto tu non sia
         pronto a immaginare, rendendomi conto dell'impor-
         tanza della fedeltà nel matrimonio per te.
     d. *Tua moglie è meno fedele di quanto tu sei pronto
         a immaginare, rendendomi conto dell'importanza
         della fedeltà nel matrimonio per te.
         'Your wife is less faithful than you are ready to
         imagine, realizing the importance of fidelity
         in marriage for you.'

In these examples only the comparative with *non* is acceptable.
The subjectless gerundial phrase, *rendendomi conto*... must
have had *io* 'I' as subject at some point, since *rendendomi* is
a reflexive form with the first person singular clitic *mi*.
Nowhere in the surface of the sentences of 27 do we have a first
person subject which could have controlled the deletion of the
subject of the gerund. Yet this gerund is fine in 27ac[11], both
with *non*, but not in 27bd, without *non*. Thus an S whose subject
is first person singular must appear in the underlying structure
for a and c, but not for b and d. This is our abstract S, which
might have had the meaning here 'I presume/expect/think'. Note
that this gerundial phrase cannot have had its subject deleted
under identity with the subject of a deleted performative verb,
since the performative verbs would be the same for comparatives
with and without *non*.
   As further evidence that this gerundial phrase is not
dependent upon the performative verb, consider the following
sentences:

(27) e. *Rendendomi conto dell'importanza della fedeltà
         nel matrimonio per te, (io dico che) tua moglie
         è meno fedele di quanto tu non sia pronto a
         immaginare.
     f. *Rendendomi conto dell'importanza della fedeltà
         nel matrimonio per te, (io dico che) tua moglie
         è meno fedele di quanto tu sei pronto a immaginare.
         'Realizing the importance of fidelity in marriage
         for you, (I say that) your wife is less faithful
         than you are ready to imagine.'

Here we see the gerundial phrase cannot appear in sentence
initial position. However, gerunds which have had their
subject deleted under identity with some NP in an initial
performative S can appear in sentence-initial position (28ab).
But gerunds dependent upon the performative verb cannot in
fact appear after *di quanto*, in contrast to the gerund seen

in 27a (although they can appear in S-final position), as
28cd show:

> (28) a. Considerando il modo in cui agisce, (io dico
>   che) tua moglie è meno fedele di quanto tu
>   credi/tu non creda.
>   'Considering the way in which she acts, (I say
>   that) your wife is less faithful than you believe.'
>   b. Rendendomi conto del modo in cui agisce, (io
>   dico che) tua moglie è meno fedele di quanto tu
>   credi/tu non creda.
>   'Realizing the way she acts, (I say that) your
>   wife is less faithful than you think.'
>   c. *Tua moglie è meno fedele di quanto, considerando
>   il modo in cui agisce, tu credi/tu non creda.
>   d. *Tua moglie è meno fedele di quanto, rendendomi
>   conto del modo in cui agisce, tu credi/tu non
>   creda.

Note that in 28ab the gerundial phrases, which are dependent
upon the performative verb, are acceptable in comparatives
with and without *non*. This is because the performative verb,
being the same for all the comparatives, can take the same
kinds of gerundial phrases. Likewise, in 27 the performative
verb is the same for all the examples, yet the gerundial
phrase can never appear in certain positions without our *non*.
What is decisive for this gerundial, then, is the presence or
absence of our verb of presupposition. It is the presence of
this verb on which the gerundial phrase in 27 depends for both
its appearance and its position. Assuming now that the
abstract Ss shown in 24b and 25b do appear in underlying
structure, the facts seen in section 3.2 below can be accounted
for.

3.1.1. Defense of *non* in underlying structure.

The differing pragmatics of comparatives with and without *non*
have led us to propose that *non* is present in the underlying
structure of the subjunctive comparatives that appear with
non in the surface, but not present in the underlying structure
of the indicative comparatives that appear without *non* in the
surface. There are several syntactic arguments to support this
proposal, and in this section, we offer support not only for
the presence of *non* in underlying structure, but also for its
position being in S_3.
  The first argument involves the features of NPs. As is
well known, indefinite NPs in examples such as 29 can be
[±specific] in affirmative sentences but only [-specific] in
negative sentences:[12]

> (29) a. Laura ha un cane.
>   'Laura has a dog ([±specific]).'
>   b. Laura non ha un cane.
>   'Laura does not have a dog ([-specific]).'

In comparatives such indefinite NPs can be [±specific] in
indicative sentences without *non* but only [-specific] in
subjunctive sentences with *non*:

> (29)   c.   Laura ama un problema di logica più di quanto io
>   amo un problema di matematica.
>   'Laura loves a logic problem ([+specific]?) more
>   than I love a math problem ([±specific]).'
>   d.   Laura ama un problema di logica più di quanto io
>   non ami un problema di matematica.
>   'Laura loves a logic problem ([±specific]?) more
>   than I love a math problem ([-specific]).'

Thus the specificity of such an indefinite NP in a comparative
with or without *non* is the same as in a noncomparative negative
or affirmative sentence, respectively. If the interpretation
of indefinite NPs depends on the surface presence of a negative
element, then 29 supplies no argument for the underlying
presence of *non* in some comparatives. But if it depends
on the underlying presence of a negative element, then 29
gives an argument for the underlying presence of our *non* in
the comparative in 29d. Since we do not presently have a way
to determine which of these situations hold, we leave the
question open.

Second, *non* with subjunctive in comparatives may appear
with negative polarity items, while indicative comparatives
without *non* cannot. In 30a-c we see that *pur* in this particular usage is a negative polarity item which cannot appear in
a nonnegated S regardless of mood. In 30de we also see that
our *non* in comparatives allows this negative polarity item,
while nonnegated comparatives do not.

> (30)   a.   *Dico che tu *puoi* immaginarlo, pur con tutta la
>   fantasia del mondo.
>   b.   *Penso che tu *possa* immaginarlo, pur con tutta
>   la fantasia del mondo.
>   'I say/think that you can imagine it, even with
>   all the fantasy in the world.'
>   c.   Non puoi/*Puoi immaginarlo, pur con tutta la
>   fantasia del mondo.
>   'You can't/can imagine it, even with all the
>   fantasy in the world,'
>   d.   *La situazione in Africa è peggiore di quanto si
>   arriva a immaginare pur con tutta la fantasia
>   del mondo.
>   e.   La situazione in Africa è peggiore di quanto non
>   si arrivi a immaginare pur con tutta la fantasia
>   del mondo.
>   'The situation in Africa is worse than one can
>   imagine, even with all the fantasy in the world.'

The constraint on *pur* in this usage is that the VP of its clause
be negated. This constraint is on underlying structure, not on
surface structure, as we see in 30a' and 30b':

(30)   a'. *Non dico che tu puoi immaginarlo pur con tutta
            la fantasia del mondo.
        b'. Non penso che tu possa immaginarlo pur con tutta
            la fantasia del mondo.

In 30a' *potere* 'be able' is never negated at any level, thus *pur*
cannot appear with it. But in 30b' with the reading in which
negative transportation has applied, *pur* can appear, even though
potere is not negated in surface structure. Thus the constraint
is on underlying structure. Looking at 30de, we can see now that
in 30d (the indicative comparative without *non*) *arrivare* is not
negated in underlying structure, while in 30e (the subjunctive
comparative with *non*) it is.
    A third argument in favor of placing *non* in S$_3$ depends upon
the conjunction of negated sentences with *neanche*, and runs
parallel to the argument above about the negative polarity item
pur. Consider 31a:

(31)   a. Tu non sei/*Tu sei convinto che Maria è intelli-
            gente e neanche Giorgio ne è convinto.
            'You are not/are convinced that Mary is intelligent
            and George isn't convinced of it either.'

Neanche in 31a can occur only if the VP of the S containing
the same verb is negated. This constraint holds at an underlying level, not at the surface. Thus if the negative is
removed by negative transportation, *neanche* may still appear.
Contrast 31b and 31c:

(31)   b. *Non dico che tu sei convinto che Maria è intelli-
            gente e neanche Giorgio ne è convinto.
        c. Non penso che tu sia convinto che Maria è
            intelligente e neanche Giorgio ne è convinto.
            'I don't say/think that you are convinced that
            Mary is intelligent and George isn't convinced of
            it either.'

31b is out because *non* never negated *tu sei convinto che S*
at any underlying level (since *dire* 'say' does not allow
negative transportation). But 31c is fine with the reading in
which *non* has been moved by negative transportation from the
predicate *essere convinto* 'be convinced' to the predicate
pensare 'think'. Now consider the comparatives in 32:

(32)   a. *Maria è più intelligente di quanto tu sei
            convinto, e neanche Giorgio ne è convinto.
        b. Maria è più intelligente di quanto tu non sia
            convinto, e neanche Giorgio ne è convinto.
            'Mary is more intelligent than you are convinced
            and George isn't convinced of it either.'

The fact that *neanche* can occur in 32b (with *non*) but not
in 32a (without *non*) means that the first *essere convinto* in
32b is negated in underlying structure while that in 32a is
not. Thus our *non* must negate S$_3$ in 25b.

The above argument against placing *non* in S_2 in underlying
structure also applies to the placement of *non* in S_4. Another
argument against placing *non* in S_4 is as follows. If *non* were
in S_4 in 25b, then the fact that it appears in S_3 (with *credere*
'believe') in the surface might be explained by negative transportation. However, *essere convinto* is a predicate that does
not allow negative transportation, so that 33a does not have
any reading identical to that of 33b. Yet *essere convinto* can
appear with *non* in comparatives, as in 33c:

> (33) a. Tu non sei convinto che Maria è interessante.
> 'You are not convinced that Mary is interesting.'
> b. Tu sei convinto che Maria non è interessante.
> 'You are convinced that Mary is not interesting.'
> c. Maria è più intelligente di quanto tu non sia
> convinto.
> 'Mary is more intelligent than you are convinced.'

If the *non* in 33c is to be accounted for in the same way the *non*
in the surface sentence of 25b (=5b) is to be accounted for,
negative transportation cannot be the correct explanation for
the placement of *non* with *credere* in 25b. For these reasons,
we conclude that *non* negates S_3 in underlying structure.[13]

3.2.   Explanatory power of this analysis.

In this section we present several facts which follow from
our analysis and which would be difficult to explain without
such an analysis.

3.2.1.   Subjunctive

Looking at 4 and 5 one notes that when *non* appears the verb
following it is subjunctive, while without *non* we have the
indicative. These facts follow automatically if the abstract
S dominating the S with our *non* calls for the subjunctive.[14]
In many varieties of Italian the subjunctive seems to be
lexically controlled. That is, certain verbs, complementizers,
NPs, and adjectives call for the subjunctive in their complements, regardless of anyone's presuppositions about that
complement. Thus in 34a everyone knows that the world is
round, yet some speakers still use the subjunctive because
for them the lexical item *credere* 'believe' controls the mood
of the complement:

> (34) a. Maria deve credere che il mondo *sia* rotondo,
> perchè lo è.
> 'Mary must believe that the world is round,
> because it is.'

In many other varieties of Italian, the subjunctive seems to
be lexically controlled by some verbs, but presuppositionally
controlled in the complement of other verbs. Kiparsky and
Kiparsky 1970 note briefly that in German factive complements

are in the indicative while nonfactives may often be in the
subjunctive. Rivero 1971 makes similar claims for Spanish.
Saltarelli 1974ab claims for Italian that the indicative mood
occurs when a proposition has identified reference, otherwise
the subjunctive occurs.

The situation in Italian seems to us to call for an analysis
of the subjunctive slightly different from any of the above.
Certainly, many speakers use the indicative if they consider
a complement to be true (i.e. factive), thus preferring 34b
to 34a.

(34)   b.   Maria deve credere che il mondo e rotondo,
              perchè lo è.
              'Mary must believe that the world is round,
              because it is.'

However, there are other speakers for whom the 'intensity'
of the complement on the part of the higher subject is relevant
to mood. Thus, if one says:

(34)   c.   Maria crede che New York *sia* bella.
              'Mary believes that New York is pretty.'

the speaker may well believe that New York is pretty, but the
subjunctive indicates that Maria has only a vague notion of
its beauty and, most probably, has never been to New York. If,
on the other hand, one says:

(34)   d.   Maria crede che New York è bella.

the speaker may or may not agree with Maria, but the notion
Maria has is firmly in her mind and probably she has visited
New York. However, even if Maria has not visited New York,
if she firmly believes it is a pretty city, the indicative
is used:

(34)   e.   Maria crede che New York è bella--non so perchè
              se l'è messo nella testa, perchè non c'è mai stata.
              'Mary thinks that New York is pretty--I don't know
              how she got that idea in her head, because she's
              never been there.'

Certainly we cannot get into a detailed analysis of the uses
of the subjunctive mood here. All we wish to have demonstrated
is that contexts are relevant to the choice of mood for many
Italians. Thus, the claim that our abstract verb controls the
subjunctive in its complement in our comparatives with *non* is
reasonable, since it is precisely the notion of supposing but
not knowing for sure that this abstract verb conveys.[15]

3.2.2. Subjunctive without *non*.

Thus far we have given examples with *non* + subjunctive and
without *non* + indicative. The facts are not as cut and dry

as our examples might lead one to believe. Actually, the
preferences are as follows:

(35) a. Maria è più intelligente di quanto tu *credi*.
      b.*?Maria è più intelligente di quanto tu non *credi*.
      c. Maria è più intelligente di quanto tu non *creda*.
      d.(?)Maria è più intelligente di quanto tu *creda*.
(36) a. Maria è più intelligente di quanto è Carlo.
      b.?*Maria è più intelligente di quanto non è Carlo.
      c. Maria è più intelligente di quanto non *sia* Carlo.
      d.(?)Maria è più intelligente di quanto *sia* Carlo.

Everyone agrees that 35ac and 36ac are perfectly grammatical.
For some speakers 35d and 36d are fine, while for others they
are less preferable than 35c and 36c (hence the ? in parentheses). Non one has told us they would say 35b or 36b, yet
everyone thinks they might have heard someone else say it.
Our analysis of the appearance of *non* in comparatives predicts[16]
that among speakers who use the subjunctive only with lexical
conditioning, there may be some who consider the abstract
verb of our abstract S not to be in the class of verbs that
calls for the subjunctive. Thus these speakers should use
non + indicative. There should be no possibility for the
indicative with *non*, however, among those speakers who control
mood semantically. We do not know if this prediction holds
true, since we have found no speakers who use the indicative
with our *non*. But the fact that people think they have heard
35b and 36b is perfectly consistent with our analysis. The
examples marked d, then, are the only ones we have not yet
accounted for. We claim that d comes from c by way of an
optional rule deleting *non*. Semantically this seems correct
since the d examples can be used in the same contexts as c,
but not everywhere the a examples can be used.[17] This distribution would be natural if c and d were transformationally
related.
    There are also at least four syntactic arguments in favor
of deriving subjunctive inequalities without *non* from those
with *non*. First, as was noted in 3.1.1, certain indefinite
NPs may have [±specific] readings in affirmative sentences, but
only [-specific] readings in negative sentences (see 29). In
subjunctive comparatives without *non*, such indefinite NPs have
only [-specific] readings:

(37) Laura ama un problema di logica più di quanto io *ami*
      un problema di matematica.
      'Laura loves a logic problem ([±specific]?) more than
      I love a math problem ([-specific]).'

The [-specific] reading of the second *un problema* in 37 would
be explained if the comparative clause were underlyingly
negative. If there is no underlying *non* in 37, one must say
that these indefinite NPs are [-specific] in negative sentences
and in subjunctive inequalities--an unlikely set of environments.
    Second, we saw in 30 (section 3.1.1) that negative polarity

items may appear with *non* and the subjunctive, but not without
non and the indicative. These same items are marginally
acceptable without *non* when the subjunctive mood is used:

    (38)   (?) ?La situazione in Africa è peggiore di quanto si
                  arrivi a immaginare pur con tutta la fantasia
                  del mondo.

The fact that 38 is much better than 30d (indicative without
non) and that it is almost as good as 35d and 36d[18] is explained
if 38 is derived from 30d by a rule deleting the *non*. If no
such rule exists, one must say that the negative polarity item
seen in 30 and 38 can occur only with negated VPs or with a
nonnegated subjunctive inequality--again an unlikely set of
environments.
    Third, we saw in 3.1.1 that *neanche* in an example such as
that in 32 is acceptable only if the S containing the same verb
is negated. We find that *neanche* can marginally appear with
subjunctive inequalities without *non*:[19]

    (39)   (?) ?Maria è più intelligente di quanto tu *sia* convinto
                  e neanche Giorgio ne è convinto.
                'Maria is more intelligent than you may be con-
                vinced and George isn't convinced of it either.'

Again if *non* is present underlyingly in 39 the facts about
neanche conjunction follow. And if it is not, we need a
strange set of environments for *neanche*.
    And fourth, we show in section 3.2.4 below that subjunctive
comparative clauses with *non* can be introduced by the complementizer *che* as well as by *di quanto*, while indicative comparatives without *non* can be introduced only by *di quanto*. Subjunctive comparatives without *non*, as we expect by this point, can
be introduced by both, with the same degree of acceptability:

    (40)   a.(?)Maria è più intelligente che *sia* Carlo.
          b.(?)Maria è più intelligente che tu *creda*.
          'Mary is more intelligent than Carlo is/you think.'

If *non* has been deleted from the comparative clauses in 40, the
choice of complementizers here and in comparative clauses with
non in the surface is one fact. But if there is no *non* in 40
at any level, then we might try to suggest that *che* can appear
with subjunctive comparatives regardless of the presence or
absence of *non*. However, note that 35b and 36b (*non* with the
indicative) have the same degree of (un)acceptability with *che*
as with *di quanto*:

    (40)   c.?*Maria è più intelligente che non è Carlo.
          d.?*Maria è più intelligente che tu non credi.

Since *che* is not totally out with *non* in the indicative but
totally out without *non* in the indicative (see 3.2.4 below),
we must say that *che* can appear in comparative clauses with
our *non* or with the subjunctive--an unenlightening set of

environments. But if *non* is present in 40 underlying, then
we can say *che* is acceptable with our *non* in comparative
clauses.

3.2.3. Subjunctive without *non*, past tense.

The deletion of our *non* with present tense verbs is marginal
for some speakers but fine for others, as we saw in 35d and
36d. In the past tense, however, the deletion of *non* is
perfectly acceptable for many speakers we have questioned:[20]

(41)   a.   Maria è più intelligente di quanto (non) *fosse*
            suo fratello a quell'età.
       b.   Maria è più intelligente di quanto tu (non)
            credessi.
            'Mary is more intelligent than her brother was at
            that age/than you thought.'

Dwight Bolinger (personal communication) has suggested to
us that the subjunctive comparative without *non* is used when
the speaker allows for the possibility that he might be
mistaken about his presumption of other people's opinions.[21]
He suggests that if this is true, then comparatives in the
subjunctive without *non* are perfectly acceptable in past tenses
because the possibility of having mistaken a past opinion is
stronger than the possibility of having mistaken a present one.
We noted above (see note 17) that the subjunctive without *non*
seems more polite. Since allowing for the possibility of having
mistaken another's opinions is more polite than stating that
we think we know another's opinions, Bolinger's explanation
seems correct to us. Thus the rule deleting *non* operates in
polite contexts of a type found more commonly in the past tense
than in the present.
     A second interesting fact involving tense distinctions is
that *non* with the indicative sounds better in the past tense
than in the present:

(42)   a.?*Maria è più intelligente di quanto non *è* suo
             fratello.
       b.?(?)Maria è più intelligente di quanto non *era* suo
             fratello a quell'età.
             'Mary is more intelligent than her brother is/than
             her brother was at that age.'
       c.?*Maria è più intelligente di quanto tu non *credi*.
       d.?(?)Maria è più intelligente di quanto tu non *credevi*.
             'Mary is more intelligent than you believe/
             believed.'

We stated our prediction in 3.2.2 that certain speakers who
control mood entirely lexically may classify the verb of our
abstract S as taking the indicative mood in its complement;
they would produce the sentences of 42. Although we have not
found such speakers, we have noted that for many who control
mood lexically (either entirely or partially), lexical items
that require the subjunctive in a present tense complement may

accept fully or marginally the indicative in a past tense
complement. For example, consider 43, with the clause intro-
ducer *prima che* 'before', an element that controls mood:

   (43) a. Prima che Maria *faccia* quello, io faccio così.
           b. *Prima che Maria *fa* quello, io faccio così.
              'Before Mary does that, I'll do thus.'
           c. Prima che Maria *facesse* quello, io facevo così.
           d.?(?)Prima che Maria *faceva* quello, io facevo così.
              'Before Mary did that, I was doing thus.'

In 43ab we see that the present indicative is out after *prima
che*. But in 43cd, we see that some speakers fully accept the
past indicative while others do not reject it completely after
prima che. Thus the fact that the indicative with our *non*
in inequalities is much better in the past tense than in the
present is parallel to the fact that the indicative after
elements that lexically control the subjunctive is better in
the past tense than in the present. These two facts are,
indeed, one if 42bd are alternatives to 41ab, which is our
claim.

3.2.4. Choice of complementizers.

The comparative complementizer, *di (quanto)*, can appear in
comparatives with or without *non*, as we saw in 4 and 5.
For many Italians the complementizer *che*, however, can appear
with the *non* comparatives but not with the comparatives
without *non* in the indicative:

   (44) a. *Maria è più intelligente che è Carlo.
           b. Maria è più intelligente che *non sia* Carlo.
   (45) a. *Maria è più intelligente che tu *credi*.
           b. Maria è più intelligente che tu *non creda*.
             'Mary's more intelligent than Carlo is/you think.'

Looking back at the structures proposed in 24 and 25 we
see that the abstract S_2 present in comparatives with *non* is
introduced by the same complementizer that introduces S_2 in
the comparatives without *non*. We also see that S_3 embedded in
S_2 is introduced by the unmarked complementizer *che*. Thus
the two complementizers, *di* and *che*, are separated only by
the abstract elements of S_2, which are subsequently deleted,
leaving behind S_3. The question, then, is what happens to
the complementizers on either side of the deletion site. Note
that when subjunctive clauses stand alone in Italian, they
may or may not be introduced by a complementizer:

   (46) (Che) le avessi comprate!
        'Oh, if only I had bought them!'

The subjunctive in Ss like 46 is exactly the kind that Lakoff
1968 proposes higher abstract verbs to account for. If there
is a higher abstract verb underlying 46, then when it is
deleted, the *che* introducing its complement may optionally be

deleted as well.

Perhaps the abstract elements of S_2 in 24b and 25b delete,
optionally taking with them the *che* complementizer that
introduces S_3. If *che* is deleted, *di (quanto)* surfaces as
the complementizer. If it is not, then we have two complementizers back to back, and since they introduce only one S,
one of them is deleted. Thus *di (quanto)* might be deleted,
yielding *che* in the surface in 44b and 45b. Nick Clements
has pointed out to us that since the complementizer *di* is
homophonous with a preposition, a rule deleting *di* before *che*
is similar to preposition deletion before complementizers
in various languages. Certainly such a rule is independently
motivated in Italian (*Ho paura di lui* 'I am afraid of him'
vs. *Ho paura (*di) che venga* 'I am afraid (*of) that he may
come').

Che can never arise in the comparatives without an abstract
S_2 (i.e. the indicative comparatives without *non*) because we
will never get the situation of two complementizers 'fighting'
for one position. Without an underlying extra abstract S in
the comparatives with *non*, it is difficult to imagine how
the choice of complementizers might be accounted for. But
with the abstract S, the data is more understandable.

3.2.5. Repetition and clitics.

In comparatives of the type seen in 4, the element which is
compared need not be deleted:

> (47) a.   Maria è più intelligente di quanto è intelligente
>   Carlo.
>   b.   Maria è più intelligente di quanto non sia
>   intelligente Carlo.
>   'Mary's more intelligent than Carlo is intelli-
>   gent.'

There is a distinct difference in the tone and possible uses
for 47a and 47b, however. The second *intelligente* in 47a is
said more slowly than its counterpart in 47b. In 47a there
is a strong sense of repetition, while in 47b it is much less
noticeable. 47a might be found in a context like the following:

Context 7 (for 49a)

Paolo: Maria e Carlo sono una coppia speciale: lei è
intelligentissima e lui è bellissimo.
       'Mary and Carlo are a special couple: she is very
intelligent and he is very handsome.'
Dario: Ma lei è più intelligente di quanto è bello lui,
no?
       'But she is more intelligent than he is handsome,
isn't that so?'
Paolo: No! Lui è il più bello del mondo! Però, lei è
più intelligente di quanto è intelligente lui.
       'No! He is the most handsome man in the world!'

But she is more intelligent than he is intelligent.'

47b, on the other hand, sounds fine in the same contexts as
4b (see context 2 above). Note that if 24a is the structure
underlying 47a, then the first instance of *intelligente* is
in S_1, while the second is in S_2. The structural proximity
may make the deletion of the second *intelligente* automatic in
most contexts. If 24b is underlying 47b, however, the two
instances of *intelligente* are in S_1 and S_3. The greater
structural distance between them may allow for an optional
deletion of the second *intelligente*.

This explanation is supported by the facts on clitics.
Predicate adjectives may be replaced by the clitic *lo*, as
in 48a. When *lo* replaces a predicate adjective a quantifier
may remain behind, as in 48b:

    (48)   a.   *Dario:* È intelligente Maria?
                         'Is Mary intelligent?'
               Paolo: Sì, lo è.
                         'Yes, she is (that).'
          b. Sì, lo è molto.
              'Yes, she is (that) a lot.'

Clitics never receive stress in Italian. If the second
occurrence of *intelligente* in 47a requires a context in which
it is lengthened or otherwise emphasized while that in 47b
does not, we would expect that the second *intelligente* of
47a could not be replaced by the unstressed clitic *lo*, while
that of 47b could. This is, in fact, the case:

    (49)   a. *Maria è più intelligente di quanto lo è Carlo.
          b. Maria è più intelligente di quanto non lo sia
              Carlo.
              'Mary's more intelligent than Carlo is (that).'

Without a structural difference between 47a and 47b we cannot
see how the cliticization facts in 49 can be accounted for.
But with our abstract S, they follow.

Another fact about clitics is that the *lo* replacing
predicate adjectives can appear only with the surface complementizer *di quanto*, never with *che* (3.2.4 above), as shown
in 50ab. This is because the repetition of the predicate
adjective can occur after *di quanto* as in 47 but not after
che (50c).

    (50)   a. Maria è più intelligente di quanto non (lo) sia
              Carlo.
          b. *Maria è più intelligente che non lo sia Carlo.
          c. *Maria è più intelligente che non sia intelligente
              Carlo.

From 50c we see that a predicate adjective cannot appear in
the comparative clause after *che*. This is the case even when
we compare clauses with different predicate adjectives:

(51) a. Maria è più intelligente di quanto è furbo Carlo.
     b. Maria è più intelligente di quanto non sia furbo
         Carlo.
     c. *Maria è più intelligente che non sia furbo Carlo.
         'Mary is more intelligent than Carlo is sly.'

We think that 51c, 50c, and 50b are out because a predicate
adjective in a comparative clause is not admissible except
in the presence of the comparative quantifier *quanto*. Since
quanto must either move into complementizer position or delete,
and since the presence of *che* blocks *quanto* from moving into
complementizer position, *quanto* can never co-occur with *che*,
nor can a predicate adjective appear in a comparative clause
after *che*. The restriction on the occurrence of predicate
adjectives only with *quanto* is perhaps some sort of 'compre-
hensibility' (surface?) constraint, since we see no syntactic
reason for it.

3.2.6. Reduction

Comparatives like 4a are fully acceptable, but they are
unusual. One prefers to use a briefer comparative like 52:

(52) Maria è più intelligente di Carlo.
      'Mary is more intelligent than Carlo.'

52 can be used in any context in which 4a can. It does not
have presuppositions of the type conveyed by comparatives
with *non*. Thus, if 52 is a reduced form of a longer comparative, it seems that it is reduced from 4a rather than 4b.
   Some speakers have another alternative way to form
comparatives, seen in 53:

(53) Maria è più intelligente che Carlo.
      'Mary is more intelligent than Carlo.'

We did not find many speakers who use 53. Still, it seems
that for those who use it, it is appropriate in the contexts
in which 4b and 5b are, i.e. it is reduced from a comparative
with *non*. In fact *non* may appear with marginal acceptability:[22]

(54) ?Maria è più intelligente che non Carlo.

Thus it seems that for many speakers only indicative comparatives can be reduced to NPs, while for others both indicative
and subjunctive (i.e. those with *non*) can. We do not know
why subjunctive comparatives can be reduced to NPs only in
certain varieties of Italian.

3.3. Obligatory negation in S_3

We have proposed that S_3 in 24b and 25b (comparative clauses
with *non*) are negated in underlying structure. This amounts
to claiming that our abstract verb takes only negative complements. Such a claim is totally consistent with the grammar of

Italian, for there are many verbs that require their complement
to be negative, just as there are many others that require
their complement to be affirmative. For example, in 55 *stare
all'erta* in the sense of 'watch out' can take only negative
complements, while in 56 *proibire* 'prohibit' can take only
affirmative complements:

(55)   a.   Sta all'erta che non ti sorprenda.
            'Watch out that he doesn't surprise you.'
       b.   *Sta all'erta che ti incontrino in quel posto.
            'Watch out that they meet you in that place.'
(56)   a.   Proibisco che Giorgio parli.
            'I forbid that George speak.'
       b.   *Proibisco che Giorgio non vada a scuola.
            'I forbid that George not go to school.'

Our abstract verb, then, is in a class of predicates with
stare all'erta which take only negative complements.

4.   *Non* in other constructions.

If our analysis of *non* is correct, its appearance depends on
the presuppositions of the speaker and not completely on the
syntax of comparatives. Therefore, we would expect to find
other syntactic environments in which our *non* can appear.
Consider a and b of the following sentences, all of which
involve indirect questions:[23]

(57)   a.   Chissà che ti sposi.
       b.   Chissà che non ti sposi.
            'Who knows if he'll marry you/if he might not
            marry you.'
(58)   a.   Non sono sicura se io debba vederlo lunedì.
       b.   Non sono sicura se io non debba vederlo lunedì.
            'I'm not sure if I should/shouldn't see him Monday.'
(59)   a.   Ci domandiamo se dobbiamo riconsiderare la
            nostra analisi di *non*.
       b.   Ci domandiamo se non dobbiamo riconsiderare la
            nostra analisi di *non*.
            'We wonder if we should/shouldn't reconsider our
            analysis of *non*.'
(60)   a.   Chissà se vale la pena (di) comprarlo.
       b.   Chissà se non valga la pena (di) comprarlo.
            'Who knows if it's worth/if it's not worth the
            trouble to buy it.'

The b examples are used when the speaker expects the negated
proposition to surprise someone or be contrary to previous
expectations. Note that the subjunctive is used with or
without our *non* in 57-59, thus our *non* sounds the same as in
these sentences as the regular *non* (of 1b, 11, and 14); in
fact b of 57-59 are ambiguous as to whether one is unsure
about the affirmative or negative possibility of the embedded
clause. However, 60 takes the indicative without our *non*,
but the subjunctive with it. If this is truly an example

of our *non*, then there should be a corresponding sentence
with *non* + indicative which contrasts with 60b in the same
way 11 contrasts with 12 (section 2.2). Indeed, there is such
a sentence, contrasting in the expected way:

> (61)   Chissà se non vale la pena (di) comprarlo.
>   'Who knows if it isn't worth the trouble to buy it.'

We believe that these examples can be translated into
English without losing the presuppositions in the Italian.
Thus the negative element discussed in this paper is not found
solely in Italian (or solely in Romance), but in English as
well. We expect it can be found in many languages.

5.   Conclusions.

In this paper we have argued that the *non* of comparatives in
Italian is present only when the speaker holds certain presuppositions. This *non* is not pleonastic, but rather a bona fide
negative. In order to explain many syntactic and semantic
facts, we have proposed an abstract verb in an abstract
sentence dominating the complement in which the *non* appears.
Finally, we have shown that this *non* appears in other constructions besides comparatives in both Italian and English. We
have given no account of why our abstract S of presupposition
can appear in certain syntactic environments but not in others.
In specific, we do not know why comparatives and indirect
questions (like those seen in section 4) provide environments
for this presuppositional sentence, but other types of
structures do not. Perhaps the presence of the *wh*-word in
both the comparatives and indirect questions is crucial. Also,
we note that generating an S that is never lexically realized
in embedded position is a new proposal and has serious
theoretical implications. However, the proposal of this S has
allowed us to account for at least five sets of facts (in 3.1,
the gerund facts, and in 3.2, the facts on mood, choice of
complementizers, clitics, and repetition) which would go
unrelated in either a presuppositional-dependent syntax model
or an interpretive approach. Thus this analysis has strong
explanatory power in its favor. Furthermore, we hope to have
presented enough syntactic and semantic evidence to support our
proposal and raise the question of the possibility of such
underlying structures.

If our analysis is anywhere near correct, this *non* is
one more example of a presuppositional fact that is accounted
for by a certain syntactic analysis. Thus we may hope that
presupposition-free syntax can still be defended.

NOTES

*We would like to thank Dwight Bolinger, Guglielmo Cinque, Nick Clements, Richard Kayne, and Emily Norwood for many helpful suggestions and insights. We thank, as well, our most patient informant, Antonio Cosenza. And a final thanks goes to Stephanie Jamison, Bob Rodman, and the class of Linguistics 362, spring '75, UNC.

[1] Huckin 1974 argues that in comparatives of inequality in English *than* is a negative element. We discuss Huckin's proposal with respect to Italian in note 13 below.

[2] Dwight Bolinger (personal communication) has brought to our attention some examples in French with two negatives: *Jean n'est pas plus beau qu'on ne pense.* 'John is not handsomer than anybody thinks.' *Jean ne peut pas être plus beau que vous ne pensiez.* 'John can't be handsomer than you thought.' The corresponding Italian examples are out: **Gianni non è più bello di quanto non si pensi. *Gianni non può essere più bello di quanto voi non pensiate.* We think the Italian Ss are out for semantic reasons. Thus, either the semantics of the French Ss are different from those of the corresponding ones in Italian, or we are wrong and there is indeed some kind of syntactic constraint against two negatives which we do not understand. Note also that the negative *non* of 3 (occurring only in the presence of some other negative element) cannot appear in the lower clause if the matrix is negated in a comparative: *Maria non è più intelligente di nessuno.* 'Mary isn't more intelligent than anyone.' **Maria non è più intelligente di quanto non è/non sia nessuno.* Mary is not more intelligent than no one is.' Why this should be so is not clear to us. We see no semantic reason for excluding the indicative comparative of the last sentence, especially in light of the acceptability of 14. We leave these facts and the questions they pose open for further research.

[3] Apparently this is not so for French. Dwight Bolinger (personal communication) has brought to our attention the following example: *Il est aussi bon qu'ils ne puissent l'être.* 'He's as good as they may be.' The corresponding Italian sentence is out: **È tanto buono quanto non lo possono essere loro.*

[4] Antinucci & Puglielli 1971 talk of COINCIDENZA as an element in comparisons of equality, but NON COINCIDENZA in comparisons of inequality. They then derive the *non* of 4b and 5b from NON COINCIDENZA and 4a and 5a from the same source with an optional rule deleting *non*. It is very difficult to tell exactly how they intend these rules to operate and exactly what status (semantic, syntactic, abstract, real lexical item) is assigned to the elements COINCIDENZA and NON COINCIDENZA. We have taken these elements to bear semantic information. However, if they are syntactic markers of some sort, the objection to this analysis raised immediately below

in the text may not be valid. Still, their analysis fails in
that 4ab and likewise 5ab should not be derived from the same
structure, given all the semantic and syntactic evidence
presented in this paper.

[5] We do consider Saltarelli's proposals important because
they shed light on the use of the subjunctive in general.
(See 3.2 for a brief discussion of the subjunctive.)
His proposals are important also for the analysis of comparatives in specific, since they suggest that comparatives with
the indicative (which he does not mention) are semantically
distinct from comparatives with the subjunctive, a suggestion
we fully agree with.

[6] Our notion of precision is distinct from Saltarelli's
notion of identified reference, as 23e shows in contrast to:
Voglio che lui creda con assoluta certezza. 'I want him to
believe with certainty.'

[7] The most convincing of these examples is the deletion of
the future auxiliary *will*, an example he credits Kim Burt
with. Note that his example involving comparatives (337) does
not call for an explanation involving presuppositions if the
analysis of comparatives by Bresnan 1973 is correct.

[8] There is evidence that *più* derives from underlying *più
tanto*. For a detailed analysis of the head of comparative
clauses in Italian, see Nespor (forthcoming). For an analysis
of comparatives in English, see Bresnan 1973. Also, at a
deeper level, the comparative S forms a constituent with the
comparative quantifier *più (tanto)* (see Bresnan 1973). For
our purposes, the exposition of our arguments is clarified
by beginning at the underlying level seen in 24 and 25.

[9] Lakoff (1972:923) notes that some embedded clauses in
Latin appear with the subjunctive or the indicative, and that
the choice of mood depends upon the context. Thus, if the
speaker 'assumes responsibility' for the assertion of the
clause, the indicative is used, and otherwise the subjunctive
is used. Lakoff claims that these facts are evidence that
linguistic facts cannot be described solely by grammatical
means, but that the context in which language is spoken must
be considered. We are not familiar with the situation in
Latin, but perhaps positing an embedded abstract S that domi-
nates the clause which appears in the subjunctive when the
speaker assumes no responsibility could be justified. In
such a case the S might have the meaning 'I am not sure if...'
or 'I do not take credit for...'

[10] Only surface subjects that are not derived subjects may
control a gerund: *Maria è stata vista da te guidando per
la strada.* 'Mary was seen by you driving (you/her) down the
street.' And in fact, NPs that are not subjects may control
the subject deletion of gerunds, such as the dative *mi* 'me'
with the psychological verb *sorprendere* 'surprise': *Mi
sorprende che sia così basso, considerando l'altezza del papà.*
'It surprises me that he is so short, considering the height
of his father.' Exactly how these facts on deletion of the

subjects of gerunds may be handled is touched on briefly in
Napoli (forthcoming). Note that these gerunds are not to be
confused with the progressive form of the verb. They do not
derive from underlying *stare Vndo* 'be Ving', as the meanings
of S above and the following show: *Studiando si può imparare
tutto.* 'By studying, one can learn everything.'

[11]27a sounds a bit awkward, although it is perfectly acceptable when read slowly with heavy pauses around the gerundial
phrase. Probably this is because of the length of the
gerundial, which makes one prefer to postpose it as in 27c.

[12]The following argument is used by Huckin 1974 to support
the proposal that *than* is negative in English. Note that
the facts in Italian differ from those of English, so that our
conclusion is the opposite from Huckin's, namely, some comparatives are underlyingly negated and others are not in Italian.

[13]For speakers of English there may be many questions
floating around at this point. First, Ross 1966 noted that
ever and *any* appear in English comparatives, while negative
elements like *nobody* do not. For this reason he proposed an
underlying *not* which gets deleted. There are no facts in
Italian parallel to these. Furthermore, negative elements
may appear in comparatives in Italian: *Non è più alto di
nessuno.* 'He isn't taller than anyone (no one).' And we
point out that *never* and *not at all* appear in English: *Better
late than never. (*ever), It's better that he did it late
than not at all (*It's better that he did it late than at all).*
And for some speakers a comparative like the following is
acceptable: *She's taller than you wouldn't believe.*

Second, Grosu 1972 has pointed out that Coordination
Reduction in English behaves differently depending on negativity. Inequalities, he points out, act like negated Ss
with respect to Coordination Reduction. In Italian, however,
Coordination Reduction is the same regardless of negativity.
Thus there is no argument for or against our analysis based
on Coordination Reduction.

Third, Huckin 1974, in a study that covers the Ross and
Grosu arguments as well as many others, has pointed out that
normally negated elements like *can't stand* or *can't help*
appear without the *not* in comparatives and that affirmative
polarity items like *already* and *still* are excluded from
comparatives in English. In both cases the facts in Italian
are different. Note that *già* 'already' is not an affirmative
polarity item in Italian; it may appear in the indicative only
with affirmative verbs, but in the subjunctive with negated
verbs: *L'ha già fatto.* 'He's already done it.' **Non l'ha
già fatto.* 'He hasn't already done it.' *Penso che (non)
l'abbia già fatto.* 'I think that he has/hasn't already done
it.' Likewise, *già* may appear with *non* in subjunctive comparatives as well as without *non* in indicative ones: *Ha avuto
un successo maggiore di quanto ha già avuto nel passato* (ind.).
**Ha avuto un successo maggiore di quanto non ha già avuto nel
passato* (ind.). *Ha avuto un successo maggiore di quanto non
abbia già avuto nel passato* (subj.). 'He had a greater success

than he already had in the past.' Note also that certain
negative polarity items like *affatto* 'at all' cannot appear
with our *non* in comparatives: *Maria è più alta di quanto tu*
non creda affatto. 'Mary is taller than you don't believe
at all.' This is because *affatto* requires a precise knowledge
of the listener's belief, but the *non* shows that the speaker
does not have such precise knowledge (see 23 and the comments
preceding). Thus the sentence is self-contradictory and,
therefore, unacceptable.

Given the above contrasts between English and Italian, it
may well be that one analysis cannot suffice for the comparatives in both languages. Still, there may be some slight
difference between the two languages causing all these
apparent gross differences. Huckin 1974 notes that many
distinctions often alleged to depend on the affirmative/
negative contrast in English may well depend instead on a
modality contrast. If this is so, the data on English
presented in this note may suggest only that the modality of
English comparatives is like that of negated Ss, rather than
that English comparatives of inequality are indeed negated.
We would like to point out that, while proposing a semantic
reading of *John is taller than Bill*, *John is -er much tall*
than Bill is not -er much tall, as Huckin 1974 does, seems
plausible, we cannot imagine what the parallel semantic
reading of *John is less tall than Bill* would be. Thus the
analysis of English inequalities which claims they are
negative meets many problems.

[14]Dwight Bolinger (personal communication) has suggested to
us that the subjunctive may appear after *di quanto* because
quanto is an indefinite antecedent. In Italian the subjunctive
mood may be used after indefinite nonspecific NPs in certain
cases, such as: (i) *Cerco una ragazza che sappia il*
giapponese (subj.). (ii) *Cerco una ragazza che sa il*
giapponese (ind.). 'I'm looking for a girl who knows Japanese.'
For all speakers *una ragazza* is [-specific] in (i). For
some speakers *una ragazza* is [±specific] in (ii), while for
others it must be only [+specific]. If it is *quanto* that
triggers the subjunctive, then we would expect that for those
speakers who read *una ragazza* in (ii) as being only [+specific],
only the subjunctive could be used after *quanto*. However, this
is not true. All speakers we have found accept both the indicative (without *non*) and the subjunctive (with *non*) in
these inequalities. Thus, unless one argues that the *quanto*
of subjunctive inequalities is [-specific] and the *quanto* of
indicative inequalities is [+specific], one cannot explain
the possibility for the indicative mood after *quanto*. The
same objection holds for comparatives of equality, where
quanto is used but the indicative is the only acceptable mood.
For these reasons, we are suspicious of Bolinger's suggested
solution. And, once we consider the syntactic facts presented
in section 3, we reject this solution in favor of the abstract
S solution.

[15]Sometimes a modal verb following our *non* may be indicative
or subjunctive, with no clear difference of acceptability:

È più alto di quanto tu non possa/non puoi immaginare. 'He's taller than you can imagine.' Since modality may be expressed either by a modal verb or by mood, this fact is not surprising for those speakers whose use of mood is presuppositionally controlled. However, one problem with our analysis is that many speakers who lexically control the subjunctive after verbs such as *credere* do not allow the indicative even with modal verbs in the complement of such verbs as *credere*. Yet these speakers do accept the S above with and without the subjunctive. We have no explanation for these facts.

[16]We are grateful to Emily Norwood for pointing out this prediction to us.

[17]For some speakers there is a slight preference to delete the *non* when the situation calls for extreme politeness. The kind of subtle difference such a choice implies between the subjunctive comparative with and that without *non* is not atypical of many choices between applying transformations or not. For example, Bolinger 1968 has pointed out the preferred use of the passive when one wishes to avoid responsibility. Many other similar cases are well known.

[18]38 may be slightly worse than 35d and 36d because of the presence of the negative polarity item in the surface, which makes one expect a *non* in the surface.

[19]Again the lower acceptability of 39 than 35d and 36d may be because of the presence of *neanche* in the surface, which makes one expect a *non* in the surface.

[20]Note that there is good syntactic evidence that *non* has been deleted from the subjunctive comparatives in the past tense: (i.a) *(?)La situazione in Africa è peggiore di quanto si arrivasse a immaginare pur con tutta la fantasia del mondo* (subj.). (i.b) **La situazione in Africa è peggiore di quanto si arrivava a immaginare pur con tutta la fantasia del mondo* (ind.). (ii.a) *(?)Maria è più intelligente di quanto tu fossi convinto e neanche Giorgio ne era convinto* (subj.), (ii.b) **Maria è più intelligente di quanto tu eri convinto e neanche Giorgio ne era convinto* (ind.). (iii.a) *(?)Maria è più intelligente che tu credessi* (subj.). (iii.b) **Maria è più intelligente che tu credevi* (ind.).

[21]We do not mean to suggest that Bolinger agrees with our rule deleting *non* from these comparatives. We are merely relating his suggestions about the differences between the subjunctive with and without *non*.

[22]Note that the corresponding sentence with *di* is totally out: (i) **Maria è più intelligente di non Carlo.* This does not mean that 54 is derived from a comparative having *non* with *che* while a comparative having *non* with *di (quanto)* cannot reduce. Rather, (i) is out because *di* can be followed only by NPs, pronouns, and numerals in the surface of reduced comparatives. Any other element (ADV, VP, PP, etc.) must be preceded by *che*: (ii.a) *Maria è più intelligente che/*di furba.* 'Mary is more intelligent than sly.' (ii.b) *Mi piace*

di più nuotare che/*di fare i tuffi. 'I like swimming better
than diving.' (ii.c) *Va più spesso al cinema che/*di in
biblioteca.* 'He goes to the movies more often than to the
library.' Thus (i) is out because *non* cannot follow *di*.
Differences between *di* and *che* in reduced comparatives are
discussed in Nespor (forthcoming).

While many speakers do not accept 54, most accept: (iii)
È più studioso che (non) intelligente. 'He's more scholarly
than intelligent.' Battaglia and Pernicone (1951:497) note
that the *non* is kept in (iii) when one wants to 'underline
more strongly the defect of intelligence'. We believe, rather,
that this *non* is our *non* of presupposition.

[23]Another example might be: (i.a) *Dubito che Carla abbia
capito.* (i.b) *Dubito che Carla non abbia capito.* 'I doubt
that Carla has (not) understood.' Certainly (i.b) is ambiguous (as are 57-59 in the b examples in the text below), but
it does have one reading similar to that of (i.a). We have
not included (i) in the text, however, because it may
exemplify a separate phenomenon that Jespersen (n.d.) calls
'paratactic negation'. Jespersen points to cases in which 'a
negative is placed in a clause dependent on a verb of negative
import like *deny, forbid, hinder, doubt*'(75), and he gives as
an example: (ii) *It never occurred to me to doubt that your
work...would not advance our common object in the highest
degree.* Dwight Bolinger (personal communication), on the
other hand, has suggested that *doubt* today might be analyzed
as *raise the doubt*, as in: (iii) *I raise the doubt that he
is (not) here*, (iv) *I raised the doubt about his (not) being
here.* Certainly (iii) and (iv) seem to give examples of our
negative of presupposition. And the Italian example (i.b)
with the reading given there is used in contexts similar to
that for our *non* of comparatives. Thus (i.b) might be used
when the speaker knows Carla is very intelligent and usually
understands, therefore the idea that she might not have
understood in this instance is unlikely. Still, there is
enough evidence to make the speaker think Carla has indeed
not understood. So the speaker raises his doubt while still
letting you know he expects people to be surprised at it.

REFERENCES

Antinucci, Francesco and Annarita Puglielli. 1971. Struttura
    della quantificazione. Grammatica trasformazionale
    italiana, ed. by Medici and Simone, 47-62. Rome: Bulzoni.
Battaglia, S. and V. Pernicone. 1951. La grammatica italiana.
    Torino: Chiantore.
Bolinger, Dwight. 1968. Aspects of language. New York:
    Harcourt, Brace and World, Inc.
Bresnan, Joan. 1973. Syntax of the comparative clause

construction in English. Linguistic Inquiry 4:3.275-344.

Chomsky, Noam. 1971. Deep structure, surface structure, and semantic interpretation. Semantics, ed. by Steinberg and Jakobovits, 183-216. Cambridge: Cambridge University Press.

Grosu, Alexander. 1972. The strategic content of island constraints. Working papers in linguistics. Columbus, Ohio: Ohio State University.

Horn, Laurence. 1969. A presuppositional analysis of *only* and *even*. CLS 5.98-107.

Huckin, Tom. 1974. Abstract negation in the English comparative sentence. The Fourth Western Conference on Linguistics, October, 1974 (unpublished) University of Washington.

Jespersen, Otto. (n.d.) Selected writings of Otto Jespersen. London: George Allen and Unwin Ltd.

Karttunen, Lauri. 1973. Presuppositions of compound sentences. Linguistic Inquiry 4:2.169-93.

Keenan, Edward. 1971. Two kinds of presupposition in natural language. Studies in linguistic semantics, ed. by Fillmore and Langendoen, 45-54. New York: Holt, Rinehart and Winston, Inc.

Kiparsky, Paul and Carol Kiparsky. 1970. Fact. Progress in linguistics, ed. by Bierwisch and Heidolph, 143-73. The Hague: Mouton.

Lakoff, George. 1971. Presupposition and relative well-formedness. Semantics, ed. by Steinberg and Jakobovits, 329-40. Cambridge: Cambridge University Press.

Lakoff, Robin. 1968. Abstract syntax and Latin complementation. Cambridge, Massachusetts: MIT Press.

_____. 1972. Language in context. Language 48:4.907-27.

Morgan, Jerry. 1969. On the treatment of presupposition in transformational grammar. CLS 5.167-77.

Napoli, Donna Jo. Forthcoming. Indefinite subject sentences in Italian.

Nespor, Marina. Forthcoming. The head of the comparative construction in Italian.

Rivero, María Luisa. 1971. Mood and presupposition in Spanish. Foundations of language 7.305-36.

Ross, John Robert. 1966. A proposed rule of tree-pruning. NSF 17.IV-1 to IV-18.

Saltarelli, Mario. 1974a. Reference and mood in Italian. Linguistic studies in Romance languages, ed. by Campbell, Goldin, and Wang, 203-15. Washington, D.C.: Georgetown University Press.

_____. 1974b. Postulati per una teoria semantica delle proposizioni comparative. Fenomeni morfologici e sintattici nell'italiano contemporaneo, 283-99. Rome: Bulzoni

Seuren, Pieter. 1969. Il concetto di regola grammaticale: la sintassi. Rome: Bulzoni.

THE EVOLUTION OF VARIABLE RULES: A CASE OF LEXICAL CONSTRAINTS

JOHN REIGHARD

Université de Montréal

1. Introduction

For the past several years, since Morris Halle's 1962 article
on the place of phonology in a generative grammar, much work
has been devoted to the development of a general theory of
language change within the framework of generative theory.
Weinreich, Labov and Herzog 1968 identify and discuss several
of the particular problems to which such a general theory
should seek to provide solutions. Among these is the
transition problem--the problem of the way in which a linguistic change, once begun, passes from its initial onset stage,
through some kind of transition period, to arrive finally at
a stage of completion.

Notice that most abrupt change models, like that of Halle
for example, in which minor changes occur in the grammar of
the adult, major changes in the construction of a brand new
grammar by the child, fail to account for the fact that in
documented cases of ongoing change, a discernible split
between generations is not necessarily present, and in fact
has apparently never really been observed. Even if it is
true then that the *form* of linguistic change is an added rule,

a dropped rule, a changed rule or a reordering of rules, we still need to understand in what manner a language passes from its original state to the new changed state, since this transition does not appear to be abrupt.

In recent years two transition models have been developed as a partial answer to this question: a model I am calling here the *feature dominance* model of Labov, and the *lexical diffusion* model of Bill Wang (cf. Labov 1972, Wang 1969, and Cheng and Wang 1971).

Feature Dominance. Labov has studied the evolution of change in great detail in Martha's Vineyard and in New York, and has developed a model based on his conception of *variable rules* (essentially a kind of highly structured optional rule). A change, such as an added rule, appears first in a language as a variable rule. This variable rule gradually moves to the status of a categorical (i.e. obligatory) rule through the rise in 'weight' or influence of one or more of the variable constraints to the point where they become categorical constraints. In the cases studied by Labov, what happens at that point is that the weight of the other variable constraints disappears altogether, so that the same rule, which earlier applied variably in several different environments, now applies categorically in one environment only.

Schematically, if a categorical rule can be represented as

(1) $A \longrightarrow B \; / \; C$

(that is, A becomes B in the environment C), then a variable rule can be represented as

(2) $A \longrightarrow \langle B \rangle \; / \quad \alpha \langle C \rangle, \quad \beta \langle D \rangle, \; \gamma \langle E \rangle$

That is, A becomes B variably in the environments C, D, and E, each of which may have a different weight in determining the global probability that the rule will apply.

In Labov's transition model, in the first stage of the change, alpha, beta, and gamma all have approximately equal weight, but in a second stage one environment becomes progressively more important--for example alpha increases in value-- so that the rule is operating much more frequently in environment C than elsewhere. Then finally in stage three, the value of alpha rises to the point where the rule applies obligatorily whenever C is present, and the rule has become categorical.

Lexical Diffusion. In the lexical diffusion model, developed by Wang and his co-workers at Berkeley, the linguistic change itself is considered to be abrupt and categorical. It is therefore representable as a categorical, not a variable rule. But its transition from onset stage to completion is gradual, taking place in discrete steps in individual words until it has 'diffused' throughout the entire lexicon. Thus in this view the rule is always categorical but applies at first in only a few words, spreads more rapidly to more and more words meeting the structural description of the rule until it is applying to the whole lexicon. At that point the change is completed. Thus while for Labov the transition of a change is a function of the evolving structure of the rule itself, for Wang there is no change in the rule; rather its transition is a function of the lexical domain of its application.

This paper presents some of the results of a study of Syncope in Latin and Old French (Reighard 1975). This is a change--the deletion of an internal unstressed vowel--which took several hundred years to go to completion. In its earliest stages, the change must be analyzed as a categorical rule undergoing lexical diffusion, exactly as described in the Wang model. However, at a later stage the rule is a near-perfect example of a familiar, Labov-type variable rule. In fact it is possible to get some idea of the relative weights of its variable constraints, and even to determine the direction in which the rule was evolving. This turns out to be a case of feature dominance, exactly as described in Labov's model.

The problem is that in Classical Latin the rule was operating synchronically both as a categorical and as a variable rule at the same time. In order to account for this state of affairs, we are led to recognize the existence of *variable lexical constraints*, which turn out to have some interesting implications both for a theory of language change and for a theory of language variability.

2.   The Latin rules

There is considerable disagreement about the proper analysis of Syncope as an historical change in Latin. This is because there are essentially three kinds of evidence on which one must draw. We will here determine first just what sort of rule will describe each type of data, and then afterward see why it is necessary to consider them together as a single rule. For purposes of exposition, let us call the rules associated with these three kinds of data Prehistorical, Historical and Variable Syncope, respectively.

Prehistorical Syncope. Here the data consist of forms for which the evidence of a syncopated vowel is available only in comparative or internal reconstructions:

(3)	*deksiteros	>	dexter
	*rekekidi	>	reccidi
	*praidiko	>	praeco (cf. praedicare)
	*propiter	>	propter
	*surrigo	>	surgo
	*arideo	>	ardeo (cf. aridus)
	*awikaps	>	auceps (cf. avis)
	*opifikiom	>	officium (cf. opifex, opificina)

We find that any short vowel in an internal open syllable could be deleted, and that there was no other apparent phonological or morphological condition on the rule.[1]

Note however that the rule was not a straightforward categorical rule, since it applied to only a subset of those lexical forms to which it could potentially have applied.

That is, out of all the words in the Latin lexicon containing
an internal unstressed vowel, only a hundred or so did in
fact undergo Syncope in the prehistorical period.

On the other hand the rule was not simply optional either,
since there is near-perfect consistency in Early Latin documents as to which forms are syncopated and which are not. We
have then a rule which was categorical in operation, but lexically restricted in its domain of application. The formal
equivalent of this random diachronic application is simply
some kind of *ad hoc* lexical marker which will serve to
distinguish that subset of forms which undergo the rule from
that subset which does not. This is exactly the kind of formal
device necessary in synchronic analyses to mark exceptions
to categorical rules, and it is available in the diacritic
features of Chomsky and Halle (1968:373-80). We can use such
a diacritic feature here--say [±Syncope]--and represent the
rule Prehistoric Syncope as follows:

(4) Prehistoric Syncope

$$\begin{bmatrix} V \\ -long \\ +Syncope \end{bmatrix} \rightarrow \emptyset \ / \ V \ C_1 \underline{\quad\quad} C^1 \ V$$

(that is, an internal short vowel is deleted in that set of
forms marked [+Syncope].)

Now it is most important to point out that this rule, in
addition to representing an historical change in Latin, continued to exist as such as a synchronic rule of Latin grammar.
The rule was necessary to account for such synchronic alternations as *praeco/praedico, officium/opificina, ardeo/aridus,*
etc. In terms of the generative typology of Halle 1962,
Kiparsky 1968 and King 1969, this is a genuine case of an
added rule in the grammar of Latin.

Historical Syncope. The second kind of data relevant to
vowel deletions consists of words which appear to have been
syncopated abruptly at some point in time during the period
of written Latin. That is, they are like the examples of
Prehistorical Syncope except that in this case we have the
unsyncopated forms attested somewhere in Latin documents.
Typically the break between unsyncopated and syncopated forms
occurs between the Latin of the early dramatists and the
Classical period. As in the case of Prehistorical Syncope
there is no evidence of phonological or morphological conditions other than that the vowel to be deleted must be short
and in an internal open syllable. The rule representing
Historical Syncope is therefore exactly the same as that
representing Prehistorical Syncope, the only difference being
that at this time the lexical feature [+Syncope] is now
attached to a few more lexical items. Examples are given
below in 5:

(5) EL opificina > CL officina
     EL cedate   > CL cette
     EL columen   > CL culmen
     EL objurigo   > CL objurgo

This is then exactly the state of affairs described in the
lexical diffusion model; we know independently that the
prehistorical rule continued to exist as a synchronic rule
of Latin grammar, and we now find that it has extended the
lexical domain of its operation. The rule itself however has
not changed in form. Thus the synchronic rule in this case
represents exactly the same thing as the historical rule: a
linguistic change which is still in the process of going to
completion--an ongoing change.

Variable Syncope. For the third kind of data we have a
historically attested overlap, or synchronic variability
between the unsyncopated and syncopated forms. Sometimes
both variants are found in the same author, sometimes only
in the same period. The length of time during which the
variability occurred for any single given form is not always
the same, but in any event we obviously have here a case of
synchronic variability of exactly the same type that has been
observed and described many times for many languages.

Despite the fact that the data come from a language which
is no longer spoken, we know that the syncopated variants
generally, by the Classical period and afterward, were normal,
unaffected forms, and that the unsyncopated forms usually
have something of a pedantic or purist flavor to them, especially in the post-Classical period.

Based on the available examples, such as the following:

(6) positus   ∽ postus
     opitumus ∽ optumus
     calidus   ∽ caldus
     aridus   ∽ ardus
     asperis   ∽ aspris
     infera   ∽ infra
     porrigo   ∽ porgo

there are obvious similarities to the categorical rule just
discussed. In particular the deleted vowel is short and in
an open internal syllable, usually the second, but occasionally
the third or fourth. But there are also some significant
differences in the consonantal environment of the deleted
vowel and in the position of the main accent.

First there is a clear predominance of examples with a
sonorant or *s* next to the deleted vowel. Second, while for
the categorical rule the position of the accent was of no
importance to the rule, there is considerable evidence that
the variable deletion of the vowel occurred more often when
the accent was to the right than to the left. Third, and
perhaps most important, there are clear indications of the
direction of evolution of this variable rule: as time progres-
ses the rule applies with a greater and greater global frequency, and both the sonorant/*s* constraint and the accent
constraint become more important.

Formally, the variable rule will look very much like the
categorical rule except for the introduction of the variable
constraints:

(7)   Variable Syncope: version one

$$\begin{bmatrix} V \\ [-long] \end{bmatrix} \rightarrow \langle \emptyset \rangle \; / \; V \begin{matrix} C_1 \\ {}_\alpha \Big\langle \begin{matrix} [+son] \\ \begin{bmatrix} +cor \\ +cont \end{bmatrix} \end{matrix} \Big\rangle \end{matrix} \text{———}\beta\langle +son \rangle \; \begin{matrix} c^l \\ \end{matrix} \; \gamma \langle +acc \rangle \; \begin{matrix} V \\ \end{matrix}$$

For details of the formalism, and for the calculation of the probability that the rule will apply in any given situation, I am following here Cedergren and Sankoff 1974, itself an adaptation of Labov 1969. In this formalism the global probability that the rule will apply in the different environments is represented in the formula 8:

(8) $p = 1 - (1 - p_0)(1-\alpha)(1-\beta)(1-\gamma) \; \ldots$

Here, each variable is given a numerical value ranging between zero (if it has no effect on the rule's operation) and one (if it has a 'categorical' effect--that is if the rule is obligatory in the presence of that variable). In this formula p_0 is taken to represent all non-linguistic constraints taken together, such as the age, social status and sex of the speaker, style of discourse adopted, etc. Alpha, beta, and gamma then represent the relative 'weight' of the various linguistic constraints. In the case of Syncope, these are the type of consonant adjacent to the short vowel and the position of the accent.

Notice now that the Cedergren-Sankoff formalism describes very neatly the historical evolution of this rule. As time went on, Syncope became more and more frequent in the indicated environment, to the point where in Old French we find it has become completely categorical in the sonorant/s environment. What happens in the Cedergren-Sankoff formalism is simply that the numerical value associated with that constraint increases gradually to one, at which point of course, the probability of rule execution becomes one, independently of the values of other constraints. And this is a situation exactly analogous to those discussed by Labov, in which in the early stages of the rule, a change is made variably in several different environments, but later categorically in one environment only.

Notice too that once again we are faced with a rule that represents at one and the same time an historical change and a continuing, synchronic rule of Latin grammar. Both of these rules then, the categorical one and the variable one, represent a genuine point of contact between the historical evolution of the language and its purely synchronic structures.

3.   Two rules or one?

Now since these two rules share obvious similarities, the question naturally arises whether they do represent in fact two different changes, or two different synchronic rules. What are these similarities? First they both leave a lexical residue, neither applying throughout the lexicon. This means

that a list of lexical exceptions would have to be given twice
in any analysis in which the rules remained distinct. Second
they both share the obvious phonological similarity of deleting
a short vowel in a second, occasionally in a third or fourth,
open syllable. Third, neither has any other strict phonological
condition determining which word the rule applies to and which
it does not. The variable rule 'favors' a sonorant and accent-
right environment, but does not apply exclusively in these
environments. On the other hand the categorical rule can
apply in any kind of environment, including that 'favored'
by the variable rule. Fourth, there is no strict morphological
or syntactic condition on either rule. One can point out
such unsystematic pairs as the following, where one word with
phonological, morphological or syntactic properties very
similar to another has been syncopated while the other has
not, and that either categorically or variably:

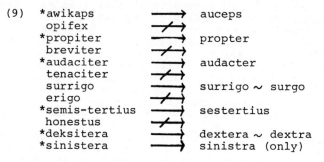

(9)   *awikaps   ⟶   auceps
       opifex   ⟶̸
       *propiter   ⟶   propter
       breviter   ⟶̸
       *audaciter   ⟶   audacter
       tenaciter   ⟶̸
       surrigo   ⟶   surrigo ∼ surgo
       erigo   ⟶̸
       *semis-tertius   ⟶   sestertius
       honestus   ⟶̸
       *deksitera   ⟶   dextera ∼ dextra
       *sinistera   ⟶   sinistra (only)

On the other hand of course there are obvious differences
between the two rules: one is categorical in operation with
lexical restrictions, while the other is variable in operation
and subject to certain variable constraints. I have discussed
elsewhere the appearance of the variable constraints, the result
of a grammatical restructuring in which three originally
independent rules were collapsed into one, and will not return
to this question here.[2] What should concern us here however
is the difference between the categorical and variable operation of the two rules. Let us see first then whether the
distinction is real enough to prevent us from considering the
two rules as one single process.

Categorical vs. Variable Operation. Now the evidence for
the distinction between categorical and variable operation in
the Latin data is simply the time of attestation of the
syncopated and unsyncopated forms of a given example: when
these times overlap it is clear that they were synchronic
variants, but when they do not overlap the data give the
appearance of an abrupt change having occurred. But there
is no principle governing this classification other than that
provided by the accidents of history. That is, there would
be nothing surprising in the discovery of a manuscript which
suddenly proved synchronic variation for any of the examples
classified up to now as categorical. Indeed it is no chance
that these 'categorical' examples come overwhelmingly from the

preliterary period, in which little or no documentation is
available.

It is for the same reason that there is an inherent difficulty in classifying definitively any given form where ample
documentation is lacking. Unsyncopated *opitumus* disappears
from the beginning of the Classical period for example, but
shows up in one inscription from the first century A.D. Is
this isolated example to be taken as an instance of synchronic
variation, demonstrating that *opitumus* and *optumus* varied for
150 years? Or is it to be taken as a spurious example of an
archaizing language, in which the author has deliberately
returned to a form 150 years old?

Thus the distinction between categorical and variable
Syncope is an artifice of the analysis, the accidental result
of using historical data which are almost entirely lacking
for part of the period studied, and only incompletely documented
for the literary period. In such circumstances, where the
documentation exists, it will necessarily give evidence
primarily of the change *as completed* and not in progress.

More particularly, the claim being made here is that Syncope
always proceeded, in every period, by variable stages, but that
it was progressively categorized--became an obligatory rule--
within a progressively larger lexical subset of all those forms
to which it could potentially apply. This is a slight modification of the lexical diffusion hypothesis: instead of a
categorical rule which at any given point in its historical
development makes a sharp distinction between the subset to
which it applies and the subset to which it does not apply,
there is a fuzzy edge between the two subsets which consists
of forms to which the rule applies variably.

This suggests that the rule of Variable Syncope is in fact
the current variable stage, the 'fuzzy edge' of Historical
Syncope. This also explains why the two rules are so similar,
and why they both continue to operate in Latin. At all points
in time they have a double function: they constitute a
synchronic rule of grammar, and at the same time an ongoing
change.

4. Variable lexical constraints

In order to represent both the historical evolution of Syncope
and its dual function in the synchronic grammar of Latin, a
formal means is needed to collapse the categorical rule and
the variable rule. As a first approximation one might propose
simply combining them as a variable rule, but including the
lexical feature [Syncope] which we used for the categorical
rule:

(10) Variable Syncope: version two

$$\begin{bmatrix} V \\ -long \\ +Syncope \end{bmatrix} \rightarrow \langle \emptyset \rangle \ / \ (\text{same as 7})$$

But this rule, while it allows for the variable deletion of

a vowel within a lexically defined subset, does not allow for
the *categorical* deletion of the vowel within a subset of that
subset.   In other words, it cannot represent the progressive
lexical categorization of Syncope, nor the three-way lexical
split in the synchronic grammar of Latin.

   But now let us suppose that, instead of having only binary
values, the lexical feature [Syncope] is instead multi-valued,
and counts just as other variable constraints in the calculation of the global probability of application of the rule,
according to the Sankoff-Cedergren formula.   Then, when a
given form is marked [0Syncope] (i.e. lacks the feature) it
has no effect at all on the rule; when it is [1Syncope] it has
the effect of cancelling out the contribution of all other
variables, and the rule applies categorically.   When the diacritic has some value between zero and one, it contributes
no more or less than any other variable constraint on the rule.

   But such a solution will still not *exclude* those words to
which Syncope never applies at all.   This is because when
the diacritic has the value zero, rather than cancelling the
rule, it simply has no effect, and the rule will continue to
apply variably.   We can however put a condition on the rule,
to the effect that whatever the value of [Syncope], it must
be greater than zero.   Then those words to which Syncope never
applies simply carry no value for the feature [Syncope]; those
to which it applies variably have some value between zero and
one; and those to which it applies categorically are marked
[1Syncope].   Then, to write the rule, we can simply enclose
the feature [Syncope] in angled brackets to denote its function
as a variable constraint, just like other variable constraints:

   (11) Variable Syncope: version three

$$\begin{bmatrix} \text{V} \\ \text{-long} \\ \langle \delta \, \text{Syncope} \rangle \end{bmatrix} \;\; \rightarrow \;\; \langle \emptyset \rangle \;\; / \;\;\;\; (\text{same as 7})$$

           Condition: $\delta > \emptyset$

5.   Implications

We are led then to introduce two formal innovations: the use
of a multi-valued *lexical* feature as a variable constraint on
rule application, and a condition that the *absence* of this
feature entails non-application of the rule.   There are at
least three predictions implicit in these innovations:
first, they imply that the three-way classification of the
Latin lexicon with respect to the rule of Syncope--words that
must syncopate, words that never syncopate, and words that
syncopate variably--is a normal state of affairs, and that we
should expect to find such cases in natural languages;
second they imply that a variable lexical constraint behaves
in a way different from that of other variable constraints,
since its absence entails non-application of the rule; third
they imply that all other things being equal, a variable
lexical constraint is an independent constraint on the rule,

of equal rank to other constraints. That is, it is predicted
that the value given to the lexical feature for a given form
affects the global probability of rule execution *to the same
extent* that other variable constraints do. Although lexical
variability has not, to my knowledge, been studied in this
framework before, there exists considerable evidence that it
does in fact behave this way.

First, the condition that [0Syncope] entails non-application
of the rule, together with the interpretation that [1Syncope]
entails categorical application of the rule, is a consequence
of the discovery that the lexical subset of Latin which meets
the structural description of the rule (i.e. all forms
containing a short vowel in an open, internal syllable) in
fact behaves in three different ways with respect to the rule:
in one subset it always applies, in another it never applies,
and in a third it applies variably.

But this three-way lexical classification can be found
elsewhere. In Modern French the well-known rule of schwa
deletion operates categorically in some forms, variably in
others, and for some speakers at least, not at all in others:

(12) a. Categorical Elision
          vous donnɇrez   (cf. vous donneriez)
          raisonnɇment   (cf. gouvernement)
      b. Variable Elision
          la pɇlouse   la pelouse
          avec cɇ plat   avec ce plat
      c. Impossible Elision (for some speakers)
          belotte   (cf. pɇlote)
          chevet   (cf. chɇval)
          guenon   (cf. guɇnille)
          venin   (cf. vɇnir)

Another example comes from Labov's 1972 study of vowel
raising in New York City, where the rule itself is reasonably
well-ordered, but where there is considerable variation in the
selection of lexical items to which it applies. The rule
behaves systematically for vowels before voiceless fricatives,
voiced stops and non-velar nasals (e.g. in *pass*, *bad* and the
noun *can*), but does not normally apply 'to auxiliaries and
other function words which can have schwa as the only vowel in
unstressed position (weak words). Nor does it apply in open
syllables as in *fabric* or *dragon* except when an inflectional
boundary follows, as in *draggin*'' (134). But exceptionally
avenue is included 'by almost every New Yorker' (159), and
there is a 'tendency of weak nasal words like *am* or *can* to
be raised by younger speakers', and a 'tendency of polysyllabic
forms with š--*fashion, passionate*--to be tensed' (159).
Finally, there is 'random decomposition' in the case of the
two words *razz* and *jazz* which are 'lexically unpredictable'
(141). (For the same rule in Philadelphia, incidentally,
words ending in voiced stops are normally not raised, but
three forms *bad, mad* and *glad* are exceptionally included (107)).

In short, even within the lexical subset which meets the
structural description of the rule, there are forms to which

the rule simply does not apply.

Zwicky's 1972 study of Allegro English provides a third
example similar to Latin Syncope. His Rule Slur deletes a
surface schwa in rapid English before *r*, *l*, or *n* and an
unstressed vowel but shows some non-systematic lexical
exceptions:

    (13)   Zwicky's Slur

        a. Categorical Slur
            business
            camera
            every
            chocolate
        b. Variable Slur
            robbery
            summary
            effeminate
            fattening
        c. Impossible Slur
            snobbery
            summery
            feminine
            monotony

In each of these cases, as in Latin, some means is necessary
to distinguish lexical subsets with respect to a variable rule.

The second of the implications discussed above is that the
lexical variable behaves differently from other variables,
in that its absence entails non-application of the rule. But
since two different kinds of variability are involved, there is
no reason *a priori* to expect them to behave in exactly the
same way. One kind determines the probability that a rule
will apply in some defined phonological environment, and
therefore to some lexical subset. But lexical variability
determines the probability that the rule will apply to some
particular member of that subset meeting the structural
description. Since the bases on which these probabilities
depend are different, it should not be surprising that their
formal representation be different and have different properties.

The third implication is that a lexical variable can determine, *independently* of other variable constraints, the probability of rule execution. That is, we should expect to find
cases where the probability of application of a rule depends
at least as much on the lexical selection of a given form as
on the presence of other constraints.

There is some evidence of the independence of the lexical
constraint in Latin. The variation between *calidus* and *caldus*
is more frequent and more widely attested than that between
viridis and *virdis*, although both are common adjectives
(Baehrens 1922, 14-6). Similarly, Syncope is common in
aridus and its compounds, but relatively rarer in *solidus*.

For New York vowel raising, Labov notes that while *avenue*
is raised for 'almost all New Yorkers', *razz* and *jazz* behave

quite irregularly. And in Zwicky's examples, he points out that while the Rule Slur does not normally apply before *m*, 'a few words--*Quadragesima*, *handsomer*, perhaps *unanimous*-- are good even in only moderate fast speech'. That is, the probability of application of the rule is a function, among other things, of the lexical selection made at the time of application.

Note finally that the introduction of variable lexical constraints is not far removed from variable grammatical constraints. It is known that variable rules may be sensitive not only to various phonological variable constraints, but also to the grammatical function (if any) played by elements in the environment of the rule. Cluster Reduction in English, for example, is sensitive to the grammatical role of past tense markers *t* and *d*, and consequently the probability of their deletion cannot be calculated on the same basis as that of *t* and *d* which occur as parts of other morphemes. As another example, in Spanish *d*-deletion operates much more frequently in past participles, and *r*-deletion more frequently in infinitives, than elsewhere (Cedergren 1972). Thus if grammatical function can affect the probability of application of a variable rule, it should not be surprising that lexical selection can do so as well.

In addition to the points raised above, a further implica- tion of the use of lexical constraints is that one of the ways a rule can evolve from a variable stage to a categorical stage is by the gradual rise of the value of the constraint in individual lexical items. As was pointed out earlier, this is a modified version of the lexical diffusion hypothesis. But it provides a diachronic explanation for all those cases discussed above where certain lexical items behave non-syste- matically with respect to the application of a rule of grammar.

Note however that we are not claiming that lexical diffusion is the only way a rule can categorize; Labov has shown in detail how categorization can take place in one of several variable constraints. But formally, this means only that *any* of the variable constraints on a rule--including the lexical constraints--may behave in this way. Thus the lexical diffu- sion model, which in appearance looks quite different from the kind of linguistic evolution discussed by Labov, turns out to be in fact only a variant of the same kind, given the formal conventions adopted here.

NOTES

[1]All these rules, and interpretations of the data on which they are based are discussed at length in Reighard 1975. The rules are somewhat simplified here, details being irrelevant to the point at issue.

[2]See Reighard 1974 for an overview and Reighard 1975 for
details. The three rules in question are Samprasarana and
Anaptyxis, both of which inserted a vowel in certain clusters
with sonorants, and the combined Syncope rule discussed in
this paper, which created sonorant (and other) clusters.
The point is that the synchronic outputs of the three rules
are indistinguishable from each other, so that there is no
reason to suppose that speakers of Classical or Late Latin
maintained them as separate rules, especially since all vowel
oppositions were neutralized in precisely these environments.

REFERENCES

Baehrens, W.A. 1922. Sprachlicher Kommentar zur vulgärlatein-
  ischen Appendix Probi. Halle.
Cedergren, H.J. 1973. On the nature of variable constraints.
  New ways of analyzing variation in English, ed. by C.J.
  Bailey and R.W. Shuy. Washington, D.C.: Georgetown
  University Press.
_____ and D. Sankoff. 1974. Variable rules: performance as
  a statistical reflection of competence. Language 50:2.333-
  55.
Cheng, C.-C. and W.S.-Y. Wang. 1971. Tone change in Chao-
  Zhou Chinese: a study in lexical diffusion. POLA Reports,
  Series II (Berkeley) 12. CW1-CW21.
Chomsky, N. and M. Halle. 1968. The sound pattern of English.
  New York: Harper and Row.
Halle, M. 1962. Phonology in generative grammar. Word 18.
  54-72.
King, R.D. 1969. Historical linguistics and generative
  grammar. Englewood Cliffs, N.J.: Prentice-Hall.
Kiparsky, P. 1968. Linguistic universals and linguistic
  change. Universals in linguistic theory, ed. by E. Bach
  and R. Harms. New York: Holt, Rinehart and Winston.
Labov, W. 1969. Contraction, deletion and inherent varia-
  bility of the English copula. Language 45.715-62.
_____. 1972. The internal evolution of linguistic rules.
  Linguistic change and generative theory, ed. by R.P.
  Stockwell and R.K.S. Macaulay, 101-71.
  Indiana University Press.
Reighard, J. 1974. Variable rules in historical linguistics.
  First International Conference on Historical Linguistics.
  Edinburgh.
_____. 1975. The history of a variable rule: syncope in
  Latin and Old French. Chicago: University of Chicago
  dissertation.
Wang, W.S.-Y. 1969. Competing changes as a cause of residue.
  Language 45.9-25.
Weinreich, U., W. Labov, and M. Herzog. 1968. Empirical
  foundations for a theory of language change. Directions

for historical linguistics, ed. by W. P. Lehmann and Y.
    Malkiel.   Austin: University of Texas Press.
Zwicky, A.   1972.   Note on a phonological hierarchy in English.
    Linguistic change and generative theory, ed. by R. P. Stockwell
    and R. K. S. Macaulay.   Bloomington: Indiana University Press.

OBLIGATORY VERSUS OPTIONAL RULES IN PEDAGOGICAL TEXTS: THE PARTITIVE CONSTRUCTION IN ITALIAN[1]

JUDY SCARPELLA-WALLS

Western Kentucky University

1. Current status of the partitive in pedagogical texts

Among linguists with a special interest in applied linguistics, there seems to be general agreement that there are many factors involved in the preparation of a pedagogical text for a language course.[2] The selection of a text depends on factors such as the objectives of the course, the age and intellectual maturity of the students, the length and intensity of the study, and the degree of contrast between the foreign and native languages. For the purpose of this study, I would also like to add the feature of naturalness of speech in the case of a conversation course. Depending on the individual situation, there are probably many more factors, but the above-mentioned are the ones on which I wish to concentrate.

The instructor of Italian who has considered all these factors and is looking for a text for his course soon discovers that not all these criteria are met. (See Table 1 for the treatment of indefinite articles and the partitive in Italian pedagogical texts.) The instructor who is also a linguist has the additional responsibility of being familiar with the

descriptive grammars as well as pedagogical grammars which
include data from student performance, and he wants the
pedagogical materials to represent the best analysis of native
speech that is currently available. No text can realistically
hope to satisfy all needs, and an instructor must be able to
fill in where he feels there is something missing. Materials
prepared for conversation courses, especially those which
suggest a direct method approach such as Cavagna's *Lo Dica in
Italiano* (1971) often use samples of native speech for which
there is no explanation in the simplified grammar they provide
for the student, and they often pass up an opportunity to
include a particular grammatical form in the presentation of
other related or similar linguistic phenomena.

A point in question is the partitive construction in Italian.
If the length and intensity of the course are such that we
are not able to teach all the grammar in the first year,
certain choices will have to be made. Does a person who takes
a first-year Italian conversation course really need to be
able to use the preterit, the subjunctive or even the conditional? I think not. However, as a natural class, pronouns
and the pro-complements[3] which have the same privileges of
occurrence are a significant part of the grammar, and since
many of them do not have structural equivalents in English
they do meet the criterion of a degree of contrast. In Italian,
the pro-complement *ne* 'of it, of them' which replaces the
partitive in accusative complements in both affirmative and
negative statements and questions is obligatory and is one of
a large class of pro-complements which are commonly used,
as in:

(1)   Non lo so.
      'I don't know.'
(2)   Me ne vado.
      'I'm leaving.'
(3)   Ci vado stasera.
      'I'm going there this evening.'
(4)   Se volete fargli un regalo, ci sto anch'io.
      'If you want to give him a present, count me in.'
(5)   Le telefono io.
      'I'll call her.'
(6)   Non ci credo.
      'I don't believe it.'
(7)   Non li conosco.
      'I don't know them.'   (m. pl.)
(8)   Ne ho due.
      'I have two (of them); I am two years old.'
(9)   Mi dici che è molto ricco. Non è vero, non lo è.
      'You're telling me that he's very rich. It's not
      true.'

According to Agard and DiPietro 1965, the proper use of
these pro-complements constitutes a major problem for the
English-speaking student since English does not have the equivalent in all cases and lacks the mechanism for replacing
complements in verb phrases. They claim that as an accusative

complement the partitive in 10 is in free stylistic variation
with 11, although both sentences contain *ne* when the accusative
complements are replaced by pro-complements as in 12:

> (10)   Compro delle banane al mercato.
>   'I buy bananas at the market.'
> (11)   Compro banane al mercato.
>   'I buy bananas at the market.'
> (12)   Ne compro al mercato.
>   'I buy them at the market.'

In an article written nearly fifty years ago, Vaughan 1926
contends that this optionality makes the language difficult
to master. Grammars that he surveyed stated that the word
some was frequently translated in Italian by the *preposizione
articolata* (preposition *di* 'of' + definite article) *del, della,
dei,* etc. or that it might be omitted, or that the partitive
was not used in an indefinite or general sense, nor in negative
sentences. (See Table 2 for Vaughan's English-Italian correspondences.)
The general rule in Vaughan's survey seemed to be that when
an English noun is accompanied by *some* or *any,* or when its
meaning would be unchanged by prefixing *some* or *any,* we have
a noun in the partitive sense and *del, della, dei,* etc. should
be used. This rule seems to imply that the English *some* and
any are exact semantic equivalents and that they could be
substituted for each other in any negative or question. Vaughan
did not accept this rule and Robin Lakoff 1969 in an article
on the presuppositions involved in sentences with *some* and
any seems to support his position.[4] Current research is now
trying to sort out the various meanings of *some* and *any* and
the Ø indefinite article as in 13, 14, and 15:[5]

> (13)   I don't have some time.
> (14)   I don't have any time.
> (15)   I don't have time.

and I will not attempt to solve this problem in this paper.
Suffice it to say that the generalization that the translation
of the Italian partitive is English *some* or *any* is simplistic
and inaccurate as I will show later. The feature [specific]
has been proposed to distinguish sentences with *some* from
generic sentences with *any.* Here again we are dealing with
a question of meaning and whether or not what is known to the
speaker is also known to the hearer.

2.   Definite and indefinite articles in Italian and English

Definite and indefinite articles are elements of the surface
structure in the Romance Languages, but not all have singular
forms which have structurally equivalent plural forms. The
singular indefinite is not distinguished in form from the
number *one,* but it has the additional meanings of non-specific,
generic, quantifier or classifying. French and Italian are the
only major Romance languages that use the partitive to indicate

indefinite plural and mass nouns, but the rule is much easier
in French because both the partitive and pro-complement which
replaces it, *en*, are obligatory (Valdman 1961):

   (16) J'ai un livre. J'en ai un.
         'I have a book. I have one.'
   (17) J'ai des livres. J'en ai.
         'I have (some) books. I have some.'
   (18) Je veux du vin. J'en veux.
         'I want (some) wine. I want some.'

    Aside from the obligatory-optional distinction between
French and Italian, another reason for considering the partitive an indefinite article in its own right in Italian is that
it either occurs in its preposition + article form or it is ∅.
The normative rule which many Italian grammars and dictionaries
give for not using the partitive + noun after prepositions--
because of the resulting sequences of two prepositions (*di* +
preposition)--is simply not followed as illustrated in 19, 20
and 21:[6]

   (19) Minnie investì gli spettatori con delle violenze
        verbali.
        'Minnie hurled verbal insults at the audience.'
   (20) Capuozzo riesce perfino a parlare con Napoli per
        delle ore da una cabina pubblica senza spendere
        una lira.
        'Capuozzo succeeds even in talking with Naples
        for hours from a public phone booth without spending
        a red cent.' (Terzoli and Vaime)
   (21) Queste stesse cose io le ho già udite dire a degli
        altri.
        'I already heard these same things said to others.'

Rohlfs 1968 also cautions against the use of partitives +
prepositions, but all of his examples are idioms or fixed
expressions which, as we shall see later, are not to be
considered as part of a treatment of regular grammatical
patterns.
    Both Italian and English use the concept of definite and
indefinite; articles may be definite or indefinite, singular
or plural, or ∅ with mass and count nouns. However, their
distribution is not the same in the two languages. With the
features singular, indefinite and class, we can have 22 in
English which cannot be pluralized with *some* as in 23 and retain
its meaning of a member of a group. The plural without the
article is the correct usage. The first indefinite is the class
indefinite with contrasts with the singular indefinite in 24,
which when pluralized becomes 25:

   (22) A consumer is entitled to rights.
   (23) Some consumers are entitled to rights.
   (24) A man just shot himself.
   (25) Some men just shot themselves.

Consider 26 and 27:

    (26)   Milk is good.
    (27)   Il latte è buono.

The English sentence includes a Ø article with the generic
subject while in Italian we have the definite article, the
sentence meaning both 'Milk is good (for you)' and 'The milk
(you just poured for me) is good'.   The definite article is
required in 27 and does not alternate with an indefinite or Ø
article in the singular and the plural, as in 28 and 29:

    (28)   Piero è architetto.
          'Piero is an architect.'
    (29)   Alma e Wanda sono professoresse.
          'Alma and Wanda are teachers.'

When we add an adjective, however, the situation is reversed
and we have 30 and 31:

    (30)   Piero è un buon architetto.
          'Piero is a good architect.'
    (31)   Alma e Wanda sono delle buone professoresse.
          'Alma and Wanda are good teachers.'

It is also possible to have the plural indefinite article with
the copula when there is no adjective and when the sentence
is an answer to a *wh*-question of identification.   Thus, someone
rings the doorbell and the following question and answer may
be heard:

    (32)   Chi c'è?
          'Who's there?'
    (33)   Siamo dei poliziotti.
          'We're some policemen.'

    DiPietro 1971 gives a rule for the partitive in sentence 34,
alternating with Ø in 35, both without adjectives:

    (34)   Sono dei professori.
          'They're some professors.'
    (35)   Sono professori.
          'They're professors.'

But he does not give an English translation so the reader is
led to believe that the optional principle is again accepted.
He continues with the addition of adjectives which, according
to him, makes the English and Italian parallel in that there
is no partitive or indefinite plural article used in either
language:

    (36)   Sono buoni professori.
          'They're good professors.'

However, it should be noted that native speech I have elicited

does not equate sentence 33 with the following, which refers
to members of a certain class or profession;

(37)   Siamo poliziotti.
       'We're policemen.'

Migliorini and Chiappelli 1962 have considered the problem
of definite and indefinite in the singular and plural and
feel strongly that 38 is no more definite than 39:

(38)   Mario ha comprato l'automobile.
       'Mario bought the car.'
(39)   Mario ha comprato un'automobile.
       'Mario bought a car.'

unless the context tells us specifically which car is being
referred to. The use of the articles and the partitive in the
plural gives us various degrees of meaning as in 40, 41, and
42:

(40)   Mario ha comprato le automobili.
       'Mario bought the cars.'
(41)   Mario ha comprato delle automobili.
       'Mario bought some cars.'
(42)   Mario ha comprato automobili.
       'Mario bought cars.'

Of the sentences above, 40 would be said only if it were known
that Mario was supposed to buy some cars, that is, referring
to cars one already knew about, while 41 indicates a certain
indeterminate number but not too great a number. Sentence 42
implies an indeterminate number which is not small, making one
think of a business investment. That is, one would say:

(43)   Ha comprato automobili e non motociclette o autocarri.
       'He bought cars and not motorcycles or trucks.'

The correct analysis of the indefinite articles seems to
be that they should be viewed as being part of an underlying
structure which may or may not be chosen according to the
grammatical features of the noun (in the accusative complement
noun phrase) such as count, mass, definite or indefinite,
classifying, generic, parts of the body and idiomatic expressions. As we have seen, however, we seem to need more information than has previously been given in grammars of English and
Italian. Language in context in a beginning course must be
included in our description. The underlying representations
for English *a professor* and Italian *professore* in *He's a
professor* and *È professore* must contain the features [profession]
and [modified] as in:

(44)   a. English   b. Italian

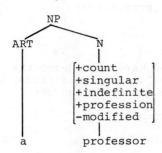
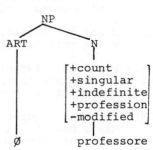

The plural nouns would need to contain similar information but also allow for 45 and 46 in Italian:

(45)   Siamo poliziotti.
       'We're policemen.'
(46)   Siamo dei poliziotti.
       'We're some policemen.'

The conditions under which the partitive would be blocked must be given in terms of rules.[7] The partitive in Italian is not used with certain idiomatic expressions, in enumerations, or as part of the subject noun phrase, when it is the first element in the sentence. Native speakers accept 47 and feel that 48 sounds stilted and too 'grammatical':

(47)   Sono venuti degli amici a trovarmi.
       'Some friends came to visit me.'
(48)   Degli amici sono venuti a trovarmi.
       'Some friends came to visit me.'

In every case examined, the plural of an indefinite singular article + noun at the beginning of a sentence was the definite plural article as in:

(49)   Un padre buono può essere severo.
       'A good father can be strict.'
       I padri buoni possono essere severi.
       'Good fathers can be strict.'
(50)   Una chiave piccola non è pesante.
       'A small key isn't heavy.'
       Le chiavi piccole non sono pesanti.
       'Small keys are not heavy.'

Nevertheless, as with 47, we have sentences like 51 and 52 as perfectly natural singular-plural pairs:

(51)   La scuola ha un'entrata.
       'The school has an (one) entrance.'
       Le scuole hanno delle entrate.
       'The schools have (some) entrances.'

(52) Ho incontrato un compagno di scuola al bar.
      'I met a school friend at the bar.'
      Ho incontrato dei compagni di scuola al bar.
      'I met some school friends at the bar.'

When other expressions of quantity, numbers or classifiers
such as *parecchio* 'a number of, a lot of', *poco* 'a little,
few', *molto* 'much, many', *qualche* 'some', *alcuni* 'some', *un
chilo di* 'a kilogram of', *due litri di* 'two liters', *quattro
metri di* 'four meters', etc. occur, the partitive is not used.
    The indefinite singular article is also restricted in
idiomatic expressions without modification as can be seen by
the expression:

(53) prendere fiato
      'to take a breath'

which is translated as 'to take breath' in the generally excellent Italian-English, English-Italian dictionary by Ragazzini
1967. When, however, the nouns in some common idiomatic
expressions such as:

(54) Ho fame.
      'I'm hungry.'
(55) Fa freddo.
      'It's cold.'

are modified, the indefinite singular article is used:

(56) Ho una fame da morire.
      'I'm starving to death.'
(57) Fa un freddo cane.
      'It's bitterly cold.'

    There are also unmodified idiomatic expressions which use
the partitive, as in:

(58) prendere dei pensionanti
      'to take in boarders'
(59) fare del bene
      'to do something good for someone'

Idiomatic expressions must be learned as lexical items and
should not be included in a presentation of grammatical
patterns of high frequency.
    The partitive is used with parts of the body in Italian
where the English equivalent would be Ø:

(60) Ha degli occhi stupendi.
      'She has stupendous eyes.'
(61) Ha delle guance come fette di lardo.
      'She has cheeks like slices of bacon.'
                                    (Terzoli and Vaime)

    In English and Italian, the choice of definite and indefi-

nite articles often depends on a larger grammatical context
rather than just on a noun subclass. Brengleman 1970 gives
the following English example:

> (62)   A man and a woman were walking down the street.
>   The man was carrying a bag.

We could not replace the second *the* with *a* unless we wished
to refer to another man other than the one just mentioned.
Rapaccini 1969 uses sentences like 63 and 64:

> (63)   Se lui vuole dei dolci, glieli porto.
>   'If he wants some sweets, I'll bring them to him.'
> (64)   Se lei vuole delle banane, gliele porto.
>   'If she (you) wants (want) bananas, I'll bring them
>   to her (you).'

Furthermore, native speakers accept them as natural speech in
the same way they accept 65 and 66:

> (65)   Se lui vuole dei dolci, gliene porto.
>   'If he wants sweets, I'll bring him some.'
> (66)   Se lei vuole delle banane, gliene porto.
>   'If she (you) wants (want) bananas, I'll bring her
>   (you) some.'

As mentioned earlier, this treatment of indefinite and
definite articles is in no way complete. But the instructor of
Italian must be aware of at least those conditions I have
listed for the use or omission of the articles and the partitive.

3. Obligatory and optional rules

DiPietro 1971 discusses the question of the hierarchies of
difficulty for language learners and reproduces Stockwell
and Bowen's sets of contrasts for the pronunciation of the
native and target languages. We might apply these criteria to
the partitive construction in Italian and its counterpart in
English since they both meet the requirement of being permis-
sible in the same environment, namely, the accusative complement. The substitution of *ne* for an indefinite noun complement would be the most difficult pattern to learn because it
is an obligatory construction in Italian and absent in English.
If we considered Ø as well as *some* and *any* as indefinite
plural markers in English and said that we had a freedom of
choice, we would have an optional pattern in both languages.
Such a pattern would certainly be low on the scale of difficulty but would not really reflect the fact that in many cases
the partitive is used in Italian where there would be a Ø
article in English as shown below:

> (67)   L'ostrica deve avere delle antenne, dei tubercoli.
>   'The oyster must have antennas and tubercles.'

(68)   Io non capisco a chi è venuto in mente di fare delle
       città in questi posti.
       'I don't understand who would think of putting cities
       in these places.'
(69)   E se non li seguivi fino al parcheggio dove ci avevano
       le spiders, li prendevi per dei barboni come me.
       'And if you didn't follow them to the parking lot where
       they had their sports cars, you took them for bums
       like me.' (Terzoli and Vaime)

These examples in addition to the data I have gathered from
native speakers support the inclusion of the partitive in a
descriptive grammar, and as samples of sentence patterns in
spoken language, they certainly ought to be part of a pedagogical text. The native speakers feel that in many cases it
is much more natural to use the partitive. The traditional
labeling of the partitive as optional in the case of statements and questions and Ø in negative statements and questions
has just meant that the students do not have to learn another
rule. Setting up a Ø-obligatory contrast between English and
Italian does increase the degree of difficulty from an optional –
optional or a Ø – Ø pattern, and if it were not for the
obligatory *ne*, one might be more inclined to dismiss it. Yet
the pressure of the pro-complement pattern is too great to
ignore. Stockwell and Bowen also consider the frequency with
which a particular contrast comes up in actual speech. My
study does not include a statistical analysis of partitives in
native speech or in contemporary literary texts containing
dialogues, but the samples I have gathered do show that the
partitive is frequently used and appears to be the spontaneous
choice in those patterns I have isolated.

4.   The obligatory proposal

My proposal for the inclusion of the partitive in a pedagogical
text would be more comprehensive than the general presentation
in the texts I have used and examined. Students today still
have difficulty with pro-complement substitution as I did when
I first started studying Italian in 1960. However, if the
descriptive grammar and the pedagogical grammar from which the
course materials are constructed give more accurate and complete
information than that which is now given, the student may have
a little better understanding of structures. We should require
an obligatory rule with the partitive used as an indefinite
singular article with mass nouns and as an indefinite plural
article with count nouns, in an accusative complement or
introduced by *C'è* or *Ci sono* 'There is, There are', and
translated into English as *some*, *any* or Ø under the conditions
stated. We can leave any semantic distinction which may be
stylistic until later, when the subjunctive and other more
complicated patterns for speakers of English are taught and
more class time can be devoted to semantic distinctions. The
instructor should be informed of recent linguistic analyses
of structures (e.g. the subjunctive, including a consideration
of meaning, as in Saltarelli 1974), but the beginning pedago-

gical text should not contain such sophisticated materials.

When the pro-complements are presented as a class, they will find their way into conversations where the pattern definite/indefinite article + noun naturally occurs as part of normal speech. If the goal is to make the student use the language from the very beginning and not just require memorization of dialogues about other people or mastery of pattern drills, the speech must be the same as the student would hear if he saw a film in Italian, traveled in Italy, or heard his instructor talking to a native speaker of Italian. The degree of fluency depends to a great extent on the ability to use patterns in a natural context, and the partitive construction and pro-complement *ne* increase this ability. The two languages do contrast on this point, and if the pedagogical materials are constructed incorporating the essential criteria we have discussed, this interference might not be so great.

NOTES

[1] I would like to thank Bill Walls, Bob Martin, Maurizio Gnerre and Gigliola Foti for their suggestions, criticisms and observations.

[2] See Rivers (1972:10) and Noblitt (1972).

[3] Hall gives the over-all term of pro-complement to substitutes for various types of verbal complements such as pronouns, pro-phrases, and pro-predicate complements.

[4] Lakoff (1969) does not agree that *I wonder if Bill would lend me some money* and *I wonder if Bill would lend me any money* are synonymous and feels instead that they are correlations of positive and negative or neutral presuppositions.

[5] The section of determiners in Stockwell, Schachter and Partee (1973) is an excellent reference for the source of articles in the structure of English. There is still no agreement on how to account for the three-way contrast of *some-any-Ø* in *I don't like some books, I don't like any books,* and *I don't like books.*

[6] Ceppellini (1962) and Paniate (1969) do not accept sentences such as *Passeggiavo con delle amiche* 'I was walking with some friends' and *Scriverò a degli amici* 'I'll write to some friends.'

[7] Even Hall (1972) agrees that rules are useful in second-language acquisition as a timesaving device at the early stages.

Table 1   Occurrences of the Indefinite Article and the Partitive in Pedagogical Texts

	Indefinite		Partitive	Statements	Neg.	Questions	Neg. Q's	*Ne*
	Singular	Plural						
Traversa	+	+	+	+	−	−	∅	+
Plant	+	∅	+	+	+	+	∅	+
*Speroni-Golino	+	+	+	+	−	−	∅	+
Bosco-Lolli	+	∅	+	⊕	−	⊕	∅	+
Hall-Bartoli	+	∅	+	+	−	+	∅	+
Hall-IFML	+	∅	+	+	X	+	∅	+
Guarnieri-Amorini	+	+	+	+	+	+	∅	+
Cavagna-IML	+	∅	∅	+	−	−	∅	+

+ used
− not used
∅ not mentioned
⊕ optional
X with mass nouns

*Graziana Lazzarino of the University of Colorado who has long used Speroni-Golino in Italian conversation classes and who has just written two workbooks for Italian 101-102 accepts both *scrivono lettere?* and *scrivono delle lettere?* and *Comprano carne?* and *Comprano delle carne?*

Table 2   The Partitive in Italian with English equivalents (after Vaughan 1926)

	Statements	Negative Statements
Italian:	Ho Ø buoni amici.	Non ho Ø buoni amici.
	Ho dei buoni amici.	Non ho dei buoni amici
English:	I have some good friends.	I don't have any good friends.
	I have Ø good friends.	I don't have Ø good friends.

	Questions	Negative Questions
Italian:	Hai Ø buoni amici?	Non hai Ø buoni amici?
	Hai dei buoni amici?	Non hai dei buoni amici?
English:	Do you have some good friends?	Don't you have some good friends?
	Do you have any good friends?	Don't you have any good friends?
	Do you have Ø good friends?	Don't you have Ø good friends?

REFERENCES

Agard, Frederick B. and Robert J. DiPietro. 1965. The grammatical structures of English and Italian. Chicago: The University of Chicago Press.

Amorini, Enzo. 1966. Esercizi e conversazioni di lingua viva ad uso degli stranieri. Perugia: A cura dell'Università Per Stranieri.

Bosco, Frederick J. and Franca Lolli. 1967. Incontro con l'italiano. Waltham, Massachusetts: Ginn-Blaisdell.

Brengleman, Fred. 1970. The English language: an introduction for teachers. Englewood Cliffs, New Jersey: Prentice Hall.

Cavagna, Giovanna Guglielmo. 1971. Lo dica in italiano, primo libro. Silver Springs, Maryland: Institute of Modern Languages.

Ceppellini, Vincenzo. 1962. Dizionario grammaticale per il buon uso della lingua italiana. 4th ed. Novara: Instituto Geografico de Agostini.

Di Pietro, Robert J. 1971. Language structures in contrast. Rowley, Massachusetts: Newbury House.

Frank, Marcella. 1972. Modern English: a practical reference guide. Englewood Cliffs, New Jersey: Prentice-Hall.

Guarnieri, Romano. 1966. Metodo di lingua italiana per gli stranieri. Perugia: A cura dell'Università Per Stranieri.

Hall, Robert A., Jr. 1958. Italian for modern living. Philadelphia: Chilton Company.

_____. 1961. Applied linguistics: Italian, a guide for teachers. Boston: D.C. Heath.

_____ and Cecilia M. Bartoli. 1963. Basic conversational Italian. New York: Holt, Rinehart and Winston.

_____. 1964. Introductory linguistics. Philadelphia: Chilton Company.

_____. 1971. La struttura dell'italiano. Rome: Armando Armando.

_____. 1972. The place of rules in linguistic analysis. Studies in linguistics in honor of George L. Trager, ed. by M. Estelle Smith, 41-3. The Hague: Mouton.

Lakoff, Robin. 1969. Some reasons why there can't be any *some-any* rule. Language 45.608-15.

Lazzarino, Graziana. 1975. Italian 101-102 workbooks. Boulder, Colorado: Department of Italian Language and Literature.

Migliorini, B. and F. Chiappelli. 1962. Lingua e stile. Firenze: Le Monnier.

Noblitt, James S. 1972. Pedagogical grammar: towards a theory of foreign language materials preparation. IRAL 10:4.313-31.

Palazzi, Fernando. 1962. Novissimi grammatica italiana. Milano: Principato Editore.

Paniate, E. 1969. Grammatica viva della lingua italiana. Torino: S. Lattes.

Plant, Derrick and Patricia Coales. 1970. A viva voce: a modern course of spoken Italian for English speakers. Bologna: Zanichelli.

Ragazzini, Giuseppe. 1967. Dizionario inglese-italiano;
    italiano-inglese. Bologna: Zanichelli.
Rapaccini, Luisa. 1969. Parlo italiano. 10th ed. Firenze:
    Le Monnier.
Regula, Moritz and Josip Jernej. 1965. Grammatica italiana
    descritta su basi storiche e psicologiche. Berna.
Rivers, Wilga. 1972. Speaking in many tongues: essays in
    foreign-language teaching. Rowley, Massachusetts: Newbury
    House.
Rohlfs, Gerhard. 1968. Grammatica storica della lingua
    italiana e dei suoi dialetti: morfologia. Torino: Piccola
    Biblioteca Einaudi.
Roncari, A. and C. Briganti. 1961. La lingua italiana
    insegnata agli stranieri. 18th ed. Milano: Edizioni
    Scolastiche Mondadori.
Saltarelli, Mario. 1974. Reference and mood in Italian.
    Linguistic studies in Romance languages. ed. by R.
    Joe Campbell, Mark G. Goldin, and Mary Clayton Wang.
    Washington, D.C.: Georgetown University Press.
Speroni, Charles and Carlo L. Golino. 1972. Basic Italian.
    3rd ed. New York: Holt, Rinehart and Winston.
Stockwell, Robert, Paul Schachter and Barbara Hall Partee. 1973.
    The major syntactic structures of English. New York: Holt,
    Rinehart and Winston.
Terzoli, Italo and Enrico Vaime. 1971. Amare significa...
    storia d'amore all'italiana. Milano: Collana Humour
    Bietti.
Traversa, Vincenzo. 1967. Parola e pensiero, introduzione
    alla lingua italiana moderna. New York: Harper and Row.
Valdman, Albert. 1961. Applied linguistics: French, a
    guide for teachers. Boston: D.C. Heath.
Vaughan, H.H. 1926. The partitive construction in Italian.
    Italica 3.5-6.

NASALIZATION AND DIPHTHONGIZATION IN MARAIS VENDÉEN FRENCH*

YVES CHARLES MORIN

Université de Montréal

We present in this paper an analysis of nasalization and
diphthongization in a dialect of French actively and widely
spoken in the northwestern part of the Vendée Department when
it was recorded between 1949 and 1953 by Lars-Owe Svenson (1959).
We shall present arguments in favor of non-phonetic abstract
underlying forms to account for a phonetically regular process
of diphthongization.[1]

1. Yod-vocalization

In this section we shall show that some occurrences of post-
vocalic *e* must be interpreted as the phonetic reflex of a more
remote *y*. This result is a prerequisite to our analysis of
diphthongization. We will just give a short description of
the phenomenon to convince the reader of the adequacy of our
analysis, without necessarily answering all the questions
raised by this analysis.

The segments *y* and *e* do not contrast in the language and
alternate both at the morpheme level and word level depending

on the position of the word in the sentence, e.g. *epay/epaes*
'épais/épaisse', *i boy/i bwe žamay* 'je bois/je ne bois jamais'.
This indicates that they have a common underlying phonological
form which can be realized as *y* or *e*. We shall take *y* to
be the common underlying form, and postulate a rule that changes
y to *e* in the appropriate context. The difficulty in stating
the phonetic distribution of *y* and *e* lies in the fact that the
contexts where *y* is realized as *e* varies with the geographical
location. We observe that *y* remains non-vocalic in word-final
position, e.g. *epay* 'épais', and becomes *e* in unstressed
syllables, e.g. *groezél* 'groseille' consistently throughout
the area. It is only in closed stressed syllables that we
observe geographic variability. Following Labov's 1972 proposal
for variable rules, we could write yod-vocalization as 1:

(1) Yod-vocalization

$$y \rightarrow \langle e \rangle \ / \ \begin{bmatrix} +\text{syll} \\ \langle -\text{stress} \rangle_1 \end{bmatrix} \underline{\quad} C$$

This rule indicates that vocalization is systematic when a
non-stressed vowel precedes (the weight attached to the occurrence of a preceding non-stressed vowel being 1 here), and
variable when it is both preceded by a stressed vowel and
followed by a consonant. Vocalization in closed stressed
syllables depends both on the geographic location and the
nature of the closing consonant. It does not take place before
an obstruent in most places, except in the Northwest, e.g. the
words *bayt, epays, rayz, žayp* 'bête, épaisse, raie, guêpe'
have for counterpart in the Northwest *baet, epaes, raez* and
žaep. Before sonorants, *y* becomes vocalic in most places,
except in the Southeast. In the Southeast *y* remains non-vocalic
before *l* and the nasals, and disappears completely before *r*,
e.g. the words *žayn, mayl, žar* 'chaîne, nèfle, chaise' in the
Southeast correspond to more general *žaen, mael, žaer*. In
the SE region where we find *žar* 'chaise' (for *žaer* elsewhere),
it is likely that the underlying form is simply *žar*. This
does not affect the analysis of yod-vocalization. In the
Southeast there would be simply no yod in *žar* to which the rule
could apply. It should be clear that the geographic indications
here only represent main tendencies, and that in some points
there can be lexical or random variation. For instance, in
St. Gervais (Center), Svenson notes *žaen* 'chaîne', but *layn*
'laine'. Extending rule 1 to cover geographic variation, we
could write yod-vocalization as 2:

(2) Yod-vocalization

$$y \rightarrow e \ / \ \begin{bmatrix} +\text{syll} \\ \langle -\text{stress} \rangle_1 \end{bmatrix} \underline{\quad} \begin{bmatrix} -\text{syll} \\ \langle +\text{sonorant} \rangle \\ \langle +\text{SE-NW} \rangle \end{bmatrix}$$

Rule 2 indicates that yod-vocalization takes place variably

before a consonant, more frequently before sonorant, and more
frequently as we move toward the Northwest pole of a Southeast-
Northwest axis.

In the example that we have shown *y* was mainly preceded by
the vowel *a*. The only other vowels that can precede *y* are
e and *o*. For these vowels we observe the same tendencies, but
slightly more complex. We shall postpone the case of *e* until
section 3. Vocalization of yod after *o* interacts with two
other phenomena, namely *glide-switching*, and *glide-formation*.
We shall postpone glide-switching until section 3 also, and
describe here only glide-formation. When the segment *o* is
followed by *e* (whether or not this *e* is from underlying yod) it
may become *w*, e.g. the expression *lœ boyt* 'il boit' is
realized as *bwet* in the Northwest, where we previously observed
that *y* is realized as *e* before *t*. We can account for these
facts by postulating a rule of glide-formation which changes
ò to *w* before a vowel. Glide-formation is blocked almost
everywhere after obstruent-liquid clusters, e.g. *groezel*
'groseille', *kroer* (sometimes however also *krwer*) 'croire'.
In some places glide-formation takes place only in non-stressed
syllables, e.g. *lœ bóet/lœ bwetúz* 'il boit/il boite'
(attested in Notre-Dame de Monts). Apparently whenever *o*
remains syllabic before vowel and it is not preceded by an OL
cluster, the stress falls on this *o* and not on the following *e*.
In the dialects where glide-formation takes place, however, *e*
is stressed. We can account for glide-formation by stating
that it applies only to unstressed *o*, and that it is the
presence of a stress on *o* which prevents its application in
dialects where we observe *bóet*:

(3)   Glide-formation $\begin{bmatrix} o \\ -stress \end{bmatrix} \rightarrow w \ / \ \_\_\_ \ V$

Rule 3 is blocked by an independent tension (derivational constraint) whenever its application would create clusters consisting of the sequence Obstruent-Liquid-Glide (c.f. Morin,
forthcoming), e.g. in *kroer*, *groezel*. This implies that stress
must be determined before glide-formation. It must also be
determined before yod-vocalization in the formulation that we
have given in 2. Underlying *boyt* receives a stress on *o* in
all dialects. When yod-vocalization applies this yields *boet*.
In the dialects where we observe *bwet*, we must postulate an
extra rule which moves the stress from the penultimate to the
last vowel in the word. This *stress-displacement* seems to
apply regularly only in two points (Beauvoir-sur-Mer and Bois-
de-Cené). Finally we observe one point (Sallertaine) where
glide-formation does not apply, whether or not *o* is stressed,
e.g. *lœ boet* 'il boit', *lœ boetuz* 'il boite'.

In this analysis we have postulated underlying *oy* on the
basis of complementary distributions. This kind of analysis
allows us to determine an underlying *oy* in words such as
mwetay 'moitié', *bwetu* 'boiteux', *lwesi* 'lessive' even though
our rules predict that its phonetic realizations will always
be *we* (except in Sallertaine) since *oy* in these words will
always be unstressed. Some versions of natural phonology

require that the segments postulated in the underlying form of
a morpheme be identical to the phonetic segments when they do
not alternate. In these words the underlying forms should then
contain *we* instead of *oy* as we have postulated here. Actually
Svenson frequently notes an alternate pronunciation *oy* in these
words, *moytay*, *boytu*, *loysi*, in slow and deliberate speech.
We can assume that in these cases each syllable is stressed.
Our analysis predicts that if *oy* is stressed in these syllables
its phonetic realization will be *oy*. In the version of natural
phonology where the invariant phonetic parts of a morpheme are
necessarily underlying, the existence of alternations such as
mwetay/moytay would then justify an underlying form with *oy*.

2.   Concerning nasalized glides as diphthongization

We will show in this section that the nasals *n* and *ŋ* observed
in the alternations *ẽ/an* and *õ/aŋ* (cf. the examples 4 and 5)
are the phonetic realizations of remote nasalized glides *ỹ* and *w̃*.

(4)	a.	do vẽ rož	'du vin rouge'
	b.	do van	'du vin'
		loe van e kʎer	'le vin est clair'
(5)	a.	la mezõ bʎãš	'la maison blanche'
	b.	la mezaŋ	'la maison'
		la mezaᵑ a bʎaŋ	'la maison de Billon'

The diphthongized variants, i.e. *an* and *aŋ* (the nasals here
will be analyzed as remote glides) are observed in word-final
syllables when they are either stressed or followed by a vowel.
We shall refer to these contexts as context B. The nondiphthongized variants are observed in unstressed syllables followed
by a consonant. We shall refer to these contexts as context A.

   The alternation *ẽ/an* is part of a larger alternation *ẽ/an/in*,
which may suggest another analysis where *n* in both of the last
two variants is underlying. We will first present this analysis,
show why it is inadequate, and finally argue for diphthongization.

   The alternation *ẽ/an* is phonologically transparent, as we
have just seen, since the distribution of *ẽ* and *an* is completely
determined by the phonological context. The alternation
ẽ/an/in on the other hand is opaque, c.f. 6, where the words 6a
are in context A, and 6b in context B.

   (6)   Alternation *ẽ/an/in*

	a.	farẽ	'brume'	fẽ	'fin (masc)'
	b.	faran	'brume'	fan	'fin'
	c.	farinu	'brumeux'	fin	'fine (fem)'

The variant *in* is observed before a vowel, e.g. *farin+u*,
and word-finally in feminine words, e.g. *fin* (fem) vs. *fẽ/fan*
(masc). It is not the case however that all words ending in
ẽ/an will be masculine, e.g. *fẽ/fan* 'faim' is feminine. But
when there is an alternation between *in* and *ẽ/an* at the end
of a word, *in* always corresponds to the feminine and *ẽ/an* to

the masculine. This shows that neither the phonological nor the morphological contexts are sufficient to determine the variant *in* or *ẽ/an* since *fin* 'fine' appears in the same contexts as *fẽ/fan* 'faim' or 'fin' and since the alternation between *in* and *ẽ/an* in feminine-masculine pairs cannot be attributed solely to gender. The lexical entries associated with *fin* 'fine' and *fẽ/fan* 'fin' will have to specify somehow that for this word the feminine is marked by alternating *in* and *ẽ/an* whereas it is not the case for the feminine word *fẽ/fan* 'faim'.

Whenever lexical solution is adopted to account for this alternation, we observe that it is paralleled by another morphological alternation where Ø and *t* alternate under the same conditions, as we can see from 7:

(7)   Alternation Ø/t/ţ

    a. do pţi let   'du petit lait'
    b. l e pţit   'il est petit'
    c. al e pţit   'elle est petite'
        ča pţit fœλ   'cette petite fille'

The final *t* in the morpheme *petit* is observed in all the contexts where *an* and *in* are found, and is deleted where *ẽ* is observed. It seems thus that the same rule (phonological or morphological) accounts for the loss of *t* and *n*.

We could for instance propose the following morphological derivation.

Underlying	fin	fin	fin	ptit	ptit	ptit
Context	A	B		A	B	
	masc	masc	fem	masc	masc	fem
Nasalization	fĩn	fĩn	–	–	–	–
Lowering	fẽn	fẽn	–	–	–	–
Truncation	fẽ	–	–	pti	–	–
Lowering-Denas.	–	fan	–	–	–	–
Phonetic form	[fẽ]	[fan]	[fin]	[pţi]	[pţit]	[pţit]

In this analysis nasalization applies to a vowel followed by a nasal consonant in the same syllable, but is lexically blocked for some feminine words (the exact mechanism of this blocking need not concern us here). The resulting nasalized vowel is lowered to become a mid-vowel. Truncation applies in context A (blocked again in some feminine words). Lastly a nasalized vowel followed by a nasal consonant is lowered again to low-position, and denasalized, thus changing *ẽn* to *an* whenever truncation has not applied.

This analysis, however, cannot be extended to account for four other morphological alternations which also share the distribution of *ẽ/an/in* and Ø/t/ţ as in the examples 8 to 11, where the words in a are in context A and the words in b in context B.

(8) Alternation ẽ/an/im

    a. vrẽ   'venim'
    b. vran   'venim'
    c. vrimu   'venimeux'

(9) Alternation ẽ/an/üm

    a. fẽ   'faim'
    b. fan   'faim'
    c. fümin   'faim'
       afümay   'affamé'

(10) Alternation õ/aŋ/un

    a. bõ   'bon'
    b. baŋ   'bon'
    c. bun   'bonne'

(11) Alternation ã/ã/an

    a. žã   'Jean'
    b. žã   'Jean'
    c. žan   'Jeanne'
       žano   'Jeannot'

It is clear from these alternations that there is no correlation between the two nasals: in 8 and 9 n alternates with m, in 10 ŋ alternates with n, and in 11 Ø (+nasalization) alternates with n. On the other hand there is a strict correlation between the nasal (or its absence) and the nature of the nasalized vowel in the transparent alternations, i.e. those alternations observed in 8a-8b, 9a-9b, 10a-10b and 11a-11b which are completely conditioned by the phonological context. One simple way to describe all the alternations observed is to adopt the variant in the opaque context, i.e. here 8c, 9c, 10c and 11c, as the morphological underlying form and postulate some morphological rules which will change in, im, üm to ẽ, un to õ, and an to ã in some lexically specified morphological context. A further phonological rule of diphthongization will then change ẽ to an and õ to aŋ in contexts B. This explains simply why ẽ always corresponds to an, why õ corresponds to aŋ, and why ã is invariant, no matter what their morphological abstract forms are.

At this point we have shown that the alternations between ẽ/an, õ/aŋ (and the non-alternation of ã in the same phonological contexts) should be accounted for independently from the further alternations in which they may take part, and in particular that the n in the alternation ẽ/an should not be related to the n in the larger alternation ẽ/an/in. We have suggested that an and aŋ should be considered as the diphthongs of ẽ and õ through a diphthongization rule such as 12:

(12) Diphthongization$_1$

$$\begin{bmatrix} \tilde{e} \\ \tilde{o} \end{bmatrix} \rightarrow \begin{bmatrix} an \\ a\eta \end{bmatrix} \Big/ \text{ context B}$$

An alternative course in which $\tilde{e}$ and $\tilde{o}$ are derived from underlying an and $a\eta$ is also possible. We will weigh the merits of both analyses later. But first we want to show that the alternations $\tilde{e}$/an and $\tilde{o}$/$a\eta$ are part of a larger phenomenon of diphthongization, which is why we have named an and $a\eta$ the diphthongized variants of $\tilde{e}$ and $\tilde{o}$.

Environment A	Environment B$_1$	Environment B$_2$
in šen d môt 'une chaîne de montre'	in šayn 'une chaîne'	
ẽ pešür 'un pêcheur'	la payš 'la pêche'	
1 pe gauš 'le pied gauche'	sõ pay 'son pied'	
	la žlay 'la gelée'	la žlay ã may 'la gelée de mai'
la mẽ gauš 'la main gauche'	la man 'la main'	
do vẽ rož 'du vin rouge'	do van 'du vin'	lœ van e kʎer 'le vin est clair'
čẽz ã 'quinze ans'	čãỹz 'quinze'	
čẽzayn 'quinzaine'		
kozey 'causer'	kauz 'cause'	
dla so fin 'du sel fin'	dla sau 'du sel'	
la mo do da 'il a mal aux dents'	lœ mau 'le mal'	la mau o pay 'il a mal aux pieds'
la mezõ blãš 'la maison blanche'	mezaŋ 'maison'	la mezaŋ a bʎaŋ 'la maison de Billon'

We observe above, besides the alternations we have already mentioned, alternations between e/ay, e.g. šen/šayn 'chaîne', $\tilde{e}$/$\tilde{a}\tilde{y}$, e.g. čẽz/čãỹz 'quinze', and o/au, e.g. so/sau 'sel', where the nondiphthongized form is observed in context A, and the diphthongized form in context B.[2] We also observe in

the language that the high vowels *i, ü, u,* and the low vowel
a are not subject to any alternation in the same contexts, e.g.
pi 'pie', *pü* 'dent de râteau', *šu* 'choux', and *gʎa* 'glace' are
invariant.   There is here clearly a common phenomenon involving
mid-vowels.   There are no reasons to consider the variation
involving the nasalized vowels separately.   First of all, the
alternation in contexts A and B is limited to mid-vowels for
both oral and nasalized vowels (we have seen that *ã* does not
alternate).   Second, the alternations *ẽ/ãỹ* and *ẽ/an* are in
complementary distribution.   The variant *ãỹ* appears in contexts
B before consonant, the variant *an* in word-final position.   This
indicates that rule 12 should be modified to 13:

(13) Diphthongization$_2$ $\begin{bmatrix} ẽ \\ õ \end{bmatrix} \rightarrow \begin{bmatrix} \begin{cases} ãỹ \ / \ \_\_ \ C \\ an \ / \ \_\_ \ \# \end{cases} \\ aŋ \end{bmatrix}$ / context B

In other words, *an* and *ãỹ* are conditioned variants.   This last
variation could be accounted for by postulating a common
remote form, e.g. *ãỹ* for both phonetic realizations *an* and *ãỹ*
and two rules; rule 14 changing *ỹ* to *n* in word-final position,
rule 15 denasalizing *a* before a nasal consonant:

(14) Yod-consonantization   ỹ → n / ___#

(15) Denasalization   V → [-nasal] / ___ $\begin{bmatrix} +cons \\ -nasal \end{bmatrix}$

Both rules 14 and 15 are transparent in the language.   The rule
for diphthongization 13 can now be rewritten as 16.   The
derivation 17 shows how the three rules of diphthongization,
yod-consonantization, and denasalization interact:

(16) Diphthongization$_3$ $\begin{bmatrix} ẽ \\ õ \end{bmatrix} \rightarrow \begin{bmatrix} ãỹ \\ aŋ \end{bmatrix}$ / context B

(17)

Underlying		dẽd 'dinde'		fẽ 'fin'	
Context	A		B	A	B
Diphthong	dẽd		dãỹd	fẽ	fãỹ
Yod-conson.	-		-	-	fãn
Denasalizat.	-		-	-	fan
Yod-vocaliz.	-	(SE)	(NW)	-	-
		dãỹd	dãẽd		

Phonetic form [dẽd] [dãỹd] [dãẽd]   [fẽ] [fan]

This analysis is further justified by the fact that in the
whole western part of the area surveyed by Svenson, instead of

the alternation *ẽ/an* we observe the alternation *ẽ/ãỹ*, e.g.
la mãỹ 'la main', *fãỹ* 'fin', etc. instead of *la man, fan*
elsewhere. Svenson also notes some variability for some speakers who can say both *mãỹ* and *man*, for instance.[3] In our analysis, western dialects would differ from the other dialects by
the absence of yod-vocalization.

The alternations *o/au* and *õ/aɲ* fall within the same paradigm
if we postulate an underlying alternation *o/aw* which applies to
both oral and nasalized vowels. Yod-consonantization must be
extended to apply to *w̃* and change it to *ɲ*. A further rule of
w-vocalization must also be posited to explain why underlying
aw becomes *au* when it is not nasalized. At this stage of our
analysis the rules of the grammar would be then as follows:[4]

(18)   Diphthongization$_4$ $\begin{bmatrix} e \\ o \end{bmatrix} \rightarrow$ a $\begin{bmatrix} y \\ w \end{bmatrix}$ / context B

(19)   Glide-consonantization $\begin{bmatrix} \tilde{y} \\ \tilde{w} \end{bmatrix} \rightarrow \begin{bmatrix} n \\ \eta \end{bmatrix}$ / ___#

(20)   Denasalization   V $\rightarrow$ [-nasal] / ___ $\begin{bmatrix} \text{-cons.} \\ \text{+nasal} \end{bmatrix}$

(21)   *w*-vocalization   w $\rightarrow$ u / a ___

Derivation 22 shows how these rules account for the alternation
o/au and *õ/aɲ*:

(22)   Underlying form

	mezõ 'maison'		so 'sel'	
Context	A	B	A	B
Diphthongiz.	mezõ	mezãw̃	so	saw
Glide-consonantiz.	-	mezãɲ	-	-
Denazalization	-	mezaɲ	-	-
w-vocalization	-	-	-	sau
Phonetic form	[mezõ]	[mezaɲ]	[so]	[sau]

It might be argued that the remote form *aw* for phonetic *au*
is ad hoc and is only here to unify the treatment of diphthongization. There are actually independent justifications for
such an analysis. Stress normally falls on the last vowel in
a word, e.g. *y u kreɔ́w* 'je le crois', *in deá* 'une dent'; the
exceptions are vowels which alternate with a consonant or a
glide, e.g. *bɛ́a/bel* 'beau/belle', *krɔ́er* 'croire', *lœ bóet/*
lœ bóyt 'il boit', *šáen/šáyn* 'chaîne'. From Svenson's
description, it appears that in the sequence *au*, *a* and not *u*
is stressed (he explicitly gives the stress in the word for
'eau' in which there are some variations: *éau* or *eáu*). This
means that when stress assignment takes place *u* does not behave
like a vowel, and that therefore it must be *w*.[5]

3. Early and late diphthongizations

Mid-vowels are not all subject to diphthongization 18. We
also observe mid-vowels which are invariant or which alternate
with other diphthongs. We shall refer to the diphthongization
described previously as the *early diphthongization* (because it
appeared historically first). We describe in this section
another diphthongization, which we refer to as the *late diphthongization*. The fact that mid-vowels can undergo two different
kinds of diphthongization indicates that there should be two
different representations at the underlying level for mid-vowels
depending upon whether they undergo the early or the late
diphthongizations. We will show that there cannot be any
phonetically based solution to this problem and that we need
a lexically marked distinction between two series of mid-vowels.
     Late diphthongization of *e* is exemplified by 23, where we
observe an alternation between *e* and *ey* in contexts A and B as
defined previously. In 23 the variant *e* is observed in
unstressed syllables and the variant *ey* in stressed syllables.

(23) a. *en ey*   'un œuf'
          en e krü   'un œuf cru'
      b. *lœ peyt*   'il le peut'
          lœ pet u faer   'il peut le faire'

Late diphthongization appears to be slightly more restricted
than early diphthongization, and in particular, there are no
instances of *ey* before liquids.
     The fact that *e* is sometimes invariant may first suggest that
there are three kinds of mid-vowels: those undergoing late
diphthongization, those undergoing early diphthongization, and
those that are invariable. Svenson's description however seems
to suggest that this is not the case, and that the difference
between the last two is not underlying, but rather due to the
fact that late diphthongization is a variable rule. First, we
never observe any invariant *e* in word-final position. All
word-final *e*'s are subject to either early diphthongization or
to late diphthongization. Second, invariant *e*'s are found
before liquids where late diphthongization does not apply, e.g.
ser 'soeur', *groezel* 'groseille'. Third, invariant *e*'s in
some areas may be diphthongizable in others. They tend to
be invariable before obstruents (and palatalized ʎ) more often
in the SE than in the NW, e.g. *aneyt/anet* 'à nuit (today)'
peys/pes 'pays (field)', *ʒeyd/ʒed* 'jatte' and *teyʎ/teʎ* 'tuile'
alternate in the NW but remain nondiphthongized in the SE.
Fourth, invariant *e*'s may still be diphthongized in some cases.
For instance, Svenson notes *aneyt* in careful speech for *anet*
'à nuit' in villages where it is not normally diphthongized.
Last, some rhymed stories show rhymes such as *vleyt* 'voulait'/
fet 'fait' between diphthongized and invariant *e*, which indicates that the two words are internalized as being identical.
It seems here that we should not distinguish at the underlying
level between *e* subject to late diphthongization and invariant
e. Phonetic [e] is observed whenever late diphthongization
does not apply, viz. in context A and also in context B,

categorically before liquids and variably before obstruents.
This can be represented as 24:

(24) Late diphthongization

$$e \rightarrow \langle ey \rangle \ / \ \underline{\quad} \left\{ \begin{matrix} \# \\ \begin{bmatrix} \langle -sonorant \rangle \\ \langle -SE-NW \quad \rangle \end{bmatrix} \end{matrix} \right\} \ / \ \text{context B}$$

It is interesting to note that the conditions under which *e*
remains invariable are exactly the same as the conditions under
which yod vocalizes. It seems possible to account for the
similar distribution by saying that *e* undergoes late diphthongization, even when it appears to be invariable; the resulting
yod would then be vocalized to *e*, and the resulting sequence
ee reduced to *e*. This would account for its appearing invariable. Another possibility would be to say that late diphthongization of *e* tends to be blocked in those contexts where
it would feed yod-vocalization, a constraint which to my
knowledge has never been suggested in phonology. We will not
pursue this any further, as it does not affect our analysis.

Just as we have seen that we should not distinguish between
invariant *e* and *e* subject to late diphthongization, we can
also show that we must not distinguish between invariant *o* and
o subject to late diphthongization. Here, however, it is much
clearer. Late diphthongization of *o* is limited to the central
dialects, and affects only word-final *o* in context B, e.g. 25.
This diphthongization could be represented as 26:

(25)   *y ã̃n avow*   'j'en avais'
       y ã̃n avo poyt   'je n'en avais pas'

(26) Late diphthongization of *o*

$$o \rightarrow \langle ow \rangle \ / \ \begin{bmatrix} \underline{\quad} \# \\ \langle +center \rangle \end{bmatrix} \ / \ \text{context B}$$

Not all instances of final *ow* are necessarily the result of
late diphthongization, but may also be the result of another
rule, namely *glide-switching*. Examples 27a, 27b, and 27c
show that diphthongization applies only in the Center, and not
in the Northern and Southern parts of the area. There are
some instances of final *ow* in the South as shown by examples
27d and 27e:

(27)   North   Center   South   Unstressed (all dialects)

   a.   bo   bow   bo   bo   'sabots (pl)'
   b.   ergo   ergow   ergo   ergo   'ergots (pl)'
   c.   la ko   la kow   la ko   la ko   'la queux'
   d.   i boy   i bow   i bow   i bwe/boe   'je bois'
   e.   doy   dow   dow   dwe/doe   'doigt'

It is important to note that *ow* in 27d and 27e alternates with

we (or *oe*) in all the contexts where yod vocalizes, and
corresponds to *oy* in the North. A simple solution could be
to postulate an underlying *oy* in the South (to account for all
the occurrences of *we* or *oe*) and a glide-switching rule which
changes *y* to *w* after *o* in word-final position. We cannot simply
say that yod is deleted and that the resulting final *o* diphthongizes since late diphthongization in the South does not normally
occur and would then have to be restricted to *o* when and only
when it is followed by yod in the underlying representation.

   We have established that we must distinguish between two
series of mid-vowels, one that undergoes early diphthongization
and the other that either undergoes late diphthongization or
remains invariant. We shall refer to these two series as (a)
the mid-vowels undergoing early diphthongization and (b) the
mid-vowels undergoing late diphthongization (somewhat impro-
perly, since in this terminology *o* undergoing late diphthongization is actually mostly invariant).

4. The non-phonetic status of the opposition e/ɛ

We have shown that we must distinguish between two types of
mid-vowels, those that undergo early diphthongization and those
that undergo late diphthongization. It would be interesting
if this could be correlated to the phonetic differences between
e and *ɛ*, and between *o* and *ɔ* noted by Svenson in this transcription. We will show in this section that it is not the case for
the opposition *e/ɛ*; the same argument would hold for the
opposition *o/ɔ*.

   The opposition between *e* and *ɛ* does not appear pertinent
since we observe considerable variations throughout the area,
e.g. *baet/baɛt*, 'bête', *šaen/šaɛn* 'chaîne', *peys/pɛys* 'pays,
šer/šɛr 'cuire', *fey/fɛy* 'feu'. The variation is not even
consistent with the location, for instance 'nuit' is *nɛyt*
everywhere, 'lit' is *leyt* in Le Vieux Cerne and *leyt* in Notre-
Dame de Monts, but 'lièvre' is *levr* in Le Vieux Cerne and *lɛvr*
in Notre-Dame de Monts. But what is more significant is the
fact that there is no phonetic opposition in unstressed
position between *e* undergoing early diphthongization and *e*
undergoing late diphthongization, both being *e* in open syllables
and *ɛ* in closed syllables (with the exception of *žamay* 'jamais'
which is *zamɛ* in unstressed position), e.g. *mãžey/mãžey*
'manger' and *mãžay* 'mangé' are neutralized to *mãže* in context A.
In other words there are no phonetic justifications whatever
to posit two different underlying front mid-vowels to account
for the two diphthongizations.

5. Underlying forms: phonetic solutions

Since the phonetic opposition *e/ɛ* and *o/ɔ* cannot serve as a
possible underlying opposition to account for the two kinds of
diphthongization we shall examine the other possible phonetic
solutions. We will adopt here the condition that the segments
postulated in the underlying form of a morpheme must appear in
at least one of its phonetic realizations.

   In the alternation *ē/an*, we can immediately eliminate the

solution in which the underlying form is /an/, because of many
words with invariant *an* in contexts A and B, e.g. *žan* 'Jeanne',
gan 'canne'. In the framework we chose for this section the
underlying form must be /ẽ/, and we must postulate rules that
will change *ẽ* to *an* in contexts B. In the alternation *e/ey*,
the form *ey* is never observed before a liquid, and therefore in
words such as *ser* 'soeur', *groezel* 'groseille', *e* is invariant
and should be the underlying form. In the alternation *o/ow*, the
form *ow* is observed only in the central dialect in word-final
position, *o* therefore should be the underlying form wherever
there are no alternations. This in turn leads to the adoption
of *ay* as the underlying form of the alternation *e/ay* in words
ending with a liquid, e.g. *mayl/mel* 'nèfle', since *e* in the
same position is invariant.

These are the only restrictions on the possible underlying
forms when we adopt the condition that the segments postulated
in the underlying form of a morpheme must appear in at least
one of its phonetic realizations. For all the other alternations the diphthongized or the nondiphthongized form could be
arbitrarily chosen as the underlying form. Other principles,
more or less precisely understood, are often invoked in the
phonological analysis of a language which will here restrict
further the possible underlying forms for this analysis. One
is often referred to as the principle of economy, and another
as the principle of symmetry.

The economy principle will lead us to adopt *e* and *o* as
the underlying forms for the alternations *e/ey* and *o/ow*,
since we have shown that we need the underlying forms *e* and *o*
for words such as *ser* and *bot* 'sabot (sg)' and that adopting
the underlying forms *ey* and *ow* in words such as *ey/e* 'œuf',
bow/bo 'sabots (plur)' would unnecessarily increase the inventory of underlying forms. The same principle will lead to the
adoption of *ay* as the underlying form for the alternation *e/ay*,
since we have been led to adopt *ay* in words such as *mayl/mel*
'nèfle'.

The symmetry principle will lead us to analyze in the same
way the alternation *e/ay* and *o/au* since they are conditioned
by the same phonetic contexts and correspond to the same type
of phonetic alternations. That is, we could not take *e* as
the underlying form for *e/ay* and *au* for the alternation *o/au*
even if historically this might have been the case. It is
normally assumed that if two phenomena share the same description and the same conditioning they are somehow the 'same'
phenomenon within the language. The alternations *e/ay*, *ẽ/ãỹ*,
ẽ/an, *e/ey* have the same phonetic conditioning, and share the
same phonetic characteristics and somehow behave identically
within the language. The symmetry principle requires that the
underlying forms be in all cases the diphthongized or the
nondiphthongized form. We have seen that the diphthongized
form is excluded for the alternations *e/an* and *e/ey*, but that
the nondiphthongized form is excluded from the alternation
e/ay. This leads us here either to reject the symmetry
principle or to reject a phonetic solution for this problem.
If we reject the symmetry principle, we are unable to express
a genuine regularity in the language. For instance, if we

choose *ay* to underlie the alternation *e/ay* and *ē* to underlie
both alternations *ē̃/ãỹ* and *ē̃/an*, it appears as an accident
that the two alternations *e/ay* and *ē̃/ãỹ* are identical. If
on the other hand we choose *ay* to underlie the alternation *e/ay*,
ãỹ to underlie the alternation *ē̃/ãỹ*, and *ē̃* to underlie the
alternation *ē̃/an*, it is an accident that underlying *ãỹ* and *an*
are in complementary distribution. We are thus led to a
nonphonetic analysis.

6. Underlying forms: abstract solution

The economy and symmetry principles require that there should
be two series of underlying mid-vowels. We have already shown
the absence of any phonetic bases for such a distinction. The
only alternative left is a diacritic solution in which some
mid-vowels will be marked as undergoing one of the diphthongizations, all the others undergoing the other diphthongization.
Following Kiparsky 1968, we predict that one of the alternations is necessarily unproductive since the absence of phonetic
opposition between the two series of mid-vowels make this
opposition hard to learn. This prediction appears to be
correct: the alternations *e/ay*, *ē̃/ãỹ*, *ē̃/an*, *o/au* are not
productive, while the alternations *e/ey* and *o/ow* are. The
economy and symmetry principles in this case make the correct
prediction, since they disallow a phonetic analysis (which
otherwise would have been possible), making it necessary for
at least one of the alternations to be unproductive. We
propose then to distinguish between *e* and *ē* and between *o* and
ō, the marked vowels undergoing early diphthongization and
the unmarked ones late diphthongization.
   The last section of this paper will give a sketch of the
historical development of diphthongization which shows that
early diphthongization is unproductive but late diphthongization is productive.

7. Historical development of diphthongization

7.1 Alternation *e/ay* and *e/ey*

There are at least three sources for the modern alternation
e/ay: (a) contraction of historical *ay*, e.g. *aysi/esi*
'essieu' < Lat. *axis*, *tayzey/tezey* 'taire' < Lat. *tacere*;[6]
(b) diphthongization of *e* in word-final position, e.g. *pay/pe*
'pied' < Lat. *pede*, *bay/be* 'bien' < Lat. *bene*; and (c) diphthongization of some *e* in stressed syllables before consonant, e.g.
fraer/frer 'frère' < Lat. *frater*, but *per* (invariant) 'père' <
Lat. *pater*. These historical changes took place only when the
proper conditions of stress were present, i.e. contraction
took place only in unstressed syllables followed by a consonant, thus accounting for the alternation *e/ay* in contexts
A and B, and diphthongization took place only in stressed
syllables or when *e* was word-final before a vowel. We observe
that diphthongization never applied other than in word-final
syllables. Therefore the alternation *e/ay* in words such as
aysi/esi could only have been caused by contraction. On the

other hand, it is not always possible to determine whether an
alternation observed in word-final syllables is due to the
effect of an historical diphthongization of *e* or a contraction
of *ay*, since the result of the contraction of *ay* is *e* which
would undergo diphthongization in any case. For instance the
alternation *e/ay* in *vray/vre* 'vrai'< Lat. *veracu* could be
due to the contraction of *ay* or the diphthongization of the
resulting *e*. Historical early diphthongization occurs
regularly in closed stressed syllables when *e* has been lengthened after the loss of a tautosyllabic *s*, e.g. *paytr/petr*
'paître'< Lat. *pascere, frayn/fren* 'frêne'< *fraxinu, tayt/tet*
'tête'< Lat. *testa,* *žayp/žep* 'guêpe'< Lat. *vespa, epays/epes*
'epaisse'< Lat. *spissa*. It occurs variably in stressed syllables ending with *r*, *v*, and *ž* (i.e. lengthening consonants,
apparently) as for example in *aer/er* 'aire'< Lat. *area,*
taer/ter 'terre'< Lat. *terra, ayv/ev* 'eau' Lat.<*aqua,*
vayž/vež 'vienne (subj. of venir)'< Lat. *venia(m)*, but not in
prœmer 'première' Lat. *primaria, ler* 'lierre'< *l* + Lat.
hedera, lev(r) 'lièvre'< Lat. *leporu*. Early diphthongization
never occurs in other stressed closed syllables. In these
syllables historical *ay* always becomes *e*, which might suggest
in fact that contraction of *ay* to *e* occurred in all stressed
syllables and that later the resulting *e* diphthongized in
exactly the same conditions as the other historical *e*'s, e.g.
let 'lait'< Lat. *lacte, set* 'sept'< Lat. *septe, met* 'mettre'<
Lat. *mittere*. In particular when a plural marker *-s* is added
to an open syllable, the diphthongization which could take
place in the singular is blocked in the plural. Eventually
final *s* will drop, and the resulting final *e* will be subject
to late diphthongization, which accounts for the modern
opposition *ay/ey* between singular and plural forms, e.g.
pay/pe 'pied(sg)', *pey/pe* 'pieds (pl)', *nay/ne* 'nez (sg)',
nay/ne 'nez (pl)'. In many words this nonphonetic alternation
has been leveled, the singular form or the plural form being
extended to cover both forms, e.g. *žay/žey* 'chien (sg/pl)' is
leveled to *žay* except in two points (out of fifteen), *ray/rey*
'rais (sg/pl)' to *ray* in eleven points, *rey* in three points,
pray/prey 'pré (sg/pl)' is leveled to *pray* in two points,
fusay/fusey 'fossé (sg/pl)' to *fusay* in two points, and
pay/pey 'pied (sg/pl)' is leveled to *pey* in two points and to
pay in one point.
　One of the sources for the modern alternation *e/ey*, as
we suggested previously, is also diphthongization of word-
final *e*. Since early diphthongization affected all occurrences
of word-final *e*, a new final *e* had to emerge in the language.
This was the result of the loss of a final consonant in closed
syllables that were not subject to early diphthongization.
We have mentioned the loss of final *s*; another important consonant loss was that of final *r* (everywhere after *e* except on
the West coast), e.g. *aštey* (*ašter* on the West coast)
'acheter' vs. *aštay* 'acheté'. Another source for *e* was the
change of *ø* to *e* (or *ü* variably), hence *ey* (or *ü*) 'œuf' <
earlier *ø*, *bey* (or *bü*)< earlier *bø*. In non-word-final syllables historical *ey* became *oy/oe/we*, and does not participate
in the alternation *e/ey*. Therefore there can normally be only

undiphthongized *e* in unstressed syllables, e.g. *eron* 'araignée' < Lat. *aranea*, or *etwel/etoyl* 'étoile' < Lat. *stella*. In word-final syllables there were some historical *ey*'s which have remained as such, when they are stressed, throughout the area, e.g. *leyt/let* 'lit' < Lat. *lectu*, *peys/pes* 'pièce' < *pettia*, *freyt/fret* 'froid' < Lat. *frigidu*, *teyt/tet* 'toit' < Lat. *tectu*, *etreyt/etret* 'étroit' < Lat. *strictu*, *neyt/net* 'nuit' < Lat. *nocte*, and *čeys/čes* 'cuisse' Lat. < *coxa*. Besides historical *ey* in word-final syllables which reduces to *e* in context A, there were many undiphthongized *e*'s in stressed syllables, e.g. *fet* 'fait' < Lat. *factu*, *set* 'sept' < Lat. *septe*. From Svenson's data it appears that these *e*'s progressively diphthongize, and that this is actually an ongoing variable rule. Late diphthongization seems to affect only syllables closed by at most one consonant and to be more widespread on the West coast. For instance *teyd/ted* 'tiède' < Lat. *tepidu* is diphthongized almost everywhere, *peyt/pet* (or *püt*) 'peut' is diphthongized in the North and on the West coast, *žeyd/žed* 'jatte' < *gabita* and *neys/nes* 'nièce' < Lat. *neptia* are diphthongized on the West coast only. Some words such as *geret* 'guéret' < Lat. *vervactu*, *lev(r)* 'lièvre' < Lat. *leporu*, and *než* 'neige' < *nežey* < Lat. *nivicare* do not diphthongize.

As we mentioned before, our analysis predicts that there should be some reanalysis from *ē* to *e* if late diphthongization is a productive phenomenon. But the leveling of the opposition *ay/ey* between singular and plural nouns is not indicative of such a reanalysis, since in this case it is a paradigmatic regularization, not an instance of unmotivated reanalysis. In the leveling of the opposition *pay/pey* to *pay* for instance both forms were present and one has been chosen as the normal form. All instances of non-paradigmatic reanalysis are in the sense of *ē* to *e*, and never the opposite. The examples that we have noted are: *eysi* for *aysi* 'essieu', *teyzey* for *tayzey* 'taire' (these examples show the development of the diphthongization *e/ey* in non-word-final syllables, and are observed in slow speech only), *peys* 'pays (field)' for historical **pays* < Lat. *page(n)sis*, *šer* for *šaer* 'chaise' in two points, *direy* for *diray* 'dirai' in three points, *mey* for *may* 'mai' in four points, *žey* for *žay* 'geai' in four points, *vrey* for *vray* 'vrai' in three points, *a(h)ey* for *ahay* 'haie' in two points.

Our analysis also predicts that borrowings with diphthongizable *e* should undergo late but not early diphthongization. The only certain instance of borrowing is the French word *pøpliye* 'peuplier', which is borrowed as *poepli(y)ey* with final *e* undergoing late diphthongization, except in two points where the informants have been able to repress this diphthongization and produce a final *e*: *poeplie*, the only case of nondiphthongization of word-final *e* in Svenson's description.

7.2 Alternations *ẽ/an* and *ẽ/ãỹ*

The set of processes involved in the creation of the alternation *e/ay* are potentially the same in the creation of the alternation *ẽ/ãỹ(an)*. There were three possible sources:
(a) contraction of historical *ãỹ(n)*, but this cannot be

ascertained because it appears only in word-final syllables
where it would normally become ẽ and would be then subject
to diphthongization; (b) diphthongization of word-final ẽ,
e.g. fan/fẽ 'fin (masc)'< fẽ(n) < fĩ(n) < Lat. finu; and
(c) diphthongization of ẽ in word-final syllables, e.g. dãỹd/
dẽd 'dinde'< dẽd. If we assume that all nasalized vowels were
long in word-final closed syllable, as they are now in most
French dialects, then this is the same historical process as
was previously involved in the diphthongization of e in word-
final closed syllables. Svenson gives dẽd as an invariant form
in three points (where unmarked e does not normally diphthongize before t, d). This could then be reinterpreted as a
reanalysis of ẽ to ẽ. On the other hand it could also be an
archaism.⁷

When late diphthongization became operative, there was no
ẽ on which it could feed, and this is why we normally do not
observe any alternation ẽ/ẽỹ(en), with the exception of one
village, Bouin, where the alternation õ/aɲ has been systematically replaced by the alternation ẽ/ẽỹ (yod-consonantization does not occur in this town, hence en mezẽỹ 'une maison',
la mezẽ bλãš 'la maison blanche'. This clearly indicates that
the alternation ẽ/ẽỹ(en) is potential, but that there simply
were no vowels to which it could have applied.

7.3 The alternation o/au and o/ow

The alternation o/au seems to have had only one historical
source, namely the contraction of Romance aw to o in unstressed
position, e.g. top/taup 'taupe'< rom. *tawp< Lat. talpa; there
were apparently no final o's to which a diphthongization
similar to the diphthongization of e could have applied; words
like ko(w) 'queux'< Lat. cote, or bo(w) 'sabots (pl)' then
had a final consonant. There were no stressed long o's
either because they had been systematically raised to u, e.g.
kut 'côte'< Lat. costa, u 'os'< Lat. ossu. Late diphthongization on the other hand affects all final o's that have appeared
later through the loss of a final consonant in the Central
dialect (four/five points on the map), hence bot 'sabot (sg)'
but bow 'sabots (pl)'.

Our analysis predicts that there could be some reanalyses
of õ as o, i.e. changes from au to ow, but not of o as õ, and
this is verified. We observe in one of the central towns a
change of eau 'eau' to eow (this is the only instance of final
au in the Atlas), but no change of final ow to au (there are
many instances of final ow in the Atlas.

7.4 The alternation õ/aɲ

The only sources of the alternation õ/aɲ is the diphthongization of word-final õ. We cannot determine from the data
presented by Svenson whether this diphthongization also
affected õ in word-final closed syllables, as all the instances
of õ in word-final closed syllables, e.g. õz 'onze', frõk
'furoncle', are drawn from locations where ẽ does not diphthongize either, cf. dẽd 'dinde' for dãỹd elsewhere.

Concerning the various forms taken by the alternation õ/aɲ
throughout the area, it cannot be determined whether they are
cases of reanalysis or archaism. Actually there is considerable
variety with respect to the alternation õ/aɲ . We have seen
previously that in Bouin it was changed to ẽ/ẽɣ̃. We observe
elsewhere the manifestations õ/ãɲ, õ/ẽɲ, and õ/õɲ. The first
alternation õ/aɲ appears to be an archaism if we assume that
the alternations ẽ/an and õ/aɲ come from an earlier alternation
ẽ/ãn and õ/ãɲ. In most dialects ã was denasalized before a
nasal consonant, in the dialect where the alternation õ/ãɲ has
been preserved, denasalization was limited to nasalized vowel
before n and did not apply before ɲ. The alternation õ/ẽɲ can
be accounted by an historical and synchronic rule which changes
ã to ẽ everywhere in these dialects, except when it is stressed
and followed by ɣ. This alternation is always observed in
dialects where ã has been systematically replaced by ẽ, e.g.
mẽžey 'manger' for mãžey elsewhere, except in stressed syllables
before ɣ̃, e.g. dãɣ̃d 'dinde' where it remains ã. The last
alternation õ/õɲ can be either a reanalysis of õ to õ, or
an archaism if we suppose that the development of õ to aɲ went
through the steps õ> õɲ> ãɲ> aɲ.

NOTES

*The research presented here was supported in part by the
Canada Council under grant S73-1781. I would like to thank
Jonathan Kaye and John Reighard who both helped improve this
paper considerably.

[1]Some of the characteristics of this dialect, of which
there shall be no further mention in this paper, are the
following: (a) palatalization of l after obstruents, e.g.
fλatey 'flatter', (b) palatalization of the dentals l, n, t
and d before i, e.g. λir 'lire', ñigau 'nigaud', țiret
'tirette' and (c) palatalization of the velars k and g before
(historical) i, e, and ü, e.g. čüray 'curé', ãžil 'anguille'.
There does not appear to be any significant difference
between open and closed mid-vowels (see section 4 for a discussion of the opposition e/ɛ) nor between posterior and
anterior a. Finally ə and œ are not distinguishable. We
shall therefore have the following vowel system:

oral vowels	i	ü	u	nasal vowels	ẽ	õ
	e	œ	o			
		a				ã

Stress falls predictably on word-final syllables and is not
always indicated in the transcriptions.

[2]It should be noted here that contexts A and B are not only
defined syntactically, but can vary within syntactic construc-

tions with stylistic pauses and stress in the speaker's
speech. Svenson observed variations such as *y e mãže do pan/
y e mãžay do pan* 'J'ai mangé du pain' with a slight pause after
mãžay in the second variant, and *esi/aysi* 'essieu', *sotlet/
sautlet* 'sauterelle' with a contrastive stress on the first
syllable in the second variant.

[3]Svenson actually gives the phonetic forms *mãy, fãy* where
the final yod is not nasalized. It could be that the nasalization of yod is hard to perceive in these positions, or
simply that *g̃* is denasalized in word-final position (if it was
ever nasalized). This does not affect in any way our analysis.

[4]Our formulation of glide-consonantization predicts that *õ*
should alternate with *ãw̃* in word-final closed syllable. This
could not be verified; Svenson only presents examples of
underlying *o* in final closed syllable from villages where as
we shall see later diphthongization of nasalized vowel never
applies, e.g. *dẽd* 'dinde', *õz* 'onze'.

[5]Another justification for the remote representation *aw*,
rather than the more phonetic *au* for example, is the fact that
there exists some words with *au* which never become *o* in non-
stressed position. Svenson observes words such as *auʎey*
'ouiller' (in which the phonetic sequence *au* is historically
different from the sequence alternating with *o*) where the
sequence *au* never alternates with *o*. This requires then that
the two *au*'s have two different underlying representations,
for instance *aw* and *au*.

[6]Some of the sources for historical yod in this dialect
appear to be the same as in standard French, viz. velars *k*
and *g*, as in Lat. *axis > *aysis > aysi*, Lat. *veracu > vray*, and
metathesis of yod before continuants and affricates, e.g.
Lat. *area > *arya > aurə > ayr*, Lat. *tacere > *tatsyer >
taydz(y)er > tayzer > tayzey.

[7]Two points on the map show the alternation *dẽdaŋ/dẽỹdaŋ*.
This is simply a change from *ã* to *ẽ* which is systematic in
these two points, cf. *mẽgot* for *mãgot* 'manchot'.

REFERENCES

Kiparsky, Paul. 1968. How abstract is phonology? (Unpub-
    lished).
Labov, W. 1972. The internal evolution of linguistic rules.
    Linguistic change and generative theory, ed. by R.P. Stockwell
    and R.K.S. Macaulay, 101-71. Bloomington: Indiana Uni-
    versity Press.
Morin, Yves-Charles. Forthcoming. Phonological tensions in
    French. Current studies in Romance linguistics, ed. by M.
    Luján and F. Hensey. Washington, D.C.: Georgetown
    University Press.

Svenson, Lars-Owe.   1959.   Les parlers du Marais Vendéen.
   Göteborg.

VOCALIC ALTERNATION IN THE SPANISH VERB: A REANALYSIS

DAVID NASJLETI

Harvard University

The root vowel [RV] and the thematic vowel [ThV] alternations of second and third conjugation verbs, displayed in Tables 1 and 2 below, have received concentrated attention.

Table 1. *RV alternations in second and third conjugations*

Environment	I $[(\overline{\text{-stress}})] \, C_0 \left\{ \begin{matrix} i \hat{v} \\ \acute{a} \end{matrix} \right\}$	II $[\overline{\text{-stress}}]$	III $[\overline{\text{+stress}}]$
1.1 v*i*vir	i	i	í
1.2 pedir	i	e	í
1.3 sentir	i	e	yé
1.4 perder	e	e	yé
1.5 beber	e	e	é

Table 2. *Thᵥ alternations in second and third conjugations*

Environment	I [-stress] 6	II [-stress]	III [+stress]		
			(i) i. ii. iii.	(ii) Inf. Imperat. 1st pl. Pres. 2nd pl. Pres.	(iii) Imperf. Pret. Part.
				Gerundive Past Subj. (Fut. Subj.) (3rd pl.) Pret.	
2.1 sentir	y	e	í	yé	í
2.2 perder	y	e	é	yé	í

In this paper an attempt is made to account for these alternations avoiding the rule proposed in Harris 1969 which raises
all nonlow RV's in third conjugation verbs, with results to
be examined presently, and also avoiding the raising rule
advanced in Brame and Bordelois 1974, and its direct antecedent,
the 'Breaking-Raising' rule of Brame and Bordelois 1973. The
immediately following critique of these analyses will justify
the revision attempted here.

The following raising rule was proposed in Harris 1969:

$$(1)\begin{bmatrix} V \\ -low \end{bmatrix} \rightarrow \begin{bmatrix} +high \\ +tense \end{bmatrix} / \begin{bmatrix} \overline{3\ conj} \end{bmatrix}\ C_0V \Big]_V$$

As pointed out in Brame and Bordelois 1973 this rule unnecessarily raises segments which will eventually have to be
lowered by a minor rule so that the surface phonetic realization may be correctly generated. In short, some of the
relevant vowels go through derivations like those sketched
in 2a, b, where the front vowel stands also for its back
counterpart:

(2)   a. Diphthongizing RV: e → i → í → É → yé
      b. Monophthongal RV: e → i → e

Additionally, the behavior of the diphthongizing third conjugation RV (in a verb like *sentir*) becomes highly idiosyncratic
as compared with that of a first conjugation or second conjugation diphthongizing RV. In the case of the latter conjugations (in verbs like *defender* and *sentar*) the underlying
unstressed RV requires only tensing for its proper surface
manifestation. But the RV in third conjugation verbs requires
additional lowering.

The following raising rule from Brame and Bordelois 1974
specifies two different sets of incorrect derivations:

$$(3)\quad Raising\quad \begin{bmatrix} +syl \\ -low \\ +S \\ -pres \end{bmatrix} \rightarrow [+high] / \begin{Bmatrix} \overline{[+stress]}\ C_0^{\ C_0V} \\ \underline{\quad}C_0\ {}^{ív}_{á} \end{Bmatrix}$$

The feature [+S] in this rule brings about the first set of
unwanted results. [+S] is the diacritic feature which in
Harris 1969 identifies the subset of the lexicon subject to
laxing of intervocalic obstruents, laxing of certain vowels,
diphthongization, and so forth. Rule 3 will raise the RV of
[+S] stems like *lee*, *corroe*, *posee*, *comete*, etc. with such
undesirable results as *lío for *leo*, *líes for *lees*, *líen
for *leen*, etc. Also because of the feature [+S] in the rule,
the RV of *elegir*, which has a [-S] stem, will not be raised
under stress so that instead of the required *elíjo*, *elíges*,
elígen, *elíja*, *elíjas*, *elíjan*, etc., Rule 3 incorrectly generates *eléjo*, *eléges*, *elégen*, etc. Finally, because of [+S],
the RV of [+S] second conjugation stems, which should show up

as [e] or [o] on the surface if unstressed, will be incorrectly
raised in the last environment specified by the rule, namely
that of the first person plural present subjunctive forms.
As a result, *pirdámos for perdámos is just one example of a
class of incorrect forms specified by Rule 3.

The second set of unwanted results are brought about by
the feature [-pres]. This feature is included in the raising
rule so that the ThV in second conjugation verbs will be raised
under stress but not in the first person plural present indicative form. The intent of the specification of [-pres] is
shown in 4, where PN stands for person-number morpheme:

(4)   Preterit   Imperfect   Participle

    comé + PN's   comé +ba + PN's   comé + to
    [-pres]   [-pres]   [-pres]

      í   í   í   (Raising)

    First Plural Present

    comé + mos
    [+pres]   (Raising does not apply)

The status of the highly suspect feature [-pres] will not be
questioned here. The inclusion of this feature, however,
prevents all the RV's in [+pres] stems from raising. Therefore, this rule specifies the incorrect forms *médo for mído,
*médes for mídes, *méden for míden, etc. and similar incorrect
derivations in all other relevant third conjugation stems.

Some of the inadequacies of the 'Raising-Breaking' rule
of Brame and Bordelois 1973 have been discussed in Harris
1974. Suffice to mention here that I, like Harris, consider
the formalism of Brame and Bordelois 1973 excessively powerful.
The set of 'conditions' I-IV that define precisely the environment where the effective part of their rule applies have as a
possible net effect the erasing of the undesirable results of
the overgeneralization embodied in the rule. The use of
diacritic features allows also for generalizations that would
not be expressed as easily in terms of phonological features.
The result of the abuse of diacritic features is a false
appearance of simplicity and the masking of the phonetic nature
of the processes involved. The use of the diacritic [+3 conj]
(which identifies membership in a morphological class)
obscures the fact that the feature in question uniquely relates
to the ThV i. As a direct consequence of the use of the
diacritic, no relationship is established between the assimilatory processes in the conjugation and the feature constitution
of the pertinent sounds.

In this presentation I am assuming your acquaintance with
the Spanish conjugation. I will not deal with derivational
morphology. Therefore, I will not attempt to cover the phonological processes that relate verb stems to other stem classes.
I believe, though, that what is said here about Spanish verb
morphology and phonology could be made an integral part of a

comprehensive description of Spanish. Because the internal
structure of the verb stem is not relevant to the specific
rules that I will propose, no attempt will be made here to
discriminate between various constituents of the verb stem.
Specifically, no boundary is set up between a verb root and a
thematic or conjugational vowel.

The label 'thematic vowel' is then an informal reference
to the last syllabic of the verb stem. Informally, too, the
morphological structure of verb forms, as they will be considered here, consists of the elements displayed in 5:

$$(5) \begin{bmatrix} [\text{Stem}]_{\text{Stem}} \\ \text{Verb} \end{bmatrix}_{\text{Stem}} \begin{Bmatrix} \begin{bmatrix} + \text{ Ending} \end{bmatrix}_{\text{Verb}} & & \text{(Nonfinite)} \\ \begin{Bmatrix} + \text{ Tense-} \\ \text{Mood-} \\ \text{Aspect} \end{Bmatrix} \begin{bmatrix} + \text{ Person-} \\ \text{Number} \end{bmatrix}_{\text{Verb}} & & \text{(Finite)} \end{Bmatrix}$$

Irregular and suppletive forms are not considered. The verbs
in Table 1 above are listed in 6 next to the informal underlying representation of their stems. The precise identification of the consonants in these stems is not attempted.
Throughout, regular orthography is used whenever possible,
although stress is indicated in most citation forms:

(6)   Verb   Stem

      vivir   bibI
      pedir   pEdI
      sentir   sEntI
      perder   pErdE
      beber   bebE

In 7, the syllabic segments represented by upper- and lower-
case letters above and the balance of the syllabics are tabulated along with a specification of those features directly
involved in the alternations under study:

(7)

	i	I	e	E	a	O	o	U	u
syllabic	+	+	+	+	+	+	+	+	+
high	+	+	-	-	-	-	-	+	+
ATR	+	-	+	-	-	-	+	-	+
back	-	-	-	-	+	+	+	+	+
CP	-	-	-	-	+	-	-	-	-

A list of the informal representation of verb suffixes is
presented in 8. All of these suffixes are either [+FIN], i.e.
absolute verb-final when they are constituents of a verb, or
[-FIN]. The latter represent a formative which, loosely
speaking, is nonfinal in syntactic structure. I have chosen
this diacritic feature over others of a more syntactic
character suggested in the past, because it is a more logical
choice than a strictly syntactic feature and also because it
seems to mesh better with the rules proposed here. Doubtful
phonological representations of a formative are indicated by

a question mark:

(8) Tense-Mood-Aspects (TMA's)

Present (Indicative): $\emptyset$

(Present) Subjunctive:
$$\begin{cases} \overset{e}{[-\text{FIN}]} \ / \ ]St_{+1\ conj} + \underline{\quad} \\ \overset{a}{[-\text{FIN}]} \ / \ ]St_{-1\ conj} + \underline{\quad} \end{cases}$$

Imperfect: $\overset{ba}{[-\text{FIN}]}$

Preterit: $\overset{I}{[-\text{FIN}]} \ / \ \underline{\quad} + $ 1st sing.

$\overset{ste}{[-\text{FIN}]} \ / \ \underline{\quad} + $ 2nd

$\overset{U}{[-\text{FIN}]} \ / \ \underline{\quad} + $ 3rd sing.

$\overset{I}{[-\text{FIN}]} \ / \ ]St_{-1\ conj} + \underline{\quad} + $ 1st pl.

$\emptyset \ / \ ]St_{+1\ conj} + \underline{\quad} + $ 1st pl.

$\overset{ro}{[-\text{FIN}]} \ / \ \underline{\quad} + $ 3rd pl.

Past Subjunctive: $\overset{ra}{[-\text{FIN}]} \quad (\ \overset{se}{[-\text{FIN}]}\ )$

Future Subjunctive: $\overset{re}{[-\text{FIN}]}$

Imperative:
$$\begin{cases} \emptyset \ / \ \underline{\quad} + \text{2nd sing.} \\ \overset{tE}{[+\text{FIN}]} \ / \ \underline{\quad} + \text{2nd pl.} \end{cases}$$

Endings

Infinitive: $\overset{rE}{[+\text{FIN}]}$

Participle: (?) $\overset{to}{[-\text{FIN}]}$

Gerundive ('Gerundio'): $\overset{ndo}{[-\text{FIN}]}$

Person-number (PN's)

1st singular: $\overset{o}{[+\text{FIN}]} \ / \ $ Present (Indicative) $ + \underline{\quad}$

$\emptyset$ elsewhere

2nd singular: Ø / $\left.\begin{array}{l}\text{Preterit}\\\text{Imperative}\end{array}\right\}$ + ____

        s   elsewhere
    [+FIN]

3rd singular: Ø

1st plural: mos
          [+FIN]

2nd plural: Ø / Imperative + ____

        Is elsewhere
        [+FIN]

3rd plural: n
         [+FIN]

The first rule, displayed in 9a, 'tenses' the ThV of second and third conjugation stems before a [+FIN] formative. This rule generates the correct ThV for the infinitive, the first and second plural present (indicative), and the imperative plural as shown in 9b:

(9)

a. R1 $\begin{bmatrix} V \\ -CP \end{bmatrix}$ → [+ATR] / $\underline{\quad\quad}\Big]_{St}$ + $\left[[+FIN]^3_0 \right]_{Vb}$

b. Infinitive   1st pl.   2nd pl.   Imperative
                Pres.   Pres.   pl.

    bibI+rE   bibI+mos   bibI+Is   bibI+tE

      i   i   i   i   (R1)

The stress rule, displayed in 10, embodies the observation that in some forms the stress falls on the RV and in all other forms the stress falls on the ThV or its replacement and that this stress distribution depends on the phonological makeup of the verb suffixes:

(10)

R2 [+syl] → [+stress]/$\underline{\quad}$ $\left\{\begin{array}{l} (C_0 \ (V)) \Big]_{St} + \begin{bmatrix} V \\ -high \\ -FIN \end{bmatrix} + \begin{bmatrix} -syl \\ +FIN \end{bmatrix} \\ \ ]_{St} \end{array}\right]_{Vb}$ i ii

Case i of the rule accounts for most of the forms with penultimate stress. It does so without making reference to syllables, by predicting that the stress will fall on the RV in the three cases displayed in 11, as in 11a, where a vocalic TMA ([-FIN]) is followed by a consonantal PN ([+FIN]); as in 11b, where a single vocalic suffix follows, as is the case when the (present) subjunctive or the first person singular is added; and as in 11c, where a consonantal suffix or no suffix occurs:

(11)

	Stem	TMA [-FIN]	PN [+FIN]	
a. (Present) subjunctive	cóme +	a +	s	2nd sing.
(Present) subjunctive	cóme +	a +	n	3rd pl.
b. (Present) subjunctive	cóme +	a +	-	1st/3rd sing.
Present (indicative)	cóme	- +	o	1st sing.
c. Present (indicative)	cóme	+	s	2nd sing.
Present (indicative)	cóme	+	n	3rd pl.
Present (indicative)	cóme	-		3rd sing.

Case *ii* of the stress rule specifies that the stress falls on
the ThV in all cases not covered by case *i*. After all the
subsequent rules have applied, this ThV stress will occur on
the ThV itself, as shown in 12a; on any vowel or diphthong that
takes its place, as in 12b; or on the adjacent vowel, with
which the ThV forms a diphthong, as in 12c:

(12)

	Stem	TMA (or Ending)	PN	Surface
a. Infinitive:	comé + rE			comér
Imper. pl.:	comé + tE			coméd
Pres. 1st pl.:	comé	+ mos		comémos
Pres. 2nd pl.:	comé	+ Is		coméys
b. Participle:	comé + to			comído
Pret. 1st:	comé + I	(+mos)		comí(mos)
Pret. 2nd:	comé + ste	(+Is)		comíste(ys), etc.
Imperfect:	comé + ba	+ s, etc.		comías
Pret. 3rd pl.:	comé + ro	+ n		comyéron
Past Subj.:	comé + ra(se)	+ s, etc.		comyéra, etc.
(Fut. Subj.):	comé + re	+s, etc.		comyére, etc.
Gerundive:	comé + ndo			comyéndo
Subj.1st,2nd pl.:	comé + a	+ mos, Is		comámos, comáys
c. Pret. 3rd sg.:	comé + U			comyó

The major raising rule, R3, raises all third conjugation
RV's under stress and all stressed second conjugation ThV's
that precede a [-FIN] TMA. Case *i* also tenses the unstressed
[-ATR] RV's that will not undergo any further change, namely
those of first and second conjugation stems. This rule raises
only segments that are [+high] in the phonetic output:

(13)

$$
\text{R3}\begin{bmatrix}-\text{ATR}\\-\text{CP}\\-\text{high}\end{bmatrix} \rightarrow \begin{bmatrix}\alpha\text{high}\\-\alpha\text{ATR}\end{bmatrix} / \underline{\quad}\left\{\begin{array}{l}C_0\begin{bmatrix}V\\\alpha\text{high}\\-\text{back}\end{bmatrix}\text{St} \qquad i\\[2ex]\Big]_{\text{St}}\ [-\text{FIN}] \qquad ii\end{array}\right\}
$$

Rule 3 is not just a raising rule. Case *i* specifies a change
in the [-ATR] RV's so that the values of both [high] and [ATR]
are affected by the height of the ThV. Of singular importance

is the fact that subrule *i* of R3 sets a contrast between the
[-ATR] RV of third conjugation stems and its counterpart in
the first and second conjugations, both in stressed and unstressed positions. As can be seen in 14, after case *i* of R3,
not only the ThV's but also the RV's of second and third
conjugations are different (schematically, the first vowel is
the RV and the second, the ThV):

(14)   Before R3   After R3, case *i*   After R3, case *ii*

3rd ⎰É ... I   Í ... I   Í ... I
conj.⎱E ... Í   E ... Í   E ... I

2nd ⎰É ... E   É ... E   É ... I
conj.⎱E ... É   e ... É   e ... Í

The RV has thus taken on some of the burden of distinguishing
second from third conjugation stems. When subrule *ii* erases
the now superfluous distinction between high and mid ThV's,
the process which started with the assimilation to the height
of the ThV, specified by case *i*, is simply carried out to a
natural conclusion. Consider an earlier proposal present in
part as 1 above and here in full as 15:

$$(15) \quad \begin{bmatrix} V \\ -low \end{bmatrix} \rightarrow \begin{bmatrix} +high \\ +tense \end{bmatrix} \Big/ \left\{ \begin{array}{c} \underline{\hspace{1cm}} \ [+past] \\ [\overline{3conj}] \ C_o \ V]_V \end{array} \right\}$$

The first case of this rule raises ThV *e* to *i* and thus erases
the distinction between second and third conjugation stems.
For this reason, the use of a superfluous diacritic becomes
necessary for the application of subsequent rules.

Rule 3 has also set the stage for the series of shared
changes that characterize the derivations of both the [+high,
-ATR] RV (of some third conjugation stems) and the [+high, -ATR]
ThV (of both second and third conjugations). A subset of each
of these vowels will surface as high, 'tense' vowels, and
another subset will diphthongize. Rule 4, *e*-Epenthesis, is
the first step in the diphthongization process.

$$(16)$$
$$R4 \quad \emptyset \rightarrow e \ / \ \begin{bmatrix} -ATR \\ -CP \\ +stress \\ \langle +high \rangle \end{bmatrix}_{St} \underline{\hspace{1cm}} \left\langle \left\{ \begin{bmatrix} -syl \\ -obstr \\ +cor \\ +ant \end{bmatrix} \left(\begin{bmatrix} -syl \\ +ant \end{bmatrix} \right) \right\} \right\rangle \begin{array}{l} i \\ + \ se \quad ii \end{array}$$

The feature [-ATR], which triggers *e*-Epenthesis, is not sufficient in the case of the high vowels, which require a special
consonantal environment in addition to the special case
provided for the past subjunctive *se*--I have met with obstacles
trying to bring the past subjunctive into line with the generalization expressed in terms of features, and this aspect of my

analyses requires further work. The special consonantal
environment required by the high vowels is specified here so
as to exclude *erguir* but not *servir* from undergoing *e*-Epenthesis.
These stems are not only odd by virtue of their peculiar behavior
vis-à-vis R3 and R4, but also by virtue of their unpredictable
pattern of alternation (cf. *serv-*, *sirv-*, v. vs. *siervo*, n.,
and *írgo* vs. *yérgo*, *írgues* vs. *yérgues*, etc.). The fact that
the idiosyncratic behavior of these stems is not the general
rule but rather the absolute exception corroborates the view
that R3 and R4 capture genuine generalizations. The additional
fact that the behavior exhibited by these stems is governed
by one or the other of those two rules is evidence confirming
the plausibility of the rules. *Servir* is [-R4]; nondiphthong-
izing *erguir* (a) is perfectly regular, while the diphthongizing
erguir (b) is exceptional by being [-R3,*i*]. Notice that this
exception to raising does not prevent *erguir* (b) from diphthongizing. Instead, its RV remains [-high] and thus meets the
general environment for *e*-Epenthesis specified by R4. As a
result, R4 does apply and the RV in *erguir* (b) epenthesizes
under stress. Contrary to the main thesis of Brame and Bordelois 1973, these rules assert that raising is not a prerequisite
for *e*-Epenthesis (and other subsequent processes leading to
diphthongization).

Some of the effects of the operation of R3 (Raising) and
R4 (*e*-Epenthesis) are shown in 17a,b:

(17) a. pErdE+mos   pErdE   sEntI   pEdI+$\begin{bmatrix} ro \\ ra \\ re \end{bmatrix}$

```
            e                 e                            (R1)
            é            É             É           Í       (R2)
       e                          Í           Í           (R3)
                         Ée            Íe           Íe      (R4)
```

perdémos   piérde   siénte   pidié$\begin{Bmatrix} ro \\ ra \\ re \end{Bmatrix}n$. Surface

b. pEdI+I   bebE+I   bebE+ndo

```
      Í            É             É            (R2)
                   Í             Í            (R3)
                                 Íe           (R4)
```
                                              .

pedí   bebí   bebiéndo   Surface

Rule 5 accounts for the surface representation of the ThV
in the context of preterit *i* and *u*. It is displayed in 18a
followed by R6, which deletes an unstressed high vowel following a stressed [-CP] V. The effects of both rules are shown
in 18b:

(18) a.
$$\text{R5} \quad \begin{bmatrix} V \\ +CP \end{bmatrix} \rightarrow \begin{bmatrix} -\text{high} \\ \alpha\text{back} \end{bmatrix} / \underline{\quad} + \begin{bmatrix} V \\ +\text{high} \\ \alpha\text{back} \\ -\text{FIN} \end{bmatrix}$$

$$\text{R6} \quad \begin{bmatrix} V \\ -\text{stress} \\ +\text{high} \\ \alpha\text{back} \end{bmatrix} \rightarrow \emptyset / \begin{bmatrix} V \\ -CP \\ \alpha\text{back} \end{bmatrix} + \underline{\quad}$$

b. amá+I   amá+U   comÍ+I   comÍ+I+mos

é	ó			(R5)
∅	∅	∅	∅	(R6)

⋮

amé   amó   comí   comímos   Surface

The rule shown in 19 raises the unstressed [-ATR] RV of third conjugation stems in the environment of a following stressed [+high, -ATR] V next to another V:

(19)
$$\text{R7} \quad \begin{bmatrix} V \\ -\text{ATR} \\ -\text{stress} \end{bmatrix} \rightarrow [+\text{high}] / \underline{\quad} C_0 \acute{\text{i}} V$$

Rule 7 raises the RV before the vowel sequences listed in 20 next to the surface forms which exhibit this raising.

(20) RV raised
      before...   Raised RV appears in

      íu   *sintió, pidió, murió, pudrió*, etc.
      íe   *pidiéndo, pidiéron, pidiéra*, etc.
      ía   *pidámos, pidáis*

Rule 8, shown in 21, has the effect of 'tensing' the stressed [-ATR] RV *I*'s that have not yielded an epenthetic *e* by R4 and all the stressed [-ATR] ThV *I*'s immediately followed by an obstruent (or nothing):

(21)
$$\text{R8} \quad \begin{bmatrix} V \\ -CP \\ +\text{high} \end{bmatrix} \rightarrow [+\text{ATR}] / [\overline{+\text{stress}}] \left\{ \begin{matrix} C_0 \; V]_{St}\cdots \\ ]_{St}(CV\cdots) \end{matrix} \right\} \# \begin{matrix} i \\ ii \end{matrix}$$

The results of applying R8 are shown in 22:

(22)   case *i*   case *ii*

       rÍi   pÍdi   pEdÍ   pErdÍ+ste   pErdÍ+mos
       í   í   í   í   í   (R8)

⋮

       ríe   píde   pedí   perdíste   perdímos   Surface

Rule 8 not only generates the correct surface phonetic representation of the vowels it operates on but also prepares the way for R9, Stress Shift, which operates on those [-ATR] V's spared by R8, namely the stressed [-ATR] V's which epenthesized through R4, and the stressed [-ATR] ThV preceding the vocalic subjunctive suffix, and the vocalic preterit suffix of the third singular person [-1st conj.]:

(23)

$$R9 \quad \begin{bmatrix} -ATR \\ -CP \\ +stress \end{bmatrix} \quad [+syl] \rightarrow [-stress] \; [+stress]$$

$$ 1 \qquad\qquad 2 \qquad\qquad 1 \qquad\quad 2$$

Forms which undergo R9 are shown below:

(24)   pidÍ+U   pidÍ+a$\begin{Bmatrix} mos \\ Is \end{Bmatrix}$ pidÍe+ndo   pÉerde

     I Ú   I á   Ié   Eé   (R9)

  pidió   *pidá*$\begin{Bmatrix} mos \\ is \end{Bmatrix}$ *pidiéndo*   *piérde*   Surface

The above formulation of Stress Shift, because of the feature [-ATR] of the segment losing the stress, explains why forms such as *ríe, varía, continúa, coméis,* etc. do not undergo Stress Shift. When Stress Shift applies, the relevant vowel in these forms and the classes of forms exemplified by them is [+ATR].

The ThV is cancelled out by a following 'tense' V by R10 shown in 25a,b together with examples of its application:

(25)

    a.   R10   V $\rightarrow$ Ø / ___ + $\begin{bmatrix} V \\ \alpha ATR \\ -\alpha CP \end{bmatrix}$

    b.   bebI+á+mos   pEérde+o   ama+é+mos

             Ø   Ø   Ø   (R10)

       bebámos   *piérdo*   *amémos*   Surface

It is possible that the deletion of the *b* of the imperfect morpheme and the voicing of the intervocalic obstruents that turns the *t* of the participle and of the imperative plural into *d* may be effected with a single rule. This question will be left unresolved, and an informal formulation is presented below:

(26)   (?) R11   b $\rightarrow$ Ø /   segment í ___

         (?) R12   t $\rightarrow$ d   under certain conditions

A 'mirror image' (MI) R13 will now turn the unstressed

vowel in hiatus into a glide.

(27)

    a. (MI) R13 $\begin{bmatrix} -ATR \\ -stress \\ -CP \\ \alpha high \end{bmatrix} \rightarrow \begin{bmatrix} -syl \\ \alpha ATR \end{bmatrix}$ / ___ $\begin{bmatrix} +syl \\ +stress \end{bmatrix}$

    b. riI+Ú   sIénti   pEérde   pEdí+Is

        y   y   Ẹ   y   (R13)

The lowering of the high V's in the last syllable of verbs depends on stress and backness as seen in 28a, b:

(28)

    a. R14 $\begin{bmatrix} V \\ \alpha stress \\ \alpha back \end{bmatrix} \rightarrow \begin{bmatrix} -high \\ +ATR \end{bmatrix}$ / ___ C_o #

    b. riyÚ   syénti

        ó   e   (R14)

Apocope applies to forms with a final E:

(29)

    a. R15 $\begin{bmatrix} V \\ -ATR \\ -high \\ -CP \end{bmatrix} \rightarrow \emptyset$ / ___ #

    b. pEdí+dE   pEdí+rE

           ∅   ∅   (R15)

By R16 a high glide is absorbed by a preceding palatal segment:

(30)

    a. R16 $\begin{bmatrix} -syl \\ -cons \\ +high \end{bmatrix} \rightarrow \emptyset$ / $\begin{bmatrix} +high \\ +ATR \end{bmatrix}$ ___

    b. riyó   pEdíys   tiñyó

         ∅   ∅   ∅   (R16)

The turning of the mid glide into a high one is accomplished through R17:

(31)

    a. R17 $\begin{bmatrix} -syl \\ -cons \\ -CP \end{bmatrix} \rightarrow \begin{bmatrix} +high \\ +ATR \end{bmatrix}$ / ___ $\begin{bmatrix} +syl \\ +stress \end{bmatrix}$

    b. pEérde

        y   (R17)

All unstressed syllabics are tensed by R18, the consequences of which have not been thoroughly investigated:

(32)

    a.   (?) R18 $\begin{bmatrix} +\text{syl} \\ \alpha\,\text{CP} \end{bmatrix} \rightarrow \begin{bmatrix} -\alpha\text{ATR} \end{bmatrix}$

    b. pEdímos   sEntído

        e   e   (R18)

In conclusion, three main points must be made. First the complex patterns of partial complementation of mid and high root and thematic vowels, particularly those of third conjugation stems, have been accounted for without recourse to diacritics of dubious phonological status. Second, the feature [ATR] has been shown to play a decisive role in the formulation presented here. Whether a more straightforward account can be given without it is a matter that deserves investigation. Finally, whether or not the feature [S], used in Harris 1969 and other subsequent analyses in the environment of various rules, is a needed diacritic is a matter left for separate treatment.

QUANTIFIERS AND AMBIGUITY: LOOKING ACROSS DERIVATIONS

JEAN CASAGRANDE AND LINDA JACKSON

University of Florida

1. Introduction

For some years, a large number of empirical facts have been
brought to light which require that the classical model be
modified. Among these are constraints which require the
application of rules in ways other than the local application
which is the hallmark of Classical Transformational Grammar. We
are, of course, referring to global and transderivational
constraints.

It is well known that Classical Transformational Grammar as
illustrated by Chomsky's *Aspects of the Theory of Syntax* was so
constrained as to allow rules to apply only to adjacent trees
in a derivation. A number of arguments have demonstrated that
all rules cannot be so constrained, that some rules are
required to apply to nonadjacent trees in derivations, and
that some rules need to apply across derivations. The purpose
of this paper is to demonstrate a need for transderivational
constraints based on empirical data not previously examined
in this light. These data are taken from French and Italian.

The syntactic rules discussed are *Quantifier Movement* (Postal's *Q-Float*), and *Clitic Placement*. Recent discussion of *Quantifier Movement* as it applies to French and Italian can be found in Kayne 1969, Fauconnier 1971 and Napoli 1974. For our purpose we will refer to this rule as *R-tous*, because, following Kayne, we want to distinguish it from *L-tous*. *L-tous* is a leftward movement which does not interest us here; *R-tous* is the rightward movement which parallels the English and Italian rules. Basically, the argument is of the following type. There are rules which are capable of creating strings that are identical to strings derived from different sources. Such rules can be prevented from applying--for no apparent reason other than the fact that ambiguity would be created. It follows, then, that the constraint in question must have access to some information in one derivation while it operates a blocking in another.

As we looked at the evidence we found that this type of constraint is somewhat unstable, from speaker to speaker, as witness the three to four dialect splits we found relating to it.

We will first survey the two rules and their interrelationship regardless of dialect. Then we will turn to dialect differences.

2. Quantifier movement and ambiguity

French, then, has a rule *R-tous* which relates sentences like 1 to 2 and 3 to 4:

(1)   Tous les anarchistes s'abstiendront de voter.
(2)   Les anarchistes s'abstiendront tous de voter.

(3)   Toutes les électrices voteront.
(4)   Les électrices voteront toutes.

In some cases the new position of the moved quantifier is the same as the position of a homonymous item in a string of a different derivational origin, in which case ambiguity may result, depending on dialects:

(5)   Les voitures sont toutes démolies.
(6)   Tes amies aiment toutes ces robes.

Sentence 5, resulting from *R-tous* is ambiguous with the same string where *toutes* is an adverbial intensifier. Sentence 6, resulting from *R-tous* is ambiguous with the string where *toutes* quantifies the object. Sentences 7 and 8 are not ambiguous. Given that a quantifier must agree in gender with the NP it modifies, it is clear that the quantifiers in 7 and 8 have been moved by *R-tous*. *Tous* and *toutes* in 7 and 8 cannot refer to the objects in these sentences:

(7)   Les hommes aiment tous ces robes.
(8)   Les femmes aiment toutes ces films.

Given this, we would predict ambiguity in 9 and 10 where it is possible for the quantifiers to modify the objects in their

respective sentences. Indeed, 9 and 10 are ambiguous in some
dialects:

(9) Les hommes aiment tous les films.
(10) Les femmes aiment toutes ces robes.

When the object NP is pronominalized it is subsequently moved
to preverbal position by the rule of *Clitic Placement*. This
rule relates sentences like 11 and 12:

(11) Nous appellerons les témoins.
(12) Nous les appellerons.

If *Clitic Placement* operates in the derivation of 9 and 10 we
get 13 and 14 respectively:

(13) Les garçons les (masc pl) aiment tous.
(14) Les femmes les (fem pl) aiment toutes.

We would expect 13 and 14, resulting from derivations A or B
below, to be ambiguous (at this point we are not concerned with
the relative ordering of *Pron, Clitic Placement,* and *R-tous)*:

(15) Derivation A
      a. Les hommes aiment tous les films.   *Pron*⟶
      b. Les hommes aiment tous les *Clitic Placement*⟶
      c. Les hommes les aiment tous.

(16) Derivation B
      a. Tous les hommes aiment les films.   *Pron*⟶
      b. Tous les hommes aiment les *Clitic Placement*⟶
      c. Tous les hommes les aiment. *R-tous*⟶
      d. Les hommes les aiment tous.

A few speakers find 13 and 14 ambiguous. They constitute one
dialect. A second, larger set of speakers, accepts only one
reading for all these sentences, that in which *tous/toutes*
quantify the direct object. This is the most restricted
dialect. For the speakers of this second dialect 13 and 14
would be translated respectively as 'The boys like them all'
and 'The girls like them all'. A third set of speakers accepts
5 and 6 as ambiguous but not 13 and 14. In addition, there are
speakers for whom 13 and 14 present different possibilities of
interpretation. For these speakers, the *tous* of 13 may refer
either to the subject or object NP depending on context,
whereas the *toutes* in 14 may only quantify the object NP, never
in any context the subject NP.
   Our goal here is to argue for the derivational constraints
suggested above in such a way as to take into account the
relatedness of these dialects. In other words we expect
dialectal differences, which we presume are small, to be matched
by correspondingly small adjustments in the derivations.
   Let us first consider the primary issue, that of accounting
for the nonambiguity.

3.   Nonambiguity

An important notion to take into account is that nonambiguity
in sentences like 13 and 14 means effectively that the rule
which moves the quantifier from presubject position rightwards,
that is *R-tous*, is blocked. Our task, then, is to define the
situation where the rule is blocked. It would seem to be
something like this:

(17)   The rule is blocked when the masculine or feminine
       quantifier would end up in sentence final position
       and where the object clitic *les* is understood as
       being of the same gender and number.

How do we formulate this constraint?

4.   A transderivational constraint

Jorge Hankamer 1973 claims that a transderivational constraint
is the only mechanism powerful enough to account for single
readings for gapped sentences where the grammar predicts
ambiguity. He found that in numerous cases of sentences where
items had been deleted by *Gapping,* the resulting sentences
could theoretically have had two or more derivational histories:

(18)   Jack wants Mike to wash himself and Arnie to shave
       himself.
(19)   Max wanted Ted to persuade Alex to get lost, and
       Walt, Ira.

A strictly local grammar of English would predict that 18 can
be paraphrased by either 20 or 21, but in fact only 21 is an
appropriate paraphrase:

(20)   Jack wants Mike to wash himself and Arnie wants Mike
       to shave himself.
(21)   Jack wants Mike to wash himself and Jack wants Arnie
       to shave himself.

Similarly, 19 would be predicted as a paraphrase of either 22,
23, or 24, but it only has the reading of 22:

(22)   Max wanted Ted to persuade Alex to get lost and Max
       wanted Walt to persuade Ira.
(23)   Max wanted Ted to persuade Alex to get lost and Walt
       wanted Ira to persuade Alex to get lost.
(24)   Max wanted Ted to persuade Alex to get lost and Walt
       wanted Ted to persuade Ira to get lost.

Hankamer proposes one condition which would handle all cases
of this nature and therefore capture a generalization, relating
the various environments in which rules are blocked. His
condition, the 'No ambiguity condition', states the preferred
situation for the application of *Gapping* (i.e. gap at the

extreme left) and blocks any rule which would generate the same
string originating from another, less preferred source. In
order to effect the block, the mechanism must be able to
identify a string which could originate from another source.
It must, therefore, have access to information from derivations
other than its own. This is clearly a strong device and should
be used to account for certain language phenomena only if more
traditional mechanisms cannot handle them.

Ambiguity is by definition a multiderivational concept since
it concerns a relationship, in this case identity, between
strings in different derivations. If, as in sentence 10, it is
only a result, haphazard in nature and never formally referred
to in the grammar, of two derivations yielding identical
strings, then it presents no problem to Classical
Transformational Grammar. However, if ambiguity is eliminated
it must be formally referred to in the grammar, and a
transderivational mechanism is required.

The ambiguity problem discovered by Hankamer seems to be
similar in nature to the French problem. Like Hankamer we wish
to explain lack of ambiguity where ambiguity is predicted; our
output is, in principle, derivable from (two) different sources
but only one of these sources is allowed.

Our French data is different from Hankamer's English examples
because (1) we are dealing with movement rules, not deletion
rules, and (2) there is a dialect difference to account for.
In light of the dialect variation, it will be useful to bear in
mind the questions we expect our grammar to answer and the
facts we expect it to reflect. These are:

A. Why is there no ambiguity in certain places where the
   rules predict ambiguity?
B. Both dialects should be incorporated into the
   description.
C. Their difference should be reflected by the grammar
   in the form of a small grammatical variation (i.e. no
   major theoretical difference between them).
D. Why doesn't the ambiguity-blocking mechanism operate
   to prevent sentences like 9 and 10 which actually turn
   out to be ambiguous, i.e. why doesn't it prevent *all*
   ambiguity?

5. Two dialects of French

In dialect A sentences 25 and 26 are both unambiguous as regards
the quantifier *tous/toutes*.

   (25) Tes amies les aiment toutes.
   (26) Les copains les aiment tous.

In dialect B only 25 is unambiguous; 26 is not. We will deal
with dialect B first, since this order tends to illustrate the
problem more clearly.

5.1.   Dialect B

In 26, *tous* may refer either to the subject or the object NP,
while in 25 only the object is referred to by the quantifier.
Thus, we have a situation where the feminine version has only
one reading whereas the masculine version has two. The nature
of the problem suggests that more than purely syntactic
considerations must be involved since syntactically the two
cases are exactly equivalent. Why should there be a
difference?

Consider for a moment the phonetic forms of the masculine
and feminine quantifiers. The masculine plural quantifier *tous*
has different phonetic shapes depending on whether it appears
immediately before the NP it modifies or in another position.
In other words, the masculine quantifier is pronounced
differently if it is not in prenominal position. Its
prenominal form is /tu/ while its form in any other position
is /tus/. The feminine quantifier, however, has only one
shape, /tut/. The relevance of this difference is that
whereas 9 is not ambiguous when spoken, 10 is.

The explanation should incorporate the data listed above and
at the same time fulfill the conditions laid down in A-D above
concerning adequate grammatical treatment. Let us examine the
facts systematically.

(27)   Derivation 1F
    a.   Toutes les copines aiment les voitures
       étrangères.   (-AMB)
          R-tous ⟶
    b.   Tes copines aiment toutes les voitures
       étrangères.   (AMB)
          Clitic Placement ⟶
    c.   *Tes copines les aiment toutes.   (*)

(28)   Derivation 2F
    a.   Tes copines aiment toutes les voitures
       étrangères.   (AMB)
          Clitic Placement ⟶
    b.   Tes copines les aiment toutes.   (-AMB)

(29)   Derivation 1M
    a.   Tous tes copains aiment les films
       étrangers.   (-AMB)
          R-tous ⟶
    b.   Tes copains aiment tous les films
       étrangers.   (-AMB)
          Clitic Placement ⟶
    c.   Tes copains les aiment tous.   (AMB)

(30)   Derivation 2M
    a.   Tes copains aiment tous les films
       étrangers.   (-AMB)
          Clitic Placement ⟶
    b.   Tes copains les aiment tous.   (AMB)

The clear pattern here is that there are never two transformations with ambiguous outputs in a row. When this shows signs of occurring, as in 27b → 27c, the grammar takes steps to prevent it and blocks one of the two transformations which would create the potentially ambiguous string. Thus, one reading is eliminated and the string remains unambiguous.

The vital difference between the masculine and feminine forms is that 29b is not ambiguous whereas the corresponding sentences with a feminine quantifier, 27b and 28a, are ambiguous. Thus the feminine derivation will not allow a further transformation to apply whereas the masculine derivation will. This may be formulated in a way similar to Hankamer's constraint, the main difference being that here we do not claim that structural ambiguity is disallowed but rather that once a string is structurally ambiguous no more optional movement transformations may be operated. Thus ambiguity is not eliminated but limited. The following is a tentative statement of this constraint:

If in a derivation D-1, a movement rule R-1 creates a string S-1 which is identical to a string S-2 in a derivation D-2 whose structure is preferred over D-1, no further optional movement rules can operate on S-1, subsequent to R-1. 'Preferred' in this case must be stated in terms of the structures involved. Here the preferred structure for the string *Tes amies les aiment toutes* would be something like 'where *toutes* quantifies the nearest NP or pronoun'.

How can we relate this to dialect A where there is no difference of reading between masculine and feminine versions? The limit on ambiguity discussed above will not apply to Dialect A.

5.2. Dialect A in comparison to Dialect B

In dialect B the explanation for the difference in readings between the masculine and feminine versions was that ambiguity did not arise at the same point in the derivation for both masculine and feminine. This was reflected at the surface. It seems then that any explanation involving reference to ambiguity will differentiate masculine and feminine. However, in dialect A there is not this difference, so the constraint stated above cannot apply in both dialects, if the data is analyzed as above. At this point it is useful to examine the possible orders of the rules involved, since the appearance of ambiguity in the course of derivations is highly dependent on this factor.

6. Rule ordering

Clitic Placement and *R-tous* apply independently of each other as can be seen in examining 31 and 32:

(31) a. Tous les garçons les aiment.   (*CL-PLT*)
      b. Toutes les filles les aiment.   (*CL-PLT*)

(32)   a.   Les garçons aiment. tous /tus/ les films. (*R-tous*)
       b.   Les filles aiment toutes les robes.   (*R-tous*)

Both 31a and b are unambiguous but only 32a is unambiguous.
This is so because of the phonetic change in *tous* in a position
other than prenominal. Keeping these facts in mind, let us
turn to sentences 13 and 14. These sentences can, given the
rules of the grammar, be derived in two different ways from
the same logical underlying structure, depending on the
relative order of *Clitic Placement* and *R-tous*. Consider 33
and 34:

(33)   a.   Tous les garçons aiment les films turcs.   (−AMB)
            Toutes les filles aiment les robes.   (−AMB)

       b.   Les garçons aiment tous les films
            turcs.   (*R-tous*)   (−AMB)
            Les filles aiment toutes les
            robes.   (*R-tous*)   (+AMB)

       c.   (*) Les garçons les aiment tous. (*CL-PLT*) (*)
            (*) Les filles les aiment toutes.(*CL-PLT*) (*)

(34)   a.   Tous les garçons aiment les films turcs.   (−AMB)
            Toutes les filles aiment les robes.   (−AMB)

       b.   Tous les garçons les aiment.   (*CL-PLT*) (−AMB)
            Toutes les filles les aiment.   (*CL-PLT*) (−AMB)

       c.   (*) Les garçons les aiment tous. (*R-tous*) (*)
            (*) Les filles les aiment toutes.(*R-tous*) (*)

In derivation 33 the b sentences differ from each other in
ambiguity whereas in 34 both the masculine and feminine
versions of the b sentences are ambiguous. Thus the crucial
ambiguity difference between the masculine and the feminine
which characterizes Dialect B is eliminated in the grammar of
Dialect A if *Clitic Placement* is ordered before *R-tous*.

7. The nature of the constraint

The transderivational constraint operating in Dialect A will
block *R-tous* when the application of *R-tous* would relate 34b
and c. This explains why the 34c sentences are not ambiguous.
   These two dialects then differ (1) in rule ordering and (2)
in that the constraint relating to ambiguity operates
differently in each dialect. From the point of view of the
theory, however, these dialects are highly similar. In both
cases reference must be made to a derivation other than the
one in which the blocking takes place. However, in Dialect B,
the transformation is blocked if its *input* is identical to a
string from a preferred source, whereas in Dialect A, the
transformation is blocked if its *output* is identical to a
string from a preferred source.
   In considering the evidence from Italian (Napoli 1974) we

will see that there is a constraint operating which is
identical to that of Dialect A in French.

8. Quantifier movement in Italian

Q-Float in Italian relates sentences like 35 and 36:

(35)   Tutti i ragazzi vogliono vedere i fiori.
(36)   I ragazzi vogliono vedere i fiori.

As in French, the quantifier may also appear in pre-object
position:

(37)   I ragazzi comprano tutti i fiori.

We would therefore predict that, where *tutti* has the same
gender and number as both the subject and object NP's, the
string is ambiguous as to which NP it refers to. Unlike
Dialect B of French, however, this is not the case. Sentence
37 is not ambiguous: *tutti* can only quantify the object.[1]
In Italian, as in French, the object NP may be pronominalized
and subsequently cliticized, that is, moved by *Clitic Placement*
to a preverbal position. Whether *Clitic Placement* has applied
or not, in 37 and 38 respectively, the quantifier modifies the
object only. Thus 39-40 are not related to 37-38:

(38)   I ragazzi li vedono tutti.
(39)   Tutti i ragazzi li vedono.
(40)   Tutti i ragazzi comprano i fiori.

This is further illustrated by the fact that when, as in 41,
the only possible reading is that of *Q-Float* the sentence is
ungrammatical:

(41)   *I ragazzi li vogliono tutti comprare.

However, the same sentence with an object NP, that is where
tutti is not preceded by a clitic, is acceptable:

(42)   I ragazzi vogliono tutti comprare i fiori.

This can be explained in a manner similar to that used for the
French data. We noted that in French there is a preferred
position--as near as possible to the NP a quantifier modifies.
This seems to hold for Italian too. Hence, the preferred
position is where *tutti* quantifies the nearest NP or clitic
pronoun, unless, of course, this is not possible because of
gender and number differences.
  We can say, then, basing our formulation on the French
constraint, that the reason that *Q-Float* could not have
generated 38 is that the output string of this transformation
would have been identical to another string originating from
another preferred source. This is another case where the
grammar eliminates a weaker or less preferred reading if two
strings would coincide, creating ambiguity. The reading

tutti i ragazzi is not possible in 37:   *Q-Float* is blocked because of the preferred reading *tutti i fiori*. The constraint operating here and in Dialect A of French can be formulated as follows:

> If in a derivation D-1 a movement rule R-1 creates a string S-1 which is identical to a string S-2 in derivation D-2, then R-1 is blocked.

9.   Caveat

Before turning to our conclusion we must add a warning about this formulation. There is in Napoli 1974 a sentence type which the transderivational constraint discussed here cannot account for. We believe that to account for this type of sentence an analogical rule is required.

A counterexample to our proposed transderivational analysis would be one where a rule is blocked from applying when there is no identical string provided by another derivation, i.e. where there is no constraint on ambiguity because no ambiguity exists. Such a case can be found in Napoli 1974, our example 41:

(41)   *I ragazzi li vogliono tutti comprare.

Admittedly, the unacceptability of 41 cannot be explained with the transderivational mechanism. However, 41 can be explained with an analogical rule (Aissen 1973). Under this type of analysis 41 is reanalyzed by 'flat structure identity' with 38 (*I ragazzi li vedono tutti*) and consequently undergoes the same constraint as 38, as shown in 43:[2]

(43)   a. | I ragazzi | li | vedono | tutti |
       b. | I ragazzi | li | vogliono | tutti | comprare

Note that here we are not attempting to make the constraint operating on 41 also apply to 38. On the contrary, the constraint on 38 also accounts for 41, only the result of that constraint on 41 does not need to restate the conditions mentioned in the transderivational constraint applying to 38. It applies analogically to 41.

Napoli's solution, a surface perceptual strategy, seems inappropriate to us. We cannot accept the striking meaning change that such a condition imposes. To say that a quantifier underlying in the subject NP and subsequently moved near the object by *Q-Float* is perceptually identified with the object is, in our view, a claim that *Q-Float* changes the meaning of strings to which it applies. We cannot accept such a claim.

10.   Conclusions

There are cases where the rules of grammar, if allowed to operate unchecked, would create ambiguity and continue to apply to ambiguous strings. We have just seen that in three

similar but different Romance dialects (we had to limit
ourselves to a twenty-minute presentation) the grammar does
not allow ambiguity to get out of hand. We stated above that
an analysis must meet certain conditions.

The first condition is to find a mechanism which successfully
blocked certain unacceptable sentences. This condition has been
met. Secondly, the analysis needed to explain why these
sentences were blocked: our analysis incorporates constraints
where rules are blocked subject to existing or potential
ambiguity. Our third condition stated that evidence in related
languages or dialects should reflect the nature of the relationships. We have shown dialects A and B in French as well as
Italian to be similar in their basic goals (limiting ambiguity)
to use the same linguistic mechanism (the transderivational
constraint), and yet to vary in some respects (i.e. in the amount
of tolerance of ambiguity).

A further important consideration is that because the
transderivational mechanism is more powerful than the
uniderivational one, it should be used only if no satisfactory
analysis can be found uniderivationally. Since any
uniderivational explanation, even global constraints, not only
cannot account for the facts but also fails to explain why the
constraint is at work, we conclude that the transderivational
mechanism is the more adequate solution. It is also the case
that logically, since the reason for the constraint seems to
be to limit ambiguity, which by definition concerns a
relationship between strings of two or more derivations (that
of identity) there *cannot* be a solution which does *not* make
use of a transderivational mechanism.

By claiming that the aim of the grammar in this case is to
limit ambiguity and that to do this any derivation has access
to information from other derivations, we are able to account
for a large and seemingly variant mass of unexplained data in
a cohesive way, and to furnish satisfactory answers to a
number of basic questions about certain phenomena. If our
claim is accurate, we may expect to find that this kind of
analysis applies elsewhere.

NOTES

[1]That 37 was not ambiguous was stated in Napoli 1974. We
found an Italian speaker who agrees with Napoli. However, she
has subsequently found (personal communication) that to some
speakers of Italian this sentence is indeed ambiguous.

[2]The line between *I ragazzi* and *tutti* suggests a
relationship between these words and the X across the line
shows that such a relationship is unacceptable.

REFERENCES

Aissen, Judith. 1973. Shifty objects in Spanish. CLS 9.

Chomsky, Noam. 1965. Aspects of the theory of syntax.
    Cambridge, Mass.: MIT Press.

Fauconnier, Gilles. 1971. Theoretical implication of some
    global phenomena in syntax. San Diego: University of
    California dissertation.

Hankamer, Jorge. 1972. Analogical rules in syntax. CLS 8.

_____. 1973. Unacceptable ambiguity. Linguistic Inquiry
    4.17-68.

Kayne, Richard. 1969. The transformational cycle in French
    syntax. Cambridge, Mass.: M.I.T. dissertation.

Napoli, Donna Jo. 1974. The no-crossing filter. CLS 10.

COMPLICATION IN OLD FRENCH PHONOLOGY*

DOUGLAS C. WALKER

University of Ottawa

1.   Introduction

Since the proposal, in *Syntactic Structures*, of an evaluation
rather than a decision or a discovery procedure as the most
attainable goal for linguistic theory, the question of
simplicity[1] in linguistic description has received considerable
attention. While it is not possible to enter into a full
discussion of the extensive literature on this subject, it may
be noted that there has been what might be called a
progressive complication of the subject of simplicity, and an
adoption of competing and sometimes conflicting underlying
principles. In certain cases, moreover, it is possible to see
the abandonment of simplicity or simplicity-related criteria
as motivating factors in particular analyses. Rather than
exploring superficially the broad implications of the
evaluation metric, I will concentrate instead on several
problems of historical phonology[2] where simplicity and other
matters are in conflict, and where historical changes
illustrate the need for a modification of certain theoretical
positions. In particular, the notions of 'natural rule',

'inverse rule', 'rule order', and 'analogy' will be briefly
considered.

In the initial application of generative phonology to the
description of historical change, innovations were usually
seen as simplifications of the grammar, particularly of the
rule component. Thus, rule generalization, loss, or
re-ordering (assuming the notion of marked and unmarked order)
were paramount, while restructuring and especially formal
complication were minimized. Kiparsky 1965, for example,
restricts phonological change to simplification and imperfect
learning (the latter a general term encompassing several
possibilities). Kiparsky (1968:175-6) suggests that we
'think of linguistic change in roughly the following terms.
Grammars are subject to changes of two kinds: the addition of
new rules to them and the simplification of them'. Finally,
King (1969:65) hypothesizes that 'the transmission of a
grammar through time or geographic space, is in general
accompanied by equal or increased simplicity, and not by
complication (reduction in generality)'.

Examples from the history of French, interpretable in the
foregoing terms, are easy to find.[3] The loss of Latin *h* in
forms like *hominem* > **omne, prehendere* > **preendere, hora* >
ora and so on can be described historically as the addition
of a rule $h \rightarrow \emptyset$. Assuming the rule to be neither chronologically
nor lexically instantaneous in its effects, there would be a
period of variation in which particular forms or lexical
domains alternate between the presence or absence of *h*, such
alternation described by an optional or variable rule. As the
loss of *h* was generalized (that is, as underlying
representations were restructured to occur without *h*), the
need for the synchronic presence of the rule diminished.
Finally, as a result of its ultimate loss, both the rule
component and the underlying representations become simpler.

Less trivial examples than this case of rule addition and
subsequent loss can be found, involving, for example, the
retention but generalization of a synchronic rule. In first
conjugation verbs in Old French, a thematic vowel follows the
second and third person singular stem in the present indicative,
but is not found after the first person stem. Then in Middle
French 'the isolated forms produced in the first person
singular...were replaced by analogical forms ending in ę [ə],
made ordinarily on the radical that was in use in the second
and third singular' (Pope 1934:353). When this analogy is
viewed from the perspective of the synchronic Old French
morphological rule assigning thematic vowels, a different type
of change is taking place:

(1)   Thematic vowel $\longrightarrow$ ə /
$$\begin{bmatrix} +\text{Class 1} \\ +\text{Indicative} \\ -\text{Plural} \\ -\text{First Person} \end{bmatrix}$$

From this point of view, the thematic vowel rule has simplified
or generalized by dropping the final feature from its

structural description, thereby extending this thematic vowel
to all persons in the singular.[4]

2. Naturalness and simplicity

As soon as we move away from such straightforward examples,
however, the exclusively simplifying picture of historical
change is modified. The first problem arises when the notion
of natural rule is considered. While the precise definition
of 'natural' remains somewhat obscure (see, in this regard,
Schane 1972), it is certainly the case that many clearly
natural rules (whatever the criteria) are more complex in
formal terms than their unnatural counterparts. A rule
nasalizing vowels before all consonants is less satisfying
than one having the same effect just before nasal consonants,
even though the former is considerably more general.
    Historically speaking, moreover, the change from the complex
to the simplified form of such a nasalization rule would be a
particularly surprising type of innovation. Now, it is
possible to modify the formalism for writing rules so that
natural rules end up as less complex (in terms of their feature
composition) than unnatural rules. One means of accomplishing
this is to have the evaluation metric ignore the various
environmental conditions or exceptions involved in a rule (as
is advocated in Schane 1973a). Another is to link the rule
to some universal meta-rule or schema whereby its progressive
development is seen in terms of a hierarchy of contexts (as
in much of the recent work of Chen, for example). I will not
explore further the possible links between simplicity and
naturalness, in part because it appears that a purely formal
approach--counting features--has certain weaknesses as a way
of accounting for rules or changes that are determined by
intrinsic properties of the human articulatory or perceptual
mechanisms. More important in this context, however, are the
following considerations. First, a frequent consequence of
historical change involves the formal complication of the
grammar, even though the result is more 'natural' when viewed
against traditional conceptions of linguistic structure.
Secondly, the direction of historical change is frequently
from natural to unnatural rules, whether the latter are
simpler or not. These claims will be substantiated with
reference to two different developments, one involving the
question of natural and unnatural diphthongization rules, the
second involving rule order and analogy.[5]

2.1. Complication and diphthongization in OF

Let us consider certain aspects of diphthongization in the
history of French. The diphthongization of both pairs of mid
vowels, ɛ-ɔ and e-o, can easily be considered a natural
process.[6] As expected, it is stressed and long (or tense)
vowels which diphthongize, and the change largely affects
these vowels in open syllables (in Gallo-Romance). The quality
of the glide that developed is determined by properties of the
associated vowel, in a type of assimilatory relationship.

The phonetic (i.e. natural) conditioning of these innovations
is clear, and in accord with cross-linguistic studies of
analogous phenomena. The synchronic correlates of these
diphthongizations, functioning initially as automatic
morphophonemic rules (or perhaps even as allophonic rules)
account for the following alternations, among others (where ´
indicates stress):

(2)		
	achiévent-achevóns	'terminate'
	chiéent-cheóns	'fall'
	criévent-crevóns	'burst'
	liévent-levóns	'get up'
	buéglent-boglóns	'sound (a bugle)'
	cuévrent-covróns	'cover'
	despuéillent-despoillóns	'skin'
	muélent-molóns	'grind'
	adeísent-adesóns	'touch'
	beívent-bevóns	'drink'
	esfreíent-esfreóns	'be agitated'
	séivrent-sevróns	'separate'
	avoúent-avoóns	'admit'
	coúsent-cosóns	'sew'
	laboúrent-laboróns	'work'
	noúrent-noróns	'bring up, educate'

We see, then, that synchronic rules for the following
alternations are necessary: ε-jε, ɔ-we, e-ej, o-ow (the
interpretation of the orthography as indicating these
alternations poses no major problems). What happens to these
rules in terms of their historical development? The most
obvious outcome is that, while the rules originally applied
under clearly specifiable phonetic conditions, subsequent
changes modify the conditions for rule application. For
example, syncope of many post-tonic vowels leads to clusters
of consonants following many diphthongs, such clusters
violating the original phonetic context, i.e. open syllables:
aourt, adeist, cruest, esmiert, third singular subjunctive of
'adore', 'touch', 'hollow out', and 'purify', respectively.
Other changes have simplified consonantal groups or geminate
consonants that originally blocked diphthongization, leading
to non-diphthongized vowels in open syllables, again contrary
to phonetic expectations: *apele, halete, cor, met*, third
singular of 'call', 'beat (wings, heart)', 'run', and 'put',
respectively.
    The diphthongization rules, then, have become opaque in two
ways: apparent application in contexts where they should be
blocked, and non-application in contexts where they should
apply freely. Rule opacity is a frequent and normal outcome
of historical change (as may be inferred from the huge
literature on phonemic split or 'phonologization'). How would
a generative phonology handle the Old French situation, aside
from a simple list of cases where the rule applies and where
it does not? One possibility (the standard one in the major
generative treatments of Romance phonology, c.f. Schane,
Harris, Saltarelli) is to introduce an underlying tense-lax

distinction or an *ad hoc* diacritic feature into the vowel
system, and to use the new opposition to condition the
application of the diphthongization and other rules. While it
is not possible here to enter into the details motivating such
an analysis for French (see Schane 1968, 1973b), we may note
that historical innovations have led to a large complication
of the phonological component and the lexicon. First, a new
underlying distinction must be widely marked in the vowel
system, increasing the complexity of lexical representations.
Second, the diphthongization rules must also be complicated so
as to become sensitive to the tense-lax feature. As a result
of historical innovations of a well-known and common type,
therefore, the grammar has been greatly complicated, contrary
to the hypotheses outlined above.

Various arguments have been raised against the use of a
tense-lax morphophonemic distinction in French, however, and
the status of the distinction is somewhat questionable at the
moment. Thus, it may not be totally fair to base arguments on
this analysis. Let us, therefore, not presuppose it in further
discussion, but simply accept that historical change often
complicates grammars (a result that is independent of whether
the tense-lax solution is adopted). We saw above that
simplicity and naturalness are not necessarily equivalent.
Perhaps historical change leads to natural if not simple
grammars. Here again the Old French diphthongization case is
instructive. We may note first that one result of historical
change involves synchronic rules of diphthongization in closed
syllables in Old French. Such a restriction cannot be ruled
out *a priori* as unnatural (Spanish is, after all, a 'natural'
language), but it is the first step in the development of
totally unnatural diphthongization rules in the modern language.
We will not examine all the intermediate stages of the
historical development in minute detail, since a comparison of
the Modern French and Old French rules is sufficient to show
the progressive *loss* of naturalness through historical change.
Grossly summarized, the diphthongs with which we are concerned
changed as follows.[7]

(3)   Simple V   Diphthong⟶   Modern Form

ɛ	jɛ				jɛ
ɔ	wɔ	wɛ	œ		œ
e	ej	oj	we	wa	wa
o	ow	ew	œ		œ

At each stage, various alternations justify the linking of the
simple vowel (or its descendent) with a diphthongal alternate.
Finally, at the Modern French stage we see, among others, the
following alternations (*o* having been dropped from this group
of alternating vowels):

(4)   e-wa   (crédibilité-croit)
      ɛ-jɛ   (bénir-bien, venir-vient, with additional

adjustments to the simple vowels)

ɔ-œ   (volonté-veulent, mort-meurent).

In the modern language (Schane 1968:20-45), there is a single *telescoped* diphthongization rule which accounts for the front vowel-diphthong pairs, and a rule of vowel fronting which treats the ɔ-œ (and, in addition, the a-ε) alternation. But where the Old French rule was a natural one, consider its Modern French descendant. In terms of rule naturalness there is no reason why front vowels should diphthongize while the corresponding back vowels shift front. Nor is there any phonetic reason why the height of the vowel should condition the frontness or backness of the inserted vowel. We might just as well expect ε-wε, e-je alternations. The most that can be said is that the rule is the shortest route between the surface alternates, but none of the proposed simplicity or naturalness arguments takes this into account.[8]

3.   Rule inversion

If we look once again at the continuous modification of the synchronic diphthongization rules, we can see clearly how an important type of historical change, *rule inversion*, comes about. Let us limit ourselves principally to the *e-wa* case, although the lower mid vowels present an analogous development. In the initial stages of diphthongization, the rule is phonetically conditioned and essentially without exceptions (transparent in generative phonological terms). Later, because of subsequent historical changes modifying its environment, the rule begins to have exceptions of two types: non-application in contexts where it should apply, and application where its structural description is apparently not met.[9] In addition, other factors contribute to the opacity of the rule. First, the importation of loan words, sporadically at first but gaining considerable momentum in Middle French, contributes forms that contradict the rule and increase its opacity. Secondly, the role of analogy should not be underestimated, since analogical leveling, from the earliest Old French times, has tended to reduce paradigmatic alternations and create further exceptions to the diphthongization rules. Thus, *voyons* instead of *veons*, or *pleuvoir* instead of *plouvoir*, by analogy with stressed *voit* and *pleut*, show diphthongs in unstressed position, while *prouve* instead of *prueve*, *trouve* instead of *trueve* by analogy with *prouvons* and *trouvons* show non-diphthongized vowels in stressed position. We have, then, what might be called sporadic, paradigmatic, and stratal exceptions to diphthongization, some of which have been present almost since the rule's inception.[10]
Far from simplifying the grammar, these types of exception require that the formal mechanisms, both in the lexicon and in the rule component, become greatly complicated. At the same time, further historical innovations affect the *structural change* of the diphthongization rules leading to unnatural synchronic alternations through the need to recapitulate

several changes at one leap, as it were: consider the *e-wa* rule in Modern French. We find, then, a synchronic rule that may be highly unnatural, and heavily laden with exceptions of both a sporadic and a systematic nature (where, for example, whole morphological classes affect the application of the rule). As the erosion of the rule's domain proceeds, the rule may very well become a *minor* rule, whereby forms undergoing it must be specifically marked, rather than the forms not undergoing it. We may assume that this is the stage immediately preceeding *rule inversion*. At the stage where the minor rule applies, the forms undergoing it are less numerous than those which do not. More-over, the forms most divergent from the underlying representation and consequently subject to the rule are the frequent, inflectional, non-learned, unmarked forms--just those which should not be secondary and not derived by minor rule. They should rather furnish the basic or underlying vowel, with the learned or derivational forms being obtained from the opposite class.11 In this specific case, the underlying vowel would be /œ/ or /wa/ on the basis of inflectional forms such as *veulent, croit*, and the derived vowels which show up in forms such as *volonté* or *crédibilité* would be /ɔ/ and /e/. We then have an inverted rule deriving /ɔ/ and /e/ from underlying /œ/ and /wa/ in contexts that are the opposite of those of the original historical change, and which are found in a peripheral lexical domain.

This example is a greatly abbreviated sketch of the genesis of an inverted rule, but the general development seems clear. Much interesting work remains to be done, particularly concerning the actual implementation of inversion. When, exactly, does the switch from a standard to an inverted rule take place--is there a period where both types co-exist? What sort of changes do inverted rules undergo? Are there differences here between inflection and derivation, etc.? One strong point in favor of inversion is the fact that such a mechanism is sensitive to the arbitrary nature of phonological and lexical relationships and the presence of subregularities and suppletion in any synchronic lexi-con. As one end point in a progression from allophonic or automatic morphophonemic rules through various degrees of opacity, then to minor rules to inverted rules, the mechanism of rule inversion has interesting implications for historical linguistic discussions. Another aspect of the concept of rule inversion is the demonstration that simplicity and naturalness are not suffi-cient, and in fact are secondary, in accounting for the historical changes in the diphthongization rules. Finally, I would like to discuss how another pair of notions from the recent generative literature--unmarked rule order and paradigm regularity--may conflict in terms of the claims they make about historical change.

4. Rule ordering and analogy

Briefly, the situation is this: Kiparsky 1968 extended the notion of markedness to the ordering relationships between phonological rules,12 showing that these relationships could also be viewed as marked or unmarked (more or less complex). Two rules are in a less marked ordering relationship if rule A creates (or does not destroy) representations to which Rule B

can apply. If rule A modifies (or fails to create) representations to which B is applicable, then the ordering relationship
between the two contributes more highly to the complexity of
the grammar. In the course of historical change, the
principles governing the complexity of grammars require that
rules re-order from marked to unmarked (bleeding to feeding)
order, if they are to re-order at all. Subsequent to
Kiparsky's original article, at least two functionally oriented
constraints have been superimposed on these re-ordering
considerations: the preservation of rule transparency and the
notion of paradigm regularity. It is this latter constraint
that interests us here, since King (1973:559) has claimed that:
    The fundamental principle governing re-orderings seems to
    be one we may term rather generally as a 'tendency toward
    uniformity.' One aspect of this tendency is that
    allomorphic variation within paradigms is minimized...
It is to be expected, therefore, that any change in rule order
will not result in the introduction of increased allomorphic
variation.13 This claim is contradicted by further Old French
facts.
    There was in Old French a rule of consonantal epenthesis
which inserted a stop between a fricative, nasal, or lateral
consonant followed by *l* or *r*.14 This rule accounts, in the
earliest Old French period, for alternations like those in 5:

    (5)   me*n*d*r*e-menour   'smaller'
          grai*n*d*r*e-graignour   'bigger'
          ance*s*t*r*e-ancessour   'ancestor'
          pre*n*d*r*e-prenons   'take'
          co*s*d*r*e-cousons   'sew'
          nai*s*t*r*e-naissons   'be born'
          va*l*d*r*a-valeir   'be worth'
          do*l*d*r*a-doleir   'suffer'

as well as many others in perfect verb forms and elsewhere.
The forms which most concern us here end in a stem-final labial
nasal *m*, and show, at this stage, the following alternations:

    (6)   raiembre-raemons   'buy back'
          criembre-cremons   'fear'
          giembre-gemons   'groan'
         *friembre-fremons   'tremble'
          priembre-premons   'press'

Very early, however, these forms start to show up with a
stem-final *dental* nasal, traditionally explained (Fouché 1967:
143-4) as due to the analogical influence of *plaindre* and
feindre, and this may well be the impetus for the change. Its
formal implementation, viewed against the background of a
generative phonological analysis of Old French, raises several
further questions. Formally, the 'analogy' involves the
re-ordering of the epenthesis rule and another well-established
rule of Old French, nasal assimilation, which makes nasal
consonants homorganic to following consonants. Consider the
derivations for the earlier and later stages in the Old French

period:

(7) Early   Later
     criembre   *criembre*

       /krem+r/   /krem+r/
Epenthesis   b   Assimilation   n
Assimilation   Epenthesis   d
       [kr(i)embrə]   [kr(ai)ndrə]

The 'analogical' changes affecting stems in -*m* are the
result of a change in rule order from epenthesis preceding
assimilation to assimilation preceding epenthesis. Both rules
are firmly established productive rules in the grammar of this
period, and the general shift of all verbs in -*m* is best seen
as a systematic event governed by rule re-ordering. Given
this re-ordering, however, we must return to King's claim that
'the fundamental principle governing re-orderings seems to be
one we may term rather generally as a 'tendency toward
uniformity''. In fact, the result of this re-ordering is less
uniformity, because in addition to stem-final -*m* (*cremons*) we
now have derived -*n* (*craindre*). Actually, the situation is
even more intricate, since additional factors must be considered.
First, re-ordering allows for substantial formal simplification
of the epenthesis rule, and for assimilation to be formulated
more naturally as a regressive rather than as a progressive
change.[15] This, plus the existant pressures from outside the
paradigm (*feindre, plaindre*), the presence of other instances
of derived -*n* through nasal assimilation (*criens, crient,
crensis* 2sg. and 3sg. pres.; 2sg. perf. respectively) and the
fact that the re-ordering is governed by Kiparsky's original
principle of the maximization of feeding order all illustrate
the complex interplay of several factors in cases of
'analogy'. We see, then, that King's restriction on re-ordering
is not relevant to this case, where a more refined notion of
the interaction between the phonological and morphological
domains is required.

5. Conclusions

What conclusions do the preceding examples motivate? They do
not show that the concepts of simplicity, naturalness,
markedness, re-ordering, paradigm leveling, and so on, taken
individually, have nothing to contribute to our understanding
of historical change. Such a negative demonstration would be
particularly surprising given the favorable results of these
mechanisms in isolation and often in concert, and the fact
that most or all of the devices are present in approaches
prior to or simultaneous with generative phonology. The
difficulties arise, I believe, when we try to reduce these
various factors to single (or a small number of) principles,
or to rank them in a fixed order of importance. The most
obvious problems arise with simplicity and naturalness, which
are postulated to underlie so many innovations. We have seen
that simplicity fails to account for several changes, even

though it often gives insightful results. Analogous comments
apply to the link between analogical leveling and re-ordering,
and no doubt for others. If we consider that languages may
change, in general terms, for phonetic, grammatical,
psychological, and sociological reasons, it is not likely
that this multiplicity of factors will be neatly and
hierarchically arranged cross-linguistically. There is no
need to fix, once and for all, the possible interactions
between the multiple causes of linguistic change. This does
not imply, however, that one should not study these interactions;
just that the relative importance of causes will change with
changing conditions. The value of the Old French and Romance
material is to show that previously suggested relationships
between theoretical concepts, valid elsewhere, must be
modified to account for new and easily documented exceptions
to standard generative formulations.

NOTES

*Research for this paper was supported by grant S7-0757 from
the Canada Council. I would like to thank Noel Corbett,
Merle Horne, and Marisa Rivero for helpful comments on an
earlier version.

[1]Few areas are as subtle and as subject to diverse
interpretations as that of simplicity. On a metatheoretic
level, Bunge (1967:377) mentions syntactic, semantic,
epistemological, and pragmatic simplicity, as well as formal
economy. All of these are conceivably relevant to particular
grammatical descriptions (theories of a language). Within
generative grammar, formal economy of a specific type is
considered the most important, although one may lose sight of
the fact that the goal of the investigation is *correct*
descriptions, not simple ones, and that 'correct' is defined in
empirical rather than in formal terms.

[2]Already this historical orientation marks a change from the
initial generative notion of simplicity. Originally, simplicity
was determined by counting the number of feature specifications
needed to represent lexical items or to write phonological
rules in a synchronic description (with the warning that the
grammar as a whole, rather than isolated 'pieces' of the
grammar, was to be evaluated, since a simplification in one
area could be overcompensated by increased complexity in
another). Historically, however, it was noticed early that
considerations of rule order, among others, were also important.
Kiparsky 1968 is the first to attempt to apply notions of
markedness to the ordering relationships among rules.

[3]Though it is not always clearly stated, a distinction must
be drawn between simplification in the structural description

of a rule, and simplification in the structural change. Only the former, correlated with an increase in the generality of the context where the rule applies, is usually evaluated, cf. the examples in King (1969:58-63, passim.). It is certainly not the case that changes in the structural *change* of a rule invariably lead to simplification (in formal terms), although there may be clear phonetic motivation for them. Consider an entirely typical example involving palatalization: $ki \longrightarrow kji \longrightarrow$ $\check{c}i \longrightarrow \check{s}i$, where the context ($-i$) remains constant and the progressive modifications in the structural change involve first increase and then decrease in formal complexity.

[4]This example shows that some instances of analogy can indeed be reduced to formal simplifications of the grammar. In this case the 'analogy' was no doubt facilitated by the fact that verb stems ending in consonant-liquid clusters would already contain a final [ə] even in the first person, because of a general constraint blocking CL sequences in final position (as in [uvrə], *ouvre* 'I work'). We see, then, that phonological (in this case, phonotactic) and morphological phenomena may complement each other in affecting change.

[5]It is clear that these illustrations go beyond naive questions of formal simplicity in order to consider more refined matters such as markedness and certain functional constraints. This trend toward expansion of the data considered is a healthy one. We will see, however, that in certain cases the use of markedness, naturalness, and so on is still insufficient; in particular, some of the relationships proposed between formal and functional criteria are still in need of modification.

[6]We will not consider here whether the proposed diphthongization of *a* through *ae* to *e* should also be linked to these developments. Much work remains to be done on the details of this question, and on diphthongization in general. Specifically, there may be differences in degree of naturalness between on-gliding and off-gliding diphthongs. If this is the case the present discussion will have to be modified to take this into account.

[7]These tables represent a gross oversimplification of the changes, and particularly of certain interactions with intersecting developments, but the substance of the arguments is not affected.

[8]In fact, when viewed in terms of the analysis in Schane 1968, the rules are even more unnatural. The difference between tense and lax vowels conditions diphthongization, but it is the *lax* vowels which diphthongize, contrary to expectations in terms of naturalness.

[9]When these exceptions are few, and where there is a large body of forms undergoing the rule, abstract and occasionally absolutely neutralized solutions are often proposed in order to try to recapture the original conditions.

[10]I have shown elsewhere (Walker 1974) that the analogical changes lead to considerable formal complexity in the grammar,

claims of standard generative treatments notwithstanding.   To
my knowledge, Harris 1970 is the first to raise the question
of the relationship between analogy and formal complexity in
the generative context.

[11]These are greatly oversimplified informal statements, and
the facts require that several overlapping inverted rules refer
to the same basic vowel, with varying derived forms resulting.
Consider the following alternations: *wa-i, froid-frigide,
doigt-digital; wa-ɔ, gloire-glorieux, victoire-victorieux;
wa-e, croit-crédibilité; wa-ü, boit-buvons,* and so on.   In
each case, the diphthong can be justified as basic to the
underlying representation on morphological grounds.

[12]I ignore as irrelevant to this particular discussion the
huge literature that has sprung up on questions of ordering in
general, particularly the claim that all ordering relationships
are to be predicted on the basis of universal principles.

[13]One could question *prima facie* this claim, since it is
certainly the case that many other linguistic changes complicate
paradigms. One would therefore have to show that rule
re-ordering is essentially different in this respect from other
possible changes. As the examples discussed below will
indicate, however, re-ordering may also contribute to the
complication of the paradigm.

[14]The formal details of this rule, while complicated and
interesting, do not concern us here.

[15]Full justification of these claims cannot be given here.
It forms part of a larger study, now under way, of the
ramifications of epenthesis in Old French phonology.

REFERENCES

Bunge, M. 1967. Scientific research I, the search for system.
   New York: Springer Verlag.
Chen, M. 1972. The time dimension: contribution toward a
   theory of sound change. Foundations of Language 8.457-98.
   _____. 1973. On the formal expression of natural rules in
   phonology. Journal of Linguistics. 9.223-49.
Fouché, P. 1967. Morphologie historique du français. Le verbe.
   Paris: Klincksieck.
Harris, J. 1969. Spanish Phonology. Cambridge, Massachusetts:
   MIT Press.
   _____. 1970. Paradigmatic regularity and the naturalness of
   grammars. Paper presented at the Winter 1970 LSA meeting.
King, R. 1969. Historical linguistics and generative grammar.
   Englewood Cliffs: Prentice Hall.
   _____. 1973. Rule insertion. Language 49.551-78.
Kiparsky, P. 1965. Phonological change. Cambridge, Massachu-
   setts: M.I.T. dissertation.

_____. 1968. Linguistic universals and linguistic change. Universals in linguistic theory, ed. by Bach, E. and R. Harms, 170-202. New York: Holt, Rinehart and Winston.

Pope, M. 1934. From Latin to Modern French. Manchester: Manchester Univ. Press.

Saltarelli, M. 1970. A phonology of Italian in a generative grammar. The Hague: Mouton.

Schane, S. 1968. French pnonology and morphology. Cambridge, Massachusetts: MIT Press.

_____. 1972. Natural rules in phonology. Linguistic change and generative theory, ed. by Stockwell, R. and R. Macaulay, 199-229. Bloomington: Indiana University Press.

_____. 1973a. The formalization of exceptions in phonology. The formal analysis of natural languages, ed. by Gross, M., M. Halle, and M. Schutzenberger, 63-70. The Hague: Mouton.

_____. 1973b. Sur le degré d'abstraction de la phonologie du français. Langages 32.27-38.

Vennemann, T. 1972. Rule inversion. Lingua 29.209-42.

Walker, D. 1974. Analogy, simplification, and the history of French. Canadian Journal of Linguistics 19.67-78.

ON COMPLEXITY AND EXPLANATIONS IN LINGUISTIC CHANGE*

BEBAN CHUMBOW

Indiana University

1. Introduction

Studies in diachronic linguistics within the generative
perspective in the last decade (since Kiparksy 1965) have been
especially interested in characterizing possible modes of
linguistic change and their implication for the theory of
language in general. In particular, evidence has been produced
to hypothesize that languages may change by one of the following
processes: rule simplification, rule addition, rule loss, rule
insertion (?), and rule reordering.
   Although there is considerable evidence in the literature
of rules becoming formally more complex at different stages,
rule complication has until recently been considered erratic,
exceptional, 'crazy' and even unnatural.[1] In a word, rule
complication is not considered a *bona fide* mode of linguistic
change. This is so apparently because it lacks a consistent
explanation within the theory. In fact, on the surface, the
existence of both rule simplification and rule complication
would presumably constitute a violation of a fundamental
requirement of scientific description: consistency.

Consistency indeed demands that explicit or implicit claims of a theory should not be in contradiction with each other. If there is contradiction, any statements directly or indirectly derived by inference from them are arbitrary or contingent. Thus, if rule complication is considered contingent, i.e. arbitrary or accidental, it is precisely because with respect to the relatively uncontroversial and statistically more important process of rule simplification, rule complication makes the contradictory claim that languages evolve in the direction of decreasing generality. Thus, it seems intuitively aberrant to consider rule complication as a systematic characteristic of natural language.

If, however, rule complication is not erratic, as recent research (Kiparsky 1971, Harris 1974) suggests, the apparent inconsistency must be resolved. One solution to this problem within the current generative theory is to provide a non-ad hoc characterization of both rule simplification and rule complication; a characterization that defines which rules may simplify and which may complicate and explains why they do so.

In this paper, evidence is discussed leading to an explanatory hypothesis for rule complication. A study of the little-known mechanism of rule complication with respect to the better-known mechanism of rule simplification shows that both modes of change are similar in certain significant respects: they follow from independently motivated formal and substantive assumptions about the form and nature of natural language. In section 2, rule simplification and rule complication are discussed. In section 3, it is shown that a previous attempt to characterize complication in terms of rule-loss (Dinnsen 1974) is falsifiable on theoretical and empirical grounds. In section 4 the basis for a *rule complication hypothesis* is discussed, and empirical evidence in support of the hypothesis is provided in section 5. In conclusion, the implications of this research for linguistic theory are discussed.

2.   Rule simplification and rule complication

2.1.   Rule simplification

Rule simplification is traditionally associated with the empirical observation that a rule at stage I of a language is essentially retained at a later stage II, such that the form of the rule in stage II is relatively simpler than in stage I. The relative simplicity in the form of rules is measured in terms of a simplicity metrics whose parameter is the number of symbols, i.e. segment features, braces, parentheses and other relevant hypothetical constructs (Chomsky and Halle 1968, Halle 1964). Two types of processes are generally associated with rule simplification: (1) rule simplification by feature loss and (2) rule simplification by rule generalization. The first is adequately illustrated by the change in the Old English Terminal Devoicing rule:

(1)   Rl   Early Old English Terminal Devoicing

$$\begin{bmatrix} +\text{obstruent} \\ +\text{continuant} \end{bmatrix} \longrightarrow [-\text{voice}]/\underline{\qquad}\#$$

R2   Late Old English Terminal Devoicing

$$[+\text{obstruent}] \longrightarrow [-\text{voice}]/\underline{\qquad}\#$$

On the surface, the change involves a loss of a feature in the innovative stage R2 and thus constitutes a simplification.

The second type of simplification is 'rule generalization' resulting from the conflation of two partially identical rules as illustrated by the following example from Bach and Harms 1968 and 1972.

A Front-Vowel Raising rule R3 was presumably added to the grammar of Old High German (circa 8th Century), and by the Middle High German period (stage III), it was generalized to R5:

(2) Stage I: Old High German Front Vowel Raising

$$R3 \quad \begin{bmatrix} +\text{voc} \\ +\text{low} \end{bmatrix} \longrightarrow \begin{bmatrix} -\text{low} \\ -\text{back} \end{bmatrix} / \underline{\qquad} \begin{bmatrix} +\text{high} \\ -\text{back} \\ -\text{cons} \end{bmatrix} \quad \text{or} \quad \begin{matrix} a \longrightarrow e/\underline{\qquad}i \\ ai \longrightarrow ei \end{matrix}$$

Stage II: Back Vowel Raising

$$\begin{bmatrix} +\text{voc} \\ +\text{low} \end{bmatrix} \longrightarrow \begin{bmatrix} -\text{low} \\ +\text{back} \end{bmatrix} / \underline{\qquad} \begin{bmatrix} +\text{high} \\ +\text{back} \\ -\text{cons} \end{bmatrix} \quad \text{or} \quad \begin{matrix} a \longrightarrow o/\underline{\qquad}u \\ au \longrightarrow ou \end{matrix}$$

Stage III: Middle High German (General) Raising

$$R5 \quad \begin{bmatrix} +\text{voc} \\ +\text{low} \end{bmatrix} \longrightarrow \begin{bmatrix} -\text{low} \\ \alpha\text{back} \end{bmatrix} / \underline{\qquad} \begin{bmatrix} +\text{high} \\ \alpha\text{back} \\ -\text{cons} \end{bmatrix} \quad \text{or} \quad \begin{matrix} a \longrightarrow \begin{Bmatrix} e/\underline{\quad}i \\ o/\underline{\quad}u \end{Bmatrix} \\ \begin{bmatrix} ai \\ au \end{bmatrix} \longrightarrow \begin{bmatrix} ei \\ ou \end{bmatrix} \end{matrix}$$

Rule 5 constitutes a generalization of the raising process initiated by R3 in that in R3, a is raised only under the influence of a high front vowel whereas in R5, it is raised under the influence of both front and back high vowels. The standard interpretation for generalizations like R5 is that a conflatable rule R4 was added at the intermediary stage II, similar enough to an existing rule R3 to be conflated (by use of variables).[2] Note that the two processes of rule simplification result in increased generality for the innovative stage. In the case of Old English terminal devoicing, R2 is not only formally simpler than R1, it is also general since devoicing in R1 affects only fricatives whereas devoicing in R2 affects all obstruents. It is therefore generally agreed that the effect of simplification seems always to be the application of the rule to a wider range of environments in the later stage. Thus rule simplification claims that languages evolve in the direction of increasing generality so that rules tend to become less restricted (i.e. more general) at a later stage.

Dinnsen 1974 has correctly pointed out that the
characterization of rule simplification in terms of two
distinct mechanisms of change--in terms of feature loss and by
addition of a conflatable rule--is unmotivated. Indeed, such
a distinction postulates empirical differences where none can
be justified. He thus suggests that all cases of rule
simplification be accounted for by the second mechanism
involving the addition of a conflatable (transitional)
'complement rule'. A complement rule is defined to operate on
some complementary set of segments or environments. The
ultimate conflation of complement rules, by means of appropriate
notations, necessarily derives a simpler, more general rule.
In the Old English example, traditionally accounted for by
feature loss, we may assume therefore that as in the German
example, R1 was generalized to R2 by the addition of an
intermediary complement rule (R') to the grammar of Old English:

(3) R1 $\begin{bmatrix} \text{+obstruent} \\ \text{+continuant} \end{bmatrix} \longrightarrow$ [-voice] /_____#

    R' $\begin{bmatrix} \text{+obstruent} \\ \text{-continuant} \end{bmatrix} \longrightarrow$ [-voice] /_____#

    R2 [+obstruent] $\longrightarrow$ [-voice] /_____#

The notion of complement rule is not an artifact set up for
convenience. Dinnsen cites empirical evidence from various
dialects of German in studies by Becker 1967, which indicate
that there are no direct changes such as from R1 to R2; there
is always a transition period corresponding to the intermediary
stage R'.[3]

2.2. Rule complication

Rule complication involves precisely the opposite effect of
simplification in that the rule needs more segments or features
in the later stage than in the earlier one. An appropriate
illustration would be a hypothetical dialect of Old English
where R2 preceded R1:

(4) Stage A: R2 [+obstruent] $\longrightarrow$ [-voice]/_____#

    Stage B: R1 $\begin{bmatrix} \text{+obstruent} \\ \text{+continuant} \end{bmatrix} \longrightarrow$ [-voice]/_____#

In stage A, all obstruents are devoiced but in the innovative
stage B, only fricatives are devoiced. A general characteristic
of rule complication from all accounts is that it reduces or
restricts the domain of the rule's application. Rule
complication therefore claims that languages evolve in the
direction of decreasing generality. Thus, rule simplification
and rule complication make contradictory claims about the
directionality of linguistic change.

2.3. Formalism, naturalness and plausibility

Chen 1972 has convincingly argued that the standard theory
evaluation metrics, based on formal considerations, does not
always reflect *naturalness* and *plausibility*. In many instances
there is absence of correlation between formalism and
naturalness, or formalism and plausibility. I will claim here
that the formal metrics of simplicity also makes wrong predictions
with respect to rule simplification and complication. In
particular, the notion of generality associated with both
changes is not consistently reflected in rule formalism as has
been generally assumed. Consider the following example:

(5)   i   u
      e,ø   o
      ε,œ   ɔ
      a   ɑ

(6)a. $\begin{bmatrix} +\text{syll} \\ +\text{high} \end{bmatrix} \longrightarrow [+\text{stress}]/\underline{\hspace{1cm}}\#$ $\{i,u\}$

   b. $\begin{bmatrix} +\text{syll} \\ +\text{mid} \end{bmatrix} \longrightarrow [+\text{stress}]/\underline{\hspace{1cm}}\#$ $\begin{Bmatrix} e,ø,o \\ ε,œ,ɔ \end{Bmatrix}$

Given a language with the vowel system in 5 and the two rules
in 6, the simplicity criteria predicts that a and b are equally
simple and equally general. However, b is clearly more general
than a but this fact is obscured by the formal evaluation
metrics. In fact, since different features may represent
varying numbers of segments, feature (or symbol) count may not
always reflect the relative simplicity or generality of two
rules.

That the formal criteria may also fail to mirror the
direction of generality in linguistic change can be illustrated
by the changes in 7 below (the rules are assumed to be formulated purely on the basis of synchronic evidence available at
each stage):

(7)a. i.   [+cont] $\longrightarrow$ [-voice]/V$\underline{\hspace{1cm}}$V
       ii. [+obst] $\longrightarrow$ [-voice]/V$\underline{\hspace{1cm}}$V

   b. i.   [+obst] $\longrightarrow$ [-voice]/$\underline{\hspace{1cm}}$#
       ii. [-cont] $\longrightarrow$ [-voice]/$\underline{\hspace{1cm}}$#

In 7a, intervocalic voicing of fricatives is generalized at a
later stage to include intervocalic voicing of stops as well.
In 7b, word-final devoicing of obstruents is later restricted
to word-final devoicing of stops. The change in 7a is in the
direction of increased generality and would qualify as rule
simplification. The change in 7b is in the direction of
decreased generality and would qualify as rule complication.
There is, however, no way of making the relevant distinction
between the two changes on formal grounds alone. This suggests
that formalism is deceptive with respect to the intuitive
significance of the notions of rule simplicity and rule

complexity in linguistic change.

It is generally acknowledged that rule simplification is statistically more frequent, i.e. more expected and more plausible than rule complication. It has been observed here, that the only stable property associated with rule simplification is the tendency towards generality. What appears to be plausible in the process of 'rule simplification' is not so much the unreliable, unpredictable formal considerations of simplicity as the direction of the change with respect to generality. Thus the question of resolving the apparent inconsistency in the existence of rule simplification and rule complication in natural language consists of explaining why some rules change in the direction of *decreasing* generality instead of increasing generality.[4] I shall henceforth use 'rule simplification' to refer to rule generalization (resulting in increased generality) and 'rule complication' to refer to rule restriction (resulting in decreased generality).[5]

3.   Rule complication and the rule-loss constraint

3.1. The rule-loss principle and complication

Equally concerned with an explanatory characterization of rule complication, Dinnsen 1974 claims that 'all putative rule generalization and rule complication are deductively derivable from the independent and necessary principles of rule addition and rule loss (respectively)'. Whereas--as observed in the preceding section--rule generalization is deductively derivable from rule addition of a complement rule, it will be argued here that all cases of rule complication cannot be derived from rule loss nor can rule loss constitute the ultimate explanation for all cases of rule complication.

Dinnsen's explanation of rule complication in terms of rule loss is based essentially on the complication of vowel nasalization in French. In Old French all vowels were nasalized before any nasal consonant, as in R9, but in Modern French vowel nasalization is more complex, as in R12, which involves decreased generality with respect to R9:

(8)   R9 $V \rightarrow [+nas] / \underline{\hspace{1cm}} \begin{bmatrix} +cons \\ +nas \end{bmatrix}$

      R12 $V \rightarrow [+nas] / \underline{\hspace{1cm}} \begin{bmatrix} +cons \\ +nas \end{bmatrix} \begin{Bmatrix} \# \\ C \end{Bmatrix}$

Between Old French and Modern French a number of rules were added to the grammar related to, or interacting with, vowel nasalization R9 in various ways. One of these was a Consonant Deletion rule R11 deleting nasal consonants word-finally before a pause or before another consonant:

(9)   R11 $[+cons] \rightarrow \emptyset / \underline{\hspace{1cm}} \begin{Bmatrix} \# \\ C \end{Bmatrix}$

To explain the complication of R9 to R12, Dinnsen observes that vowel nasalization R9, as a synchronic rule, abbreviates a number of subdomains or subrules including the following:

(10)   R9   a.   V⟶[+nas]/_____ $\begin{bmatrix} +cons \\ +nas \end{bmatrix}$ V   transparent

        b.   V⟶[+nas]/_____ $\begin{bmatrix} +cons \\ +nas \end{bmatrix}$ C   opaque

        c.   V⟶[+nas]/_____ $\begin{bmatrix} +cons \\ +nas \end{bmatrix}$ ##   opaque

The introduction of Rll renders R9 opaque in subrules b and c. Comparing Rl2 with the ancestral R9, it can be said that Rl2 is derived from R9 by loss of subrule a and a subsequent conflation of subrules b and c.

However, since the loss of R9a entails the loss of a transparent rule contrary to King's rule-loss constraint, by which only opaque rules can be lost (King 1973), Dinnsen proposes a refinement of the rule-loss constraint to account for this as well as other cases of rule loss:

A rule may be lost if and only if its defining schema is rendered opaque and the rule is transparent with respect to some forms.

This constraint is purported to be 'capable of explaining the facts of rule complication exclusively in terms of rule loss'. Thus, for instance, in the case just discussed, the introduction of Consonant Deletion Rll renders some parts of R9 (b and c) opaque, and R9a which is transparent with respect to some forms is lost.

3.2.   The insufficiency of the rule-loss constraint

In spite of its apparent intuitive appeal, the explanation of rule complication in terms of rule loss can be falsified on theoretical and empirical grounds. I shall present the arguments for the insufficiency of this explanation in order of increasing importance.

The refined rule-loss constraint, which provides the basis for the explanation of rule complication in terms of rule loss, does not follow *directly* from any known principle of language as does the original rule-loss constraint. King's proposal that only opaque rules can be lost follows directly from the independently motivated opacity condition (Kiparsky 1971), whose content is essentially that opacity adds to the cost of grammar and consequently tends to be minimized. A constraint that allows opaque rules to be lost is a natural consequence of the tendency to minimize opacity.

With the refined rule-loss constraint, although it is observed that opacity is a necessary condition for rule loss, the presence of opacity does not have an explanatory value. Why is it that in an opaque schema the transparent subrule is lost instead of the opaque subrules (which add to the cost of grammar)?[6]

The choices of subrules a, b, c to explain the complication is arbitrary, since, following the reason underlying the breaking up of R9 into subrules, the number of possible subrules that R9 abbreviates is well near infinity. In other words, it is also true that R9 abbreviates not only a, b, c but also d, e, f, and others:

(11)   R9 $V \longrightarrow [+nas] /$ ___ $\begin{bmatrix} +cons \\ +nas \end{bmatrix}$

a. $V \longrightarrow [+nas] /$ ___ $\begin{bmatrix} +cons \\ +nas \end{bmatrix}$ V   transparent

b. $V \longrightarrow [+nas] /$ ___ $\begin{bmatrix} +cons \\ +nas \end{bmatrix}$ C   opaque

c. $V \longrightarrow [+nas] /$ ___ $\begin{bmatrix} +cons \\ +nas \end{bmatrix}$ ##   opaque

d. $V \longrightarrow [+nas] /$ ___ $\begin{bmatrix} +cons \\ +nas \end{bmatrix}$ VC   transparent

e. $V \longrightarrow [+nas] /$ ___ $\begin{bmatrix} +cons \\ +nas \end{bmatrix}$ CC   opaque

f. $V \longrightarrow [+nas] /$ ___ $\begin{bmatrix} +cons \\ +nas \end{bmatrix}$ C#C opaque

.

.

.

A choice of subrules other than a, b, c would make the wrong
predictions with respect to the form of the contemporary
Nasalization rule, R12. In fact, in accordance with the rule
loss constraint, the transparent rules a and d would be lost,
followed by a conflation of the remaining opaque rules,
including e and f. This would result in a monstrous and
incorrect nasalization rule for Modern French. Although it can
be countered that d, e, f may be subsumed by a, b, c respectively,
there is, under these assumptions, nothing which prevents the
independent existence of d, e, f, etc. on the same level as
a, b, c.[7]

Furthermore, the atomization of Nasalization R9 into subrules
with each subrule reacting independently with respect to the
other rules of the grammar implicitly claims that nasalization
did not constitute a unified process in the language. This
explanation, in other words, conceives a metatheory that would
value and accept a synchronic grammar of Old French that
presented the facts of nasalization in terms of three or more
rules. Such a claim is unmotivated and contradicts the
better-motivated assumption of standard theory that rules such
as 9a, b, c have no independence of existence in the linguistic
conscience of a speaker or hearer. Just like rules abbreviated
by braces, rules like 9a, b, c are subjected to the same set
of lexical exceptions and do not undergo separate changes and
thus constitute a unified process.

In any science, the strongest argument against a claim is
to grant it all its basic assumptions and still show that,
even then, the claim is untenable. In addition to the above
theoretical arguments, there is empirical evidence, from other
cases of rule complication, which invalidates the rule-loss

constraint; even granting the refined rule-loss principle in
its integrality, all initial rules of cases of rule
complication cannot be atomized into subrules of a schema from
which the complication is derivable. Diphthongization from
Proto-Romance to Early Old French (discussed in section 5) is
an example of rule complication where the initial rule cannot
be meaningfully conceived as an aggregate of subrules.

4.   Towards an explanation for complication

In this section, it will be demonstrated that rule complication
is derivable in a way similar to rule generalization, i.e.
from independent assumptions about the form and nature of rules
of language.

Although rule simplification and complication are
distinguishable in terms of their direction with respect to
generality, the empirically based requirement of an
intermediary stage reflected by an appropriate rule must be
true for both processes, since direct changes from cases such
as Rl to R2 and vice versa are impossible without a transition.[8]
Thus, assuming the notion of transitional rule, the two
processes can be restated as follows:

(12)   Rule Simplification

a. $\begin{bmatrix} +\text{obstruent} \\ -\text{continuant} \end{bmatrix} \longrightarrow [-\text{voice}]/\underline{\quad}\#$

b. $\begin{bmatrix} +\text{obstruent} \\ +\text{continuant} \end{bmatrix} \longrightarrow [-\text{voice}]/\underline{\quad}\#$

c. $[+\text{obstruent}] \longrightarrow [-\text{voice}]/\underline{\quad}\#$

Rule Complication

d. $[+\text{obstruent}] \longrightarrow [-\text{voice}]/\underline{\quad}\#'$

e. $\begin{bmatrix} +\text{obstruent} \\ +\text{continuant} \end{bmatrix} \longrightarrow [+\text{voice}]/\underline{\quad}\#$

f. $\begin{bmatrix} +\text{obstruent} \\ -\text{continuant} \end{bmatrix} \longrightarrow [-\text{voice}]/\underline{\quad}\#$

In the above, b and e are transitional rules, but b is a
complementary rule while e a noncomplementary one. The
parallelism in both processes of linguistic change, based on
the empirical motivation provided by Baker 1967 and Labov
1965, indicates a symmetry in their mechanism of change, a
symmetry which is not devoid of empirical content.

There are in fact at least two reasons why in the case of
the generally accepted process of rule simplification we would
readily agree that the addition of b to the grammer should
naturally result in a 'restructuring' of the grammar to yield

the more general and simplified rule c. First, there is the
partial similarity (and related formal considerations) between
rules a and b, giving the latter the status of a complement
rule, which by definition is conflatable. Second, there is
the fact that the addition of b to the grammar renders a opaque,
and, assuming with Kiparsky that opacity adds to the cost of
grammar, we will expect it to be obliterated subsequently. The
conflation of a and b to c has precisely this effect.

Note that rule complication in turn results from a similar
development except that the added rule e, although related to
d, is not a complement rule. Nevertheless, f has the same
effect as c in that the 'restructuring' of d and e, yielding
f, obliterates the opacity created by the addition of e to the
grammar. This similarity of mechanism and effect in both
processes of linguistic change, previously obscured by the
general tendency to focus uniquely on formal considerations,
suggests that both simplification and complication are
desirable means of achieving a higher objective in the dynamics
of linguistic change, namely, *minimization of opacity*
(resulting from rule addition).

These observations are, of course, based on a systematic
study of cases of rule simplification and rule complication
from a variety of languages, but to illustrate the mechanism of
change involved, the examples above were chosen for their
simplicity. I will characterize rule complication, now that
the facts have been put in perspective, and then discuss some
of the empirical evidence that constitutes the basis for the
characterization.

The Rule Complication Hypothesis. Rule complication, like
rule simplification, results from rule addition. In both
processes of change, the added rule is an agent of opacity in
that it renders some rule in the language opaque. Both the
opaque rule and the agent of opacity are subsequently
'restructured', i.e. conflated, coalesced, or collapsed as the
case may be, resulting in a generalization (simplification) or a
restriction (complication). The only difference between the
two processes is that where the agent of opacity is a
complement rule, which appears to be generally the case, the
resulting restructuring yields a case of rule simplification;
but where the agent of opacity is a noncomplementary rule, the
process results in complication. Note that in the process of
restructuring, the agent of opacity loses its formal identity,
and can be said to be lost from the system (as a *sui generis*
rule) once its function is assumed by the generalized or
complicated rule.

5. Rule complication and the rule complication hypothesis

5.1. French diphthongization and nasalization

French diphthongization in its earlier development provides a
case of rule complication that not only illustrates the
mechanism of complication discussed above, but invalidates an
explanation of complication uniquely in terms of the loss of

a subrule (cf. section 3).

In Proto-Romance, ε and ɔ were lengthened to ε: and ɔ: respectively as a result of increased stress on the former in Late Latin. From all accounts (e.g. Bourciez 1930, Pope 1934, Walker 1971), the stressed vowel thus lengthened diphthongized in open syllables by the Gallo-Roman period, as witnessed by the following alternations:

(13)   R13   *Sing.*   *Plural*
              ljέf   levóns   'raise'
              krjέm   kremóns   'fear'
              fjέr   feróns   'celebrate
              trwɔ́f   trovóns   'find'
              wɔ́vr   ovróns   'work
              mwɔ́l   molóns   'grind'

In Gallo-Roman, the facts of Diphthongization are capturable by R14:

(14)   R14   Diphthongization

$$\begin{bmatrix} +voc \\ +high \\ +mid \\ \alpha back \\ +stress \end{bmatrix}_1 \longrightarrow \begin{bmatrix} -syll \\ -cons \\ \alpha back \end{bmatrix} + 1/\underline{\qquad}(C_0^1 V)$$

Insert a glide in front of a stressed ε or ɔ in open syllable, a glide which agrees with these vowels in backness, i.e. stressed ε and ɔ in open syllable diphthongize to jε and wɔ respectively.

This is a natural process and according to Schurr 1936 and Spore 1972 attested in other Romance languages as well. Subsequently, the diphthong wɔ was modified to wε, a fact which is capturable as the addition of a vowel adjustment rule to the grammar:

(15)   R15   Vowel Adjustment

$$\begin{bmatrix} +voc \\ -high \\ +mid \end{bmatrix} \longrightarrow \begin{bmatrix} -round \\ -back \end{bmatrix} / \begin{bmatrix} -syll \\ -cons \\ +back \end{bmatrix}\underline{\qquad}$$

Rule 15 is a dissimilation process with respect to backness, less plausible, perhaps, than the previous assimilatory process but presumably with an independent and plausible phonetic motivation.[9]

A synchronic observation of the facts at the Late Gallo-Roman or Early Old French period shows that there is no evidence to justify a vowel adjustment rule separable and distinguishable

from the diphthongization process. The synchronic grammar at
this period must have the facts formulated as in R16 (see
Walker 1971):

(16)   R16   Diphthongization

$$
\begin{bmatrix} +voc \\ +high \\ +mid \\ \alpha back \\ +stress \\ 1 \end{bmatrix} \longrightarrow \begin{bmatrix} -syll \\ -cons \\ \alpha back \end{bmatrix} + \begin{bmatrix} -back \\ -round \\ 1 \end{bmatrix} / \underline{\hspace{1cm}} (C_0^1 V)
$$

Stressed ɛ and ɔ in open syllable diphthongize
to *jɛ* and *wɛ* respectively.

Diphthongization R16 constitutes a case of rule complication
with respect to the ancestral Diphthongization R14. Note that
the addition of Vowel Adjustment R15 renders Diphthongization
R14 opaque. Note also that with the complication of
Diphthongization R14 to R16, R15 is no longer attested; R16
diphthongizes as well as performs the vowel readjustment
function originally performed by R15, and with R16 in the
grammar, the opacity introduced by R15 is obliterated. It
follows that some time after the introduction of R15--a
noncomplementary rule and an agent of opacity--there was a
restructuring in the nature of a grammar optimization process
which fused the functions of both rules R14 and R15, leading
to a complication, R16. Once the function of Vowel Adjustment
is assumed by Diphthongization R16, Vowel Adjustment R15 no
longer has any *raison d'être* in the system and is lost. Thus,
the introduction of opacity led to a complication of the rule
in order to minimize opacity.[10]
        Notice however, that the initial Diphthongization R14 by its
nature and form differs significantly from the Nasalization R9,
and cannot be split up in such a way as to recover the more
complex R16 from it in the manner proposed by Dinnsen. This,
and apparently complications involving rules of metathesis not
anticipated by the refined rule-loss principle, would not be
amenable to 'a rule schema explanation'.
        Let us take another look at nasalization in French. It will
be recalled that Nasalization R9 in its initial stage in Old
French was a simple process affecting all vowels preceding a
nasal consonant as exemplified in 17:

(17)   R9   V $\longrightarrow$ [+nas] / $\underline{\hspace{1cm}}$ $\begin{bmatrix} +cons \\ +nas \end{bmatrix}$

			Latin	*Old French*	*Late Mid. French*
a.	i.	unu(m)	ũn	ũ (œ̃)
	ii.	plenu(m)	plẽin,plẽn	plẽn (plẽ)
	iii.	san(i)tate(m)	sãnte	sãnte (sãte)
	iv.	bon(i)tate(m)	bõnte	bõnte (bõte)

b.	i.	una(m)	ũnə	ünə
	ii.	plena(m)	pleĩnə, plɛnə	plenə, plɛn
	iii.	femina(m)	fẽmə, fãmə	famə
	iv.	bona(m)	bõnə	bɔnə

A fact not taken into consideration in Dinnsen's analysis is
the occurrence of a denasalization process in Late Middle
French whereby nasal vowels of Old French immediately preceding
an intervocalic nasal were denasalized as evidenced by 17b.
This fact is accounted for by the addition of a Denasalization
Rule, R11 at this period:

(18)   R11   Denasalization

$$\begin{bmatrix}+\text{voc}\\+\text{nas}\end{bmatrix} \longrightarrow [-\text{nas}]/\underline{}\begin{bmatrix}+\text{cons}\\+\text{nas}\end{bmatrix}\begin{bmatrix}+\text{voc}\\-\text{cons}\end{bmatrix}$$

Note that denasalization R11 has the effect of restricting the
domain of Nasalization R9.

Evidence from Pope 1934 and Bourciez 1930 indicates that a
Final Nasal Consonant Deletion Rule was added to the grammar
and progressively incorporated into a general Final Consonant
Deletion Rule, R10:

(19)   R10   C $\longrightarrow$ Ø/$\underline{}\begin{Bmatrix}\#C\\\#\#\end{Bmatrix}$

Rule 10 deletes a consonant before another consonant with or
without intervening word-boundary or in absolute final position.
Given Middle French pronunciation from Pope 1934, the relevant
examples are derived as in 20:

(20)   Late Middle French

	a. ##bɔn##	b. ##bɔn+ə##	c. ##bɔn#ami##	d. ##bɔn#livrə##
Nas R9	#bɔ̃n##	#bɔ̃n+ə##	#bɔ̃n#ami##	#bɔ̃n#livrə##
FCD R10	#bɔ̃ ##			#bɔ̃ #livrə##
Den R11		#bɔn+ə##	#bɔn#ami#	
	[bɔ̃]	[bɔnə]	[bɔnami]	[bɔ̃livrə]

Notice that Denasalization R11 renders Nasalization R9 opaque
as in b and c, where [bɔnə] and [bɔnami] indicate that R9 is
opaque by subcase i of opacity (Kiparsky 1971) and that the
Final Consonant Deletion R10 also renders R9 opaque as in a
and d, where [bɔ̃] and [bɔ̃livrə] render Nasalization R9 opaque
by subcase ii.

By the Early Modern French period, when the variations that
gave Denasalization the status of an optional rule in Middle
French were no longer attested, and when the synchronic
evidence no longer permitted a separate rule, the facts of
nasalization are capturable by R12:

(21)   R12

$$V \longrightarrow [+nas]/\underline{\hspace{1cm}}\begin{bmatrix}+cons\\+nas\end{bmatrix}\begin{Bmatrix}\#\\ [+cons]\end{Bmatrix}$$

Let us recapitulate by recalling a number of relevant facts:

1. Nasalization R12 is a case of rule complication with respect to Nasalization R9.
2. Denasalization R11, a noncomplementary rule added to the language in Middle French, created opacity (along with R10).
3. Denasalization is no longer attested at this period as a *bona fide* rule of the grammar.[11]
4. When it was productive, Denasalization had the function of restricting the domain of Nasalization R9 by disallowing nasal vowels in certain environments where they previously occurred in Old French. It is evident that Nasalization in Early Modern French achieves precisely this effect, i.e. it nasalizes and restricts nasalization to precisely the environments predicted by both Nasalization R9 and Denasalization R11.

It follows that a restructuring passed the function of the Denasalization rule on to the Nasalization rule and the former is dropped from the grammar, since it now lacks motivation. Here again, as in the case of Diphthongization in Romance, the complication achieves a minimization of the opacity created in the Middle French period. In a study of cases from a variety of other languages (Chumbow forthcoming), complication consistently and persistently follows this pattern of development. Cases examined include Slavic Umlaut, Late Middle Korean Vowel Harmony and Icelandic 'Breaking' rules.

5.2. Phonotactically motivated cases of complication

There is another type of rule complication which appears to be in a class by itself with respect to the mechanism of change involved but also proves to be similar to the cases above. These are phonotactically motivated cases of complication, resulting from the introduction or development of surface phonotactic constraints in the grammar. This type can be exemplified by the development of Glide Formation in French.
    Before the 13th century, glide formation was a simple and general process whereby high vowels became glides when immediately followed by any high vowel, as in R19:

(22)   R19   Glide Formation (Old French)

$$\begin{bmatrix}+syll\\+high\\ \alpha F\end{bmatrix} \longrightarrow \begin{bmatrix}-syll\\ \alpha F\end{bmatrix} / \underline{\hspace{1cm}}[+syll]$$

sciait siɛ $\longrightarrow$ [sjɛ]
ouvrier uvrie $\longrightarrow$ [uvrje]

> A high vowel preceding any vowel becomes a corresponding
> glide (with respect to backness and roundness).

By the 13th Century, a constraint against Obstruent, Liquid
and Glide (OLG) clusters emerged in the system, as a result of
the interaction of forces irrelevant to our analysis (discussed)
in some detail in Morin 1974 and also in Chumbow forthcoming).
In Modern French, glide formation must be constrained to avoid
having glides after OL clusters as shown by the differences in
the alternations in 23a and 23b:

(23)   a.   scie [si]   sciait [sjɛ]
            sue [sy]   suait [sɥɛ]
            noue [nu]   nouait [nwɛ]
            monter [mɔ̃te]   montions [mɔ̃tjɔ̃]

       b.   trie [tri]   triait [trijɛ]
            flue [fly]   fluait [flyɥɛ]
            troue [tru]   trouait [truʷɛ]
            montrer [mɔ̃tre] montrions [mɔ̃trijɔ̃]

R22   Glide Formation (Modern French)

$$\begin{bmatrix} +syll \\ +high \\ \alpha F \end{bmatrix} \longrightarrow \begin{bmatrix} -syll \\ \alpha F \end{bmatrix} / \underline{\quad}[+syll] \sim /OL\underline{\quad}$$

A high vowel preceding any vowel becomes a glide,
except after sequences of Obstruent and Liquid.

Rule 22 constitutes a complication with respect to the
ancestral Glide Formation R19, but what is the mode of
complication involved?   It has been claimed in section 4 that
all modifications of rules in the form of generalization or
restrictions are effected not by some abstract loss or addition
of features but by rule addition.   Is this true for
phonotactically motivated cases of complication, or do they
constitute an exception?
     Morin 1974 has shown that phonotactic constraints behave
like rules in that they may be added to the grammar, create
opacity like any rule, and motivate rules which are
subjected to the same set of lexical exceptions.   On this basis,
the complication of Glide Formation in French may be viewed as
a direct result of the addition of the OLG constraint.   The
constraint renders R19 opaque, forcing it to become complicated
in order to minimize opacity and also in order to be consistent
with the demands of the constraint.   If these are all the facts,
then we are led to the conclusion that the mechanism of
complication for phonotactically motivated instances of
complication is different from that of other cases.   Here, the
opaque rule complicates by simply incorporating an appropriate
portion of the phonotactic constraint as a restriction.
     Morin notes, however, that once OLG clusters were set up as
a constraint, various changes occurred apparently geared towards

modifying them. Two of these changes are exemplified in 24
(Note that the traditional Glide Vocalization is actually a
surface reflex of a transitional Glide Insertion rule).

(24)   Glide Vocalization   OLG⟶OLV   uvrje--⟩ uvrije
       Loss of Glide   OLG⟶OLØ (OL) brjɛf--⟩ brɛf

R21   Glide Insertion

$$\emptyset \longrightarrow \begin{bmatrix} -syll \\ -cons \end{bmatrix} / OL \begin{bmatrix} +syll \\ +high \end{bmatrix} \underline{\quad\quad}$$

The addition of R21, a noncomplementary rule, renders R19
opaque, and the subsequent complication of R19 to R22
eliminates the opacity.
    This would suggest that the added constraint does not
occasion complication directly but motivates a rule which,
being a noncomplementary rule and an agent of opacity, triggers
the complication as predicted by the rule complication
hypothesis. However, the scarcity of phonotactically motivated
cases of rule complication and the paucity of descriptive
information on the two cases available (i.e. French Glide
Formation and French Cluster-schwa Deletion), make a definite
characterization of the mechanism of change involved premature.
The latter characterization, consistent with the mechanism
outlined earlier, would be more plausible, but only a discovery
of more such cases and further study would clarify the
situation.[12] Whatever the specific modality of change may be
in this as well as in all the other cases examined, rule
complication is consistently geared towards minimization of
opacity.

5.3. Formal complexity and rule generalization

In section 2, it was observed that the formal evaluation
metric makes wrong predictions with respect to rule
simplification and rule complication. On the basis of those
observations, some rules, considered cases of rule complication
in the literature on the basis of their relative formal
complexity alone, turn out to be defensible cases of rule
generalization.
    Consider for instance the complication of Diphthongization
in Chicano Spanish discussed by Harris 1974:

(25)   R24   Diphthongization (Standard Spanish)

$$\begin{bmatrix} e \\ o \end{bmatrix} \longrightarrow \begin{bmatrix} je \\ we \end{bmatrix} / \underline{\quad\quad}_{[+stress]} \qquad \text{(minor rule)}$$

Stressed *e* and *o* diphthongize to *je* and *we*
respectively.

R25
$$o \longrightarrow we/\ldots \left[\begin{bmatrix} X[+back]C_o \\ 1 \text{ conj} \end{bmatrix}_{stem}\right]_{verb}$$

o (stressed or unstressed) in a first conjugation stem diphthongizes to *we*.

R26   Diphthongization (Chicano Spanish)

$$\begin{bmatrix} e \\ o \end{bmatrix} \longrightarrow \begin{bmatrix} je \\ we \end{bmatrix} / \left\{ \begin{array}{l} \overline{[+stress]} \\ \left[X \; [+back]C_o \atop 1 \text{ conj} \right]_{stem} \end{array}\right]_{verb} \right\} \begin{array}{l} \text{(a)} \\ \\ \text{(b)} \end{array} \text{ minor rule}$$

e and *o* diphthongize if (a) they are stressed and (b) if *o* is a first conjugation verb stem.

Rule 24, diphthongization in Standard Spanish, is a simple phonological rule affecting stressed *e* and *o*. In Chicano Spanish, stressed *e* and *o* as well as any *o* in first conjugation stems are diphthongized. Rule 26 is a morphologized rule, formally more complex than the ancestral R24. In light of our knowledge of the mechanism of rule change, R26 presupposes the addition of a rule like R25. A subsequent restructuring collapses R24 and R25, yielding R26.

Note that although R26 is formally more complex than its ancestor R24, it is more general in that the domain of diphthongization now stretches beyond stressed *e* and *o*. Note also that the added R25 is a complement rule and its addition naturally results in rule generalization. Rule 26 is therefore a *bona fide* case of rule generalization, for the mechanism by which it is derived and its effect in the system are characteristic properties of rule generalization. This again indicates clearly that the formal evaluation criterion is deceptive. Since *increased generality*, a characteristic of rule simplification, is a plausible condition in linguistic change, we can now understand why morphologized rules like Chicano Diphthongization and Latin Rhotacism (Kiparsky 1971) do occur; they are plausible or natural processes although they occur only under special conditions.

Both Kiparsky 1971 and Harris 1974 observed that these rules are paralleled by a concomitant compensation in paradigm regularity. They therefore conclude that the relative formal complexity of rules like R26 can be explained by the *Principle of Paradigm Regularity,* namely that 'allomorphy tends to be minimized in paradigms' (Kiparsky 1971). I have claimed that the complexity of this type of rule follows from an independent assumption about the nature and form of rules of language: the empirically well-motivated assumption that partially identical rules ('complement rules') constitute a unit and are therefore conflatable or collapsible.[13]

Note that R24 and R25, functioning separately, have the effect of regularizing paradigms. They do not need to be merged in order to produce this effect in the system, but it is necessary for R25 to be added in order to produce it. This shows that the Paradigm Principle is relevant not as an explanation for the formal complication of R26 but specifically as an explanation for the addition of R25 to the grammar. In other words, R25 is added to the grammar with a particular function (minimization of allomorphy), but because it happens to be a complement rule, generalization must take place and the specific function of R25 is carried over into the more generalized R26.

6. Conclusion

In this paper, evidence was provided for the rule complication hypothesis, which defines what rules may be complicated and explains why they become complicated. Only rules in an opacity relation may complicate and they do so in order to minimize opacity. The mechanism of complication is generally as follows: A noncomplementary rule, y is added to the grammar. Rule y renders another rule of the grammar x opaque. A subsequent restructuring merges x and y yielding $x + y$. Then y is lost as a rule, but its function is assumed by the complicated rule $x + y$. Rule $x + y$ is a complication with respect to the ancestral rule x but the opacity introduced by the addition of y to the grammar is obliterated. Rule complication is therefore compatible with the Opacity Principle (Kiparsky 1971). There is no incompatibility in the existence in natural language of both processes of rule simplification and complication since they are each predictable: the former from the addition of a complement rule and the latter from the addition of a noncomplementary rule that is at the same time the agent of opacity. Another point made in this paper is that all changes in the form of a rule in a diachronic process, i.e. all simplifications and complications, are effected by rule addition. In other words, the loss or addition of features or segments of traditional descriptions in generative historical linguistics are actually surface observations of the effect of rules incorporated into the grammar adding or deleting features or segments.

This paper has also contributed to the position that formal considerations of simplicity cannot carry the burden of explanations in phonology, for certain phenomena can be adequately explained only by recourse to substantive principles that characterize natural language and override formal considerations (Kiparsky 1971). In particular, it was observed that the formal criteria cannot consistently distinguish between rule simplification and rule complication, and that the substantive principle of *Increased Generality* was most relevant to this distinction. Some cases of formal complication are shown to be in reality instances of rule simplification. Finally, it follows from the study, that all empirically defensible cases of rule complication are compensated for by an increased optimization in the grammar, in that opacity, which adds to the cost of grammer, is minimized.

NOTES

*I am grateful to Daniel Dinnsen, Albert Valdman, Fred Householder, Sam Rosenberg and Ashley Hastings for their valuable comments on this paper.

[1] See, for instance, Darden 1970, Walker 1971, Bach and Harms 1972, and Chumbow 1973, among others.

[2] Bach and Harms have correctly observed (as evident in the change from R3 to R5) that variable coefficients (α, β, etc.) should be valued simpler than a + or - coefficient since the variable reflects greater generality.

[3] Support for this position also comes from language variation. Often two varieties of a language, a standard (or a conservative form), and a nonstandard (or an innovative form) coexist at a certain point in time. Thereafter, the standard form gives way to the nonstandard form or to a reanalyzed form that incorporates the innovative form (Labov 1965 and 1972). This empirical evidence reflects Dinnsen's observation that the complement rule exists first as an optional rule in a transition period before conflation.

[4] Increased or decreased generality involves reference to increased or decreased number of natural classes or members of natural classes (i.e. segments). Since it has been argued that increased generality is a measure of plausibility, it follows that changes involving natural or more plausible processes (assimilation, preferred syllable structure, maximum differentiation, Schane 1972), would be more general than changes involving less natural processes.

[5] On this basis, some putative cases of rule complication would be shown (in section 5.3) to be in reality instances of rule generalization.

[6] Actually, some transparent rules (not subrules) do get lost (see sections 4 and 5), and King's rule-loss principle stands to be modified on empirical grounds. For further discussion, see Chumbow forthcoming where the modified rule-loss principle is motivated and shown to follow directly from the *opacity condition*.

[7] To eliminate the possibility of considering subrules d, e, f, an additional convention which allows some subrules to be subsumed by others would be required. There is no independent motivation for such a convention. Besides, this in turn raises the question of what convention would appropriately allow all and only the relevant subrules to be subsumed in all possible cases of rule complication.

[8] The evidence in note 4 is equally valid here. Language being a rule-governed system, only the assumption that features, segments, etc. are added or lost from a rule by the addition to the grammar of another rule, which carries out these

additions of features or segments, has any appeal with respect
to psychological reality. Besides, what is the basis for
assuming linguistic change by feature loss or feature addition?
By what mechanism are these features or segments added or lost,
and what is the psychological reality of such a mechanism?

[9]Presumably the principle of maximum differentiation
(Martinet 1955, Schane 1972) is the motivation for the
dissimilation.

[10]The Diphthongization rule later undergoes a series of
changes apparently involving the interaction of simplification
and complication with other processes.

[11]In spite of apparent exceptions to Nasalization, there is a
general consensus that there is no Denasalization rule in
Modern French. Schane 1968 considers the exceptions as
idiosyncracies, Dell 1971 accounts for them by local ordering,
and Hanzeli 1970 accounts for them by readjustment rules.
Even those who have attempted to motivate a Denasalization rule
for Modern French (Schutt 1973) agree that it is unrelated to
the Denasalization rule of Middle French.

[12]In a theory of phonology with a level of phonotactics at
which Surface Constraints may be presented, rules like the
French Glide Formation would not be cases of rule complication.

[13]For more on alleged cases of rule complication that turn
out to be cases of rule generalization, see Chumbow forthcoming.

REFERENCES

Bach, E. 1968. Two proposals concerning the simplicity metrics
    in phonology. Glossa 2,2.128-49.
Bach, E. and R. Harms. 1972. How do languages get crazy rules?
    In Stockwell and Macauley, 1972.
Becker, D. 1967. Generative phonology and dialect studies:
    an investigation of three Modern German dialects. Houston:
    University of Texas doctoral dissertation.
Bourciez, E. 1930. Précis historique de phonétique française.
    Paris: Klincksieck.
Chen, M. 1972. On the formal expression of natural rules in
    phonology. Journal of Linguistics 9,2.
Chomsky, N. and M. Halle. 1968. The sound pattern of English.
    New York: Harper and Row.
Chumbow, B. 1973. Cameroon Pidgin English and the role of
    simplification and restructuring in pidginization and
    creolization. Paper presented at the 4th annual conference
    on African Linguistics, Queen's College, Flushing, New York.
Chumbow, B. Forthcoming. A case for rule complication.
    Bloomington: Indiana University doctoral dissertation.

Darden, B.   1970.   The fronting of vowels after palatals in
    Slavic.   Papers from the Sixth Meeting of the Chicago
    Linguistic Society, 459-70.
Dell, F.   1971.   Les règles phonologiques tardives et la
    morphologie dérivationnelle du français.   Cambridge,
    Mass.:   M.I.T. dissertation.
Dingwall, W.   1971.   A survey of linguistic science.   University
    of Maryland Linguistic Program.
Dinnsen, D.   1974.   The non-complexity of linguistic change.
    Papers presented at the Summer Meeting of the Linguistic
    Society of America.
Goldin, M. et al.   1974.   Linguistic studies in Romance
    languages.   Washington, D.C.:   Georgetown University Press.
Halle, M.   1964.   Phonology in generative grammar.   In: Katz,
    J. and J. Fodor, 1964.
Hanzeli, V.   1970.   Readjustment rules in French morphophonology.
    Unpublished manuscript.
Harris, J.   1974.   Morphologization of phonological rules: an
    example from Chicano Spanish.   In: Goldin, M. et al., 1974.
Katz, J. and J. Fodor.   1964.   The structure of language:
    readings in the philosophy of science.   Englewood Cliffs:
    Prentice Hall.
Kiparsky, P.   1965.   Phonological change.   Cambridge, Mass.:
    M.I.T. dissertation.
_____.   1971.   Historical linguistics.   In: Dingwall,1971:
    577-649.
Labov, W.   1965.   On the mechanism of linguistic change.   In:
    Report of the 10th annual round table conference.   Washington,
    D.C.:   Georgetown University Press.
_____.   1972.   The internal evolution of linguistic rules.
    In: Stockwell and Macauley, 1972.
Martinet, A.   1955.   Économie des changements phonétiques.
    Berne: Francke.
Morin, Y.-Ch.   1974.   Phonological tensions in French.   Paper
    presented at the Texas Symposium on Romance Linguistics,
    Austin, Texas.
Pope, M.   1934.   From Latin to French.   Manchester: University
    of Manchester Press.
Schane, S.   1968.   French phonology and morphology.   Cambridge,
    Mass.:   MIT Press.
_____.   1972.   Natural rules in phonology.   In: Stockwell and
    Macauley, 1972.
Schurr, F.   1936.   La diphtongaison romane.   Tübingen.
Spore, P. 1972.   La diphtongaison romane.   Odense University
    Press.
Stockwell, R. and J. Macauley.   1972.   Historical linguistics
    in the perspective of generative grammar.   Bloomington:
    Indiana University Press.
Walker, D.   1971.   Old French phonology and morphology.   San
    Diego: University of California dissertation.

RHOTACISM IN LATIN: PHONOLOGICAL OR MORPHOLOGICAL RULE?

JURGEN KLAUSENBURGER

University of Washington

Generative phonology of the last decade has made no distinction
between rules that are purely phonetically conditioned and
those that are phonetically arbitrary or unconditioned. The
attempt to couch unconditioned alternations in 'phonological'
rules led to synchronically abstract formulations, such rules
often showing a propensity for diachronic recapitulation. Most
recent work, however, is more and more distancing itself from
phonological abstractness. The natural consequence has been
the addition of a morphological component to the emerging
model (cf. Matthews 1974):

Model of the 60's	*Model of the 70's*
A. Syntax	A. Syntax
	B. Morphology
	1. Inflectional sub-component
B. Phonology	2. Derivational sub-component
	(via-rules)
	C. Phonology

205

Phonological rules in the new model must meet strict criteria
of phonetic motivation and plausibility (Matthews 1973:73).
If these factors are not met by a particular rule, it must be
assigned to the morphology. It is clear that this dichotomy
is valid since it reflects the speaker's handling and
understanding of two distinct types of linguistic regularity.
An additional division seems to be necessary within morphology
between the inflectional and derivational subcomponents.
Vennemann 1972a has suggested the term *via-rule* to account for
derivational alternations including so-called learned words.
Examples from English illustrating the three-way split proposed
would be:

a. Inflectional morphology: a rule accounting for *take/took;*
b. Derivational morphology: a rule accounting for
                                    divine/divinity;
c. Phonology: a rule accounting for the plural in
                                    cats/dogs/roses.

In a number of recent studies, rules that appear to be hybrids
combining both phonological and morphological characteristics
have been discussed. The process of 'morphologization' is
attributed to Chicano diphthongization in Harris (1974:19) to
account for a paradigm such as *vuelar* 'to fly', which, contrary
to Standard Spanish, exhibits the diphthong *ue* in unstressed
position:

$$\begin{bmatrix} e \\ o \end{bmatrix} \longrightarrow \begin{bmatrix} ye \\ we \end{bmatrix} / \left\{ \begin{array}{l} \overline{[+stress]} \\[1ex] \left[\ldots \left[X \begin{array}{c} \overline{[+back]} \\ 1 \text{ conj} \end{array} C_o \right]_{Stem} \cdots \right]_{Verb} \end{array} \right\} \begin{array}{l} \text{(a)} \\ \text{minor} \\ \text{(b)} \text{rule} \end{array}$$

This rule expresses a grammatical conditioning ('1 conj verb')
for the back vowel *o*, since the phonetic condition (stress)
would not suffice in a verb like *vuelar*. A special kind of
morphologized rule may be seen in rule inversion, a category
introduced and amply documented by Vennemann 1972a. Excellent
examples of inversions are hiatus rules, one of which is needed
in the English alternations of the indefinite article *a/an.*
Vennemann (1972a:212-6) shows that the synchronic rule is

a$\longrightarrow$an/____V,

the inverted form of the historical development

an$\longrightarrow$a/____C.

The formulation given does not make the morphological aspect of
the inversion obvious. In fact, it looks like a perfectly
motivated phonological rule. However, the *n*-insertion
illustrated is restricted to the indefinite article, thus
grammatically conditioned. In Klausenburger (1974a:169) I
demonstrate that the synchronic rule of liaison in Modern French
also constitutes rule inversion,

$\emptyset \longrightarrow$C/____V,G,

consonant epenthesis, which inverts the historical deletion

$C \longrightarrow \emptyset /$ ____ $C, \#$.

Again, morphological information, which specifies which
morphemes in French take on liaison, will have to be added as
part of a complete description. Let me now present and analyze
a rule which uniquely fits into this complex of morphological,
morphologized, and phonological factors, Latin rhotacism.

During the 4th century B.C. the rule $s \longrightarrow r / V$ ____ V was added to
the grammar of Latin (Sommer 1948:190; Anttila 1972:59-60).
The effects of this change on the morphological system of Latin
were extensive, ranging from the infinitive (*amase$\longrightarrow$amare
'love'), finite forms like *esam$\longrightarrow$eram 'I was', *eso$\longrightarrow$ero 'I
will be', to declensional roots (*corposis-->corporis 'body'
gen.sg.) and suffixes (*-asom$\longrightarrow$arum fem.pl.). In Classical
Latin, a synchronic rule of rhotacism seems to be reflected in
verbal alternations like ger+ere/ges+tum 'carry' (inf./past
part.) and nominal alternations like corpus/corpor+is 'body'
(nom.sg./gen.sg.) (Matthews 1973/72). The verbal examples,
however, are clearly too restricted to serve as good evidence.[1]
Therefore, the segment of Classical Latin morphology containing
'live' rhotacizing alternations remains the 3rd declension of
nouns. The following data (of nom./gen.sg.) are presented in
three chronological layers, the first two attempting to
reconstruct the history leading up to the classical attestations:

A.   Pre-rhotacism

(1)
amos, amosis 'love'
pavos, pavosis 'fear'
honos, honosis 'honor'
labos, labosis 'work'

(2)
genus, genesis 'kind'
corpus, corposis 'body'
cinis, cinesis 'ashes'
tellus, tellusis 'earth'

(3)
flos, flosis, 'flower'
os, osis 'mouth'
ius, iusis 'law'
ros, rosis 'dew'

B.   Post-rhotacism

(1)	(2)	(3)
amos, amoris	genus, generis	flos, floris
pavos, pavoris	corpus, corporis	os, oris
honos, honoris	cinis, cineris	ius, iuris
labos, laboris	tellus, telluris	ros, roris

C. Classical Latin

(1)	(2)	(3)
amor, amoris	genus, generis	flos, floris
pavor, pavoris	corpus, corporis	os, oris
honor, honoris	cinis, cineris	ius, iuris
labor, laboris	tellus, telluris	ros, roris

Stage A illustrates paradigm uniformity in *s*, Stage B shows the
exceptionless application of rhotacism producing the alternation
s/r. Classical Latin synchrony represents the most interesting
stage, a coexistence of paradigm uniformity in 1 (in *r*) with
the alternation *s/r* in 2 and 3. Type 1 includes approximately
120 nouns of abstract nature, all of which had leveled out to
r by Classical Latin, although some are also attested with
their etymological *s* in the nom.sg. (Quellet 1969:58-61).
This leveling has been explained by Saussure (1967:221-6)
as proportional analogy to agentive nouns like *orator, oratoris*
'speaker', which contain etymological *r*. What makes the
Classical Latin situation interesting is not the leveling in 1
by itself, however, but the coexistence of 1 with 2 and 3,
bringing up the crucial question of our analysis: What rule
accounts for the *s/r* alternation in 2 and 3?

Two solutions may be offered. The first solution posits a
phonological rule, $s \rightarrow r/V\_\_\_V$, the synchronic copy of the
historical addition, for alternations 2 and 3, and the
morphological rule $s \rightarrow r/$(nom.sg.) for cases in 1. In such an
analysis, historical *s* remains underlying in Classical Latin:
if it underlies in 2 and 3 it also does so in 1, even though 1
by itself does not motivate *s* at all--hence the morphologization
of $s \rightarrow r$. A second solution considers the leveling in 1 as
decisive, thus positing restructuring with no rule for 1; as a
consequence, the remaining alternation in 2 and 3 will be
described as a rule inversion, $r \rightarrow s/$(nom.sg.). I believe
that the second solution is to be preferred and shall explain
the reasons for the choice.[2]

The leveling in 1 in the direction of *r* constitutes the most
important support in favor of rule inversion for 2 and 3.
Paradigm uniformity could have been achieved with a
pre-rhotacized *s*, in which case the phonological rule
$s \rightarrow r/V\_\_\_V$ would be motivated synchronically. Given the
restructured *r* in 1, we may, in fact, be justified in inserting
an additional stage in the development of rhotacism between B
and C, a phase B', where all alternations were accounted for by
rule inversion:

Stage A:	s ... s	Pre-rhotacism	
Stage B:	s ... r	Post-rhotacism	
Stage B':	r ... s	(a) restructuring,	(b) rule inversion
Stage C: a.	r ... s	(a) restructuring,	(b) rule inversion
b.	r ... r	(a) restructuring,	(b) loss of inverted rule
Stage D:	r ... r	(a) restructuring,	(b) loss of inverted rule

The scheme presented also suggests a Stage D where no trace of even the inversion remains, where r would be totally regularized. Although this outcome seems to be inevitable, it was never reached in Classical Latin, since the monosyllabic nouns of 3 showed unbending resistance.[3] The example *honŏr* may be used to illustrate the five steps given more concretely:

Stage A:	honōs, honŏsis	(no rule)
Stage B:	honōs, honōris	Rule: s→ r/V___V
Stage B':	honōs, honōris	Rule: r→ s/(nom.sg.)
Stage C:	a. honōs, honōris	Rule: r→ s/(nom.sg.)
	b. honŏr, honōris	(no rule)
Stage D:	honŏr, honōris	(no rule)

In addition to the *s/r* alternation, which occurs in B, B' and Ca, the example cited (and most of the other nouns involved, although this is not marked in the data) also contains a vocalic alternation *ō/ŏ*, which appears in complementary distribution with *s/r*, in A, Cb and D.[4]

As made explicit in the above diagram, the crucial point in the proposed solution consists of motivating the change from Stage B to Stage B', from a purely phonetically conditioned rule of rhotacism to the morphologized inversion. Morphological analogy in group 1 nouns has already been mentioned and may be said to constitute its external motivation. It is possible to discover what may be termed an internal motivation with the concept of rule opacity.

In a slight modification of his original (1971) definition of opacity, Kiparsky (1973:22) considers a rule P, A---B/C___D, opaque 'to the extent that there are phonetic forms in the language having either (1) A in environment C__D, or (2a) B derived by P in environment other than C__D, and (2b) B not derived by P (i.e., underlying or derived by another process) in environment C__D'. By this definition, rhotacism is doubly opaque, opaque (1) due to the existence of *causa* 'cause', *rosa* 'rose', *asinus* 'donkey', etc., and opaque (2b), since r must be counted among the underlying segments of Latin (cf. *fero* 'I carry'). According to Schindler (1974:2), opaque (2b) rules lead to restructured paradigm leveling. This is exactly what happened in Latin nouns of the type *honŏr*. It is important to stress that both paradigm leveling *and* restructuring to *r* occurred. Of course, the actual leveling was due to a rule loss. But, as has already been pointed out, the loss of rhotacism could have led to two paradigm levelings, either *s...s* or *r...r*. The fact that the second took place is due to the opaque (2b) (or doubly opaque) nature of rhotacism.[5] The difference between a rule loss resulting in restructuring and one that does not may be outlined thus (cf. Vennemann 1974: 138-9):

I. Underlying A   II. Underlying A

    1. Restructuring
    2. Rule inversion
    (3. Rule loss)   Rule loss
    Result: Underlying B   Result: Underlying A

Since 'rule loss is conceptually motivated and occurs only if a
rule is dead, both as a phonetic process and as a symbolic
process' (Vennemann 1972b:191), the loss in both I and II is
the loss of a morphologized rule, in I that of an inverted
rule, in II that of a non-inverted rule.[6]
    Ancillary to the analysis of rhotacism, but supporting the
solution defended in this paper, is the interrelationship of
rhotacism (R) with another rule of Latin, liquid dissimilation
(LD). As brought out in Watkins (1970a:525), a rule

$$-\bar{a}li- \longrightarrow -\bar{a}ri- / (...) \ 1 \ (...) \ \underline{} ,$$

'if a preceding liquid in the stem is an *l,* then the suffix is
dissimilated to *-āri-* (cf. *capitālis* 'main', but *populāris*
'popular')',must have preceded rhotacism historically in Latin,
since such dissimilation also occurred in the Oscan dialect
Vestinian (*flusare*). Watkins posits a rule insertion of the
later rhotacism ahead of liquid dissimilation in order to
explain *flōrālis* 'floral'; if the sequence were the historical
one, LD would bleed R, i.e.

       flōsālis
LD flōsāris
R   (does not apply);

but if R precedes LD,

       flōsālis
R   flōrālis
LD (does not apply),

the correct output is derived. Of course, the two rules are
'mutually bleeding', since R prevents LD from applying also.
To be exact, the rule of rhotacism must now be slightly revised
from our original (simplified) formulation, as indicated in
Dressler (1971:597), to

$$s \longrightarrow r/V\underline{}V\begin{bmatrix}C_0\\-vibr\end{bmatrix}$$

which explains why *miser* 'poor' never rhotacised to **mirer* (cf.
also Anttila 1972:59-60). Dressler (1973:204) makes the
important point that LD was an optional rule (cf. the doublet
lūmināris, lūminālis 'shining') and thus must be ordered,
synchronically, after obligatory R, the sequence also achieved
by either rule insertion or rule reordering. In any case, the

fact that R did produce *flōrālis* increases paradigm uniformity
in the direction of *r*:

A. LD/R: flōs, flōris, flōsāris
B. R/LD: flōs, flōris, flōrālis

The Classical Latin stage B exhibits only *flōs* with *s*, which
stands isolated especially if we add the proper name *Flōra* (the
goddess) which was conceivably connected to the paradigm of
'flower' by the Latin speaker (Dressler 1971:598).
   Perhaps it is appropriate to conclude the discussion of
rhotacism by considering another rule of Latin which involves
both phonological and morphological factors. In the generative
literature (for details see King 1973), Lachmann's Law has been
considered a phonological rule, lengthening vowels before
voiced stops. However, Watkins (1970b:64), following
Kurylowicz (1968), concludes that 'no phonetic conditioning
whatsoever is involved in Lachmann's Law. That 'law' simply
states that at a certain period in the pre-history of Latin
the morphological expression of the perfect passive assumed an
accessory mark of vocalic length, there where that same vocalic
length served as the distinctive mark of the perfect active'
(Contrast *ăgo, ēgi, āctum* 'act' to *făcio, fēci, făctum* 'do').
Watkins exaggerates a bit, perhaps. There does exist in Latin
a perfectly good phonetic-phonological rule of vowel lengthening
seen in *rĕgo-->rēxi* 'I rule(d)' which is to be kept separate
from the vowel lengthening in *rŭpo-->rūpi* 'I break, broke',
phonetically arbitrary and morphologically conditioned (Matthews
1972:212). If we connect the first case of vowel lengthening
with Lachmann's Law, we consider the latter another instance of
a hybrid between phonology and morphology. Thus, Lachmann's
Law may be seen as a morphologized, but non-inverted rule,
while rhotacism constitutes a (morphologized) inversion.

NOTES

[1] I could find only three other cases: *urere/ustum* 'burn',
haurire/haustum 'create', and *queri/questum* 'complain'.

[2] A third solution, one which posits the phonological rule
for the existing alternations, but restructured *r* with no rule
for *l*, ought to be eliminated due to internal inconsistency:
how can it be made plausible that Latin speakers accounted for
the given data with two underlying segments, sometimes *s* (in 2
and 3) and sometimes *r* (in 1)? (Cf. Kiparsky 1971:596-8.)

[3] Sommer (1948:369) gives a possible explanation: 'Die
Erhaltung des für das Sprachbewusstsein unregelmässigen
Zustandes speziell bei Monosyllaba mag darauf beruhen, dass
kürzere Formen sich dem Gedächtnis mehr einprägen und so
ausgleichenden Neuerungen am besten widerstehen'.

[4]Derivational examples like *honŏr/honestus* 'honest' and *arbŏr/arbustus* 'belonging to a tree' are to be accounted for by the rule inversion r⟶s/(...) functioning as a via-rule (Vennemann 1974:146).

[5]In the phonological history of French, doubly opaque rules are always lost and cause restructuring (Klausenburger 1974b: 57-60).

[6]As Lipski (1974:277) points out, however, quoting Campbell (1971:197), 'any supposed instances of rule loss can be re-interpreted as the addition of a rule which obliterates the result of some other rule'. We may express the analogy in *honŏr* in terms of a (morphological) rule addition, s⟶r/(nom. sg.), which obliterates, i.e. causes the loss of, rhotacism. For the various generative categories of phonological change, see King 1969.

REFERENCES

Anttila, Raimo. 1972. An introduction to historical and comparative linguistics. New York: Macmillan.

Campbell, Lyle. 1971. Review of Robert D. King, Historical linguistics and generative grammar. Lg. 47.191-209.

Dressler, Wolfgang. 1971. An alleged case of non-chronological rule insertion: *flōrālis*. LI 2.597-8.

_____. 1973. Nochmals zur Regelanordnung in lat. *flōrālis*. Die Sprache 19.204.

Harris, James W. 1974. Morphologization of phonological rules: an example from Chicano Spanish. Linguistic studies in Romance languages, ed. by R. J. Campbell, M. G. Goldin, and M. C. Wang, 8-27. Washington, D.C.: Georgetown University Press.

King, Robert D. 1969. Historical linguistics and generative grammar. Englewood Cliffs, New Jersey: Prentice-Hall.

_____. 1973. Rule insertion. Lg. 49.551-78.

Kiparsky, Paul. 1971. Historical linguistics. A survey of linguistic science, ed. by W. O. Dingwall, 577-649. College Park, Md.: University of Maryland Press.

_____. 1973. Abstractness, opacity, and global rules. Indiana University Linguistic Club.

Klausenburger, Jurgen. 1974a. Rule inversion, opacity, conspiracies: French liaison and elision. Lingua 34.167-79.

_____. 1974b. Historische französische Phonologie aus generativer Sicht. (Romanistische Arbeitsherte, 12.) Tübingen: Max Niemeyer.

Kurylowicz, J. 1968. A remark on Lachmann's law. HSCP 72. 295-9.

Lipski, John M. 1974. Rule interaction and rule loss. Neophilologus 58.273-82.

Matthews, P. H. 1972. Inflectional morphology. A
  theoretical study based on aspects of latin verb conjugation.
  (Cambridge Studies in Linguistics, 6.) Cambridge: Cambridge
  University Press.
_____. 1973. Some reflections on Latin morphophonology.
  Transactions of the Philological Society, 59-78.
_____. 1974. Morphology. An introduction to the theory of
  word-structure. (Cambridge textbooks in linguistics, 1.)
  Cambridge: Cambridge University Press.
Quellet, Henri. 1969. Les dérivés latins en -or. Étude
  lexicographique, statistique, morphologique et sémantique.
  (Études et Commentaires, 72.) Paris: Klincksieck.
Saussure, Ferdinand de. 1967. Cours de linguistique générale.
  Paris: Payot.
Schindler, Jochem. 1974. Fragen zum paradigmatischen
  Ausgleich. Die Sprache 20.1-9.
Sommer, Ferdinand. 1948. Handbuch der lateinischen Laut- und
  Formenlehre. Heidelberg: Carl Winter.
Vennemann, Theo. 1972a. Rule inversion. Lingua 29.209-42.
_____. 1972b. Phonetic analogy and conceptual analogy.
  Schuchardt, the Neogrammarians, and the transformational
  theory of phonological change, ed. by T. Vennemann and
  T. H. Wilbur, 181-204. Frankfurt am Main: Athenäum.
_____. 1974. Restructuring. Lingua 33.137-56.
Watkins, Calvert. 1970a. A case of non-chronological rule
  insertion. LI 1.525-7.
_____. 1970b. A further remark on Lachmann's law.
  HSCP 74.55-65.

IS THE USE OF MOOD IN SPANISH SUBJECT TO VARIABLE CONSTRAINTS?

MARY ELLEN GARCÍA AND TRACY TERRELL

Georgetown University and University of California, Irvine

1. Introduction

In Hooper and Terrell 1974 and Terrell 1974 it is hypothesized
that the use of mood in Spanish is correlated with the semantic
notion of assertion when used in embedded nominal sentences.
These studies were based on normative grammars, however, and
they may not reflect the way native speakers actually use the
indicative and subjunctive moods. If native speakers do not
use the indicative and subjunctive moods as prescriptive
grammars suggest, either the system of rules is different from
the one suggested by Hooper and Terrell, but static, or the
system is in a state of change in which case the rules relating
the semantics and syntax of the two moods must be, at least in
some part of the system, variable.

The important work to date dealing with possible syntactic
variables has followed sociolinguistic methodology using
recorded interviews. However, the variables studied, such as
be in Black English Vernacular (Labov 1972) and *que* in Canadian

French (Sankoff 1972), were of relatively frequent occurrence.
Such is not the case with the use of mood in Spanish noun
sentential complements. Therefore, we explored various methods
of soliciting native speaker judgments of the grammaticality
of the sentence types which seemed most crucial for our study.

According to the analysis proposed by Hooper and Terrell
1974, the subjunctive mood is correlated with cases of
non-assertion. Supported by syntactic and semantic evidence,
they motivate three classes of non-assertive sentences:

1. *Commands*
   Quiero que te quedes con nosotros.
   'I want you to stay with us.'
2. *Doubt*
   Dudo que te quedes con nosotros.
   'I doubt that you'll stay with us.'
3. *Subjective Comment or Reaction*
   (With complement presupposed)
   ¡Qué bueno que te quedes con nosotros!
   'How nice that you're staying with us!'

Classes 1 and 2 are fairly clear cut semantically; however,
there are certain problems with the use of the notion
'presupposition' in class 3. Terrell 1974 presented evidence
that there are two types of presupposition--weak and strong--
and that sentences with weakly presupposed complements are
also assertions while strongly presupposed complements never
are. The semantic class of matrix is also different:

4. *Knowledge*
   Supe que no lo habían completado.
   'I found out that they hadn't finished it.'
5. *Subjective Comment or Reaction*
   Me alegré de que no lo hubieran completado.
   'I was happy that they hadn't finished it.'

Although the differences between the three main classes of
matrices are clear, presupposition, even strong presupposition,
is much more closely related semantically to assertion than
are either sentences of doubt or imperatives. In the case of
assertion we assert the proposition to be true to the best of
our knowledge; with presupposition, we presuppose the
proposition to be true and react to it in some way. Thus, if
the use of mood were to be associated with a semantic notion
of 'truth' or 'fact', 3, 4, and 5 would be classed together
as opposed to 1 and 2. We therefore made the following
working hypotheses:

a. The use of mood in Spanish is subject to variable
   constraints.
b. The linguistic constraints are correlated with and
   based on the semantic notions of assertion,
   presupposition, doubt, command as developed by
   Hooper and Terrell.

    c. The extra-linguistic correlations of variability
        include geographic area of residence, socio-economic
        level, and stylistic range.

The evidence we will present speaks most directly to b, but
there are enough indications in support of c to suggest that
future research will be fruitful.

2.1.   Survey 1: Mexican and Mexican-American students in the
       El Paso-Ciudad Juarez area

A list of sentences which included all four semantically based
types proposed by Hooper and Terrell (assertion, presupposition,
doubt, and commands) was made with mood forms occurring randomly.
The sentences were then taped and a response sheet was made up
to facilitate their judgment by native speakers of Spanish.[1]
It was felt that by measuring the reactions of speakers in
large enough numbers one could obtain a fairly accurate
representation of the grammaticality of the sentences to these
groups, thereby getting closer to the actual use of the subjunctive and the real rules behind it.
    The tape was fifteen minutes long; the response sheet
contained the number of the sentence, but not the written
representation, so that respondents would respond only to the
oral utterance. The instructions were to mark 'Yes' or 'Si'
if the sentence corresponded to something they would say or
would hear and that sounded natural to them. They were asked
to mark 'No' if it sounded like something that they would not
say or that would sound odd or strange to them. It was made
clear that this had nothing to do with grammar books, but with
how they themselves spoke.
    The tape was presented to high school students aged 13-19
in the El Paso-Juarez area on the Texas-Mexico border.[2] The
schools were all in El Paso, but because the cities are
literally adjacent to each other, the Mexican students often
lived in Juarez while attending school in El Paso during the
day. Over 200 students participated and, from that number,
195 were used as valid data, with 117 Mexicans and 78 Mexican-
Americans giving the results presented here.[3]

2.2.1. The data and analysis

In order to determine semantic class correlations, we examined
each class in terms of the average acceptance of indicative
mood verb forms in sentences which, prescriptively, require
subjunctive:

	Mexicans	Mexican-Americans
Commands	8%	26%
Doubt	25%	47%
Subjective Comment	48%	56%
(Presupposition)		

To these figures we can compare the average acceptance of
subjunctive forms in assertive sentences:

Assertion   19%   29%

From even these data we can conclude that there are at least
three clearly delineated classes in terms of variability and
possible change.   In addition, it is also clear that Mexican-
Americans, as represented by the sample we studied, do use
mood following the same system of constraints as Mexicans, but
in different proportions.[4] We suggest that the mood distinction
is being lost and that the rate of change has been accelerated
among Mexican-Americans who are not as exposed to the
normative pressures of Mexican society.   The remainder of this
section will be devoted to a more detailed examination of these
data with reference to these hypotheses.

2.2.2.   Imperatives

It is instructive to note that the semantic class of commands is
the 'Bastion' of the subjunctive mood.   Even assertions with
subjunctive forms are accepted more often than are commands
with indicative forms.   There are certain syntactic factors
which may support the retention of this structural and formal
pattern.   The imperative-assertive contrast is the basic formal
contrast of independent sentences; mood signals the distinction:

> El señor Gomez estudia inglés.
> Sr. Gomez, ¡estudie inglés!

This same contrast is maintained in embedded sentences:

> Creo que el señor Gomez estudia inglés.
> Quiero que el señor Gomez estudie inglés.

Because of this basic correlation, there are minimal pairs in
sentences with matrices which can serve to report either
assertions or commands:

> Nos dijeron que se quedarían una semana más.
> Nos dijeron que nos quedáramos una semana más.

This network of command-subjunctive correspondence would
theoretically support very strongly the maintainance of the
subjunctive forms in imperative sentences.
   In the examples which occur throughout the rest of this
paper, we give *acceptance rates*.[5] That is, the two percentage
figures to the right of the sentence indicate the degree of
its acceptability, the first figure representing the Mexican
group and the second, the Mexican-American group.   An asterisk
indicates statistically significant differences between
dialects, using a chi-square analysis based on a 95% confidence
level.   Since in our many years of contact with native speakers

of Spanish we had never heard an indicative form in these
sentences (e.g. 'I want', 'prefer', 'advise', 'order', etc.),
we supposed that the examples in this category would serve
primarily as a reliability test for the survey. As expected,
a majority of Mexicans and Mexican-Americans accepted sentences
of volition with subjunctive forms and rejected those with
indicative forms.

The highest rate of rejection of any sentence in the sample
for both Mexican and Mexican-Americans is found in sentences
with *querer* followed by the indicative mood. This is very
obviously the most common verb of volition and its
incompatibility with the indicative corresponds to the strong
preference of the subjunctive forms in the imperative
sentences:

(1)	Quiero que se casa conmigo.	*3%	10%
(2)	Quiero que me lo pagas mañana.	*5%	17%

In the other examples, perhaps not as strongly volitional, the
majority of both groups rejected the sentences, the Mexican-
American group doing so consistently to a lower degree:

(3)	Preferimos que apagas la televisión.	*8%	23%
(4)	Es necesario que llegas antes de las ocho.	*6%	27%
(5)	¿Le aconsejaste a María que no lo hacía?	*14%	38%
(6)	Piden que lo pagamos ahora mismo.	*11%	41%

Examples with the subjunctive were accepted by both groups as
expected:

(7)	Prefiero que no lo hagas de esa manera.	*86%	74%
(8)	Sugiero que lo hagas mañana.	*90%	58%

It may be that the low acceptance rate for 8 was due to *sugiero*
which for Mexican-Americans is perhaps used only infrequently.

2.2.3. Doubt

Although on a semantic level sentences of doubt are clearly not
assertions, the syntactic reinforcement which may operate in
imperatives is not present. First of all, the mood contrast
in embedded sentences is almost always redundant; there are no
common matrices which may be followed by an affirmation or a
doubted proposition.[6] Secondly, the only independent sentences
of doubt are those with the adverbials *tal vez, acaso, quizás*.
Even in these sentences, however, the indicative mood is quite
common. Affirmations with embedded indicatives are accepted
and those with embedded subjunctives are rejected by both
groups. Again, however, the differences in acceptance or
rejection rates are significant:

(9) Nos aseguraron que estarían allí
     a las ocho en punto.   *96%   73%
(10) Creo que es un problema muy difícil
     de solucionar.   *92%   63%
(11) Es mi opinión que deben de practicar
     más de hacer la presentación.   *81%   72%

In three cases the sentences were accepted by Mexicans but
rejected by Mexican-Americans. These differences may indicate
a real dialectal difference in Mexican-American Spanish where
these lexical items possibly are used only infrequently:
juzgamos que, concluyo que, sostengo que.
   Examples of affirmation followed by subjunctive were largely
rejected, as indicated by the low percentage of acceptances
shown below:

(12) Creo que no se hayan bañado.   *11%   46%
(13) Pensaba que me levantara temprano.   *11%   32%
(14) Es verdad que se acostara.   *20%   34%
(15) Opino que no fuera muy fácil.   32%   33%

Surprisingly, both groups accepted sentence 16. We have no
sure explanation for this striking difference; however, it
should be relevant that the sentence 'It is (not) obvious that
we did it quickly' on one reading is presupposed:

(16) Es obvio que lo hiciéramos
     rápidamente.   *71%   59%

Sentences of doubt followed by subjunctive were uniformly
accepted:

(17) No creo que Juan se corte el pelo.   88%   88%

Sentences of doubt followed by indicative were variably
rejected by Mexicans and variably accepted by Mexican-Americans.
It is probable that the relative degree of doubt perceived by
the speaker plays a role in these sentences since 18 and 19
are more emphatically doubtful (*poco, muy*) than 20 and 21:

(18) Es poco probable que trabajaron todo
     el día.   *10%   40%
(19) Es muy dudoso que voy con Uds. esta
     noche.   21%   24%
(20) Dudo que van a estar muy felices con
     este regalo.   *27%   54%
(21) No estoy seguro que tenían el
     dinero.   *41%   70%

Doubt also plays a very important part in sentences which
present certain problems for a straightforward semantic analysis.
The verb *suponer*, for instance, which conveys the very
uncertain state of mind of 'supposing', is rejected with the

subjunctive. This indicates that what is supposed, in Spanish
at least, is taken as an assertion in the linguistic sense and
not really a matter of doubt:

> (22) Supongo que vayamos.   38%   32%

The matrix *probable* also seems to work like *suponer,* in that it
is an affirmative view of what will happen. Used with the
indicative, it is acceptable to the majority of both groups:

> (23) Es probable que los precios allí
>   serán mas bajos.   63%   60%

When *posible* is used, however, it makes a difference to the
Mexican group. This expression, then, must imply a greater
degree of uncertainty than does *probable,* although its degree
of acceptability indicates that this does not hold for the
whole group:

> (24) Es posible que comprarán la
>   televisión a colores.   *43%   60%

   Apparently, doubt played a very minor role in determining
the mood of the following sentence. The acceptance of this
sentence must have been due to its assertive property rather
than its possible doubt:

> (25) ¿Dudas que ya lo hice?   *74%   56%

A similar sentence could be construed to have a presupposed
complement. Cast in the indicative, it was neither overwhelmingly accepted nor rejected:

> (26) No es muy evidente que Juan es
>   el mejor para el puesto.   50%   46%

   On the basis of this evidence, though by no means conclusive,
we propose that the differentiation of mood is also being lost
in sentences that are more affirmative than doubtful. That
is, where the subjunctive is now prescriptively called for, it
is in reality not obligatory, for speakers can react to a
partially assertive property and use the indicative.

2.2.4. Subjective comment

As we noted, sentences of subjective comment contain presupposed
complements and are semantically most like assertions. If the
mood system is changing, and if the Hooper-Terrell hypothesis
is valid, it must be this category which shows the most
variation. That is, the verb in such a presupposed complement
is variably accepted both in the subjunctive and indicative.
Examples with subjective comment plus the subjunctive are
accepted in the same degree by both groups:

(27) Es triste que se vaya tan pronto.	84%	78%
(28) Me pareció muy raro que llegaran antes que usted.	87%	68%
(29) Nos encantó que usted haya podido pasar este mes en nuestra casa.	74%	64%

Examples of subjective comment plus indicative are also acceptable to both groups, with Mexicans favoring the constraint that the verbs in the complement clause be preterite:

(30) ¡Que extraño que no nos llamaron!	*83%	68%
(31) Me extrañó mucho que no consiguieron los libros que buscaban.	57%	62%
(32) Me sorprendió que ustedes no pudieron ayudarnos con el plan.	52%	54%
(33) Siento mucho que has estado enfermo.	44%	57%
(34) Es bueno que tenemos tiempo para visitar a Juan también.	*31%	60%
(35) Da vergüenza que sigue andando con ese muchacho.	*36%	54%

Inevitably, each of these sentences contains other factors which possibly influence judgments. Such factors may contribute to the variability in this class, but they do not cancel the validity of the data. We should note that a greater degree of rejection would have been expected if the mood system was static and operated according to the rule found in prescriptive grammars.

3.1. Survey 2: Mexican college students

Since the highest indices of variability are found in sentences of subjective comment we decided to examine this type of sentences in more detail. Because the informants and certain extra-linguistic factors are different, the results are not strictly comparable; however, we believe the data to be relevant. Twenty-five written sentences, all containing matrices of subjective comment and therefore prescriptively to be allowed only with subjunctive forms, were distributed randomly to students of the Universidad Ibero-Americana in Mexico City. The survey was completed in the cafeteria of the school under very informal conditions. The students were told that the survey sheets contained sentences from compositions written by American students of Spanish and were requested to indicate sentences with errors and correct them to natural spoken Mexican Spanish if they so desired. We received a total of 180 survey sheets, most with written corrections.

The students were all between the ages of 17 and 25 and belonged to the middle and upper classes. This group was chosen precisely because it was thought that stigmatized forms, or forms reflecting uneducated usage, would be present to a low degree especially in the formal context of 'grammar correction' but that nonstandard, but nonstigmatized forms, might pass unnoticed if they were commonly used by this group of speakers.

The previous data forced us to certain methodological conclusions. Because of the high rejection rate in the first survey we simplified the sentences in terms of vocabulary and syntax as much as possible. Moreover, in this survey we were able to calculate the number of cases in which a sentence was rejected because of factors other than mood. The rejection rate for reasons other than mood was fairly high ranging from one to a high of 67 out of 180 responses. Such changes were usually either lexical substitutions (*hizo sol>salió el sol* or *hubo sol* was very common) or tense substitutions (*Es natural que Juan se quedara en casa > Era natural*... or ...*que se haya quedado*...). One particularly frequent correction was in sentences with subordinating matrices such as *se enojó de que, se alegró de que, estaba contento de que,* and *estaba furioso de que*. These were quite often changed to coordinate sentences with *porque* (e.g. *se enojó porque),* which may indicate that where possible, the subjunctive is avoided altogether. In any case these results explain to some extent the relatively high rejection rates in the first survey.

3.2.   The data and analysis

Propositions with subjunctive forms were usually accepted, but a small percentage of speakers actually crossed out the subjunctive forms in the following sentences and changed them to indicative forms.

		% mood changed
(36)	Siento mucho que no vaya con nosotros mañana.	1%
(37)	Qué redículo que se acuesten tan temprano.	1%
(38)	Es triste que coma demasiado.	2%
(39)	Juan lamenta que no haya podido ayudarles más.	2%
(40)	Es natural que Juan se quedara en casa.	4%
(41)	Me pareció muy extraño que siempre le llevara la comida.	4%
(42)	Es bueno que Uds. hayan llegado temprano.	7%
(43)	Se enojó de que viniera sin llamar.	9%
(44)	Estaba contento de que viniéramos.	13%
(45)	¡Qué bueno que lo recibas mañana!	22%

In sentences 42-45 the change was normally to either preterite (42-44) or to future forms (45). This led us to re-examine tense-mood correlations. There are in Spanish no subjunctive tenses which are formally marked for subsequence, i.e. future and conditional or for perfectivity at a specific past point in time, i.e. the preterite. Thus, we hypothesized that within the category of subjective comment, tense form is a variable restriction.

Turning to sentences with indicative forms, the average acceptance for this group was 45%, which compares strikingly

well with 48% for Mexicans in the first survey. In that
survey there were indications that preterite forms had an
unusually high acceptance rate in these sentences. The
acceptance rates of sentences 46 and 47 show that this is a
correct conclusion:

(46) Al padre de Isabel le enojaba que
      ella salía con aquel chico.   6%
(47) Se alegró de que no llovió.   67%

Of the past tenses surveyed (perfect, imperfect, preterite),
it is only the preterite which is accepted to a higher degree:

(48) Es bueno que Ud. no llegó ante ayer.   51%
(49) Es una lástima que no hizo sol ayer.   54%
(50) Qué extraño que no nos llamaron.   88%

Sentences with future forms are also more likely to be accepted:

(51) Qué raro que no llegará a tiempo.   52%
(52) Qué interesante que Uds. llegarán antes
      que nosotros.   66%
(53) Qué bueno que saldrán mañana.   85%

On the other hand, sentences with present, perfect or
imperfect forms were usually rejected:

(54) Siento mucho que has estado enfermo.   4%
(55) Al padre de Isabel le enojaba que ella
      salía con aquel chico.   6%
(56) Es una lástima que sus hijos no los
      visitan más.   17%
(57) Era muy extraño que seguía visitándolo
      todos los días.   26%
(58) Es interesante que Ud. sigue con el
      mismo trabajo.   37%

It seems clear from both surveys that it is precisely in
the tenses for which there are no direct subjunctive forms--
preterite and future--that the distinction of mood is being
ignored to a greater degree.

4.1. Survey 3: Mexicans in Mexico City

Sentences which are grammatical, i.e. accepted by native
speakers, may or may not be produced by these same speakers in
a natural context. As a final test of the preceding results,
we asked 20 students (all under the age of 25) to complete
sentences with matrices of subjective comment:

1.   Siento mucho que...
2.   Juan lamenta que...
3.   Me molestó que Jorge...

The first 17 sentences contained matrices which are normally followed by a presupposed complement. The last three sentences represented the three other semantic categories:

18. Prefiero que... (Command)
19. Dudo que... (Doubt)
20. Es seguro que Juan... (Assertion)

The students were asked to complete the sentences in any way they wished. The interviews were taped. Most of the survey was conducted with a group of onlookers (who became the subsequent informants) and the entire survey was quite relaxed with friends trying to outdo each other creating 'clever' sentences. It was obvious that very little, if any, attention was paid to 'grammatical' considerations.

4.2. The data

Of a total number of 340 dependent clauses the use of tenses was distributed as follows:

Past Perfect Indicative	1
Imperfect Indicative	1
Future	1
Present Indicative	5
Preterite	33
Present Subjunctive	67
Imperfect Subjunctive	91
Perfect Subjunctive	102
Omitted	14
Other constructions (Inf., etc.)	25

Of the indicative forms only the use of the preterite is really significant. There were five sentences in which no one used preterite forms (*me gusta que, no nos sorprendió que, es extraño que, es bueno que, es muy natural que*). In addition, six of the twenty informants used no preterite forms at all. With just the data we have collected, we assume this to be a result of insufficient data and not a meaningful gap in the structural pattern.

An additional experiment was tried during these interviews. The interviewer proposed to complete the test sentences, and the group of students listening were to correct any errors. All sentences with present indicative brought immediate reaction and correction to present subjunctive. No preterite forms were corrected or even commented on.

5. Conclusions

a. The evidence supports the hypothesis that mood choice in Spanish is subject to variable constraints.
b. The linguistic constraints include at least the following. *Semantic classification of sentence*: indicative forms are acceptable most in sentences of subjective comment (with

presupposed complements) and least in imperative sentences; they are acceptable in sentences of doubt to a lesser degree than in sentences of subjective comment, but more often than in imperatives; in sentences of doubt the use is variably correlated with the relative intensity on the assertion-doubt continuum. *Verb tenses*: forms with no formal subjunctive correspondences are more acceptable than those with such corresponding tenses in the subjunctive mood; past indicative forms are more acceptable than present.

   c. The mood system is used by Mexican-Americans following the same constraints as Mexicans; however, the contrasts and correlations are less categorical in every case. There are two possible interpretations: mood system is variable at certain points but usually static for Mexican speakers while Mexican-Americans are losing the mood contrast. Or, the mood system is variable for all speakers and Mexican-Americans being least subject to normative pressures represent the most advanced state of these tendencies.

Future investigations can shed more light on these specific changes in Spanish and, more importantly, will be a solid contribution to our understanding of the mechanisms of syntactic change in natural languages.

NOTES

[1]This survey method was developed by García in her analysis of the adverbial use of *para* in the Spanish of Mexican-Americans as distinct from that of Mexicans. Since the results from that survey revealed interesting constraints on its usage, it was felt that a similar approach could also yield valuable data for analysis in this case.

[2]The schools that participated were: The Lydia Patterson Institute, Father Yermo High School, and Canutillo High School. We would like to thank them for their cooperation.

[3]The results were tabulated on a computer which correlated responses with dialect group. It also performed a chi-square test of statistical significance between the groups. Differences between dialects were considered significant at the .05 level.

[4]In reality, without extensive surveys with the same individuals we could not show that the use of mood is variable for an individual, but only that it varies within a group. Such variation could, theoretically, be produced by categorical rules.

[5]It became all too obvious that sentences were rejected for many reasons other than mood--lexical items appeared to be often a factor. We will return to this problem in the following section.

[6]Some linguists have claimed that such contrasts are possible in certain cases. See Rivero 1971:

    ¿Te parece que venga?
    ¿Te parece que viene?

However, even if Rivero's assertion is true, it is difficult to see how one could show that the contrast is valid for a large group of people instead of a small group of linguists.

REFERENCES

García, Mary E. Forthcoming. *Para* and *pa* in Chicano Spanish. Proceedings of the Texas Symposium on Romance Linguistics, 1974.

Hooper, J. and T. Terrell. 1974. A semantic-based analysis of mood in Spanish. Hispania.

Klein, P. 1974. Observations on the semantics of mood in Spanish. Seattle, Wash.: University of Washington dissertation.

Labov, W. 1972. Language in the inner city. Philadelphia: University of Pennsylvania Press.

Rivero, M. L. 1971. Mood and presupposition in Spanish. Foundations of Language 7.305-36.

Sankoff, G., R. Sarrasin, and H. Cedergren. 1972. Quelques considérations sur la distribution sociolingustique de la variable QUE dans le français de Montréal. Paper presented at the 39th Congress of the French Canadian Association for the Advancement of Science.

Terrell, Tracy. Forthcoming. Assertion and presupposition in Spanish complements. Proceedings of the Texas Symposium on Romance Linguistics, 1974.

PRE-LATIN LANGUAGES AND SOUND CHANGES IN ROMANCE: THE CASE OF OLD SPANISH /h-/

HERBERT J. IZZO

The University of Calgary

Probably for as long as people have had written records that
allowed them to compare their own speech with that of their
ancestors (and possibly even before that), some of them have
been aware of linguistic change. We know, for example, that
certain writers of classical times, e.g. Cicero and Quintilian,
were aware of changes in pronunciation in their language. In
the Renaissance, writers on language were already aware that
the Romance languages were modern descendants of Latin, and they
speculated on the reasons for linguistic change. (As I have
been busy with some of those Renaissance authors recently and
have then considered present-day attempts to explain linguistic
change, I have sometimes wondered whether we have made any
progress.)
    The idea that linguistic change is the result of laziness,
that change is in the direction of ease of articulation, is
such an obvious and simpleminded one that it has probably been
around forever. Not long ago, when everything non-linguists
'knew' about language was automatically labelled linguistic
folklore, it was customary (perhaps even de rigueur) for

linguists to laugh at any appeal to ease of articulation.[1]
Although I myself used to scoff at the idea, I now believe
that, properly understood, ease does play a part in linguistic
change;[2] but as a general explanation it is obviously
deficient in several respects. First and most obvious, if
languages are moving toward ease, why don't they ever reach
it? To me Modern English seems infinitely simpler and easier
than Old English, of course. In fact Old English seems so
unreasonably complicated that I wonder how the language a
thousand years before it could possibly have been spoken at
all; and if simplification continues at the same rate in the
future as in the past, a thousand years hence English ought to
be so plain and uncomplicated that even a set of ordered rules
will be able to describe it 'adequately'. Extrapolating
forward and backward from what appears (to present-day native
speakers) to be the simplification of familiar languages in
historical times, one can easily end up with an absurdity like
Mark Twain's on the Mississippi River:

> In the space of one hundred and seventy-six years
> the Lower Mississippi has shortened itself two
> hundred and forty-two miles. That is an average of
> a trifle over one mile and a third per year.
> Therefore, any calm person, who is not blind or
> idiotic, can see that in the Old Oölitic Silurian
> Period, just a million years ago next November, the
> Lower Mississippi River was upwards of one million
> three hundred thousand miles long, and stuck out over
> the Gulf of Mexico like a fishing rod. And by the
> same token any person can see that seven hundred and
> forty-two years from now the Lower Mississippi will be
> only a mile and three quarters long, and Cairo and
> New Orleans will have joined their streets together,
> and be plodding comfortably along under a single mayor
> and a mutual board of aldermen. There is something
> fascinating about science. One gets such wholesale
> returns of conjecture out of such a trifling investment
> of fact.[3]

Of course, we know that the seeming simplicity of Modern
English (for example) is an illusion arising only from our
familiarity with it, that the simplification of English noun
morphology has been at least compensated for by the complication
of verbal syntax, that King Alfred probably would have thought
our language as unnecessarily difficult as we find his. If
most of us find the structure of Latin more difficult than that
of Spanish, we do not find it more difficult than the less
familiar Rumanian, with its apparently complicated vowel
alternations (*frumos* m., *frumoasă* f. 'beautiful'; *negru* m.,
neagră f. 'black'; *poate* 'he can', *putem* 'we can', etc.) and
seemingly capricious plurals (*casă/case* 'house(s)', *masă/mese*
'table(s)', *stradă/străzi* 'street(s)', *brînza/brînzeturi*
'cheese(s)', etc.). In short, there is no objective evidence
that linguistic change leads, overall, to greater ease or--

despite the opinion of such a great linguist as Jespersen
(cf. Jespersen 1894 and 1923:337-66)--progress. In fact, not
only do languages never become easy, but sometimes we find
diametrically opposed changes (e.g. voicing and devoicing)
have occurred in different languages or even in different
periods of a single language. Obviously we cannot maintain
that opposite tendencies both result in greater ease.

Moreover, there is the problem that ease is an ever-present
cause. Why does it sometimes take thousands of years for it to
produce an effect? Why don't languages become as simple as
possible at once?

Finally, even if the other objections could be explained
away, ease could not account for divergent development of a
language when groups of its speakers become isolated from each
other. What is easy in one place ought to be easy in another,
so languages should change but not become dialectalized.

An equally naive but to me even less satisfactory
explanation of language change--though Henry Sweet and Edgar
Sturtevant held it (cf. Sturtevant 1917:33-7)--is that it
results from imperfect learning by children. Although Robert
Hall is surely correct in his insistence in several recent
publications (e.g. Hall 1968:17-32) that the child's linguistic
system is never an exact replica of any one of his adult models
(and that nobody's language is completely systematic), children
appear, at least, to learn the sounds perfectly, as has often
been noted. Even if they did not (or perhaps do not), we
would still have no explanation for why changes occur at one
time and not another; and no explanation for dialect variation:
'No permanent factor can account for specific changes which
occur at one time and place and not another' (Bloomfield 1933:
386). Moreover, unless we incorporate ease theory, we cannot
explain why, if children deviated from the adult norm, their
deviations would not be random and therefore cancel each other
out.[4]

The influence of climate and physical environment--people
avoid open-mouthed sounds in cold climates, speak in a lazy
way in hot climates, use aspirates in mountainous country
because they breathe heavily from so much climbing, etc.--is
too obviously and absurdly folkloristic to require comment.
Yet as an explanation of sound change it is superior to the
preceding in one respect: it proposes a specific cause for
a specific effect. (That the same alleged 'cause' may
correspond to completely different 'effects' in different cases
is, of course, another matter.)

A change in physical environment and especially a change in
cultural environment can and does cause lexical and semantic
changes. Since the triumph of the automobile, *hood, trunk,
dashboard, fan,* and *lane* have changed their primary meanings
considerably, while *withers, gaskin, fetlock,* and *pastern* have
become obsolete for most of us. But it is difficult to see how
changes in institutions or even attitudes or social structure
could produce changes in grammar or phonology--except by
altering the status of already existing class dialects, whose
original differentiation would still be unexplained.

The Praguean functional structuralism propounded and developed in the work of Martinet, Juilland and Haudricourt, Harald Weinrich, and others has attractive features; and it explains sound changes--in a certain sense. But it can justly be looked upon as a very refined version of the ease theory, and it fails to satisfy for the same reasons: if languages are always tending toward symmetry, economy, toward optimal phonological systems, why do they never achieve them? How or why do they get out of joint? Especially why do changes occur at one time rather than another, and how do dialects arise? In fact, some of the practitioners of functional structuralism do not attempt to answer these questions within the system but rather assume that external factors must provide the initial disequilibrium, as we shall note later.

Functional structuralism, with its attempts to establish universal laws about what kinds of phonological systems are possible, what sorts of conditions are necessary for various kinds of changes, what further changes are induced by initial changes, etc. would clearly seem to be an *explanatory* system, even if one may not think it a *correct* explanatory system. It is notable then that the generativist view of Martinet's processes is that they 'describe (n.b. *not* explain) the covarying shifts often enough encountered in the evolution of phonetic systems' (King 1969:194; emphasis in original). One cannot help wondering what 'explain' is intended to mean in generative historical linguistics when one finds that a change is 'explained' by a rule which in fact merely restates the change in a pseudo-algebraic formula. It appears that we are supposed to understand that the change is caused by the rule rather than that the rule is a description of the change. Where the speakers (or rather, supposedly the language itself) got the rule is not even asked, much less answered. The rules of TG linguistics have (in my opinion) as much to do with causation as the commands issued by the King of Asteroid 325 in St. Exupéry's *Le petit prince*. The king commands the little prince to do what he is about to do anyway, and thus he is always obeyed; when a sound change has already occurred, the generativist derives from the observed facts a rule (or a deletion or a reordering) which supposedly caused it.[5]

The supposition that a language may be changed by contact with other languages, however, seems intuitively satisfying at just those points where all of the preceding are not. It provides a reason why an apparently stable system should change, a reason for change that is not always at hand but acts at a given time, and a reason why a language should change differently in different places, i.e. develop dialects. Furthermore, that contact causes change is not merely a plausible supposition but an observed fact, a phenomenon that provides a fertile field for sociolinguistic research today.[6]

In Romance historical linguistics it seems to me that we have largely ignored the kinds of social, political, economic, and cultural relationships that have been found to determine the direction and sorts of inter-language influence and have preferred to operate in terms of metaphorical linguistic layers.

I have long objected to the terms substratum and superstratum.
because it has always seemed to me that, as they are usually
defined, there is no linguistically significant difference
between them. In the case of either one of them, we have at
the time of language contact what we would call by still another
layer word, adstratum, if the contact existed now. The only
difference is that the speakers of a substratum language were
already present in a particular region when speakers of the main
stratum language came in, while speakers of a superstratum
language came afterward. But, as I argued a few years ago
(Izzo 1972a), the terms often imply more than the geographical-
chronological relationship just mentioned and more than an image
of layers or crusts. Substratum speakers are usually assumed to
be conquered, socially inferior people, and the discussions
generally imply that they are numerous in relation to the
speakers of the new language, whereas a superstratum language
is assumed to be that of a conquering and therefore socio-
politically superior group (but not, or not necessarily, a
culturally superior group, since for Romance the superstrata
are chiefly Vandals, Goths, Langobards, etc.). It is also
generally understood that the superstratum groups are relatively
small.
    What is really essential, however,--and some scholars make
this explicit--is that substratum influence is *not* a form of
linguistic borrowing but rather an unwilled, probably unconscious
carryover of native speech habits into the new language. It is
the result of imperfect learning, a failure to imitate foreign
models correctly. It is also important to note, even though one
may believe in substratum explanations without holding this
view, that many leading proponents of substratum hypotheses
have held (cf. Menéndez Pidal 1950) that any people that changes
languages *inevitably* carries over to the adoptive language
certain habits of its first language. It is important to
realize this because it explains why Battisti, Merlo, Menéndez
Pidal, and others sometimes found substratum influence where
others could not. They knew that something had to have survived.
If they could find a feature unique to an area once occupied by
speakers of a pre-Latin language, that in itself was enough
evidence for them to ascribe the feature to the influence of the
pre-Latin language, without any knowledge of the language
itself. Merlo (1933:18-9) went so far as to affirm that the
only source of accurate information about the phonology of
pre-Latin languages was the dialects now spoken on the same
territory; and that, conversely, a single characteristic feature
in a modern dialect was sufficient to delimit exactly the
territory once occupied by speakers of a pre-Latin language.
It is also important to realize that at the time some of the
substratic explanations of sound changes were proposed, their
propounders believed in the inheritance of acquired
characteristics (Meillet 1938:233, Battisti 1930:253-4) and
were therefore not bothered by the appearance of a change long
after the language to which they attributed it had ceased to
exist. I think it is important to be aware of these two facts
because it seems that today some linguists try very hard to
find justifications for substratum explanations that they

probably would reject if they were not already accustomed to
them, or if the explanations were to be presented today for the
first time.

Many Romance changes and even some retentions of original Latin
sounds have been attributed to the influence of pre-Latin
languages. Most of the attributions appear plausible, but so
few withstand a careful examination that some scholars have
been tempted to reject the entire concept.

Here are some of the better known cases: the voicing of
voiceless intervocalic single consonants which occurred in
almost all the Romania except Central and South Italian and
Rumanian has been attributed to Celtic substratum, but the fact
that voicing did not occur in a small area in the Pyrenees has
been attributed to the influence of Basque. The fronting of
[u] to [ü] in French and a part of Northern Italy is also
attributed to Celtic substratum. The change of [mb] to [mm],
[nd] to [nn], [mp] to [mb], [nt] to [nd], and [ŋk] to [ŋg] in
Southern and about half of Central Italy is attributed to
Osco-Umbrian influence. The spirantization of intervocalic
/p, t, k/ in Tuscany has been attributed to Etruscan substratum.
The aspiration of syllable-final /s/, the assibilation of /rr/,
and the change of /tr/ to a retroflex affricate in the Spanish
of Chile has been thought to be due to Araucanian substratum.
The use of /rr/ in syllable-final position in Mexican Spanish
has been said to be due to Aztec substratum.

The last of these attributions is due to Bertil Malmberg,
who had previously attributed many features of Paraguayan
Spanish to Guaraní in his monograph 'L'Espagnol dans le Nouveau
Monde' in 1947 and 1948. Much later he observed that in
Mexico City *r* in syllable-final position is /rr/, not /r/.
This disagreed with his belief that syllable-final consonants
are always weak in Spanish (as indeed they are *in some dialects*).
Without first investigating the phonology of Nahuatl, he
concluded: 'No cabe duda que se trate de un fenómeno de
influencia indígena (substrato azteca), una supervivencia de
una tradición india...' (1964:242). The Mexican phonetician
and dialect geographer Lope Blanch (1967) replied that Aztec
has no sound comparable to Spanish /rr/. I should not be
surprised if by now someone has made the very absence of the
sound in Aztec the cause of the pronunciation observed by
Malmberg: the Aztec speakers must have overcompensated; in
their efforts to imitate Spanish /rr/, they used it even where
Spanish speakers did not. But the fact is that Malmberg's
explanation is completely unnecessary, for the use of /rr/ in
syllable-final position is by no means a special characteristic
of Central Mexico. It is used widely in Spanish America, in
Spain and even in Portuguese (both Peninsular and Brazilian).[7]
If Malmberg failed to notice this phenomenon until years after
he published his studies on American Spanish and then noticed
it only in Mexico, so much the worse for his credibility as
an authority on Spanish pronunciation.

The attribution of Chilean aspirated /s/, assibilated /rr/,
and affricated /tr/ to Araucanian influence is a much more

important and unfortunate case. The substratum assumption
was first published in German and therefore perhaps came
more quickly to the attention of scholars who were less
likely to realize its absurdity, more slowly to the attention
of Spanish speakers, who published their refutations in
Spanish, and were not read by some who accepted the original
attribution--hence the idea gained wide currency and survived
for a long time.[8] The view that 'in the main, the Spanish
spoken by the common people of Chile is Spanish with Araucanian
sounds' was put forth by Rudolf Lenz in 1893. It was accepted
by Meyer-Lübke who put it into the first edition of his
Einführung in 1901, thus, of course, helping its spread greatly,
and by Jespersen, who discussed it as a clinical case of
substratum influence in his *Language* of 1923. That Lenz
succeeded in convincing Meyer-Lübke and Jespersen, who were
both generally skeptical of substratum influence, is to the
credit of his ability to present a persuasive case, but not at
all to the credit of his competence as a Hispanist.

It would seem that Lenz came to Chile with a good knowledge
of phonetics but with only a classroom knowledge of Spanish.
He observed features in the pronunciation of Chile that he had
not known about and he presented them in several studies
totalling nearly 200 pages, along with his ideas about the
conditions of the Spanish conquest and settlement of Chile as
justification for the survival of Araucanian speech habits.[9]
The fact that Lenz considered the aspiration of syllable-final
/s/ ([mímmo, bóhke, áhta] for *mismo, bosque, hasta*) to be 'the
most notable of all the Chilean changes' and 'the most curious
aspect of Chilean phonetics' would be enough to make anyone
even moderately acquainted with Spanish dialectology suspicious,
for this phenomenon is common to much of southern Spain and to
most of the lowland areas of Spanish America. In normal,
unaffected speech it is probably used by more speakers than
the nominally normal [s]. All of the other supposedly
Araucanian substitutions in the Spanish of Chile are also
widespread in the Spanish-speaking world, all of them occurring
both in Spain and at other, widespread points in Spanish
America. Several Spanish and Latin American scholars spoke
against Lenz's thesis almost at once, but it did not receive
its coup de grâce until 1939, when Amado Alonso examined and
refuted every detail of it (cf. Alonso 1953:332-98). One
cannot help lamenting the effort that was required to undo what
never should have been done.

The spirantization of intervocalic /p, t, k/ in Tuscan is a
question I myself have dealt with at length (Izzo 1972b), and
I shall not repeat the details of the problem here. Let it
suffice to say that on the surface the substratum case looks
strong: the so-called 'aspiration' occurs in Tuscany, which
is approximately the same as the territory of ancient Etruria,
the land of the Etruscans, who, according to the evidence of
inscriptions, had aspirated stops in their language. A look
below the surface shows almost everything is wrong. Etruscan
speakers may have been only a ruling minority. In any case,
their cities were concentrated in an area where 'aspiration'
does not occur. Tuscan 'aspiration' turns out to be

spirantization, and it occurs partly where Etruscan settlements
were sparse, partly where there were no Etruscans at all.
There is evidence (not conclusive, but reasonably strong) that
the aspirate letters of Etruscan did not represent aspirated
sounds, i.e. that Etruscan did not have any aspirates. There is
direct testimony, in the form of clear phonetic descriptions,
that Tuscan had spirantized only /k/, not /p/ and /t/, as late
as the sixteenth century. Finally there is considerable
indirect evidence that even /-k-/ was probably not spirantized
before the fourteenth or fifteenth century. And the paucity of
Etruscan lexical influence on Tuscan makes Etruscan influence
on *any* aspect of Tuscan pronunciation appear unlikely.10
     The Southern Italian assimilations of stops after nasals
(*quanno, sembre, banga* for standard *quando, sempre, banca*) seem
to have aroused less controversy than most other substratum
problems having to do with such a large territory, but not
everyone has accepted Osco-Umbrian causation of the changes,
even though Hall, who is among the most critical of substratum
explanations, has written in favor of it (Hall 1949). Two
things about this problem strike me especially. The first is
that although students of Italic posit an Oscan and Umbrian
change of /nd/ to /nn/ to account for words like *upsannu* and
sakrannu, corresponding to Latin *operandum* and *sacrandum,* Oscan
texts are otherwise full of *mp, nt, nc; mb, nd, ng,* in many
cases corresponding to Latin words with the same sounds (or at
least the same letters). If, as Conway proposed in 1891,
Whatmough affirmed in 1949, and Poultney has just reaffirmed
this year, the Oscan and Umbrian gerundive in *-nn-* and the
Latin gerund and gerundive in *-nd-* both came from IE *-ny-,* one
does not have to assume a change *-nd- > -nn-* (although Poultney
does so), and the substratum thesis is left with little
foundation. The second striking fact is that if it is true
that Oscan-Umbrian had undergone a complete assimilation of
voiced stops after nasals and voicing of voiceless stops, it
is easy enough to see why Oscans and Umbrians might have
substituted [mb, nd, ŋg] for Latin (mp, nt, ŋk], which they
wouldn't have had in their own system; but it is *not* easy or
even possible to see why they would have substituted [mm, nn]
(and [ŋŋ]?) for Latin [mb, nd] (and [ŋg]?), which they did have
in their system. It is as if needing a pair of gloves and
finding only two left-handed ones, one were to put one of them
on one's right hand and throw the other away.
     I shall add a third thought, although it is still rather
tentative. In searching through early Italian texts, I have
so far found no examples of any of the above-mentioned
substitutions before the thirteenth century; and my earliest
examples are from Rome, not from Oscan territory.
     The attribution to Celtic influence of the change of Latin
[u] to French [ü] is indeed controversial. Since there is no
evidence that the Celtic of Gaul had the sound [ü], much less
that it had [ü] and lacked [u], the 'hypothesis' is really only
a conjecture. When one sees that French (which unlike almost
all of the rest of the Romance languages palatalized [k] and
[g] even before [a], even in borrowings from Germanic) did not
palatalize them before Latin [u] (*culus > cul, cupa > cuve,*

acutus > aigu); that words like *cŏctus* and *hŏdie*, which
presumably came to Gaul still having [ɔ] or [o] as their tonic
vowel, underwent the same fronting as [u] (and became modern
cuit, hui, etc.), that early borrowings from French into Old
High German have [u] not [ü], that Frankish and even Norse
loanwords in Old French underwent the change of [u] to [ü], one
cannot help thinking that the change must have occurred well
after the first learning of Latin by Celtic speakers and therefore is probably unrelated to Celtic phonology.

In earlier discussions of possible substratum influence, the
criteria for decision were sometimes developed in the course
of the presentation but more often were merely implied or were
taken for granted. More recently, for example in Hall's and
Pulgram's papers of 1949, scholars have generally been more
explicit about what, in their opinion, constitutes a valid case.
Not surprisingly, however, the criteria vary from one scholar
to the next; for some are much more willing to admit substratum
causation than others. I believe that as long as we must deal
with language transfers that occurred nearly two millenia ago,
for which we can never hope to have the testimony of 'ear-
witnesses' and for which there will always be large lacunae in
the record between the time of the transfer and ourselves, we
will never be able to prove with absolute certainty that any
phonological feature is or is not a survival from a pre-Latin
language. I do believe, however, that in some cases we should
be able to establish that pre-Latin survival is so highly
probable or so completely improbable that the alternative is
not worth entertaining.
  It seems clear then that we need two sets of criteria, one
by which to establish that a feature is in all probability a
pre-Latin survival and another set by which to establish that
it probably is not, although perhaps if the criteria for
admission of pre-Latin influence are strict enough to satisfy
the substratophobe and the criteria for exclusion strict enough
to satisfy the substratomaniac, the majority of cases may remain
undecided for a long time.
  The papers on linguistic substrata in Italy published by Hall
and Pulgram in 1949 proposed fairly similar criteria for judging
the validity of allegations of substratum influence. Hall
listed the following points (which I quote from a more recent
revised statement (Hall 1974:63), and not from the 1949
articles):
  1. The languages involved must be shown to have been in
      sufficient contact for a period of bilingualism to
      have existed;
  2. The period of bilingualism must have been long enough
      to have affected one or more generations of speakers;
  3. It must be demonstrated that the alleged substratum-
      language actually had the structural feature(s)
      ascribed to its influence on the later language.
Pulgram (1949:243) stressed especially the necessity of
non-linguistic evidence (Hall's points 1 and 2): '[Substratum
influence can be claimed] obviously only in places where

non-linguistic evidence, historic and prehistoric, actually
shows that the members of a social group, at a certain time,
acquired en masse the language of another group and adopted it
as their own. But non-linguistic evidence *must* be produced, in
addition to linguistic. Linguistic agreements by themselves
prove nothing'.

These criteria are, I think, perfectly reasonable. But even
though they are distinctly more stringent than the assumptions
with which scholars like Menéndez Pidal, Merlo, Devoto,
Terracini, and others had been operating, they are not in fact
sufficient either to confirm or disprove. By applying them
alone one would have as much reason to maintain that Spanish
/θ/ is due to Gothic as to attribute OFr. /h/ to Frankish.[11]
If one can demonstrate all three of Hall's points, one shows
that substratic survival *may* have occurred but not that it *did*.
If one cannot demonstrate one or more of the points, it is not
shown that substratum survival is impossible (although I, like
Hall and Pulgram, would throw the case out of court). To do
that, one must demonstrate that at least one of the three points
did *not* obtain.

Fredrick Jungemann in his *Teoría del sustrato y los dialectos
hispano-romances y gascones* (1955:418) allows the possibility
of substratum causation of a sound change only if (1) the
substratum language had a feature which can be related to the
change in question in structural terms, (2) the change cannot
be accounted for in terms of 'internal' factors alone, (3) there
was a long period of bilingualism, (4) the group in question
was isolated from important centers of influence or was itself
an area of influence and prestige.

The first of these conditions is the same as the first of
Hall's. It is a necessary condition but not a sufficient one.
A feature that the substratum language did not have, cannot, of
course, have survived. The second, which seems to figure in
every functional-structuralist discussion, is completely
inadmissible. Given the ingenious flexibility of this system,
there is probably no change that could be produced by the
carry-over of the phonology of one language to another that
could not also be attributed to internal factors. For example,
devoicing of final obstruents in English is explicable
structurally, and in fact a tendency in this direction has been
observed in various places. But what linguist discovering
regular, complete devoicing of final English obstruents in a
group of known recent German provenence and showing other
aspects of German 'accent', would hesitate to attribute the
devoicing to German influence? One might just as reasonably
establish as a principle of criminal investigation that if it
is possible that a victim could have fallen or jumped from a
window, it is thereby proven that he was not pushed.

The third condition is, of course, like the first, necessary
but not sufficient. Without contact there can be no transfer,
but the transfer of any given feature is not assured by contact,
no matter how prolonged. The fourth condition can be assumed
to make native-language carryover more likely, but it does not
assure it, nor does its absence prevent it.

Malmberg (1959:258) proposed these principles of phonological change:

1) Une explication générale est préférable à une explication spéciale. 2) Une explication interne est préférable à une explication externe (interférence). 3) Si une altération implique une perte de distinctions et d'unités fonctionnelles, il est préférable de l'expliquer comme une réduction à la périphérie, plutôt que recourir à l'influence d'un substrat possible. 4) Le substrat (l'interférence) ne doit être allégué comme explication que si l'innovation implique une augmentation du nombre d'oppositions ou une réinterprétation des relations entre celles-ci. 5) Le substrat ne doit être invoqué que dans les cas où la situation sociologique d'une population est telle que l'adoption de faits d'interférence par les couches socialement dirigeantes semble probable.

The first of Malmberg's principles (that a general explanation is preferable to a special one) is an important principle of all sciences, but it must be subordinate to the even more important principle that a correct explanation is preferable to a wrong one. I don't see how it helps to make any decisions concerning the correctness of a substratum hypothesis. The second (that an internal explanation is preferable to an external one) is purely dogmatic, a statement of Malmberg's faith. The third and fourth of Malmberg's principles are approximately the converse of each other. The fourth is counterintuitive and (if the foreign language learner may be taken as a micro-model of language transfer in a speech community) also counterempirical. It is *possible* for the learner to identify the variants of a single phoneme in the target language with two or more separate phonemes of his native language and thus introduce new distinctions (as, for example, an English-speaking learner could conceivably identify the occlusive and spirant varieties of Sp. /d/ [*cuando/nada*] with English /d/ and /ð/; but what is much more often observed is that the learner fails to perceive and reproduce some of the distinctions of the target language, identifying two or more target-language phonemes with one of his own, as when the English speaker makes homonyms of Sp. *carro* and *caro,* or *astilla* and *hastía,* or when the Spanish speaker conflates English /č/ and /š/, /iy/ and /i/ in *cheap~ sheep~chip~ship*. This is precisely what we regularly find in normal linguistic borrowing, as for example in the case of Medieval Spanish borrowings from Arabic, in which the Arabic glottal, pharyngeal, and velar spirants all come out with the same Spanish /h/.[12]

Only the fifth of Malmberg's principles is really admissible, but it is almost circular (i.e. substratum survival is probable only under those sociological conditions under which it is probable), and it is clearly not a criterion of decision (although it is stated as such) but only of probability.

In my *Tuscan and Etruscan* I wrote:

> If we find that a feature of a modern dialect, which
> represents a distinct innovation in the core-stratum
> language (as it was spoken before it was introduced
> to the region of the modern dialect), was certainly
> present in the substratum language; that the
> relationship between the sub- and core-stratum
> phonological systems was such as to make the use of
> the feature highly probable in the substratum speakers'
> initial attempts to speak the core-stratum language;
> and that the territory inhabited by speakers of the
> substratum language is known, with reasonable certainty,
> to be the same as that covered by the modern feature:
> then we must, if there is no valid counter-evidence,
> consider substratum origin of the feature extremely
> probable. But if it is clear that the feature first
> arose long after the substratum language ceased to be
> used, all other 'evidence' becomes spurious and
> substratum origin of the feature must be excluded.

This paragraph introduced a section on chronological
considerations. It was not intended as a specification of the
minimum conditions under which I would admit the possibility of
substratum influence (as one reviewer somehow supposed) but
rather as a statement of the *strongest* case we could hope to
make for the survival of a phonological feature from a pre-
Latin language in Europe. For present purposes I would modify
this statement by incorporating into it some of the provisos
or amplifications that I then had scattered throughout the
discussion.

First, the innovation referred to need not appear in the same
form in the modern dialect as in the pre-Latin language, but
there must be a clear relationship: suppose there is good
evidence that the pre-Latin language introduced a voiceless stop
at a new point of articulation; if a voiced stop appears at that
point of articulation in the modern dialect, the connection of
the one with the other is taken as demonstrated if in this dialect
all voiceless stops regularly became voiced. Second, the geographical coincidence must be understood in the sense of Pulgram's
1949 insistence on the necessity for non-linguistic information:
territorial coincidence means nothing unless we have good reason
to believe that there were no major shifts of populations; or if
there were such shifts that can be certainly determined, the idea
of territorial correspondence must be interpreted accordingly.
Finally, I would incorporate the chronological exceptions or
exclusion into the affirmative statement: if the other conditions are fulfilled and if in addition we have evidence that the
innovation was continuously present from the time of the introduction of Latin, we can consider substratum origin of the
innovation to be as certain as it is possible for anything of
this nature to be. Where such continuous evidence is lacking (as
in all cases it is likely forever to be), substratum origin is
still worth considering if there is no evidence that the

feature was *absent* at any time after the disappearance of the
pre-Latin language--providing the other criteria are met.

If the other criteria are not met, in my opinion any
substratum argument becomes a useless speculation about
infinite possibilities. If we know the name of a tribe and
roughly where it lived but know nothing about its language,
anything or nothing in modern dialect could be due to its
influence. If we know a language but know nothing about the
history of its speakers, we can populate the Romance world with
them wherever any coincidence between one of its features and
a feature of a modern dialect appears. We could be right. We
could also hit a one-inch target at a hundred yards with a
pistol--blindfolded, or call our aunt in San Jose by dialing
random numbers. The chances of success seem more or less
comparable. (Many people will not agree with me. Clemente
Merlo, as I mentioned earlier, claimed he could discover both
the phonology and the location of pre-Latin languages by
studying modern Romance dialects.)

To prove a substratum hypothesis *all* of several conditions
must be demonstrated. To disprove one, only *one* of several
conditions needs to be shown. The pro-substratist may think
this unfair, but it is in the nature of things. A car needs
wheels *and* a motor *and* a transmission. Remove any one of the
three and you ain't got no wheels.

If it can be shown that a pre-Latin language did not have
the feature which it is alleged to have passed on to Latin,
substratum survival of that feature from that language is
excluded. If it can be shown that there is no historical
connection between the speakers of a pre-Latin language and the
speakers of a modern dialect, substratum survival from that
language is excluded. If it can be shown that a given feature
arose after the pre-Latin language became extinct, substratum
origin of that feature is excluded.

Unfortunately, no criteria for decision can solve problems
when the evidence is unclear, as it often is in these matters.
I would like to suggest two subcriteria. First, although
socio-politico-economic relationships cannot tell us what did
happen, they can tell us what is likely to have happened; and
therefore they must be taken into consideration, in so far as
they can be determined in a non-circular way.   Second,
uncertainties piled upon uncertainties do not make certainties
or even probabilities. On the contrary, they make
improbabilities. If there is only a 50% chance that speakers
of dialect X are descendants of speakers of language Y, a 50%
chance that language Y had feature Z, and a 50% chance that
feature Z is not a fairly recent innovation in dialect X,
there is by no means an even chance that feature Z is a
survival from language Y. There is only one chance in eight,
which is to say that non-relationship is eight times more likely
than relationship; and this is certainly not the kind of thing
we should refer to as probable, because it is improbable.

After this long preamble the reader will no doubt expect that I
intend to reward his patience by telling his whether the Spanish

change of [f] to [h] was caused by the influence of a pre-Latin
language. Unfortunately I don't really know, at least not with
certainty.

In 1971 Paul Lloyd referred to the Spanish change of [f] to
[h] as 'without doubt one of the best proven cases of
interference'. In my opinion it is without doubt one of the
most confused. It is not merely a question whether the change
was caused by a pre-Latin language but, if so, what language
it was caused by and what the nature of the change was; and,
if not, whether it was because the change occurred too early or
too late to have been caused by substratum influence.
Jungemann's previously cited book of 1955 reviews more than
three dozen previous discussions of the problem and comes down
cautiously on the side of Basque influence as it was interpreted
by Martinet in 1952 (incorporated into Martinet 1955). I do not
agree with him.

The facts about Spanish /f/ itself, as accurately as I am
able to determine them, are the following: in north central
Spain, sometime before the eleventh century (how much before
we shall discuss later) Latin /f/ began to be pronounced [h]
(approximately) in word-initial position, or in fact wherever
it occurred, unless it was followed by a consonant or the
diphthong [we] (see 1 below); but the letter f continued to be
written for a long time after, probably because there was no
possibility of confusion (and because orthographic traditions
change very slowly):

(1) Spanish reflexes of Latin /f-/

Latin		Spanish
fŏcus	>	fuego
fŏcacia	>	hogaza
fŏllis	>	fuelle
fŏllicare	>	holgar
fŏnte	>	fuente
fageus	>	haya
fatu	>	hado
facere	>	hacer
frŏnte	>	frente
frĭcare	>	fregar

As Castile came to dominate more and more of the Peninsula, the
[h] spread south. Before [h] had reached the extreme south--
perhaps about the end of the fourteenth century but possibly
much earlier--[h] became silent in the north; but the spread of
[h] continued south from the political center in the center of
the Peninsula, which at that time still consisted of four
separate kingdoms. A couple of centuries later, when Spain was
a single nation and the loss of [h] had reached a large part of
it, a new sound [x] arose from another source (viz /š/ and /ž/)
and spread so rapidly that in part it overtook and fused with
[h] from /f/, chiefly in the extreme south. The preservation
of [h] from /f/ is substandard today, but it is fairly
widespread, in America as well as Spain. One of the best known
areas is Puerto Rico, where jaula and habla begin with the

same sound. Some words with [h] (from /f/) preserved have
been borrowed back with /x/ into dialects in which [h] is lost,
and even a few doublets exist. For instance, *jamelgo* from
famelicus is a Standard Spanish word for 'broken down nag',
borrowed back from Andalusian. *Juerga* 'a noisy party' is the
Andalusian (and now also common Spanish) form of *huelga*
(<*follicare*) 'a period without work, a strike'. Central
Mexican, in which [h] from /f/ is otherwise dead, has *jalar* 'to
pull' (corresponding to Standard Spanish *halar*) as a normal,
correct word. But another substandard pronunciation, occurring
widely, is the change to /x/ of the initial /f/ that is still
preserved before /we/ in standard dialects. It has been
reported for Mexico, Columbia, Peru, Argentina, and a part of
Northern Spain. Thus, for example, in the speech of a Gaucho
fuego 'fire' and *juego* 'game' may be homonymous.13 Finally,
/f/'s which are preserved--/f/ before /r/ (*frío, frente*), /f/
in Latinisms (*fácil, difícil*), in borrowings from Arabic
(*azafata, azafrán*), from Portuguese, Catalan, or French (*faca,
faena, jefe*)--may all be pronounced with bilabial [ɸ] almost
anywhere by people of any class, not only in areas which have
undergone the normal Old Castilian aspiration and/or loss but
also (I get this information from the ALPI) in many places in
Galicia and Portugal, where /f/ is regularly retained. This
bilabial /f/ is not noted in studies of Standard Spanish
pronunciation like T. Navarro's *Manual,* but it has been noted
in many descriptions of dialects (cf. Boyd-Bowman 1960:64-5).

   Aspiration of /f/ also occurs in the southwest corner of
France, in the part of Gascony bordering on Spain. Most
people think this is significant for the question of substratum
origin of the phenomenon. But farther away, about as much
farther away as you can get, [f] > [h] also occurs in Macedo-
Rumanian (or Aromân), in two small areas in northern Italy, in
a fairly considerable area of Calabria, southern Italy, and
in part of eastern Sardinia. There is, of course, no direct
connection between these and the Iberian case; but they are
important because they prove--in case anyone should doubt it--
that the Spanish change does not have to have been caused by
the influence of a particular substratum language.

As for the pre-Latin languages of Spain, ancient authors have
left us the names of more than two dozen tribes, which
archeologists have struggled to locate on the map, to identify
with rather meager material remains and with very meager
inscriptional remains. For many years the prevailing view was
that of von Humboldt, supported by Schuchardt and others,
according to which pre-Roman Iberia was occupied by just two
main linguistic groups, Celts and (non-IE) Iberians, plus a
mixed Celt-Iberian group (cf. Arribas 1964:21-6). The Basques
were thought to be the last survivors of the once widespread
Iberians. (There were and are various theories about the
origins of the Iberians and about the relationship of Iberian
or Basque to other languages, but they contribute nothing to
the solution of the present problem--cf. Michelena 1968.)

When, about fifty years ago, the writing system of the 'Iberian inscriptions finally began to be understood, it became clear that they represented at least three different languages, none of which was genetically related to Basque (cf. Hubschmid 1960:34-6, Tovar 1960:17). Some proponents of substratum origin of [f] > [h] refused to accept the finding that Iberian was not proto-Basque, but that finding really did not weaken their case, for the inscriptions considered to be Iberian come exclusively from an area where the change of [f] to [h] has never occurred (cf. Tovar 1949:194-210, Arribas 1964:98).

The original version of the substratum hypothesis (which was never given up or modified by Menéndez Pidal) was that the Basques (i.e. the Iberians), having no /f/, replaced Latin /f/ directly by their own /h/. For many this hypothesis was unacceptable on phonetic grounds alone. Meyer-Lübke (1935), who opposed the substratic explanation, cited cases of loanwords in Slavic languages having no [f] at the time of borrowing, in which [f] was replaced by [p]. Von Wartburg (1950:7-12), who supported this and many other substratum hypotheses, proposed that the Basques, having no [f] and in doing their best to imitate Latin, must have produced [ɸ], and this sound later became [h]. Martinet (1955: 304-15) presented a much more involved and ingenious scheme. For him too the direct replacement of [f] by [h] was unacceptable for essentially the same reason as for Meyer-Lübke: speakers of a language having no [f] will always replace [f] by some other labial, not by [h]. Martinet proposed that at the time of Romanization Basque must have had a complete series of aspirated stops and that Basque speakers learning Latin must have substituted Basque /ph/ for Latin /f/. The borrowed /ph/, along with the /th/ and /kh/ of Basque (assumed not to have been transferred into Basque-influenced Latin), later became [h] and then dropped. Martinet supports this rather far-fetched proposal by pointing out that in Modern Basque an unusually large number of words begin with vowels. This abundance of initial vowels is to be explained, Martinet suggests, by the assumption that a whole series of consonants disappeared. Since Martinet's theory is the one that Jungemann found acceptable out of all those he reviewed, it is worth pointing out in some detail why it is not acceptable.

First of all, it assumes that those Basque speakers who learned Latin would have made the same phonological changes in their new language, *over several generations,* as other Basque speakers who did not learn Latin made in their language. Such an assumption is clearly unfounded and unsupported by any evidence (except other equally doubtful substratum cases). But even more important is that Martinet's scheme leads to the wrong results. Latin words borrowed by Basque at the earliest period now have /b/ (or in some dialects /p/) for Latin /f-/:

(2)   Latin loanwords in Basque

Latin		Basque
pĭcem	>	bike
pacem	>	bake
ceresia	>	geresi
cella	>	gela

regem	>	errege
parcere	>	barkatu
cristianu	>	giristinu
fatum	>	batu, patu
familia	>	pamili
ferrum	>	berra, perra
fagus	>	bago
fava	>	baba
ficus	>	biku
tempora	>	dembora
voluntate	>	borondate
altare	>	aldare

They should, of course, have zero. Moreover, Martinet assumes
that Proto-Basque had a second series of stops, the voiceless non-
aspirates /p, t, k/, which became voiced in initial position. If
we assume that Basques learned to speak Latin with Basque phonology,
we must assume either that they identified Latin /p, t, k/ with the
Basque aspirates and Latin /b, d, g/ with the Basque non-aspirates
or else that they identified both Latin series with the Basque
non-aspirated series. In the first case, according to the
development Martinet assumes, Latin initial /p, t, k/ should all
have become [h] and then disappeared in Spanish. In the second
case they should have become /b, d, g/. But Latin initial /p, t,
k/ are alive and well in Spain to this day. As for the anti-
substratist position, I shall mention first the theory of John Orr
(1936), since I said earlier that one anti-substratum contention
was that the change occurred too early, while another was that it
happened too late.

Considering the fact (well known to Latinists but apparently
not to Romance scholars) that there was a certain confusion of /f/
and /h/ in Latin, and finding a considerable number of French
place-names with /h-/, corresponding (Orr believed) to others with
/f-/, Orr claimed that [f] > [h] must have been a pan-Romance
change going back to low-class speech in Rome itself; [f] was later
restored by learned influence in most Romance territory but not in
Gascony and north-central Spain. This thesis, put forth in 1936,
was opposed by influential scholars (not all of whom were sub-
stratophiles), and it is rarely mentioned today. I believe,
however, that Orr's position, although certainly exaggerated,
contains some points which should be taken into consideration.

That [f] > [h] occurred too late to have had a substratum
origin was the position taken by Meyer-Lübke, and it is the one
I shall attempt to demonstrate here. I believe that there is
much evidence that supports this view and none that conflicts
with it.

First, it is to be noted that intervocalic /f/, like *all*
intervocalic voiceless consonants, became voiced in Spanish.
It did *not* become [h] or fall (except in a few special cases).
The voicing of intervocalic consonants may have been fairly
early--the date is disputed--but it clearly had not yet taken
place when Latin came to Spain, even to those parts conquered
last (as is proved, perhaps ironically, by Basque borrowings
from Latin like *biku < ficu, errota < rota)*. Intervocalic /f/,

having become voiced, remained and still remains in Modern
Spanish--as the bilabial [ƀ], throughout its known history
identical with the sound that developed from Latin /-b-/.
Apparently /f/ was still [f] (or perhaps [ɸ]?), not [h], when
voicing occurred:

(3) Spanish reflexes of Latin /-f-/ and /-ff-/

Latin		Spanish		
cŏfanu	>	cuévano		
*trifinium	>	Treviño		
profectu	>	provecho		
Stephanu	>	Estevan		
trifol(i)u	>	Trébol		
bifera	>	bevra	>	breva
*affictare	>	ahitar (cf. It. affittare)		
*affundare	>	ahondar (cf. It. affondare)		
*affurcare	>	ahorcar (cf. It. afforcare)		
*affocare	>	ahogar (cf. It. affogare)		

Intervocalic /ff/ did become [h], like initial /f/. Generally
in Spanish (as generally in the other western Romance languages)
medial double consonants and initial consonants had the same
development. I think we can (in fact, must) assume that /-ff-/
remained (like other doubles) while the voicing of intervocalic
singles was in progress and only later changed to [h], like
initial /f/.

Initial /f/ did not become [h] before the diphthong [we]. It
seems only reasonable to conclude that [f] > [h] occurred
after /ŏ/ had become [we]. That /f/ was restored by the
influence of the diphthong, as has sometimes been suggested, is
not reasonable, especially in view of the fact that /f/ was
also preserved before /r/ and usually before [je] (</ĕ/),
where there is no labiality to invoke as the cause of restoration
of the labial consonant.

Internal evidence of a relatively late occurrence of [f] >
[h] agrees perfectly with the evidence of loanwords. No Spanish
words borrowed from Gothic preserved /h/:

(4) Visigothic loanwords in Spanish

Gothic	Spanish
hilms	elmo (OSp.) (cf. Fr. heaume)
harpan	arpar (cf. OFr. harper)
hanka	anca (cf. Fr. hanche)
*fat	hato
*falw	hovero (OSp.), jovero (Mod. dialectal)
Harjamunds	Arcemundo
Friþunands	Hernando

This obviously suggests that Spanish Latin had no /h/, that in
Spain then, as in Italy today, [h] was heard as nothing. But
in the few Gothic loanwords which had /f-/, /f-/ was changed to
[h], like the /f-/ of Latin words. It seems necessary to

conclude that [f] > [h] had not yet occurred at the time when
Visigothic was spoken in Spain.

Later, during the period of strong Old French influence
in Spain (because of the pilgrimage route, the Camino Francés,
to the shrine of Santiago de Compostela), Old Spanish preserved
both the /h/ and the /f/ of words which it borrowed from Old
French. This would seem to indicate that by then (about the
tenth century) Spanish had a sound with which its speakers
could identify Old French /h/ and that /f/ was no longer
changed to [h]:

(5) OFr. loanwords in OSp.

Old French	Old Spanish
hardi	hardido, fardido
hache	hacha
honte	honta, fonta
heraut	haraute, faraute

Spanish borrowings from Arabic present a somewhat confused
picture, but one generally in agreement with what we should
expect if in fact [f] > [h] occurred between the time of
Visigothic domination and the time of Old French influence; for
that is exactly when the Arabs came onto the scene. In the
majority of cases Arabic /f/ is preserved, and Arabic /h, ḥ/
and /ḫ/ all become Old Spanish /h/; but that majority is not
so overwhelming as one might like it to be:

(6) Arabic loanwords in Spanish

Arabic	Spanish
faras	alfaraz
kafal	alcáfar
safat	azafate
kāfur	alcanfor
zafarân	azafrán
ḥâfiz	hafiz
fulân	fulano
ḥurr	horro
muḥadda	almohada
baḥrî	baharí
but	
ḥanǵar	alfanje
ḥomra	alfombra

That some Arabic /f/'s became Spanish /h/'s is easily explained
by the assumption that the change either had not yet occurred
or was still in progress at the time of the earliest
borrowings--which could have been as early as the first half of
the eighth century. More difficult are the cases--fairly
numerous--in which Arabic /h, ḥ, ḫ/ became Spanish (and
Portuguese and Catalan) /f/. I think we can consider these a
kind of hypercorrection. Speakers of /f/-preserving dialects,
accustomed to equating Castilian /h/ with their own /f/, may
have done the same with Arabic words. This explanation would

seem to gain at least some support from the fact that Portuguese and Catalan changed Arabic /h, ḥ, ḫ/ to /f/ in more cases than did Spanish. (But this is a problem that requires further investigation. There are over 4,000 Arabic words in the languages of the Iberian Peninsula. They obviously cannot all be handled in a few minutes.)

Returning now to Basque and the Basques, I would like to point out some reasons, other than the apparently late date of the change, why I think that Basque had nothing to do with it.

First, in spite of many attempts to demonstrate the contrary, there is little or nothing about Basque phonology that agrees with the historical development of Spanish. It is not known whether early Basque had [h] or not. Of the modern dialects, only those spoken in France have. But in any case, Latin /f/ of early borrowings always appears as /b/ or /p/, never as /h/, in the surviving words. We noted that Basque has preserved Latin /-p-, -t-, -k-/; Spanish voiced them (cf. Spanish *hado, higo* vs. Basque *batu, biku*). Basque has kept Latin /k, g/ as velars before front vowels; Spanish palatalized and spirantized them (cf. Latin *pace* > Basque *bake*, Spanish *paz*). Basque regularly voiced Latin /p, t, k/ after nasals and /l/; Spanish did not (cf. Spanish *tiempo*, Basque *dembora*). Basque generally inserted epenthetic vowels between stops and liquids (*fronte>boronde*); Spanish did not. Basque did not dipthongize /ĕ/ and /ŏ/; Spanish did. Basque merged /ĭ/ with /ī/, /ĕ/ with /ē/, /ŭ/ with /ū/, /ŏ/ with /ō/; Spanish merged /ĭ/ with /ē/ and /ŭ/ with /ō/, keeping /ĕ/ and /ŏ/ (as well as /ī, ū/) separate. And, as I mentioned in connection with Martinet's discussion, Basque voiced initial /p, t, k/ while Spanish preserved them.[14]

As for historical connection (in the sense of the first speakers of /f/-less Ibero-Romance having been descendants of speakers of Basque), available evidence does not support the substratist position. The study of place names suggests that the greatest area ever occupied by Basque speakers was only slightly more extensive than the Basque Provinces of today. This would seem to indicate that no very large number of Basque speakers became speakers of Romance. Moreover, while some formerly Basque-speaking territory is in Old Castile, more of it is in Navarre, where /f-/ still survives.

Defenders of the hypothesis of substratum origin of [f] > [h] have spoken of intimate contact between the Basque territory and Castile and have said that Basques initiated the Reconquest of Spain from the Arabs. (It is not clear that these allegations support the assumption of substratum [= imperfect learning] influence. They seem rather to support the assumption that [f] > [h] was a borrowing from Basque, an adstratum or superstratum influence.)

As for the first point, it is true that the northern part of eastern Castile was generally bounded by Basque territory and that in later times (i.e. after about the beginning of the thirteenth century) the Kingdom of Castile included the western part of the Basque lands; but Navarre *always* included more than half of the Basque territory and until the thirteenth century included all of it (cf. Shepherd 1956:54, 82-3). Pamplona, the

capital of Navarre, is barely outside the Basque-speaking area,
which in fact formerly encompassed it. Yet, as already
mentioned, Navarrese Spanish did not change /f/ to /h/.

The second point, that the Basques were the initiators of the
Reconquest, seems to have even less foundation. According to
both popular tradition and scholarly history, the first
counteroffensive against the Arabs came from the nascent kingdom
of Asturias, whose capital was at Cangas de Onís, 175 kilometers
west of the present border of the Basque provinces and at least
125 kilometers west of the most extreme limits assumed for
Basque speakers in previous centuries on the evidence of place
names (cf. Masías 1943:99-100). Moreover, it would be
incongruous to imagine the Basques as leaders of an anti-Islamic
crusade (thereby gaining the prestige that supposedly caused
their peculiarities of pronunciation to be imitated by others)
at a time when they themselves probably had not yet been
Christianized (cf. Gallop 1970:10-11).

The reasons why the Basque language has been able to survive
and the Basques have been able to maintain their separate
identity to the present century are also reasons why it is
unlikely that the Basques could have had much influence on the
development of Spanish. They remained isolated and
non-participating on land that no conqueror was much interested
in taking over and exploiting. Their complete lack of political
unity is reflected in the fact that on a territory of 60 by 160
kilometers there are eight major dialects and an uncounted number
of subdialects (cf. Tovar 1957:106-9). The major dialects differ
from each other so widely that speakers from different provinces
often cannot understand each other's native dialects and must
communicate with each other in Spanish or French.[15] The English
Bascophile Rodney Gallop wrote (1970:12-3): 'In the main the
Basques took no part in the historical events of which the
Basque Country has been the scene, and they held coldly aloof
from these innumerable wars and princely passages. Basque
history is the history of independence of the Basque provinces'.
The distinguished Spanish philologist-historian Americo Castro
(1966:151), speaking of the Navarrese Basques of the twelfth
century, opines that, 'El no haberese romanizado
lingüísticamente descubre, sin más, su escasa participación en
la vida del resto de la Península'.

To sum up the case for [f] > [h] as a carryover of the
pronunciation of a pre-Latin language in reference to the
criteria suggested earlier in this paper, we have found that

1.   The claimed phonological correspondences are
     implausible or, at best, doubtful;
2.   A convincing historico-territorial relationship
     cannot be demonstrated;
3.   The change appears to have occurred too late to
     have been caused by substratum influence;
4.   Our knowledge of social and political conditions of
     early Spain does not give us reason to think that even
     if Basque speakers had substituted [h] for [f] when
     they began to speak Romance, this feature would have
     been accepted by non-Basque speakers of Romance and

have eventually become the national norm.
Pre-Latin origin of the change is, of course, not disproved;
but it certainly appears unlikely.

If time permitted, I should like to deal with two more points:
a possible non-substratic explanation of [f] > [h] and (since I
have rejected every substratum hypothesis mentioned here) the
question of whether substratum influence on pronunciation is
possible at all. But time does not permit. Allow me to say in
regard to the first only that I do think a non-substratic
explanation is possible, that my explanation is partially similar
to Haudricourt and Juilland's, but it is also related to Orr's
in that I think [ɸ] may already have existed in the Latin
brought to Spain.[16] In regard to the second, I would say that
I do indeed believe that there are conditions under which native
sounds can (and do) continue in a new language learned by a
whole group, but it does not appear that such conditions existed
in the Romanization of any of the present Romance-speaking lands.
The influence of the pre-Latin languages seems to have been
limited to lexical and toponomastical borrowings, like the
influence of Spanish on the English of the American Southwest.
Any influences on phonology must have been either too subtle to
be traced or lost in the many successive spontaneous sound
changes and demographic shifts.

NOTES

[1]This has not always been the case, however. The ease theory
has been in and out of fashion many times. Whitney, Curtius,
Jespersen, and Bourciez, among others, believed in it; and even
Bloomfield conceded (1933:386) that 'a great deal of sound change
is in some way connected with this factor'; but Leskien and
Sievers rejected it as worthless, as did most American linguists
of recent decades.

[2]By 'ease properly understood' I mean to say that at least
the following must be kept in mind: (1) Ease of articulation is
always in conflict with ease of comprehension (the tendency to
slur and mumble is restrained by the speaker's need to be
understood), with the desire to be emphatic, and with the need
to fill pauses with meaningless noise while the speaker thinks
(hence, *at this point in time* for *now*, etc.). (2) There is
something like a Newton's Second Law of Motion in language: if
a language is squeezed at one place it may bulge out in another.
(When English dropped the /-g/ of words like *thing, song,* etc.
it gained the new phoneme /ŋ/, and *longer* and *stronger* became
irregular comparatives.) (3) At any given moment probably any
particular sound contrast is dispensable, but not more than a
few contrasts can be given up at a time. This means that the
'decision' to give up a contrast or series of contrasts is
equivalent to a 'decision' to retain other contrasts--for the

time being. (4) Like physical, chemical, or biological processes, linguistic changes take time.

If these factors and perhaps certain others are taken into consideration, the idea that ease may be a causative factor in linguistic change will not appear incompatible with the fact that languages never really become easy and never stop changing any more than the fact that water evaporates from the oceans is incompatible with the fact that the oceans don't dry up.

[3]From *Life on the Mississippi*, Chapter 17.

[4]Cf. Sapir 1921:157-61 on random variation, Jespersen 1923:140-5 on children's apparently perfect conformity with the norm in the matter of phonology. Andersen 1973, developing and formalizing the principle (already discussed in, for example, Jespersen 1923:172-80) which he calls abductive change, gives an account of the reinterpretation of facets of a language as it passes from generation to generation that answers the objection of randomness (cf. also Maher 1976); but abduction explains semantic and grammatical change more satisfactorily than phonetic change.

[5]Generativists would of course object that I have distorted their claims, but their ways of expressing themselves certainly invite one to assume that they believe that rule changes cause rather than describe linguistic changes. Cf. again King (1969:197): 'These changes can be explained in terms of rule simplification as follows. First, we assume that Rule 8.3 was added as an innovation in Southern Yiddish: ... Rule 8.3 is then simplified ... The resultant rule now affects both back rounded vowels, creating the drag chain $\bar{u}>\ddot{u}$ and $\delta>\bar{u}$'. Cf. the comments on this matter in Andersen 1973:766-7.

[6]But I should like to point out that the study and many of its findings are not new. Although it is customary to make a respectful reference to Uriel Weinreich's excellent summation of two decades ago, it is not often remembered that two decades before *Languages in Contact* Bloomfield had given an insightful synthesis in the three chapters of *Language* called 'Cultural Borrowing', 'Intimate Borrowing', and 'Dialect Borrowing'; and that before Bloomfield, Jespersen, Vendryes, the now forgotten George Hempl (and perhaps many others that I am unaware of) had said things that are still interesting and valid. The mere idea that language contact causes change (but without any working out of specifics) goes back at least to the 16th century. (Cf. the interesting but fanciful statements about the influence of Etruscan on Italian by Pier Francesco Giambullari in his *Origine della lingua fiorentina* of 1549. See Rea 1976 for the substratum and superstratum ideas of the 16th-17th century English mathematician Edward Brerewood.)

An erroneous tradition ascribes to Graziadio Ascoli the invention of the theory of substratum influence or 'ethnic reaction' near the end of the 19th century (e.g. Amado Alonso 1954:315 and Tagliavini 1964:64). Curtis Blaylock (1960) notes that Diez was aware of the possibility of substratum influence, and he refers in a note to the article in which Niels Nielsen attributes the invention of the idea of substratum influence to

Jakob Bredsdorff in 1821; but Nielsen was mistaken. Carl L.
Fernow had already proposed in 1808 that the influences of
pre-Latin languages had caused certain phonological changes in
the Romance languages, as had Carlo Denina in 1804; and, as
already mentioned, the idea of sub- and superstratum influence
already existed, at least in vague form, as early as the 16th
century.

[7]One can easily verify this by listening to some of the
readily available recordings (e.g. Folkways FL 9930 for standard
Peninsular stage pronunciation and Folkways FL 9927 for a
variety of Argentinian). In the varieties of Brazilian
Portuguese with which I am acquainted /r/ is a tap [r], but /rr/
is [x]. This makes the presence of syllable-final /rr/ (e.g.
[gwaxdáx] *guardar*) obvious even to the untrained ear. (Cf.
also Cassano 1973 on this question.)

[8]In fact it is not quite dead even today. Rosetti (1968:205)
refers to it as an established case of substratum influence, and
Tagliavini (1964:114) speaks favorably of Lenz's work, warning
only that Lenz exaggerated the Araucanian influence somewhat.

[9]Lenz's papers published in five installments in two
different journals in 1892 and 1893 were brought together,
translated into Spanish, and published (Lenz 1940) by Amado
Alonso.

[10]See Pulgram 1957 for a discussion of the relative ease with
which different elements of linguistic structure can be passed
from one language to another. For justification of the other
points cf. Izzo 1972b.

[11]Frankish and Visigothic are, of course, superstrata, not
substrata, for French and Spanish. I cite them here because the
facts in this case are far more certain than any substratum case
known to me.

[12]Cf. in this connection also Martinet's observations (1963:
211) on the nondistinction of /ɑ/ and /a/ in southern France.

[13]Examples of this phenomenon can be heard in the previously
cited Folkways FL 9927 and can be found in many literary works
(e. g. Gaucho poetry) that imitate popular speech.

[14]For Basque phonology cf. Gavel 1920, Gavel 1929, Tovar 1957,
Michelena 1961.

[15]Cf. Castro 1966:10: 'En 1921 yo oí leer un discurso en
vizcaíno que, por supuesto, yo no entendía, ni tampoco un
vasco quipuzcoano sentado junto a mí'. Cf. also Gallop
1970:81-2.

[16]Looked at formalistically--through the grid of a feature
matrix for example--the change of [f] to [h] seems an extreme
one and seems to require a complicated explanation; hence
suggestions (e.g. Naro 1972) of an intermediate stage or stages.
From an articulatory point of view the change is simple: if a
speaker fails to make sufficient labial constriction to produce
friction noise but changes nothing else, [h] is the automatic

result. (I assume that this was also the mechanism of the much
later change of [s] to [h] in southern Spain and lowland
Spanish America.)

REFERENCES

Alonso, Amado. 1953. Estudios lingüísticos: temas
hispanoamericanos. Madrid: Gredos.
_____. 1954. Estudios lingüísticos: temas españoles.
Madrid: Gredos.
Andersen, Henning. 1973. Abductive and deductive change.
Language 49:765-93.
Arribas, Antonio. 1964. The Iberians. New York: Praeger.
Battisti, Carlo. 1930. Aspirazione etrusca e gorgia toscana.
Studi etruschi 4:249-54.
Blaylock, Curtis. 1960. Substratum theory applied to
Hispano-Romance. Romance philology 13:414-9.
Bloomfield, Leonard. 1933. Language. New York: Holt.
Boyd-Bowman, Peter. 1960. El habla de Guanajuato. Mexico:
Universidad Nacional Autónoma de México.
Cassano, Paul V. 1973. A critique of Bertil Malmberg,
Tradición hispánica e influencia indígena en la fonética
hispanoamericana. Canadian journal of linguistics 18:31-45.
Castro, Américo. 1966. La realidad histórica de España.
3rd ed. Mexico: Porrúa.
Conway, Robert S. 1891. The origin of the Latin gerund and
gerundive. Classical review 5:296-301.
Gallop, Rodney. 1970. A book of the Basques. 2nd ed. Reno:
University of Nevada Press.
Gavel, Henri. 1920. Éléments de phonétique basque. Paris:
Champion.
_____. 1929. Grammaire basque. Bayonne: Imprimerie du
Courrier.
Hall, Robert A., Jr. 1949. Nasal+homorganic plosive in central
and south Italian. Archivum linguisticum 1:151-6.
_____. 1968. An essay on language. Philadelphia and New
York: Chilton.
_____. 1974. The external history of the Romance languages.
New York and Amsterdam: Elsevier.
Haudricourt, André and Alphonse Juilland. 1970. Essai pour une
histoire structurale du phonétisme français. 2nd ed. The
Hague: Mouton.
Hempl, George. 1898. Language-rivalry and speech-
differentiation in the case of race-mixture. Transactions
of the American Philological Society 29:31-47.
Hubschmid, Johannes. 1960. Lenguas prerromanas de la península
ibérica: lenguas no indoeuropeas--testimonios románicos.
Enciclopedia lingüística hispánica, ed. by Manuel Alvar et
al., 1.27-66. Madrid: Consejo Superior de Investigaciones
Científicas.

Izzo, Herbert. 1972a. The layer-cake model in historical
    linguistics. General linguistics 12:159-68.
_____. 1972b. Tuscan and Etruscan: the problem of
    linguistic substratum influence in central Italy. Toronto:
    University of Toronto Press.
Jespersen, Otto. 1894. Progress in language. London.
_____. 1923. Language; its nature, development, and origin.
    London and New York: MacMillan.
Jungemann, Frederick H. 1955. La teoría del sustrato y los
    dialectos hispano-romances y gascones. Madrid: Gredos.
King, Robert D. 1969. Historical linguistics and generative
    grammar. Englewood Cliffs: Prentice-Hall.
Lenz, Rudolf. 1940. El español de Chile. Biblioteca de
    dialectología hispanoamericana 6:79-258.
Lloyd, Paul M. 1971. L'action du substrat et la structure
    linguistique. Actele celui de al XII-lea Congres
    Internaţional de Lingvistică şi Filologie Romanică 2.953-63.
    Bucharest: Academia Republicii Socialiste România.
Lope Blanch, Juan. 1967. La -r final y el sustrato nahua.
    Thesaurus 22:1-20.
Maher, J. Peter. 1976. The source of Italian *tardi*, with notes
    on the transformational-generative paradigm. Italic and
    Romance: linguistic studies presented to Ernst Pulgram, ed.
    by H. Izzo. Lisse: Peter de Ridder.
Malmberg, Bertil. 1959. L'extension du castillan et le
    problème des substrats. Actes du Colloque International de
    Civilisations, Littératures et Langues Romanes, 249-60.
    Bucharest: UNESCO.
_____. 1964. Tradición hispánica e influencia indígena en la
    fonética hispanoamericana. Presente y futuro de la lengua
    española, OFINES, 2.227-43. Madrid: Ediciones Cultura
    Hispánica.
Martinet, André. 1955. Économie des changements phonétiques.
    Bern: Franke.
_____. 1963. Éléments de linguistique générale. 3rd ed.
    Paris: Armand Colin.
Masías, Angeles. 1943. Introducción a la historia de España.
    Barcelona: Apolo.
Meillet, Antoine. 1938. Esquisse d'une histoire de la langue
    latine. 4th ed. Paris: Hachette. (Reprinted 1966.)
Menéndez Pidal, Ramón. 1950. Modo de obrar el substrato.
    Revista de filología española 34:1-8.
Merlo, Clemente. 1933. Il sostrato etnico e i dialetti
    italiani. Italia dialettale 9:1-24.
Meyer-Lübke, Wilhelm. 1935. Lat. *F* im Baskischen, Span.,
    Gaskogn. *h* aus Lat. *F*. Archiv für das Studium der neueren
    Sprachen 166:50-68.
Michelena, Luis. 1961. Fonética histórica vasca. San
    Sebastián: Seminario Julio de Urquijo.
_____. 1968. L'euskaro-caucasien. Le langage, ed. by
    André Martinet, 1414-37. Bruges: Gallimard.
Naro, Anthony J. 1972. On *f* > *h* in Castilian and Western
    Romance. Zeitschrift für romanische Philologie 88:463-82.

Navarro Tomás, Tomás. 1953. Manual de pronunciación
    española. 4th ed. New York: Hafner.
Nielsen, Niels. 1952. La théorie des substrats et la
    linguistique structurale. Acta linguistica 7:1-7.
Orr, John. 1936. *f > h*, phénomène ibère ou roman? Revue de
    linguistique romane 12:10-35.
Poultney, James W. 1976. The phonology of the Latin gerundive.
    Italic and Romance: Linguistic studies presented to Ernst
    Pulgram, ed. by H. Izzo. Lisse: Peter de Ridder.
Pulgram, Ernst. 1949. Prehistory and the Italian dialects.
    Lg. 25:241-52.
_____. 1957. Linguistic expansion and diversification.
    Studies presented to Joshua Whatmough, ed. by Ernst
    Pulgram 239-52. The Hague: Mouton.
Rea, John A. 1976. Linguistic speculations of Edward
    Brerewood (1566-1613). Linguistic and literary studies in
    honor of Archibald A. Hill, ed. by Mohammad Ali Jazayery
    et al., 257-62. Lisse: Peter de Ridder.
Rosetti, Alexandru. 1968. Istoria limbii române. Bucharest:
    Editura pentru Literatură.
Sapir, Edward. 1921. Language. New York: Harcourt, Brace
    and Co.
Shepherd, William R. 1956. Historical atlas, 8th ed. New York:
    Barnes & Noble.
Sturtevant, Edgar. 1917. Linguistic change. Chicago:
    University of Chicago Press.
Tagliavini, Carlo. 1964. Le origini delle lingue neolatine.
    4th ed. Bologna: Pàtron.
Tovar, Antonio. 1949. Estudios sobre las primitivas lenguas
    hispánicas. Buenos Aires: Coni.
_____. 1957. The Basque language. New York: American Book Co.
_____. 1960. Lenguas prerromanas de la península ibérica:
    lenguas no indoeuropeas--testimonios antiguos. Enciclopedia
    lingüística hispánica, ed. by Manuel Alvar et al., 1.5-26.
    Madrid: Consejo Superior de Investigaciones Científicas.
Vendryes, Joseph. 1921. Le langage. Paris: La Renaissance
    du livre.
Wartburg, Walter Von. 1950. Die Ausgliederung der romanischen
    Sprachräume. Bern: Franke.
Weinreich, Uriel. 1953. Languages in contact. New York:
    Linguistic Circle of New York.
Weinrich, Harald. 1958. Phonologische Studien zur romanischen
    Sprachgeschichte. (Forschungen zur romanischen Philologie,
    Heft 6) Münster: Aschendorffsche Verlagsbuchhandlung.
Whatmough, Joshua. 1949. On gerund grinding. Classical
    weekly. 43:20-1.

GENDER, SEX, AND SIZE, AS REFLECTED IN THE ROMANCE LANGUAGES

YAKOV MALKIEL

University of California at Berkeley

1. Preliminaries

Let me attempt to circumscribe from the start the intended
scope of this paper. It is to contain no announcement of any
sensational discovery. The threads that lead from the
examination of grammatical gender to the study of naive
statements about size, or of suggestions of size, with some
background attention paid to sex, allow us to piece together
the fascinating story of a protracted scholarly dialogue. The
discussion started in low gear almost a century ago; it reached
a much higher plateau of intensity from the early twenties to
the late forties, and some of the participants of that debate
are still with us, while others passed away not so long ago.
New voices, including young ones, have been heard over the last
few years, though no new chorus has yet emerged. My paper, then,
concerns a classic issue in Romance linguistics, one which
abounds in implications for general linguistics--an issue
distinctly better defined and understood at present than it was
half a century ago, but by no means exhaustively solved in all
its complexity. I shall exercise my right to offer, here and

there, bits of criticism and certain slight qualifications, but
I shall not presume to settle all such ramifications of the
chosen problem as have been left dangling.

The relation of sex to gender--in those languages which accept
gender as a separate grammatical category--varies from culture
to culture. In this respect, the configuration of English, in
which, poetry and allegory apart, *he* stands for 'male', *she* for
'female', and *it* for 'inanimate', is fairly exceptional. Some
major languages of the world, German included, do not even
possess separate terms to distinguish between 'gender' and
'sex', between 'masculine' and 'male', or between 'feminine'
and 'female'; the same lexical items, *Geschlecht, männlich,* and
weiblich, each perform the same dual function. Russian
separates 'gender' from 'sex' (*rod* vs. *pol*), but not, e.g.
'masculine' from 'male'. The Indo-European languages are,
thus, characterized by a partial overlap of 'gender' and 'sex'.

This overlap is particularly easy to observe in the older
(or modern but traditionally-patterned) Indo-European languages.
In Classical Latin, for instance, a grammatically masculine·
word may designate a male animate being (say, *puer* 'boy') or
some inanimate object (say, *lapis* 'stone'); and the same holds
for the feminine (witness *puella* 'girl' vs. *mēnsa* 'table');
neuters do not refer to animate beings in Latin (typical
examples being *bellum* 'war' and *mare* 'sea'); but in Russian
they may occasionally do so (e.g. *ditja* 'baby, child'),
although in all other relevant typological respects Russian
coincides with Latin. The gender in practically all Indo-
European languages can often be recognized by sharply
characterized forms of qualifiers that accompany the nouns at
issue, including articles if these are available, or by pronouns
substituted for these nouns; in certain languages the ending of
the given word supplies reliable or at least probabilistic
concomitant information. Thus, in Latin, despite a few tricky
cases, such as *socrus* for 'mother-in-law' and *nūrus* for
'daughter-in-law' (or, for that matter, *domus* 'house'), the
ending *-us* is normally a safe guide to the masculine gender,
as in *hortus* 'garden' and *exercitus* 'army'; also, *-a* in the
singular, except for tiny, neatly-delimited groups of exceptions,
is practically a guarantee of feminine gender, though the state
of affairs is entirely different in the plural, where *-a* is
associated with the neuter, far beyond the confines of Latin.
Other endings are inconclusive as to gender. In Spanish and
Tuscan you find to this day a very similar situation; it is,
incontrovertibly, *el tío* 'uncle' ~ *la tía* 'aunt', *lo zio* ~ *la
zia,* but what about *arte* and *fin(e)*? Small wonder that here
predictability is at its lowest and the decisions of the
speakers sometimes appear not only arbitrary but hesitant,
within the same language--as between Sp. *el arte gótico,* but
las bellas artes or between It. *la fine* 'end' and *il fine*
'purpose'--but even more so if one compares one language with
others: Sp. *la sangre* 'blood' vs. Ptg. *o sangue,* It. *il sangue.*
In French, on the other hand, the shape of a noun, in general,
and its final segment, in particular, cast only faint light, or
no light at all, on the gender. We happen to know that *oncle*
is masculine and *tante* is feminine, but it is not the respective

sequences of sounds that offer us these clues.

Many more such elementary facts could be recapitulated here, but my assignment at this point calls for a switch of attention to the linguistic correlates of size. In the parent language, as well as in its congeners, special modifying suffixes were available for suggesting a half-hypocoristic (or -ironic), half-diminutive message; thus, *rēgulus* (from *rēx*) could mean 'small king', 'charming little king', 'petty king', and the like. The daughter-languages developed a whole network of hypocoristic-miniaturizing and derogatory-augmentative suffixes; their genesis and diffusion is an intricate problem, into which we need not delve. Can size be linguistically suggested in yet other ways? Otto Jespersen, a firm believer in the effects of sound symbolism, once remarked in a celebrated short note that the vowel /i/, cross-culturally, was apt to evoke diminutiveness, an idea to which Joseph H. Greenberg, not so long ago, reverted, by no means disapprovingly, in his stimulating *Essays in Linguistics*. Meillet was willing to endow, at least in an individual language such as Latin, the *a* of the adjectival root-morpheme with a suggestiveness of comparable latitude.

At this juncture there arises the question whether the inventory of size-suggestive devices, in a family or rather subfamily of languages such as Romance, could also have included the mechanism of gender-switch. For instance, could the existing label for a 'large container', particularly if that label was equipped with an ending sharply characterized as to gender (say, -*a* in Spanish or Italian), give rise to the name of a tag for a 'small container' through substitution of -*o* for -*a?* Posed in these terms, the issue is difficult enough, involving as it does a grammatical plus a referential ingredient and appealing as it must to the straight linguist and to the student of material civilization steeped in *Wörter-und-Sachen* analysis. The problem is bound to be further complicated if one adds the element of sex, as observed especially in humans and in larger, familiar animals. Is there, in the problem at hand, a component that, for lack of a more appropriate term, one might be tempted to call, with Damourette and Pichon, 'sexuisemblance'?

It turns out that the entire multi-pronged issue is by no means new and that we have now sufficiently prepared ourselves not only for attacking it frontally, but also for critically inspecting and sifting the record of earlier tentative formulations. The one shred of information still missing is that in the course of the transition from Latin to Romance the neuter disappeared in the class of nouns (though not of pronouns), merging frequently with the masculine in the singular and/or with the feminine in the plural--producing collectives, as in It. *il dito* 'the finger' beside *le dita* 'the five fingers of one hand' (or 'the five toes of one foot'), or casting off 'ambigenerics', i.e. words masculine in the singular and feminine in the plural, as in Rumanian.

2.   The crystallization of the problem

If you search for the earliest manifestation of originality in
Romance linguistics, as displayed in the discovery of one
particularly rewarding genre of research, you will perhaps
agree with me that the ferreting-out and classification of
doublets (*doppioni*, *Scheidewörter*) was one such experiment or,
if you prefer, fad. There was an ingredient of parlor game in
this type of inquiry which, launched almost simultaneously by
a minor figure, Auguste Brachet, and by the great comparatist
Michel Bréal around 1868, spread like wildfire, catching the
imagination not only of Romance linguists, such as Ugo Canello,
Carolina Michaëlis, and Francisco Adolfo Coelho, but of
outsiders as well, witness the British etymologist W. W. Skeat.
Ordinarily, doublets (and, in exceptional cases, triplets) were
coexistent reflexes—typically, with semantic differentiation—
of the same ancestral bases, involving different channels of
transmission (say, learned vs. vernacular or borrowed vs.
indigenous), as in Sp. *mácula* 'blemish' vs. *mancha* 'spot' or in
Fr. *rigide* 'strict' vs. *raide* 'stiff, tight, taut'. But once
curiosity about such pairs had been sensitized, it was possible
to transfer it to similar configurations of semantic units.
     Thus, when the Swedish pioneer dialectologist Å. W. Munthe,
working in Western Asturias in the mid-eighties, recorded in
his field notes *bintanu* 'small window' alongside *bintana*
'window', the local counterpart of Sp. *ventana*, the brilliant
Portuguese linguist Gonçálvez Viana, reviewing Munthe's Upsala
dissertation in the opening volume of *Revista Lusitana* a few
years later, was led to expatiate on the entry, distinguishing
between two kinds of such semantically nuanced and formally
polarized pairs in standard Portuguese: either the feminine
was preëxistent and the masculine, secondarily arrived at,
involved diminution, as in *caldeira* 'caldron, kettle', *canela*
'shin bone', *cortiça* 'cork bark', vs. *caldeiro* 'small kettle',
canelo 'horse shoe', *cortiço* 'beehive'; or the masculine was
preëxistent and the feminine, representing the innovation,
was augmentative, as in *sapato* 'shoe' and *poço* 'well', vs.
sapata 'low shoe, brakeshoe' and *poça* 'shallow pool, pond,
puddle'. This laconic comment, running to a few lines,
contained the seeds of one of the most celebrated issues in
the annals of Romance linguistics.[1]
     Meanwhile, the year 1883 had witnessed the appearance on the
scene of a young scholar who was soon to influence events in
the Romance field, and of a book of major, if indirect,
relevancy to the issue under scrutiny. In his doctoral
dissertation Wilhelm Meyer—the future Meyer-Lübke—concerned
himself with the vicissitudes of the Latin neuter in Romance.
Such facets of the problem as the long coexistence of, say,
folium, sg., 'leaf' and *folia*, pl., 'leaves, foliage' (cf. Fr.
feuil ~ feuille as in OFr. *chèvrefoil* 'honeysuckle' beside
fueille) or *brac(c)hium* 'arm' and *brac(c)hia* 'arms' (cf. Fr.
le bras, the anatomical term, as against *la brace* 'fathom');
or as the relation, in Tuscan, of the singulars *dito* 'finger',
osso 'bone', *uovo* 'egg' to the peculiar collectives in *le dita*,

le ossa, le uova; or as the crystallization in Rumanian of the
two ambigeneric nominal paradigms into which eventually even
words of Hungarian and Anatolian Turkish ancestry were pressed--
oraş m. 'town'/*oraşe* f. 'towns', *dulap* m. 'closet'/*dulapuri* f.
'closets'--these and related issues, bearing on collectivity
and augmentation, were to acquire considerable prominence in
the discussion of lexical pairs differentiated as to size. On
the Indo-European side, Meyer-Lübke's study likewise fell into
place very smoothly, because here scholars of the rank of
Johannes Schmidt also, independently, busied themselves, in
the late nineteenth century, with the formation of the neuter
plurals. In his *Italienische Grammatik* of the year 1890,
Meyer-Lübke himself reaped benefit from his earlier probings,
first, by citing several pairs of nouns where the masculine,
in *-o*, designated a smaller object than the corresponding
feminine, in *-a: ber(r)etto* 'cap, headgear', *buco* 'hole',
bugnolo 'straw-plaited basket', *canestro* 'wicker basket, fruit
basket, washing basket', *cavicchio* 'bolt, peg, wooden pin, rung
of a ladder', *cerchio* 'circle, ring', *fiasco* 'glass bottle
(with straw covering)', *fungo* 'fungus, mushroom', *orezzo* (poet.)
'light breeze, cool shade' (291f.); and, second, by observing,
in another, not closely related passage (303), that feminine
primitives are accompanied by genuine diminutives in *-ina* (e.g.
casa 'house'--*casina* 'small house', *carrozza* 'car'--*carrozzina*
'small car') where the corresponding *-ino* derivative normally
reserved for this purpose has accidentally become semantically
deflected (*casino, carrozzino*). Meyer-Lübke treated both
points briefly and superficially,[2] and, alas, was to pay scant
attention to the problem and its ramifications in his subsequent
writings.[3]

Perhaps as a result of this relative indifference on the part
of the tone-setting specialist, the discussion, for thirty long
years, was to pick up momentum very slowly. To be sure,
individual observations, on a small scale, were made here and
there, e.g. by Karl Jaberg in his first introduction (1908) to
dialect geography, when he discussed the maps *chaudron* and
chaudière of the *Atlas linguistique de la France*. In reference
to Occitan usage (which marks the masculine with zero and the
feminine with *-o*), Jaberg confirmed that *pairol* ordinarily
denotes the 'small kettle' and *pairolo* the 'large kettle'.
Pairol, by way of exception, may denote the large kettle if
preceded by the qualifier *grã*, unless an entirely different
word is pressed into service for the 'small kettle'. Gilliéron
himself, the mastermind of the glottogeographic movement,
focused attention in a celebrated excursus, ten years later, on
a separate, but related problem: in reference to very young
girls, a masculine form of one of the available diminutive-
hypocoristic suffixes is attached to their names, transmuting
Louise into *Louison, Marie* into *Marion, Suzette* into *Suzon,*
this despite the fact that the less disquieting use of *-onne,*
or *-ette,* or *-ine* would, so it seems at first glance, have
been admissible. This stimulating side issue has produced a
sizable corpus of literature of its own, into which it is
tempting to plunge--but we must curb the temptation; suffice

it to state that through Gilliéron's sparkling essay gender
switch and derivational suffixation were for the first time
closely associated. The time was now ripe for a livelier
course of events, and a dialogue soon ensued.

The year Gilliéron's study, appended to his monograph on the
Gallo-Romance names of the bee, appeared in print, a Catalan
polymath or *polígrafo*, M. de Montoliu, published in a Barcelona
journal--to be specific, in the Bulletin of the Catalan
Institute--a short list of regionalisms recorded in the rural
environs of Tarragona. Two consecutive entries, given no
particular prominence, were *llangost* 'locust' and *llangosta*
'somewhat larger locust'. These entries captured the attention
of a young and, at that juncture, still little-known Swiss
Romanist, W. von Wartburg, who, conceivably under the continued
impact of his teacher Gilliéron's sensational monograph on
entomonymy, asked himself, in a tightly-packaged note which
appeared three years later, whether the root of the suggestion
of larger size by the feminine variants was traceable to the
names of living beings, e.g. insects, and could thus, in the
last analysis, go back to man's--specifically, an untutored
speaker's--observations of the facts of nature. At this point,
in 1921, the so far unsuspected possibility of a biological
element or kernel began to loom.

After briefly considering the wisdom of this explanation,
which he called 'objective' and which we would tend to associate
with conditions of 'real life', Wartburg repudiated it, in part
because biological facts failed to support it--male locusts,
at least those stationed in Spain, happen to exceed their
females in size--in part, more significantly, because the majority
of lexical pairs related to inanimate referents, e.g. Cat. *anell*
'ring' vs. *anella* 'large ring'. 'Une différence naturelle ne
peut donc plus en être la cause', argued Wartburg, casting
around for other examples of names of tools and containers,
such as Sp. *bieldo ~ bielda* 'rake, pitchfork', *panero ~ panera*
'breadbasket', 'baker's basket', *saco ~ saca* 'sack, bag', with
the feminine member of the pair consistently labeling the
bigger object (cf. also Fr. *râteau* 'rake' vs. Gasc. *rastero*
'big rake').[4] Wartburg selected as the starting point for his--
strictly grammatical--explanation the collectively nuanced
plurals of the Latin neuters--*prātum* 'meadow' vs. *prāta* 'meadows',
as reflected in Fr. *pré* vs. *prée,* arguing that the mass-noun
meaning could gradually have changed into an augmentative
meaning: from 'several adjoining small meadows' there was but
a step to 'single large meadow': 'On s'est évidemment figuré
le tout comme composé de plusieurs morceaux. Puis, peu à peu,
l'idée de la pluralité s'est effacée et l'on a conçu l'étendue
des prés comme un tout'. After choosing *saco ~ saca* as the
presumable leader words among the designations of tools and
containers and recognizing in Sp. *dedo* 'finger, toe' beside
Ast. *deda* 'big toe' an advanced stage of the development,
Wartburg rightly observed that this pattern, from the start,
was far more weakly developed in French than in Occitan and the
languages of the Iberian Peninsula, but made a serious blunder
by flatly declaring that the model was absent from Italian and,

presumably, from Rumanian--a surprising remark indeed after
Meyer-Lübke's well-documented statements to the contrary, at
least as regards Tuscan. On later occasions a more experienced
and better-read Wartburg would revert to this topic, but his
subsequent pronouncements no longer formed links in the
principal chain of events.[5]

Wartburg's 1921 note--provocative and, in part, clearly
misleading as it was--did not at once stir any controversy;
thus field workers lucky enough to discover further vestiges
of such lexical pairs failed to refer to it--it was not ignored
but simply overlooked.[6] But the related issue of the paradoxical
development of the suffix -one continued to worry scholars
throughout the twenties. In addition to the slightly piquant
problem of the French hypocoristics *Louison, Madelon, Marion,*
etc. there was that other puzzle familiar to every traveler
touring Europe: whereas in France *carafon* is a small and
carafe a standard-sized decanter, in Spain *garrafón* denotes a
large and *garrafa* a standard-sized carafe. How can one
reconcile these diametrically opposed evolutionary lines?   It.
caraffa, as an old liquid measure, stands alone; were it
accompanied by an appropriate satellite formation, Italian
usage would, on circumstantial evidence, harmonize with Spanish
preferences, leaving French alone. But aligning majorities is
not yet offering a satisfactory explanation. In 1921 E.
Gamillscheg credited the semantic peculiarity of Fr. *-on* to
Germanic influence, which indeed was stronger in Northern Gaul
than in most other provinces. Leo Spitzer, in a paper attached
to Gamillscheg's, opted for a witty, psychologizing
interpretation of the facts. Eight years later, Gamillscheg
reversed himself: he was now prepared to distinguish, in the
parent language, between an individualizing suffix $-\bar{o}$, $-\bar{o}nis$,
attached--among other uses--to certain animal names, and a
miniaturizing suffix $-i\bar{o}, -i\bar{o}nis$, appearing in the names of small,
flitting living beings (cf.$p\bar{a}pili\bar{o}$ 'butterfly' and, judging
from Fr. *poisson,* *$\ast pisci\bar{o}$* 'fish', originally 'small fish,
fishlet', which had been allowed to spread at the expense of
Class. *piscis* preserved elsewhere--It. *pesce,* Ptg. *peixe,* OSp.
peçe, etc.). The two suffixes merged, and the second, being
more copiously represented in Northern France, left its
semantic stamp on Fr. *-on,* making in the end *carafon* a small
rather than a large decanter.

3.   The peak of the discussion

In addition to engaging in research, Gamillscheg, after his
transfer to the University of Berlin in the mid-twenties,
doubtless devoted lectures to these topics and to others germane
to them. Against this background and within such an intellectual
climate, it becomes understandable why one of his best students
of those vintage years, Renée Toole, should, in her doctoral
dissertation completed by 1931 and published in 1934, as a slim
but meaty book on a point of French dialect geography, have
prepared an excursus of over fifteen pages on the topic under
discussion. Her analysis, distinctly more original and

sophisticated also on the side of documentation, and better
buttressed than anything previously offered, produced few
immediate results, for a variety of reasons,[7] even though it
was to trigger certain long-range effects.

From the start, after briefly surveying the few available
statements on the chosen category of word pairs, the author
demolished Wartburg's hasty denial of the existence of this
pattern in Italian (32-4). She then offered well-arrayed
selective lists culled from Italian (34-7), Occitan (37-9),
Hispano-Romance (40), and French (40-1) sources; each section
was so organized that primitives came first and derivatives
involving so-called modifying (in most cases, diminutive)
suffixes followed. For example, under the rubric of Italian,
one finds, at first, an inventory of pairs structured like
capanno 'small cabin' ~ *capanna* 'cabin', *cucchiaio* 'spoon' ~
cucchiaia 'big spoon' and, later, others architectured like
chies-in-o 'tiny church' vs. *chies-in-a* 'small church'
(primitive: *chiesa*), *colt-ello* 'knife' vs. *colt-ella* 'big
knife'.[8] The advantage of this approach, within the frame of
Renée Toole's thinking, will become apparent at once; one of
its liabilities, for the diachronically-oriented linguists, is
the author's failure to distinguish between original feminines
that gave rise to masculines, such as *capanna*, and the reverse
process.

Renée Toole's analysis of the data assembled (41-3) contained
several daring ideas. She felt that the switch from a collective
to an augmentative meaning was, generally speaking, rare
(witness the record of the minutely-examined suffix -$\bar{a}ta$), but
that two special circumstances expedited the transition in this
particular instance: semantically, the prevailing
tridimensionality of the object referred to; and formally, the
fact that the overwhelming majority of the cases involved nouns
already equipped with a diminutive suffix, so that the typical
feminine member of a word pair designates the slightly larger
of two varieties of a miniaturized image: '...so dass also die
feminine Form die Bezeichnung eines ausdrücklich kleinen
Raumes in semantischer Hinsicht vergrössert'. Straight
augmentative suffixes (say, -*one* or -*accio*) could not very well
have been pressed into service as an alternative here, because
they would or might have been neutralized by the preceding
diminutive suffixes. Let me immediately add, by way of
criticism, that Renée Toole's illustrations have almost all been
extracted from dictionaries--both monolingual, like Tommaseo-
Bellini, and bilingual, like Rigutini-Bulle; she did not
properly weight the factor of actual incidence, paying equal
attention in her statistics to very common and exceptionally
rare words, not a few of which may even have been manufactured
by overambitious lexicographers.

Another original idea of Renée Toole's flowed from her
preceding qualification of the switch from collective to
augmentative. The number and diversity of the factors involved
allowed, in a third evolutionary stage, never before isolated,
a new function to develop: the feminines in -*a* (or > -*e*)
become paler, retaining a merely modifying, limiting, nuancing
rather than discernibly augmentative force, as was previously

hinted at by F. Hanssen: 'Das Nebeneinanderbestehen der
Endungen -o und -a wurde dann als Mittel zur Schaffung von
Bedeutungsdifferenzen gebraucht' (129).   There was henceforth
less emphasis on the names of containers as primitives, i.e.
a lighter stress on tridimensionality.   After offering another
assortment of illustrative examples from Italian, Old Provençal,
Occitan, Spanish, and French (43-5), once more organized
according to her favorite principle, Renée Toole comes up with
a big surprise: at the extreme fringe of the nuancing function
(Stage III) one finds isolated cases of the feminine partner,
in such word pairs, denoting the smaller object.   Such stray
examples of the downright diminutive function of the feminine
are found in Italian, where *tina* designates a smaller 'vat' or
'tub' than does *tino*; the same is true of *bacchetta* 'rod,
staff', *navicella* 'small craft', and *rapa* 'turnip' vis-à-vis
bacchetto, *navicello*, and *rapo*, respectively.   The chances for
the feminine in -a to end up as a diminutive are relatively
best where the primitive has been previously expanded by the
augmentative suffix -on-:   thus, if one starts out from *camera*
'room' and *casa* 'house', a *camer-on-a* and a *cas-on-a* turn out
to be somewhat smaller than a *camer-on-e* and a *cas-on-e*.   The
symmetry to the earlier case of *chies-in-a* ~ *chies-in-o* is
transparent.   One recognizes something approaching the
configuration of a quadripartite cycle: I. Collective; II.
Weakly-Augmentative; III. Nuancing; IV. Weakly-Diminutive.   A
brilliant schema indeed, argued with passionate persuasiveness
and in scintillating German by a very young woman, barely
twenty-four years old, and one born in a different country and
into a different culture.9

Through a bizarre twist of circumstances, Mauricio Schneider's
paper--dedicated to Amado Alonso--appeared on this side of the
Atlantic the same year as Renée Toole's excursus did in Europe.
The two investigations, whose authors were unaware of each
other's involvement, shared one more peculiarity: they aroused
little immediate attention, and no third party rushed to the
foreground of events to offer any bold synthesis.   The title
of Schneider's monograph-length article was descriptive: 'El
colectivo en latín y las formas en -a con valor aumentativo en
español'.   Perhaps the claims Schneider staked out were, on
balance, too modest.   In addition to canvassing the feminine
augmentive (62-86) he also neatly set off its occasional
counterpart, the masculine diminutive (86-8), as when standard
Spanish tolerates the innovation *ruedo* 'small sphere' alongside
traditional *rueda* 'wheel', from *rota*, or as when the
Santanderino dialect in northern Spain accepts *anguilo* 'name of
a fish smaller than the eel' beside *anguila* 'eel', from
anguīl(1)a.   There is a more satisfactory balance between the
Latin prelude and the Romance drama in Schneider's article than
in any other study that has come to my attention, partly so
because his main emphasis is on the early evolutionary stage,
marked by hypertrophy of mass-noun function.   Thus, he devotes
a whole chapter--rather elaborate at that--to the so-called
'heterogeneous' nouns in Latin (we might be tempted to call
them 'ambigeneric'); i.e. nouns with a recorded gender switch

from singular to plural, which to him marked the starting point
of the entire development, e.g. *acinus* 'berry', pl. *acinī* ~
acina; clīvus 'slope, gradient', pl. *clīvī* ~ *clīva; iocus* 'jest,
joke', pl. *iocī* ~ *ioca; locus* 'place', pl. *locī* ~ *loca,* with
tendential semantic differentiation; also *armentum* 'herd',
caementum 'rough stone from the quarry', *nervus* 'sinew', whose
plurals display all sorts of irregularities in the suggested
direction. Finally, Schneider scrupulously combed the latest
Spanish Academy Dictionary then available as well as numerous
Old World and New World dialect dictionaries of Spanish in
search of fresh data, coming up in the end with a real corpus,
however limited, rather than with randomly selected illustrations.
Unlike Renée Toole, he attributed no particular importance to
any division of the Romance words affected into primitives and
diminutives.

The impetus of Bengt Hasselrot's eventual involvement in
this problem is due to the fact that his main purpose, patently,
was not to criticize or qualify opinions voiced by any
predecessors, but to offer a sliver of original thinking. In
the early forties, the Swedish scholar was slowly, but firmly
and methodically at work on his *magnum opus,* the rise and
spread of certain Romance diminutive suffixes, chiefly -*ittus*
and variations thereupon. This project was to keep him in a
state of alertness for over thirty years; he clearly was in no
hurry. The extraordinary thoroughness of his data-gathering is
evident throughout the first of his two monographs entitled
*Du changement de genre comme moyen d'indiquer une relation de
grandeur.* In that slender 1944 tract, he added to the inventory
of relevant languages Sardinian and at least two islets of
Rhaeto-Romance; drew fine lines between the separate usages of
Gascon, Provençal proper, and Franco-Provençal rather than
lumping together shreds of evidence under some such
indiscriminate label as Occitan; used dialect monographs and
glossaries, guides to hydronymy, phonetically-transcribed field
notes (in part unpublished), and maps of dialect atlases, in
addition to more conventional sources of information; and
ferreted out numerous long-hidden hints in a wide spectrum of
scholarly treatises.[10] On the technical side, his treatment
showed unrivaled mastery in 'pinpointing', and maturity of
judgment as well.

Hasselrot's starting point coincided approximately with
Renée Toole's midpoint and altogether transcended Schneider's
horizons. Taking for granted the expectation that the
suffixally-derived diminutive in Romance will normally tend to
adopt the gender of the primitive, he isolated three groups of
exceptions,[11] then focused attention (108) on the one group
involving pairs of diminutives clashing in overtly marked gender
and referring to objects of varying size--with the feminine
variant ordinarily matching the larger of two paired-off objects.
However, in the word-list that he actually supplied (108-12),
he no longer distinguished carefully between primitives and
suffixal derivatives, placing Sp. *charco--charca* 'puddle'
beside Cat. *ganivet--ganiveta* 'penknife', and he did not use
as a classificatory criterion the etymological priority of the

masculine over the feminine partner, or vice versa, in such
binomial relationships.

In the analytical section of his monograph, Hasselrot
initially accepted the standard explanation, surmising that the
feminine augmentative in Romance rested on a collective
function, and that neuters like *prātu* 'meadow' ~ *prāta* 'meadows',
'*one large meadow' paved the way for masculines like *hortu(s)*
~ V.Lat. *horta* 'garden(s)', *mūru(s)* ~ V.Lat. *mūra* 'wall(s)'.
He sensed that Classical Greek and certain Semitic languages
also illustrated the semantic switch from mass noun to
augmentative, for feminines. A few pages farther down,
however, Hasselrot--and herein lies his real originality--
rebelled against the feminine augmentative, calling its use
abnormal, or, as we would say, counter to expectation,
counterintuitive. Using as his guides Jakob Wackernagel's
celebrated lectures on comparative syntax and several bold
syntheses made over a quarter-century span by the noted
Africanist Carl Meinhof, Hasselrot now protested that in most
healthy cultures the larger size associatively goes hand in
hand with the evocation of male sex and, through the widespread
overlap of sex and gender, with the masculine gender. Listen
to his own words:

> Le féminin augmentatif, bien qu'assez répandu comme nous
> venons de le voir, constitue tout de même, réflexion faite,
> une anomalie. Dans plusieurs langues, c'est au contraire le
> masculin qui peut assumer une fonction augmentative et,
> puisque l'homme, normalement, est plus grand et plus fort
> que la femme et que le même rapport existe entre le mâle et
> la femelle dans la plupart des espèces, cela paraît plus
> normal, plus conforme à la nature des choses.

At this point Hasselrot, in the work of Hermann Jakobsohn (1926),
cited Franz Boas's sketch of Chinook, an Amerindian language
which makes large animals masculine and smaller animals
feminine, as well as African languages classing designations of
females and of smallish males with those of inanimate objects.
He also joined Grimm, Wackernagel, and Wartburg who, unlike
Brugmann, all three operated with the assumption of a far-going
'sexualisation des objets du monde inanimé', as seen in the
names of countless artisans' tools, in the technical parlance
of sailors very explicit in this regard, etc., though, let me
add on my own, it is not so much differences of sheer size as
those of configuration which appear to have been decisive in
matters of nomenclature.12

The conclusion that Hasselrot drew from the findings of yet
other scholars--botanists, students of ancient medical and
veterinary science, and toponymists included--was that the
situation was more complex than had been anticipated by the
pioneers. There has existed in Romance, on the one hand, an
augmentative feminine, which throve on an internal, grammatical
process--the disappearance of the neuter and the various
consequences which that event entailed; and, on the other hand,
there has, independently, developed an augmentative masculine,
rooted in ever-present, ever-active personification and
sexualization, to which, upon occasion, there has further been

added, as a third ingredient, the interplay of the designation of inanimate objects with suffixes ordinarily used to tag cubs and whelps. In Spain, a small river will be known as *riato*, from *río*, and one tributary of the *Duero* will be called *Durato*, involving *-ato*, the label for young animals. In France, the streams flowing through the villages *Auzon*, *Leuc*, and *Hon* will be known as *l'Auzonnet*, *le Lauquet*, *le Hogneau*, but the streamlets emptying into those streams will be *l'Auzonnette*, *la Lauquette*, and *la Honnelle*. 'Nous avons affaire ici à une combinaison des phénomènes de personnifications et de sexualisations', argued Hasselrot, 'l'affluent de *l'Auzonnet*, p.ex., était considéré, pour ainsi dire, comme sa femme et sa femelle'.

The conflict between the two patterns can be resolved in many striking ways. Ordinarily each speech community decides whether the masculine or the feminine is principally associated with aggrandizement. Because the augmentative feminine is solidly entrenched in standard Spanish and Portuguese, these languages show only minimal traces of the augmentative masculine; but individual Hispano-Romance dialects may steer a different course. In Spanish *jarra* 'earthen jar' refers to something bigger than *jarro*; but in Western Asturian *x̃arro* denotes a bigger container than *x̃arra*, and Upper Aragonese offers seven instances of the augmentative masculine. In Franco-Provençal, the spread of the augmentative masculine encountered weak resistance, because in Gallo-Romance the augmentative feminine happened to be underdeveloped.

In conclusion, Hasselrot admitted that, despite these subtle regional variations, a measure of ineradicable ambiguity had crept in. Once the natural, biological association had become grammaticized and lexicalized, it was in the way of the *prātum* ~ *prāta* scheme, which, from the start, had been a strictly grammatical device. Since neither mechanism succeeded in completely dislodging its rival, they neutralized each other, and their initially-promising advance ground to a standstill. They lost out to the more explicit—and, let me add on my own, more expressive—augmentative and diminutive suffixes: 'L'opposition masculin-féminin ne peut donc, en fin de compte, remplir convenablement la fonction d'indiquer sans ambiguïté une relation de grandeur'. In the penumbra of the gradual withdrawal or shrinkage of this device, there crystallized certain hazily-delineated relationships between doublets, in which the *-o* partner and the *-a* partner (to cite the Italian and Spanish carriers of the contrast) were semantically differentiated along an axis other than that of size. Thus, It. *berretto* and *calzetto* refer to garments worn by men, while *berretta* and *calzetta* perform the opposite service. This zigzag takes us back, as Hasselrot could not fail to observe, to Renée Toole's 'nuancing function'; but what to her had been a fairly early link in the chain of events impressed Hasselrot as being, most plausibly, the concluding link.

During the war years and immediately thereafter, no sustained dialogue ensued; for a short while it seemed to matter little whether a paper by one investigator preceded or followed upon a paper by another. No major close-knit theory nearly so

innovative as Toole's and Hasselrot's was presented by any
party; but minor gaps in documentation were randomly filled and
an occasional trial balloon was allowed to float. The corpus
of Catalan examples was slightly expanded in O. Bernhard's
otherwise undistinguished Zurich dissertation. G. Gougenheim
presented a short list of modern French formations in -ette, some
of them of very recent vintage and frankly experimental, which
seem to lack a masculine counterpart; though the paper was
written for and channeled through an American journal, the
author was unaware of the impact of mock-French American on
genuine French usage in the climate of fraternization peculiar
to 1944-45, though a hybrid like gangsterette should have
alerted him to this possibility; after all, in this country a
blonde and a divorcee even now normally refer to a woman, and
petite has been borrowed, while petit has not.[13] The well-known
Latinist Marouzeau, on one of his periodic forays into
contemporary French, raised a number of questions without
providing explicit answers, though there was no dearth of hints
in his comments. He felt that in dealing with the standard
language, psychologizing explanations with sexual overtones
were inadequate to account for change in grammatical gender:
Fr. la mer 'the sea', he argued, underwent the shift from neuter
to feminine under the pressure of its semantic opposite la terre
'the earth' (and in substandard speech l'air 'air' followed
suit),[14] without the slightest implied reference to a woman's
charm, tempestuous beauty, or fickleness. In examining
specimens of racy speech, however--on the level of 'français
argotique'--Marouzeau was less certain of his point: in
numerous stereotyped phrases involving faire and être + noun;
in characteristic sequences such as se la fouler, se la mettre,
on se la casse 'on fuit'; in newly-coined facetious postverbals,
say, la crève (from crever 'to burst') and l'épate (from épater
'to baffle, dazzle'); in derogatory references to individuals,
especially to males: canaille, crapule, fripouille, gouape,
nouille, and in certain other sharply delimited groups the
feminine was used almost exclusively, which could hardly be
due to coincidence. Had Marouzeau been writing thirty years
later, he might have allowed for a streak of 'male chauvinism'
in French society, at least at certain levels or in certain
contexts. In any event, Marouzeau's inconclusive note added
a sociolinguistic or stylistic dimension to the problem.
Finally, the discussion of the ticklish French hypocoristics
Louison, Madelon continued unabated; the controversy, started
by Gilliéron in 1918, now aroused the attention of Dauzat and,
predictably, of Spitzer, who offered heavily speculative and
psychologizing interpretations.[15]
  When the dust settled on the war and on its immediate
repercussions, the debate was resumed on an ambitious scale.
The next item in my chronologically-arrayed bibliography, a
forty-page article, straddling the years 1948 and 1949, by
Henry and Renée Kahane titled 'The augmentative feminine in the
Romance languages', was, and has remained, the single most
elaborate piece of research devoted to this problem and in
certain crucial respects, even in today's perspective, marks

the summit of the entire controversy.   It also carried with it
a few mild surprises, insofar as, first, Mrs. Kahane turned
out to be the very same person as Miss Toole; as, second, here
was for the first time a contribution written and published in
English, albeit by two scholars steeped in European learning;
and as, third, the article was editorially processed by a
newly-founded American journal.[16]

The thoroughness and maturity of the Kahane paper, on the
separate levels of documentation and of analysis, makes it
indeed a finely-chiseled masterpiece.   The fact that after such
a long search they found no vestiges of the phenomenon under
study in Balkan-Romance, including Rumanian, has become an
important negative characteristic of word-formation in that
bundle of dialects.   Their survey of earlier, necessarily
sketchier treatments of the process is, on the whole, fair in
verdicts and restrained in tone.   The one link in the chain a
reader misses is an attempt at detached self-criticism: what
did the Kahanes themselves, from their vantage of 1948, find
worthy of acceptance, of modification, or of excision in Renée
Toole's 1931-34 excursus?

Despite the tribute they paid to Hasselrot, the Kahanes, as
they were approaching the mid-century point, basically adopted
and fortified Renée Toole's earlier position.   The presentation
of the material remained, in essence, identical, though numerous
data, this time, were culled from dialect glossaries and dialect
maps, an opportune deviation from earlier practice in the dual
direction of authenticity and specificity.   The concept of
'nuancing function' originally toyed with was now replaced by
that of 'discriminative function or meaning', for which a
separate, generously-expanded dossier was prepared, which in
turn invited a good deal of accurate geographic pinpointing.
The rare instances of the diminutive feminine were once more,
with increased authority, recognized as constituting just an
unusual shade of the discriminative service performed by -a.
Finally, on the side of l'historique du problème, all
interpretations so far advanced were divided into two major
classes: the strictly grammatical ones, championed by
Wartburg, Toole, Bernhard, and Schneider, and the staunchly
psychological ones, spearheaded by Damourette and Pichon (after
an earlier advocacy by the seldom-remembered pioneer R. de la
Grasserie in 1904), with Spitzer and Hasselrot emerging as less
than entirely successful would-be mediators. The school of
psychology involved was, let me add at once, conjectural and
speculative.   The Kahanes' personal sympathies lay
indisputably with the camp of grammarians. They neatly defined,
without resorting to polemics, their limited disagreement with
Hasselrot, whom they--rightly or wrongly--viewed as influenced
by Kuhn:

> The strongest objection to Kuhn's and Hasselrot's
> interpretation seems to lie in chronological considerations:
> the diminutive feminine appears so much later than the
> augmentative feminine that it is doubtful whether in its
> incipient period natural philosophy still influenced Romance
> gender. (p.169)

With Henry and Renée Kahane's balanced analysis, proffered
in measured terms, the discussion, I repeat, reached its
all-time peak. Unfortunately, Hasselrot yielded to the
temptation of once again (indeed, more than once) entering the
fray. His chief revision, summation, and rebuttal are contained
in a 1950 article published in the Swiss journal *Vox Romanica*.
What mars this second attack on the problem--which, had it been
written in English, might well have borne some such title as
'Gender Switch Revisited'--is that most of the space is given
over to the circumstantial refutation of an extremely silly
remark dropped and, unfortunately, later reiterated by Dauzat.
The net result of the controversy is to confirm that Occitan
preponderantly coincides, as was to be expected, with Spanish
and Italian in favoring the augmentative feminine over its
masculine counterpart. In certain zones (e.g. Savoy and French
Switzerland) one encounters a good deal of confusion as between
one village and another. On the positive side, one notes
Hasselrot's success in filling one minor gap in his earlier
documentation: Central Rhaeto-Romance (specifically, the Fassa
Valley) was now firmly credited to the territory of the
augmentative feminine. In 1950, Hasselrot voiced the belief
that Northern France initially likewise belonged to that area,
but that the derivational model was subsequently eroded to the
north of the Loire through the vigorous spread of the
augmentative masculine, so that a sort of neutralization and
ultimate decay ensued: 'Le masculin augmentatif et le féminin
augmentatif s'équilibraient à peu près et se nuisaient ainsi
mutuellement au point de s'entretuer' (p.141). As regards the
kernel of the disagreement, Hasselrot, in 1950, was unwilling
to yield ground on the issue of the evocation of biological
facts: 'Le masculin augmentatif', he averred, 'doit son
origine à un rapprochement entre genre et sexe, à une
comparaison toute naturelle et spontanée entre le règne
inanimé et la relation de grandeur et de force qui existe entre
mâle et femelle dans la plupart des espèces animales qui
intéressent l'homme et surtout entre l'homme et la femme
eux-mêmes'. With respect to the feminine augmentative, he
accepted the standard hypothesis of a collectively-colored
ancient plural neuter as the bridge to the Latin ending -*a*, but,
apropos names of containers, he toyed with the possibility of
animization, indeed, personification: 'Pour ce qui est des
récipients, il peut aussi reposer sur une comparaison entre
le[s] corps des humains des deux sexes' (p.143). To put it
differently, Hasselrot was willing to operate with anatomical
imagery; on the other hand, he resolutely rejected as unproven,
indeed, undemonstrable, Spitzer's attempt to drag in popular
notions, however suggestive, of a female's psychology. He next
considered the relevant pages of Orion Bernhard's and rejected,
perhaps not strongly enough, that scholar's bizarre phono-
symbolic explanation of augmentative -*a*.[17] Only the last four
pages dealt with the article of the Kahanes, which received
unstinted praise on the side of documentation, but was
mercilessly criticized on the level of causal and chronological
interpretation.

As regards particulars, Hasselrot's rebuttal corrects a few factual inaccuracies; then reasserts his fundamental belief in a steady interaction of grammatical pressures (today some of us conceivably would use instead the word 'constraints') and ever-present animistic forces, which could perhaps have been unleashed in the intermediate zone between the animate and the inanimate realms, e.g. in hydronymy and in vernacular phytonymy. Hasselrot appeals also to folklore and even to learned allegory (*l'opinion, reine du monde*) in his search for collateral support. Reduced to a still sharper, more abstract formulation, and all details apart, Hasselrot argues that the Toole-Kahane hypothesis hinges, in the last analysis, on a single and unique state of affairs in Late Latin: *prāta* denotes not only something larger than *prātum*, but also, at least potentially, something different from *prātum*, whereas his own interpretation is essentially binary. A second ineradicable contrast between the two principal theories: whereas the Toole-Kahane analysis attaches major importance to the fact that the given word either constitutes a primitive or is endowed with certain modifying suffixes, Hasselrot disregards this circumstance entirely, but feels, by way of compensation as it were, that the semantic cleavage in the development of a few such suffixes, particularly *-one* and *-otto*, now diminutive now augmentative (depending on the dialect), constitutes a relevant parallel to such fluctuations as augmentative feminine vs. diminutive feminine--in terms of language universals.[18] Thus one finds a syntagmatic, pitted against a paradigmatic, appeal to derivational suffixes within the frame of our problem.

Hasselrot's last-mentioned remark was no doubt designedly programmatic, because he was at that point actively, almost feverishly, at work on his *magnum opus* on Romance diminutive suffixes--perhaps the last, enduring classic of old-style Romance scholarship--a book in which he reverted incidentally to the problem here at issue, as he did in a number of shorter pieces, simultaneous or subsequent.[19] But there were no longer to come any dramatic confrontations with the Toole-Kahane hypothesis, while the Kahanes themselves, of late, have apparently regarded their mission as completed, except for details that may have emerged at the surface in their far-flung *etymologicon*.

The involvement of derivational suffixes, whether in paradigmatic or in syntagmatic perspective, makes it incumbent upon me to mention very briefly several brilliant studies which may someday be called upon to play a major role if and when the discussion of our major issue reopens. Erica García, using in part statistics, in part introspection as a native speaker of American Spanish, has associated gender switch in suffixal formations with the establishment of a wider semantic gap between primitive and derivative: hierarchically, *papeleta* is more autonomous vis-à-vis *papel* than is *papelito*, and the relation of *ventana* 'window', *ventanilla* 'small window', and *ventanillo* 'peephole' can be similarly defined. Suzanne Fleischman has thrown a bridge from the denominal augmentatives in *-ón* to the action nouns in *-ón* suggestive of sudden, violent movements, such as *tirón*. Sufficient ammunition has once more become available for the battle to be resumed; let me qualify: a strictly cognitive battle.

4. A tentative conclusion

Let us attempt to draw a provisional balance sheet. Have the eighty years or so of intermittent discussion produced any tangible results? I believe that the answer should, at least in part, be positive. In all likelihood, all the major causative factors and all or, at least, most of the relevant perspectives in which the growth is amenable to observation have been identified; but the all-important concatenations of these factors and of the events produced by them remain, in most instances, a matter of continued dispute. Some of these concatenations, the simplest to describe, involve cogent chronological sequences: by what margin (if any) did the augmentative masculine precede or trail behind the augmentative feminine? Others refer to compatibility: to what extent do aggrandizement and miniaturization exclude each other?

Despite the successive appeals to statistics, phonosymbolism, animization, sexuality, and what not—only substratum influences have not yet been invoked—we still have no truly satisfactory answers to such basic facets of the problem as the absence of the augmentative feminine from Rumanian; its rarity in Northern French, as against its superabundance in Occitan and Catalan, to say nothing of Italian and Spanish; the syntagmatic or the paradigmatic role of competing augmentative and diminutive suffixes; and the wisdom of accepting or rejecting a binary schema: grammar vs. personification, which of course would imply the interplay of linguistic and extra-linguistic forces. The inventory of side issues left unsolved or, perhaps worse, incompletely solved could be generously extended.

This situation, let me conclude, is typical of Romance spatio-temporal linguistics, to the extent that it is explicative, i.e. concerned with causation. Many problems have been raised; some have, in the process, been made to appear excessively complicated through the discovery of all sorts of side issues; relatively few have actually been solved. Our intellectual appetites have been whetted; after having sampled the *hors-d'œuvre*, our generation of late-twentieth-century workers may as well sink its teeth—excuse the personification—into the *entrées*.

NOTES

[1]While Portuguese dialects later moved out of the center of discussion, O. de Pratt, in 1911, offered a very similar shred of information: Minhoto *janêlo*, in less careful speech *jinêlo*

'peephole, small window', beside *janela* 'window' [from IĀNUA 'threshold'] (Viano-do-Castelo and adjoining areas), likening it to such regionalisms as *cancêlo* beside *cancela* 'low, wooden gate'; *sete-estrêlo* 'the Pleiades' beside *estrela* 'star'; and *panêlo* alongside *panela* 'pot, pan, kettle' (see 158b-159a).

[2]Thus, he did not ask himself the key question whether only primitives ending in *-o* or *-a* can produce relevant counterparts, and, unlike Gonçálvez Viana just two years earlier, he did not bother to distinguish between masculines giving rise to feminines and vice versa.

[3]It is particularly surprising that as late as 1921--in Part 2 of his innovative *Historische Grammatik der französischen Sprache,* where he grouped derivational suffixes in semantic or functional clusters--Meyer-Lübke should have left the augmentative feminine unmentioned as a rival device in discussing *-as (-asse)*, *-âtre*, and *-aud* (§§172-5), an omission not remedied in J. M. Piel's disappointing supplement to the 1966 ed. of his teacher's handbook.   Meyer-Lübke's dictionary contained, of course, a number of relevant entries (e.g. CANISTRUM/KANASTRO, CISTUS, SACCUS), but the material offered in them was not so organized as to cast into bold relief the processes here studied.

[4]Typically Gilliéronesque was Wartburg's quip that *plato* 'plate, dish' failed to generate **plata* 'large dish' because the right to the occupancy of that latter word's niche had been preëmpted by *plata* 'silver'.   In sober fact, had **plata* 'large dish' sprung into existence at an early date, it might have blocked its homonym's entry and strengthened the precarious position of ARGENTUM to the south of the Pyrenees.

[5]Wartburg was, of course, again and again reminded of his early note by hundreds of articles, stretching over a half-century, in his monumental *Französisches etymologisches Wörterbuch.* He refrained from including the note, in its original or in any revised form, in his selection--misleadingly subtitled collection--of articles, *Von Sprache und Mensch; gesammelte Aufsätze* (Bern: Francke, 1956).

Wartburg's later 'Stellungnahme' to this problem--a summary and an elaboration at the same time--is, I regret to report, neither fair nor effective; see *Einführung in Problematik und Methodik der Sprachwissenschaft* 68 and *Problèmes et méthodes...* 66-7 (tr. P. Maillard); even in the 3d German edition (1970), brought up to date by P. Ineichen and enriched by a temporary program of collaboration with S. Ullmann, the results are unsatisfactory.   Wartburg cites his 1921 note without admitting its basic error as regards Italian; there is a reference to the shorter and less significant of the two papers by Hasselrot, while the crucial studies by R. Toole and H. and R. Kahane-- closer to Wartburg's own position--are swept under the rug; the author cites enthusiastically an opinion by J. Grimm and declares himself unconvinced by Brugmann's strictures, without either stating these objections or, at least, identifying the place where a curious reader can find them.   Above all, it remains unclear under what conditions purely formal or semantic circumstances determine the association of gender with size (and strength?).

[6]Thus, F. Belloni-Filippi, 'La lavorazione di un frantoio idraulico in territorio di Buti (Pisa)', after recording a few conspicuous cases--*canala* 'un grande canale di acqua', *coltella* 'più grande e robusta del coltello', *barroccina* 'più ampia e commoda del barroccino' (233-4)--mused: 'Curiosa questa tendenza di mettere al femminile gli accrescitivi'. He was apparently unaware of holding in his hand two trump cards: the refutation of Wartburg's arbitrary exclusion of Italy, and the proof that a masculine in -*e* could also be flanked by an augmentative feminine in -*a*.

[7]For one thing, the monograph series in which this exciting dissertation appeared was hardly known for its high quality; see my necrological essay on E. Gamillscheg; for another, the title of the dissertation led readers to expect little more than a routine interpretation of one map (818: *MARMITE*) in Gilliéron's atlas, with side glances at a few other collaterally useful maps (715: *JATTE*; 1065: *POT*; 1509: *COCOTTE*). Clearly, to spark discussion, Gamillscheg should have persuaded and helped his star pupil to separate the pan-Romanic excursus from the bulk of the booklet and to channel it through some widely-read journal.

[8]Forty years ago scholars did not operate with the concept of suffixoid, so it is hardly surprising that Renée Toole made no effort to build a bridge from *cucchiaia*, which to the average speaker has no identifiable primitive, to the more transparently carpentered derivatives in -*aia*, which she lists separately under -ĀRIUS. It is puzzling, however, why *coltell-o, -a*, equally 'monolithic'--by her standard--for the uninitiated, should appear under -ELLUS rather than among unsegmented primitives.

[9]As her philosophical guide to lexico-derivational problems of language (history), Renée Toole took the Polish scholar Jan Rozwadowski's once influential book *Wortbildung und Wortbedeutung*, on which Wartburg and other experts leaned heavily as late as the mid-forties.

[10]On gender switch in suffixal diminutives the earliest--to this day important--pronouncements by Indo-Europeanists seem to be K. Brugmann's 1906 note, 'Der Genus der Diminutivbildungen', and its critique twenty years later by H. Jakobsohn.

[11]The two groups less worthy of sustained attention involve either those primitives which, unlike their satellites, have undergone a fairly late change in gender (thus, Fr. *amourette* echoes older [fem.] *amour*) or those suffixal derivatives that have undergone the influence of their near-synonyms, as when Fr. dial. *baquette* 'small vat' (Ardennes) echoes the ending (and, inescapably, the gender) of *tinette* 'small tub'.

[12]An even greater--almost wild--allowance for the physiological and psychological implications of sex in grammar was made in many of his writings by Leo Spitzer; perhaps more

explicitly than elsewhere in his study (1921) of epicene nouns
in Romance. For a more recent and, all told, far more judicious
assessment of a closely-related (in part interlocking) problem
see Anita Katz Levy's 1973 paper on plural form vs. singular
meaning.

[13]Appended to Gougenheim's note is a brief and light-weight
editorial comment--presumably, on circumstantial evidence,
from the pen of Leo Spitzer. The two-way link between Am.-E.
and Fr. -ette was better grasped by B. Hasselrot in his second
attack (1950) on the problem. For the most successful attempt
to place the agentives in -ette within an appropriate cultural
framework see Kathleen Connors' 'Studies in feminine
agentives...'.

[14]Marouzeau, a professional Latinist but a mere amateur in
the Romance domain, was apparently oblivious of the use of *la
mar* (obsolete, poetic, figurative) in Spanish, where in the
absence of rhyme, no appeal can be made to any irresistible
pressure of *tierra*. The influence of *terra* could have been, at
most, a concomitant, as I pointed out shortly thereafter in my
paper on lexical polarization.

[15]To reconstruct in detail Spitzer's zigzagging line of
thinking one would have to examine a raft of his studies,
spanning a full quarter-century, from 'Entwicklung des
Gegensinns...' (1921) via 'Feminización...' (1941) all the way
to his lengthy essay on hypocoristics. The pervasive factor of
his reasoning was the assumed primacy of sensual associations
over grammatical mechanisms, a hierarchy which in 1950 shocked
even the outspokenly 'realistic' Hasselrot.

Specifically, in his 1946 article Spitzer expatiated on
Gilliéron's excursus and attempted to show that *Margot, Ninon*
suggested 'des garçons manqués'. Had he had access, during the
war, to A. Dauzat's earlier note in *FM* 9.161-70, he might have
thought differently: Dauzat stated (convincingly, I think) that
Marion, (Mar)goton, Margot pertain to amorous parlance, in
which the interversion of gender forms part of the general
cajolery and persiflage (I can cite on my own the colloquial
use of Sp. *¡feo!*, *¡negro!* in the sense of 'handsome!'). Dauzat
adduced as a parallel grotesquerie the emotional stress in
épOUvantable; note also the many corrections in his review (*FM*
15.75-6) of Spitzer's article.

[16]I hope I am committing no breach of discretion by
testifying to the fact that the authors, though initially eager
to see their vigorously expanding paper appear in the opening
issue of the journal, later curbed their impatience in exemplary
fashion and waited until all the evidence, down to the minutest
detail, had been scrupulously assembled and sifted. This
thoroughness at the concluding stage of the operation must be
superadded to the eighteen years or so of previous thinking and
data-gathering on the part of Renée Toole Kahane. The echoes
to the Kahane paper, as listed in A. Pietrangeli's retrospective
bibliography, were favorable but, on the whole, faint. M.
García Blanco provided a detailed summary in Spanish; M. Paiva
Boléo dramatized the chief paradox and cited the authors' own

conclusion; B. Pottier stressed the difference between the rich yield of the device in Spanish and Italian and its relative meagerness in French; G. Rohlfs was satisfied with praising the authors' industriousness (the accolade he had given fifteen years earlier to Renée Toole's thesis excursus was warmer and less hasty).

[17] Hasselrot struck a cavalier attitude toward Bernhard's bold appeal to phonosymbolism, but failed to point out just what made that appeal so grotesquely inopportune. One may argue about the propriety of so interpreting a stressed vowel, including *a* (in It. *-accio*, Sp. *-azo*, Fr. *-as*, say), but the application of this principle to unstressed final vowels receives no support from any side. Another fantastic idea of Bernhard's was to justify the link between the names of domestic animals and the device of the augmentative feminine with the argument that the females of those species, though actually of smaller size, often happen to be more useful to man, hence more valuable, and thus loom bigger.

[18] Hasselrot also feels that the referential contrast evoked by gender and by the light endings *-o* vs. *-a* (or their local counterparts) need not be slighter than the contrast suggested by the use of the heavier standard derivational suffixes, such as *-ino*.

[19] In his contribution to the Rohlfs Testimonial Volume, Hasselrot, aside from surveying, briefly or in searching detail, earlier studies (by Tobler, Gilliéron, Dauzat, Spitzer, Jaberg, Rohlfs, Herbillon, Brattö, Michaëlsson, Jacobsson, and others), proffered one original idea: the flowering of the declensional type *Hue(s)* (subj.) ∼ *Huon* (obl.), patterned on a Germanic model, in Northern France more than in any other Romance country, unavoidably restricted in that territory the range of *-on* as a hypocoristic suffix to the feminine sector of the onomasticon. Whereas *Marion* was apt to express 'cute little Mary', *Huon* could not perform a parallel service with regard to 'Hugo'. Interestingly, Hasselrot mentioned (204) the insertion of an 'antésuffixe' (i.e. interfix) like *-es(s)-*, *-ign-*, or *-ill-* as the one device that could be seized upon to protect the hypocoristic value of *-on* under such circumstances. Ch. 8 of Hasselrot's *Études sur la formation diminutive*...is also concerned with the various functions of Fr. *-on*. In his last major book (1972), confined to present-day French (*Étude sur la vitalité de la formation diminutive française au XXe siècle*), Hasselrot reverted, again and again, to such favorite themes as 'désaccord en genre entre dérivé et mot base', 'genre indice de grandeur'(see 16f., 60, 64, 79, 101), expatiating on earlier analyses of his own.

REFERENCES

A. General (in alphabetic sequence)

Damourette, Jacques, and Édouard Pichon. 1930-49. Des mots à
la pensée: essai de grammaire de la langue française. 7 vols.
Paris: Collection des linguistes contemporains.
Greenberg, Joseph H. 1957. Essays in linguistics. Chicago:
The University of Chicago Press.
Jespersen, Otto. 1922. Symbolic value of the vowel *i*.
Philologica 1.1-19. Prague & London. (Reprinted in
Meisterwerke der romanischen Sprachwissenschaft, ed. by Leo
Spitzer, 1.53-68. München: Hueber.)
Meillet, Antoine. 1928. Esquisse d'une histoire de la langue
latine. Paris: Hachette.
Rozwadowski, Jan. 1904. Wortbildung und Wortbedeutung: eine
Untersuchung ihrer Grundgesetze. Heidelberg: C. Winter.

B. Special (in chronological sequence)

1868. Brachet, Auguste. Dictionnaire des doublets, ou doubles
formes de la langue française. Paris: A. Franck.
1871. _____. Supplément [au Dictionnaire des doublets].
Paris: A. Franck.
1873. Coelho, Francisco Adolfo. Formes divergentes de mots
portugais. Romania 2.281-94.
1883. Meyer [-Lübke], Wilhelm. Die Schicksale des lateinischen
Neutrums im Romanischen. Halle: M. Niemeyer.
1887-89. Viana, [A. dos R.] Gonçálvez. Review of Å. W. Munthe,
Anteckningar om folkmålet i en trakt af vestra Asturien
(diss. Uppsala). Revista Lusitana 1.279-85, at 283.
1889. Schmidt, Johannes. Die Pluralbildungen der
indogermanischen Neutra. Weimar: Böhlau.
1890. Meyer-Lübke, Wilhelm. Italienische Grammatik. Leipzig:
O. R. Reisland.
1906. Brugmann, Karl. Der Genus der Diminutivbildungen.
Indogermanische Forschungen 19.215-6. (Cf. Grundriss der
vergleichenden Grammatik... 2^2:1.609.)
1908. Jaberg, Karl. Sprachgeographie; Beitrag zum Verständnis
des 'Atlas linguistique de la France'. Aarau: H. R.
Sauerländer.
1910. Hanssen, Friedrich. Spanische Grammatik auf historischer
Grundlage. Halle: M. Niemeyer.
1911. Pratt, O. de. Linguagem minhota. Revista Lusitana
14.145-68.
19[11-]20. Meyer-Lübke, Wilhelm. Romanisches etymologisches
Wörterbuch. Heidelberg: C. Winter.
1918. Gilliéron, Jules. Généalogie des mots qui désignent
l'abeille, d'après l'Atlas linguistique de la France. Paris:
Bibliothèque de l'École Pratique des Hautes Études. (Excursus
13 [Suffixes masculins dans les prénoms féminins] was included
in Meisterwerke der romanischen Sprachwissenschaft [2 vols.],
ed. by L. Spitzer, 1.279-89. München: Max Hueber.)
_____. Montoliu, M. de. Petit vocabulari del camp de
Tarragona. Butlletí de dialectologia catalana 6.38-51.

1920-24. Wackernagel, Jacob. Vorlesungen über Syntax, mit
besonderer Berücksichtigung von Griechisch, Lateinisch und
Deutsch. 2 vols. Basel: Kommissionsverlag von E.
Birkhäuser.
1921. Wartburg, Walther von. Substantifs féminins avec valeur
augmentative. Butlleti de dialectologia catalana 9.51-5.
_____. Meyer-Lübke, Wilhelm. Historische Grammatik der
französischen Sprache, 2: Wortbildungslehre. Heidelberg:
C. Winter. (2d ed., revised by J. M. Piel, 1966.)
_____. Gamillscheg, Ernst. Grundzüge der galloromanischen
Wortbildung, in: Gamillscheg & Spitzer, Beiträge zur
romanischen Wortbildungslehre. Biblioteca dell'Archivum
Romanicum 2:2. Genève: L. S. Olschki.
_____. Spitzer, Leo. Über Ausbildung von Gegensinn in der
Wortbildung, in: Gamillscheg & Spitzer, Beiträge zur
romanischen Wortbildungslehre.
1926. Jakobsohn, Hermann. Review of J. Wackernagel,
Vorlesungen über Syntax... Gnomon 2.369-85 (see esp. 375f).
1929. Gamillscheg, Ernst. Zur Frage der Auswahl bei der
suffixalen Ableitung. Behrens-Festschrift: Dietrich Behrens
zum siebzigsten Geburtstag dargebracht. Zeitschrift für
französische Sprache und Literatur, Suppl. 13. Jena &
Leipzig: W. Gronau, W. Agricola. (Reprinted in E. G.,
Ausgewählte Aufsätze [1]: Festschrift zu seinem fünfzigsten
Geburtstage, ZFSL, Suppl. 15 [1937].)
_____. Belloni-Filippi, Ferdinando. La lavorazione di un
frantoio idraulico in territorio di Buti (Pisa). L'Italia
dialettale 5.226-38, at 233f.
1934. Schneider, Mauricio. El colectivo en latín y las formas
en -a con valor aumentativo en español. Boletín de la
Academia Argentina de Letras 2.25-91.
_____. Toole, Renée. Wortgeschichtliche Studien: *toupin* und
bronze. Berliner Beiträge zur romanischen Philologie 3:4
(dir. E. Gamillscheg). Jena & Leipzig: W. Gronau.
1941. Spitzer, Leo. Feminización del neutro. Revista de
Filología Hispánica 3.339-71.
_____. Dauzat, Albert. Les interversions de genre à valeur
affective; les hypocoristiques du type *Marion, Margot:* leur
explication. Le français moderne 9.161-70. (Reprinted in
Mélanges de linguistique française 52-61 [Paris: D'Artrey, 1946].
1943. Bernhard, Orion. La formación de nombres por sufijos
en catalán. Zürich diss. Zürich-Altstetten: Buchdruckerei
H. Schraner.
_____. Wartburg, Walther von. Einführung in Problematik und
Methodik der Sprachwissenschaft. Halle: M. Niemeyer.
(3d ed. [revised by G. Ineichen], Tübingen: M. Niemeyer,
1970.)
1944. Hasselrot, Bengt. Du changement de genre comme moyen
d'indiquer une relation de grandeur dans les langues
romanes [1]. Språkvetenskapliga Sällskapets i Uppsala
Förhandlingar 1943-1945, pp.107-25.
1946. Gougenheim, Georges. Les féminins diminutifs en français
moderne. Modern Language Notes 61.416-9.
_____. Marouzeau, Jules. Un aspect du féminin français. Le
Français Moderne 14.241-5.

_____. Spitzer, Leo. Suffixes masculins dans les prénoms féminins en français. The Romanic Review 37.127-49.
1948-49. Kahane, Henry R. and Renée T. The augmentative feminine in the Romance languages. Romance Philology 2:2-3.135-75.
1948. Dauzat, Albert. Review of Hasselrot, Du changement de genre... [1]. Le Français Moderne 16.76.
1950. Hasselrot, Bengt. Du changement de genre comme moyen d'indiquer une relation de grandeur dans les langues romanes [2]. Vox Romanica 11.135-47.
1951. Malkiel, Yakov. Lexical polarization in Romance. Language 27.485-518.
1957. Hasselrot, Bengt. Études sur la formation diminutive dans les langues romanes. Uppsala Universitets Årsskrift 1957:11.
1958. Hasselrot, Bengt. Le type *Marion, Louison*--une monstruosité lexicale? Romanica: Festschrift für Gerhard Rohlfs, 200-7. Halle: M. Niemeyer.
1965. Craddock, Jerry R. A critique of recent studies in Romance diminutives. Romance Philology 19.286-325. (Includes rev. of Hasselrot, Études sur la formation diminutive..., and of all critical reactions to that monograph [287-310].)
1970. García, Erica C. Gender switch in Spanish derivation (with special reference to *-a → -ero, -o → -era, -a → -ín, -ón*). Romance Philology 24:1.39-54.
1971. Connors, Kathleen. Studies in feminine agentives in selected European languages. Romance Philology 24:4.573-98.
1972. Hasselrot, Bengt. Étude sur la vitalité de la formation diminutive française au XXe siècle. Studia Romanica Upsaliensia 8.
1973. Fleischman, Suzanne. Collision of homophonous suffixes entailing transfer of semantic content: the Luso-Hispanic action nouns in *-ón* and *-dela/-dilla*. Romance Philology 26:4.635-63.
_____. Levy, Anita Katz. Plural form versus singular meaning in Hispano-Romance nouns. Romance Philology 27:1.13-25.
_____. Malkiel, Yakov. One short-lived genre of glotto-historical research. Romance Philology 26:4.749-51.
_____. Malkiel, Yakov. Ernst Gamillscheg (1887-1971) and the Berlin School of Romance linguistics (1925-1945). Romance Philology 27:2.172-89.
_____. Pietrangeli, Angelina. The writings of Henry and Renée Kahane: an analytical bibliography, §§2 and 87. Issues in linguistics: papers in honor of Henry and Renée Kahane. Urbana: University of Illinois Press.
(Forthcoming). Malkiel, Yakov. The analysis of lexical doublets: The Romanists' earliest contribution to general linguistics. [To be included in a forthcoming testimonial volume.]

ON THE STRUCTURE AND ORIGIN OF CREOLE FRENCH

ALBERT VALDMAN

Indiana University

1. Introduction

The ebullient activity and intellectual ferment in evidence
today in the field of pidgin and creole studies have not yet
spread to the domain of Romance linguistics. That Romance-based
pidgins and creoles should remain neglected step-children is
ironic since, not only was this branch of linguistics launched
by a Romanist, Hugo Schuchardt, but French-, Portuguese-, and
Spanish-based creoles enjoy the widest geographical distribution
and count the largest number of speakers among existing pidgins
and creoles. In addition, since Romance linguists are blessed
with copious historical records and documentation on dialect
diversification, they are well equipped to address some of the
burning issues in the field of creolistics.
   It will be recalled that Hugo Schuchardt became attracted to
pidgins and creoles because he saw in these *mischsprachen* the
opportunity to refute two of the basic assumptions of the
Neogrammarian: (1) the impermeability of grammatical structure
to external elements and (2) the gradualness of linguistic
change.

Knowledge of the social matrix for the formation of
Romance-based creoles afforded by their shallow time-depth
makes these languages a suitable testing ground for theories of
linguistic change, or as some might say, a propitious battle-
ground for substratomaniacs and substratophobes. Henry
Hoenigswald also saw in pidgins and creoles a source of more
secure data for the diachronist (1971:473):

> If...matters of origin, change, and disappearance are more
> essentially on the surface of things in the case of pidgins
> and creoles than they are in the case of other speech forms,
> but if it were also true that the difference is only one of
> degree and not of kind, it would require no more than a
> fairly safe extrapolation to furnish the theory of linguistic
> change--so largely speculative in character--with a
> quasi-empirical foundation.

Creole French promises to be a particularly instructive source
of empirical observations and an inviting testing ground for
theories of language change. Creole French dialects are no
doubt the most elaborated of European-based creoles. They have
also been the best described, and historical records abound
that would permit the reconstruction of the social setting of
their formative period. There exists in addition a wide
spectrum of colonial varieties of French exported outside of
the metropolis during the period when Creole French sprang up,
thus affording an opportunity for comparative studies that
might delineate linguistic features distinguishing creolization
from so-called normal linguistic change. Not to be underestimated are the vast resources in the form of dialect
glossaries and descriptions of regional varieties of French
available to the student of Creole, not the least estimable of
which is von Wartburg's monumental *Französiches Etymologisches
Wörterbuch*. In the light of these opportunities, available
knowledge about the genesis and development of Creole of an
incontrovertible nature is disappointingly meager. There has
been no dearth of hypothesis formulation, some not altogether
devoid of brilliance and perceptive insight (Faine 1936, 1939),
but little testing of theories against all accessible facts.
It is my purpose today to assess current hypotheses and to
indicate directions that investigations might take which promise
to shed light, not only on the development of Creole, but on the
processes of linguistic change that have operated in their
emergence from the contact of French and substrate languages.
     Similarities and differences between pidgins and creoles are
accounted for in terms of polygenesis or monogenesis.
Polygenetecists claim that individual pidgins have developed
independently, except for the possible stimulus diffusion of
models for pidginization. The most extreme form of monogenesis
is the relexification hypothesis, according to which all pidgins
and creoles based on Western European languages are derived by
a process of massive lexical replacement from an Afro-Portuguese
contact vernacular, itself based perhaps on the Lingua Franca
of the Mediterranean. Two sets of processes have been
hypothesized to account for the emergence of pidgins from the

contact between the base and the substrate languages. For
Schuchardt, and Bloomfield after him, speakers of the base
language purposely simplified their speech to make it accessible
to beings they held intellectually limited or--in a less racist
version of the hypothesis--to facilitate its acquisition on the
part of foreign speakers. An opposing hypothesis, first put
forward by the Dutch creolist D. C. Hesseling (1934), holds
that pidginization does not differ from normal second-language
learning and reflects simply interference from the learner's
native language.

   Hypothesis-building in the field of pidgins and creoles may
be informed from three directions. First, the adequacy of a
hypothesis must be evaluated in the light of current discussions
in the area of developmental psycholinguistics and language
acquisition. Starting from the currently widely accepted
interactionist model of second-language learning, it is
tempting to view pidginization as the stabilization at a low
level of learners' approximative systems (Corder 1973). Of
equal relevance are observations on special registers, such as
baby talk or foreigner speech (Ferguson 1971, 1975), and on the
nature of expansion and correction in a free-learning environment. Second, social factors play a determining role in
second-language learning and the sociolinguistic setting in
which pidginization and creolization took place must be
reconstructed from historical evidence. Third, the proto-pidgin
or proto-creole must be reconstructed by the use of two sets of
evidence: comparative studies of current pidgins and creoles
and the reconstruction of a plausible form of the base-language
by means of extrapolation from dialect descriptions and
historical texts.

2. On the genesis and development of Creole French

In a recent paper entitled 'On the origin and chronology of
French-based creoles' Alexander Hull (1975) traces all Creole
French dialects to a West African Pidgin French derived by
relexification from an Afro-Portuguese pidgin. The emergence
of the postulated pidgin is localized precisely in time and
space; it is supposed to have developed in 1761 at Whydah, a
multi-national trading post and fort on the coast of Dahomey.
Hull also hypothesizes a very precise genetic process:
   West African Pidgin French...arose not as a compromise
   between some African language or languages, but as a
   deliberate calque of Guinea Gulf Portuguese Creole, using
   mainly Maritime French material.
I will examine this proposal from the three perspectives
discussed previously: language acquisition, social history,
and facts about present-day Creole and vernacular French
varieties.

   The sort of relexification process assumed by Hull involves
what Marius F. Valkhoff has termed 'linguistic acrobatics'
(1966:121). Mulatto and native traders, proficient in Afro-
Portuguese Pidgin, are said to have initiated the relexification
process to converse with French slavers who, themselves, had at

least a comprehension ability in it. The new pidgin was delusitanized by the French, and there developed basilectal and acrolectal varieties differing in regard to the degree of gallicization, the acrolect employed by the French and the basilect by the slaves awaiting transport to the plantation islands. Confronted with this complex acquisitional model, one is led to ask why the postulated pidgin would have arisen if Afro-Portuguese pidgin was available to both parties involved in the construction of the new speech form. Several convincing cases of relexification have been described, notably the case of Mbugu, a contact vernacular with Bantu grammatical base and non-Bantu lexicon (Goodman 1971) and convergent forms of Aryan and Dravidian languages used in rural areas of India (Gumperz 1971). But in these cases of language mixture, relexification took place over a long time span and not with the instantaneity suggested by Hull. For the relexification hypothesis to be taken seriously, its proponents must document actual cases of second-language learning involving total lexical replacement and the absence of any transfer of grammatical structure.

Robert Chaudenson, in the first detailed lexicological study of a creole French dialect (1974), adduces historical evidence which makes implausible a strict monogenetic theory for the genesis of Creole and refutes incontrovertibly a West African Pidgin French origin for the Indian Ocean dialects. Hull claims that the pidgin was introduced in Bourbon Island (present-day Réunion) and taught to Malagasy and Indian slaves. It was considerably re-gallicized when later adopted by poor white settlers. However, Bourbon was not permanently settled by the French until 1665 and the proportion of servile immigrants did not become preponderant until well into the middle of the 18th century. The 1713 census lists a population of 633 whites and 538 colored slaves; of the latter, a considerable number were of Indo-Portuguese, not Indian, origin. Given the relatively gradual influx of slaves, it can only be assumed that problems of linguistic communication would have been solved, not by the use of a pidgin, but by an attempt on the part of the slaves to acquire whatever French vernacular was in use on the island. Indeed, Chaudenson cites a deposition in Creole dated between 1714 and 1723, made by a runaway slave girl. From the point of view of linguistic form this text does not differ substantially from present-day Réunion Creole (1974:I,444; from H. Azema, *Premières peines et premiers châtiments à Bourbon*):

(1)   Moin la parti maron parce qu'Alexis l'homme de jardin
      l'étais qui fait a moin trop l'amour.
      'I ran away because Alexis the yard boy was making too
      pressing amorous advances.'

Particularly noteworthy are the use of the marker *la* and the extended verb stem to express the past, the past form *lete*, 'to be' and the use of a periphrastic construction for the non-punctual aspect, all features that characterize present-day Réunionese.

Hull's hypothesis for a West African origin of Creole rests on a single linguistic fact, the survival in Lesser Antilles

dialects of the tense-aspect markers *ka* 'non-punctual' and *ke*
'irrealis' instead of forms based on *après* and *aller*,
respectively, that occur in the other dialects. To prove his
contention that *ka* and *ke* are relics from the Guinea Gulf Afro-
Portuguese pidgin, Hull invokes back-formations on these two
particles found in such geographically distant overseas
varieties of French as Réunion Poor White speech and Windward
Saint-Barts French (and the latter's satellite community in the
Carenage section of Saint-Thomas):

(2)   li lete ki asiz.   (Réunion)   'She was sitting.'
      õn ete ki partε.   (St. Thomas)   'We were leaving.'
      õn ε ki par.   (St. Thomas)   'We're leaving.'

Hull claims that the presence of *ki* in these sentences is an
attempt on the part of speakers bilingual in French and Creole
to make sense of an inexplicable *ka* bearing progressive meaning.
A more obvious source for this construction is the wide array
of periphrastic aspectual constructions found in vernacular
varieties of French (Gougenheim 1971). Indeed, Antoine Grégoire
notes such a construction with progressive meaning in the speech
of Belgian children (147:II, 197-8):

(3)   Tit f[r]ère qui pleure.   'Little brother is crying.'
      (Petit frère pleure; Petit frère est
      en train de pleurer; Voilà petit frère
      qui pleure; Y a petit frère qui pleure)

and cites examples from colloquial French collected by Albert
Sechehaye (1926:122):

(4)   Ma poupée qui est cassée.   'My doll's broken.'
      Madame, vot' broche qui   'Lady, your brooch is
      s'décroche.   coming undone.'

    Pidginization and creolization may be viewed as special types
of second-language learning and first-language acquisition,
respectively (Bickerton 1975, Traugott 1973). The validation of
any hypothesis for the genesis of Creole involves testing its
plausibility vis-à-vis models of language learning and acquisition, and this requires necessarily the reconstruction of the
social setting of the formative period of colonial plantation
society. Though they disagree on the nature of the genetic process and on the relative contribution of such factors as universals of linguistic structure and of language acquisition, all
creolists assume that pidginization and creolization involve convergence from different linguistic systems. The obvious first
step in the elucidation of the genetic process is the reconstruction of the *terminus a quo* of creole languages, the speech
varieties employed in the contact situation. In the case of
Creole, the reconstruction of the base-language *terminus a quo*
does not entail exclusive dependence on comparative reconstruction
from extant speech forms. French creolists may, as it were,
resort to looking at the back of the book, in the form of extensive historical sleuthing to uncover accounts and transcriptions
of vernacular colonial speech and of examination of material on
the vernacular speech of the metropolis. In this effort it is

essential to abandon the implicit assumption that the French part of the *terminus a quo* was more or less equivalent to the present-day standard language.

The reconstruction of the social setting in which Creole emerged and the identification of the *terminus a quo* are inextricably linked since social conditions determine the socio-linguistic setting. First, we need to set aside the simplistic interactionist model opposing the white master to the colored slave. In such plantation colonies as Saint-Domingue there existed a chain of intermediaries between the plantation owner (often an absentee landlord) and African-born field-hands: 'Creole' house-slaves, indentured and free white servants, managers, overseers, artisans, soldiers, officials, etc. When Haitian independence was declared, half of the slaves were self-termed *natif-natal* who granted themselves privileges denied to the African-born *Dandas*. It is very doubtful that the mass of white settlers spoke the language of the Versailles courtiers or of the Paris magistrates and notables. Chaudenson ascribes the choice of SF as the frame of reference in all comparative studies in the field of Creole French to ignorance on the part of foreign scholars of the chasm that separates SF and vernacular speech. The persistence of so gross a misconception must be laid, rather, squarely in the lap of French academic purism. One of the more genial intuitions of Jules Faine, the dilettante Haitian creolist, was that Creole originated in a nautical lingua franca spoken in the French harbors of the English Channel and the Atlantic. Whether the speech of the early French settlers was a Maritime koinê, as Alexander Hull suggests (1974, 1975) after comparing New World Creole and North American varieties of French, or simply a form of *français populaire* with admixture from regional dialects, it differed considerably from the literary norm of the period and undoubtedly showed many features of so-called advanced French (Sauvageot 1962). In addition to evidence from the vernacular speech of seventeenth and eighteenth century France and that of Franco-Canadian and Acadian, the reconstitution of the speech of white settlers should be informed from the description of the speech of whites isolated in creolophone areas, such as Saint-Barts Windward, Saint-Thomas Carenage, and the Réunion highlands.

The reconstruction of the substrate languages spoken by the slaves awaiting transport in West African barracoons and those who were imported into the plantation colonies is fraught with greater perils. Heretofore, creolists have been content to compare extant creoles and pidgins with present-day African and Malagasy languages. It is no doubt the case that these languages have changed considerably over the last two centuries. The possibility must also be envisaged that Africans involved in the creation of Creole might have employed contact vernaculars. B. Heine 1975 has shown that when they become pidginized African languages undergo modifications that parallel those that distinguish the standard form of West European languages and pidgins and creoles derived from them. In the light of these uncertainties it is hazardous to claim that feature X or feature Y of Creole is transferred directly from such or such individual West African language.

At this juncture it would do well to remember that *Une langue est un système où tout se tient* (or at least, *presque tout*). To establish the incontrovertible influence by way of direct transfer or calque of a specific substrate language or particular variety of French, it is necessary to compare, not isolated features of a given dialect of Creole or of Creole in general, but whole subsystems: phonotactics, nominal deixis, tense-aspect, topicalization, etc. The most extreme example of the atomistic comparative procedure I am reproving is Suzanne Comhaire-Sylvain's identification of the post-posed definite determiner alternants -*la* and -*a* of HC with homophonous post-positions in Ewe:

(5)   *HC*   *Ewe*
         kaj-la   'the house'   ho-la
         kaj-la-jo   'the houses'   ho-a-wo
  but kaj-jo   'the houses'   ?

As attractive as this identity of form might appear, one must compare the entire nominal determiner system, including deixis and number marking, at the phonological and semantico-syntactic level. Is it the case, for example, that in Ewe, as obtains in Creole, the plural marker implies definiteness and that both 'plural' and 'definiteness' may be marked by the plural post-position only?

But if we are to compare whole subsystems of Creole with French varieties or African or Malagasy languages from which they might have sprung, we must first describe these subsystems. Although Gallo-Romance specialists may take pride in the fact that Creole French dialects are among the best and most delicately described of Creole languages, available descriptions are still relatively superficial and lacking in explicitness. They are also primarily taxonomic--using that term without any pejorative intent. That is, they fail to interrelate super-ficially disparate features and thus fall short of revealing the coherent subsystems whose parentage the comparativist might wish to determine. Once such subsystems have been identified, it becomes clear that they cannot be assumed to have been transferred *en bloc* from either the base or the substrate languages. Instead, it is necessary to assume a process of continuous elaboration by which building blocks from the base and substrate languages become integrated into complex but coherent wholes.

In the remaining part of my presentation, I will attempt to illustrate the uniqueness and the coherence of the subsystems of HC by re-examining three areas of its structure from which creolists have drawn evidence for grammatical calquing or straight-forward transfer from African languages: (1) the nasal vowel system; (2) external sandhi phenomena; (3) the tense-aspect marker system.

3. Nasalization in Haitian Creole

A superficial contrastive analysis of HC and SF would reveal

only minor differences in phonemic inventory. HC has a
triangular nasal vowel system that contrasts with the quadri-
lateral set of SF nasal vowels:

Nasal Vowel Inventories of Haitian Creole and Standard
French (Vowels indicated in parentheses have marginal
status)

TABLE I

But the two languages differ mainly with respect to the distribution and function of nasality. Were it not for a rather long
list of exceptional items and considerable variations linked to
the sociolinguistic phenomenon of gallicization in HC, vowel
nasalization could be assumed to be environmentally determined.
One might posit a morpheme structure condition defining as
nasal any vowel followed by a nasal consonant:

    HC   *SF*

1. Regressive Assimilation of Nasalization

        vẽn   'vein'   vɛn
        žõn   'yellow'   žon
        kãn   'cane'   kan
        bãnãn   'plantain'   banan
        bẽɲẽ   'to bathe'   bɛɲe
        žẽnũ   'knee'   žənu
        zarẽɲẽ   'spider'   arɛɲe

2. Exceptional Items

        mɔn   'hill'   mɔrn
        šam   'piece of magic' šarm   'charm'
        vɛn   'our glass'   vɛr   'glass'

    Nasal vs. Non-Nasal Vowel in the Environment __N

                    TABLE II

The most striking impressionistic feature of HC is its nasal
quality. It results, not only from the fact that vowels are
generally nasalized before a nasal consonant but also from the
effect of various nasal assimilation rules. One of these is
optional regressive assimilation across word and higher level
syntactic boundaries (Henri Tinelli 1974):

(6) Optional Regressive Assimilation of Nasality

m ap di jo	'I am telling them.'
m ap dĩ nũ	'I'm telling you (plural)'
li sɔti	'He left.'
lĩ mɛ̃m	'himself'
jo ba li	'They give him.'
jo bã mwɛ̃	'They give me.'
pu li	'for him(her)'
pũ mwɛ̃	'for me'
fɔ wu di jo	'You have to tell them.'
fõ m di jo	'I have to tell them.'

Optional regressive assimilation of nasality across morpheme boundary results in the appearance at the phonetic level of three additional nasal vowels, [ẽ], [õ], and [ã]:

(7)
mo nũ	[mõnũ]	'our word'
ze mwɛ̃	[zẽmwɛ̃]	'my egg'
papa m	[papãm]	'my father'

Except when they occur at the end of a word, HC nasal vowels have a more diffused nasality than their SF counterparts and, in addition to stylistic variation, there are alternations between nasal and corresponding non-nasal vowels in cognate words:

(8) Stylistic Variants:

famij	~	fãmij	'family'
demõ	~	dẽmõ	'demon'

Alternants:

amu	'pride'
fɛ lãmu	'to kiss, to make love'
amitje	'type of vine'
zãmi	'friend'
tutɔm	'everyone'
nõm	'man'

Many creolists (Hall 1950, Jourdain 1956, Alleyne 1966) have attributed this extension of the domain of nasalization and its consequent reduced differentiative role to substrate West African languages. But reflexes of an older regressive nasal assimilation rule are well attested in older stages of SF and in regional dialects (Bourciez 1950, Pope 1934, Chumbow 1975). At best one could only claim, as does Tinelli (1974:350), the emergence of a latent tendency of Northern Gallo-Romance through the catalytic effect of a convergent feature from the substrate languages. This lends support to Roman Jakobson's claim that 'a language accepts foreign structural elements only when it corresponds to its own latent tendencies'. The extension of the distribution of nasalization cannot be interpreted as a feature of the French *terminus a quo* of Creole since it is notably absent from the Mascarene varieties:

(9)
HC	Réunionese	
lãni	lanis	'anise'
sɛ̃n	sɛn	'seine'
zãmi	amiz	'friend'

kãnɔt   kanɔt   'boat'
grafinẽ   grafine   'to scratch'

Any claim for the African origin of nasalization must be backed
up by evidence showing not only that African languages X or Y have
the high nasal vowels [ĩ] and [ũ] absent from French but, more
crucially, that they show the various assimilation rules
described. Indeed, African reflexes must also be found for such
morphophonemic rules as the assimilation of *l* to *n* exhibited by
the definite determiner and the 3 sg. pronoun:

(10) Assimilation of *l*

    madãm lã   ∼   madãm nã   'the woman'
    lalin lã   ∼   lalin nã   'the moon'
    lãŋ lã   ∼   lãŋ nã   'the tongue'

and segment-hopping progressive assimilation manifesting itself
by the use of the nasalized alternant of the definite determiner
after an ostensibly oral segment:

(11) žẽnu ã   'the knee'
     mãgo mi ã   'the ripe mango'
     klinik lã   'the private hospital'
     fãmij u ã   'your family (specific)'
     kãnif lã   'the pen-knife'
     mõt lã   'the watch'
     mãsõž lã   'the lie'

4. Phonotactic structure: rule conspiracy?

The complex nature of the phonological role of nasalization in HC
has been described, at the word level, by most studies (Comhaire-
Sylvain 1938, Hall 1953, d'Ans 1968). But external sandhi
phenomena, such as the regressive assimilation rule illustrated
in 6 and segment-hopping progressive assimilation of 11, have
generally escaped notice. HC has a rich array of optional external
sandhi phenomena that have either not been observed or else
described as disparate features of individual morphemes. Unlike
French liaison and elision, they operate on surface phonemes,
rather than abstract segments, latent consonants or underlying
final consonants depending on the model chosen (Schane 1968,
Valdman 1970). Like liaison, however, they affect closed classes
of morphemes: personal pronouns, tense-aspect markers, etc. I
will attempt to show in this section that the optional external
sandhi phenomena of HC are not isolated features but constitute
a set of rules that conspire to eliminate sequences of two
consecutive unstressed vowels.
    HC had an apparent vowel elision rule which, unlike that of
French, does not present the characteristic of a natural rule
(Schane 1973). As shown in 12, this optional rule applies before
consonants as well as before vowels and immediately contiguous to
a vowel as well as across intervening consonantal segments:

(12) Personal Pronoun Elision (Consonants)

    li marje ak li   'He married her,   ḷ marje ak li
    *li marje ak ḷ   she married him.'   *ḷ marje ak ḷ
    ḷ marje avɛ li   ḷ marje avɛ l
    li ale ak li   'He went with her.' l ale ak li

(13)   Personal Pronoun Elision (Glides)

j arete l	'They stopped him.'	jo arete l
w ale	'You went.'	u ale, *wu ale
jo vini	'They came.'	*j vini
u vɔje	'You send.'	*w vɔje, *wu vɔje

If vowel elision were indeed involved in the data presented in 12
and 13, the rule would have the form: V → ∅ / ___V. We are
dealing then with a complex vowel truncation rule whose formulation
requires a statement of the features of the segments preceding
or following the truncated vowel as well as a definition of the
syntactic environment. For instance, as shown by the examples
in 13, this rule does not apply if it would produce sequences
consisting of glides plus consonants. Vowel truncation in
pronouns and in a variety of forms including tense-aspect markers,
conjunctions, and, marginally, verb stems results in the
reduction of successive unstressed vowel sequences. But it
appears to be countered by other rules whose output is precisely
VV sequences:

(14)   Post-Posed Definite Determiner

pitit la	pitit la	'the child'
dlo la	dlo a	'the water'
šẽ la	šẽ ã	'the dog'

However, VV sequences resulting from *l*-truncation (restricted
to the definite determiner *la* and the 3 sg. personal pronoun *li*)
are partially eliminated by the insertion of a glide after all
high vowels (including high-mid):

(15)   Glide Insertion

dlo a	[dlowa]	
šẽ ã	[šẽjã]	
se u	[sewu]	'It's you.'
papa u	[papawu]	'your father'
papa o	[papawo]	'Oh, father!'
but		
papa a	[papa a]	'the father'
bɔkɔ a	[bɔkɔa]	'the witch doctor'
vɛ a	[vɛ a]	'the glass'

VV sequences remain only after low vowels, as in *papa, bɔkɔ,* and
vɛ. Glide insertion also operates word-internally, but it is
clearly a different process since here it applies after the low
vowel *a* in *mai.* The distinction between glide segments and
glides introduced by the two glide insertion rules rests on the
fact that the presence of the glide is optional in items such as
kreol or *loa* but obligatory in *pijaj* or *awona:*

(16)   Glide Insertion (Internal)

kreɔl	[krejɔl]	'Creole'
pei	[peji]	'country'
mai	[maji]	'corn(maize)'
dɛjɛ	[dɛjɛ]	'back'
pijaj	[pijaj]	'give-away'

| loa | [lowa] | 'loa' |
| awona | [awona] | 'whore' |

VV sequences also result from the post-position of the 2nd
person pronoun (and possessive adjective) u--and in those
dialects where occurs the alternation *li~i*--of the 3rd person sg.
pronoun *i*. The latter assumes the form *i* everywhere except after
a consonant: *šat li* 'his cat' **šat i*. These sequences are
reduced by the formation of glides from the two high vowels:

(17) Glide Formation (Unrounded)

jo kupe i	[jo kupej]	'They cut it.'
lapo i	[lapoj]	'his skin'
sat li		'his cat'
but		

(18) Glide Formation (Rounded)

dlo u	[dlow]	'your water'
pje u	[pjow]	'your foot'
avɛ u	[avɔw]	'with you'
papa u	[papɔw]	'your father'
m ap ba u	[mapbɔw]	'I'll give you'
tu sa u vle	[tusɔwvle]	'everything you want'

That glides rather than unstressed, reduced high vowels are
formed is supported by the absence of any distinction between
papaj 'papaya', ending with the segment /j/, and the combination
papa plus *i (papa i)* 'his (her) father'. Note that in 18
assimilation of rounding results whenever *u* follows an unrounded
vowel.

A few descriptions of HC, notably Hall 1953 and Stewart 1963,
note vowel reductions taking place before the indefinite
determiner whose usual realization is õ:

(19) Vowel Truncation

| se õ mun | [sõmun] | 'It's a person.' |
| li gẽ õ šat | [l̩gõšat] | 'He (she) has a cat.' |

But that we are not dealing with an idiosyncratic phenomenon
is demonstrated by a complex set of vowel assimilations and
reductions attested in the Cape Haitian dialect.[1] In that
dialect, as in some Lesser Antilles varieties, possession is
indicated by the use of the preposition *a* between the determined
noun and the post-posed personal pronoun.[2] Vowel sequences
result which are reduced by the truncation of any word-final
unrounded vowel:

(20) Vowel Truncation (Cape Haitian)

sulje a papa	[suljapapa]	'Papa's shoes'
diri a nũ	[dirãnũ]	'our rice'
mãže a m	[mãžãm]	'my food'
pẽ a j	[pãj]	'his bread'
papa a jo	[papajo]	'their father'

Potential three-vowel sequences are formed with 2nd and 3rd person sg. pronouns. These are reduced, first, by the application of glide formation, and in the case of the 2nd person pronoun, by a vowel harmony rule changing the rounding feature. The latter rule applies before *w* in all cases:

(21)   Vowel Harmony

akew	[akow]	'with you'
lgéw	[lgṍw]	'He(she) has you.'
kõmãw	[kõmṍwje]	'How are you?'

The interaction between Glide Formation, Vowel Harmony, and Vowel Truncation is summarized in 22. No strict external ordering of rules is being claimed, but it must be assumed that Vowel Truncation applies last since *sulje a u* is realized with a low-mid rather than a high-mid vowel:

(22)   Vowel Harmony + Vowel Truncation

Input	ake u	sulje a u	papa a u
Gl. Formation	ake w	sulje a w	papa a w
V. Harmony	ako w	sulje ɔ w	papa ɔ w
V. Truncation	-----	sulj ɔ w	pap ɔ w
Output	[akow]	[suljɔw]	(papɔw]

Finally, when the preposition *a* follows a rounded vowel, Vowel Truncation does not apply. Instead, the rounded vowel is reduced to the corresponding glide:

(23)   Glide Formation ($V_{Lab}V$)

do a m	[dwãm]	'my back'
mo a m	[mwam]	'my word'
ku a nũ	[kwãnũ]	'our neck'
po a nũ	[pwãnũ]	'our bridge'

   That avoidance of vowel hiatus underlies HC phonotactics is underscored by an interesting analogical development in the Cape Haitian dialect. In Northern varieties of HC, post-vocalic *r* is generally maintained, particularly in final position. Thus, pairs such as *pɛ* 'peace' and *pɛr* 'priest', which fall together in the Western (Port-au-Prince) dialect, are kept distinct. As one would expect, the final *r* appears in the possessive construction: for instance, [sɛrãm] 'my sister' (the nasalization of the *a* is accounted for by the regressive assimilation rule illustrated in 6). But an epenthetic *r* crops up unexpectedly in forms ending with a vowel in their isolated form:

(24)   R-Insertion (Cape Haitian)

sɛr		[sɛrãm]	'my sister'
papa	[papãm]	[paparãm]	'my father'
pitapitit	[pitapitãm]	[pitapitarãm]	'my grand-child'

karako   [karakwãm]   [karakorãm]   'my nightshirt'

In Northern HC there exist, then, two mechanisms for the
reduction of VV sequences: (1) Vowel Truncation or Glide
Formation, depending on the nature of the vowels involved; (2)
R-Insertion. In most cases, either of the two alternatives are
available to speakers, although there are numerous lower-level
constraints that restrict the choice. Presumably, the choice
between the two alternatives is not 'free' but determined by
various sociolinguistic factors that require further
investigation:

(25) R-Insertion vs. Vowel Truncation

Input	sɛram	papa a m	papa a m	papa a u
R-Insertion	-----	paparam	-------	-------
Gl. Formation	-----	--------	-------	papa a w
V. Harmony	-----	--------	-------	papa ɔ w
V. Truncation	-----	--------	pap a m	pap ɔ‵w
Nasalization	sɛrãm	paparãm	papãm	--------
Output	[sɛrãm]	[paparãm]	(papãm]	[papɔw]

Related to R-Insertion is the appearance of an epenthetic
central glide in Port-au-Prince Creole:

(26) [pu γ u]   'for you'
      [se paγu]   'It's not you'.
      [se tɛ u]   'It's your land.'
      [se pa u]   'It's your part.'

The fact that the glide does not occur in forms cognate with
those containing a final postvocalic r in Northern varieties of
HC may be explained by the placement of stress on the final
vowel of the noun. In other words, the last two items of 26 do
not contain VV sequences.
    The total elimination of VV sequences toward which the
various morphophonemic rules presented here in a tentative and
informal form appear to lead is not attained in HC, if only
because these rules are optional. In the absence of descriptions of other dialects of Creole that meet the standards of
explicitness of those available for HC, it would be premature
to claim that the canonical syllable structure VCVC is most
closely approximated in normal-style HC. Nonetheless comparison
of cognate items in HC and, say, Réunion Creole, reveals that
the elimination of VV sequences is brought about by the
application of other phonological processes such as prosthesis
and apheresis:

(27) *Réunionese*   *HC*
      avalas   lavalas   'downpour'
      akute   kute   'to listen'
      amare   mare   'to tie'
      amiz   zãmi   'friend'
      asize   šita   'to sit'

Even if it were possible to demonstrate that the rich set
of external sandhi phenomena of HC conspire to achieve a CVCV
structure, this would not serve as a persuasive argument for
the French or African basis of Creole phonology. Recent
reformulations of SF elision and liaison (Klausenburger 1974)
buttress the long-held claim that French abhors vowel hiatus.
I have attempted to show by this discussion of HC external
sandhi that whatever the ultimate source of the phonotactic
basis of the language, there has been no simple carry-over of
isolated rules. The external sandhi rules of HC form a complex
integrated whole that could hardly exist in the same form in
the base or substrate languages. If Creole has inherited from
French a phonotactic structure that is CVCV 'in spirit'
(Schane 1973), the attainment of that goal takes a markedly
different form. And the integration of disparate rules into
an organic whole is precisely one of the chief features of the
process of elaboration by which a pre-pidgin or a set of
evolving approximative learner systems develop into a creole.
Such a complex set of rules with a unifying objective could
hardly have developed before the language had acquired native
speakers. From the point of view of communicative competence,
it is clear that external sandhi rules generate a wide array of
morphophonemic variants that provide speakers of the language
with the 'stylistic manoeuvre' that Sankoff and Laberge 1973
found so sorely lacking in pre-pidgins.

5.   The tense-aspect system of Creole French

It is in its verbal system that specialists of Creole have seen
a clear effect of the African substrate languages. Even Robert
A. Hall, Jr.--who could hardly be termed a substratophile, let
alone a substratomaniac--declared (1966:109):
      ...the entire inflectional system of the Haitian Creole
      verb with its loss of tense and person-and-number endings
      and its use of aspectual prefixes, is straight African.
Indeed, the verbal system of Creole contrasts strikingly from
that of SF: (1) it gives priority to aspectual rather than
tense distinctions; (2) tense-aspect categories are expressed by
free morphemes occurring before an invariable verb base rather
than by inflectional suffixes or stem alternations. Some
creolists go so far as to look for an African origin for the
phonological shapes of the pre-posed tense-aspect markers. For
example, Suzanne Comhaire-Sylvain claimed that the so-called
future marker of HC (*ava, av, a*) is derived ultimately from a
Bantu root *bia*. Morris Goodman (1964:85) found various
possible African etyma for the Lesser Antilles non-punctual
(durative) marker *ka*, which, it will be recalled, was traced to
Guinea Gulf Portuguese Pidgin by Alexander Hull: Hausa *kan*
'habitual', Mende *kaka* 'repetition in point of time', Efik *ke*
'progressive', Wolof ŋ*ga* or ŋ*ge* 'continuous present'.
      Except for the *ka* and *ke* markers of Lesser Antilles dialects,
all Creole tense-aspect markers correspond phonologically to
French auxiliaries or modals. An African origin must be sought
not for isolated forms but for the total semantactic system.

In a *troisième cycle* thesis, Alain Bentolila compares the
tense-aspect systems of several European-based creoles with
those of eight African languages (Wolof, Twi, Gon, Susu,
Maninka, Bassa, Bulu, Serer), and he suggests that they
originate in that of Fon, the simplest of the African systems.
A comparison of Bentolila's analysis of HC and Fon does
reveal a remarkable semantactic identity between the two
systems:

ASPECT	PUNCTUAL		NON-PUNCTUAL		TENSE
REALIS	∅	*ϕ*	ap	*do*	NON-ANTERIOR
	te	*ko*	t ap	*ko do*	ANTERIOR
IRREALIS	a	*na*	av ap	*na do*	NON-ANTERIOR
	ta	*na ko*	t av ap	*na ko do*	ANTERIOR

Comparison of Tense-Aspect Marker System of Haitian
Creole and Fon (Italics)

TABLE III

Each system has three markers with comparable semantic range
and, except for the anterior and irrealis markers, they occur
in the same position relative to each other.
   The other African languages surveyed by Bentolila show more
complex aspectual systems (see for example that of Maninka
displayed in Table IV). There is no reason to believe that
African slaves used the lowest common denominator system in
communicating with each other. The use of a simple aspectual
system, such as that of Fon, could only have developed if it
had been that of an African-based contact vernacular. However,
there is no evidence for the existence of such a speech form on
the coast of West Africa from the fifteenth to the seventeenth
century. Furthermore, that contact vernacular would have had
to be an elaborated pidgin, such as Tok Pisin (Melanesian
Pidgin English), for one of the characteristics of pre-pidgins
is the absence of highly developed tense-aspect systems. In
these, verbal grammatical relationships are often expressed by
the use of adverbs (Sankoff and Laberge 1973).

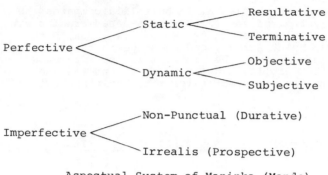

Aspectual System of Maninka (Mande)

TABLE IV

The deep-level analysis for the Creole tense-aspect system
Bentolila proposes does not account for many distinctions which
have been grammaticalized in the Mascarene dialects, notably
Mauritian Creole (MC), and which are incipient in HC. The
system presented in Table V, based on recent detailed
descriptions of Mauritian Creole by three different investigators
(Baker 1972, Corne 1973, Moorghen 1972), specifies more
accurately the categories distinguished by HC speakers. No
attempt is made to specify all occurring combinations, nor to
state the order of markers relative to each other:

ANTERIOR/NON-ANTERIOR	ti/zero
NON-COMPLETIVE:	
NON-PUNCTUAL/PUNCTUAL	pe/zero
IRREALIS:	
DEFINITE	pu
NON-DEFINITE	a
COMPLETIVE:	
DURATIVE	fin
ACTUAL	fɛk

Tense-Aspect Markers of Mauritian Creole

TABLE V

The tense-aspect system of MC shows four aspectual contrasts:
completive vs. non-completive, with the former further
differentiated between durative and actual; punctual vs.
non-punctual and an irrealis aspect, further subdivided into
definite vs. non-definite. Whereas in other dialects the zero
form implies completion, in MC that aspect is expressed overtly
by *fin (in, n)* or *fɛk*. The following examples illustrate the
distinction between the anterior marker *ti* and the two
completive markers:

(28)   letã ki li   n (in, fin) mɛt so maj dã magazẽ, lera vini,
       mãz so maj.

       'When he had (completed) putting his corn in the barn,
       Rat came and ate his corn.

(29)   nu ti ape fɛk kɔz u la.

       'We were just in the process of speaking about you.'

(30)   zã in (fin) fɛk sɔti.

       'John has just left now.'

Of the two irrealis markers, *pu* indicates the speaker's intent
to carry out an action or the certainty of the action or state.
Compare:

(31)   li pu gaɲɛn baba

       'She'll have a child (it's certain since she's already
       pregnant).'

(32)   li a gaɲɛn baba

       'She'll have a child (if she continues not taking the
       pill).'

In HC *pu* occurs within an obligative construction introduced
by *se*:

(33)   se pu u fɛ sa.

       'You have to do this.'

One can readily envisage the grammaticalization of that element
and an accompanying semantic shift from weakened obligation to
definiteness. Forms cognate to the MC completive markers *fin*
and *fɛk* also occur in HC, but they function like other modals,
such as *sɔti* 'to have' *prã* 'to be just about to' or *sa* 'to be
able to'. It would appear that in HC these two modals are
incipient tense-aspect markers, and there is some evidence that
suggests that *fɛk* is only grammaticalized in MC. For example,
its position relative to other tense-aspect markers is variable:

(30)   zã in fɛk sɔti

       'John has just left now.'

(34)   zã fɛk fin al laboutik

       'John has just now gone to the store (and hasn't
       come back yet).'

Immediately after declaring that it is impossible to account for the HC verbal system in terms of a normal evolution from French, Suzanne Comhaire-Sylvain (1936:106) makes mention of a large number of periphrastic constructions with aspectual meaning found in vernacular varieties of French. In his detailed study of these constructions, Geroges Gougenheim (1971:55ff) lists numerous constructions with durative meaning and several with prospective meaning: *être après, être après à, être à, être en voie de (en route de, en devoir de)*, etc. on the one hand, and *être pour* and *devoir*, on the other. In 3 and 4 above is illustrated another periphrastic construction with durative meaning used widely today. I would submit that a construction such as:

(35) Je suis pour y aller.

'I will go there.'

attested in SF from the Middle Ages to the seventeenth century is a plausible source for the MC definite future marker *pu*.

The existence in vernacular varieties of French of analytical verbal constructions suggests that in this aspect of the structure of Creole, as was the case for vowel nasalization, congruent features from the African substrate languages served as a catalyst for tendencies latent in Gallo-Romance. Yet there exists between the structure of the Creole and the vernacular French verbal systems a 'structural break' that cannot be bridged by normal linguistic evolution (Hull 1975:18). Even varieties of French with greatly reduced verbal morphology, such as Frenchville, Pa. or Saint-Barts Windward, exhibit some stem alternation and overt inflectional suffixes.

For Derek Bickerton 1975 such a break is a necessary consequence of pidginization. Starting from the premise that all West European-based plantation creoles are derived from pidgins elaborated by multilingual servile groups, Bickerton assumes that these pidgins, precisely because of their reduced nature, are 'unlearnable' by children. Faced with an impossible language acquisition task, children who grew up in a plantation colony setting 'created' a language by resorting to linguistic universals. In the case of the tense-aspect system Bickerton claims that natural semantax would specify precisely the three-way system illustrated in Table III: an opposition between anteriority and non-anteriority intersecting with two aspectual distinctions. He puts forward the even stronger claim that the markers would necessarily appear in the order anterior--irrealis--non-punctual characteristic of HC as well as such other West European-based creole languages as Sranan234tongo, Papiamento, and Hawaiian Creole. Bickerton's intriguing hypothesis can only be validated typologically, for to attempt to re-create the sociolinguistic conditions of plantation societies in which one might observe acquisitional development on the part of children exposed to (1) diverse natural languages and (2) a pidgin resulting from the interaction of these languages requires inhumane experimental conditions.

Bickerton's proposal does raise the issue of whether the structural breaks exhibited by creoles are a function of adult language learning (pidginization) or of child language acquisition (creolization). According to what might be termed 'standard theory', massive restructuring is located at the pidginization stage. Taking a universal grammar stance, as did Louis Hjelmslev when he spoke of the optimal nature of the grammar of creoles, and as is currently fashionable, one would account for the emergence of the tense-aspect marker system of Creole by the interplay of features of universal grammar under conditions of communicative stress (Givón 1975). Universal grammar would be highly unmarked and would be expected to show: (1) marking of categories by free particles rather than by bound inflectional endings; (2) a one-to-one correspondence between morphemes and their phonological realization; (3) the use of invariable syntactic order and particularly the perceptually preferable SVO order; (4) absence of syntactic permutations. However, markedness theory does not explain the most significant feature of the tense-aspect system of Creole, the choice of the semantic categories marked overtly.

6. Conclusion

The signal contribution of the pioneering creolists of our era--Robert A Hall, Jr., John Reinecke, Douglas Taylor--was to dispel the notion that pidgin and creole languages were inferior, broken, bastardized, or mongrelized versions of older, longer-established languages. The removal of the stigma that attached to these languages required the demonstration of the systematic and self-contained nature of their structure. I trust that I have succeeded in demonstrating to this audience of Romanists that, on the one hand, creole languages are as complex and as difficult to describe as other natural languages, and on the other, that they pose the same challenges to linguistic theory. I also hope to have shown that Creole French dialects do not constitute 'un français coulé dans le moule de la syntaxe africaine...une langue éwé à vocabulaire français' (Comhaire-Sylvain 1936:178) and that, at the same time, they are not direct reflexes of vernacular varieties of Northern French. Creole French dialects are separated from French varieties by a structural break caused by massive restructuring in a short period of time, itself the product of special social circumstances. These circumstances created, in particular, a condition of communicative stress in which foreign learners of French were obliged to use the language for communicative needs without being provided either appropriate native models or expansion of deviant speech. To put it differently, their learner-approximative systems were frozen at a very low level. Current longitudinal studies of second-language learning underscore the determining influence of language universals in the development of approximative learner systems and the relatively minor effect of conscious simplification, or even of expansion and correction, on the part of models or of transfer from the first-language, at least in the domain of grammar.

The adoption of a universalist, cognitive-interactionist view of second-language learning has, in the field of pidgin and creole studies, the advantage of enabling us to move beyond the sterile discussions pitting polygeneticists against monogeneticists and supporters of the baby talk or simplification hypothesis against proponents of language interference. The point of view that pidginization and creolization are the result of the operation of language universals does not exclude language transfer nor the use on the part of the speakers of the base language of special registers, including foreigner talk (Ferguson 1971, 1975). It is also compatible with parallel genesis in different geographical locations of pidgins and creoles from the same language and admits the role of stimulus diffusion.

The facts I have presented in this paper support, I think, the following tentative conclusions with regard to the genesis and development of Creole.

1.   Historical evidence precludes the localization of a proto-pidgin French in Africa and invalidates the relexification hypothesis. At least two distinct focal points must be recognized: the island of Bourbon in the Mascarenes and some island in the Antilles.

2.   The common base of all Creole French dialects was some vernacular variety of French relatively uniform from one plantation colony to the other. That variety of French differed from the standard language, among other things, by the reduction of inflectional categories and the preponderance of analytic over synthetic constructions.

3.   Individual dialects of Creole arose by pidginization and creolization but without the crystallization of an elaborated pidgin. In other words, they developed from pre-pidgin continua.

4.   Similarities between Creole French dialects (and between Creole and other European-based creoles) stem from the shared base in vernacular French and the operation of linguistic universals. There were also considerable contacts between the various plantation colonies, including between the Antilles and the Mascarenes, in the form of population movement and trade.

5.   Differences may be accounted for, not only in terms of language contact, for example the influence of Malagasy and Indo-Portuguese on Bourbonnais and of West African languages on Antillean varieties, but by differences in social factors. These in turn determined differential effects of French varieties on the incipient creole and resulted in differential decreolization at more elaborated stages of the language. These various factors would explain, for example, the greater complexity of the verbal systems of Indian Ocean dialects and, on the other hand, the more elaborated nature of the nominal deixis system of Haitian Creole.

These tentative conclusions are offered more as working hypotheses than as claims. To quote a Haitian proverb: *Sa sé twokèk: chay-la dèyè* 'This is the head-pad; the load is to follow'.

NOTES

[1]I am indebted to Michel Lange for the Cape Haitian data
which, however, I have not been able to verify in the field.
Yves Dejean supplied the information on which is based my
analysis of forms involving vowel harmony and vowel truncation
in Port-au-Prince (Western) HC. I am also grateful to him for
numerous discussions concerning the sandhi phenomena described
in this article, although I take full responsibility for the
interpretation of the data.

[2]Another feature shared by Cape Haitian Creole and Lesser
Antillean varieties is the realization of the 3 sg. personal
pronoun as /i/.

REFERENCES

Alleyne, Mervyn C. 1966. La nature du changement phonétique à
    la lumière du créole français d'Haïti. Revue de Linguistique
    Romane 119-120.279-303.
d'Ans, André-Marcel. 1968. Le créole français d'Haïti. The
    Hague: Janua Linguarum. Series Practica, 106.
Baker, Phillip. 1972. Kreol. London: Hurst.
Bentolila, Alain. 1970. Créoles et langues africaines:
    comparaison des structures verbales. Paris: Université René
    Descartes thesis.
Bickerton, Derek. 1975. Creolization, linguistic universals,
    natural semantax and the brain. Paper presented at the
    International Conference on Pidgins and Creoles, University
    of Hawaii, Jan. 6-11.
Bourciez, B. A. 1950. Précis de phonétique française. Paris:
    Klincksieck.
Chaudenson, Robert. 1974. Le lexique du parler créole de la
    Réunion. Paris: Champion.
Chumbow, Beban. 1975. Rule complication as a mechanism of
    linguistic change. Bloomington: Indiana University
    dissertation.
Comhaire-Sylvain, Suzanne. 1936. Le créole haïtien:
    morphologie et syntaxe. Port-au-Prince and Wetteren: Imp.
    de Meester.
_____. 1938. Contes du pays d'Haïti. Port-au-Prince:
    chez l'auteur.
Corder, S. Pit. 1973. Introducing applied linguistics.
    Harmondsworth, England: Penguin.
Corne, Chris. 1973. Tense and aspect in Mauritian Creole.
    Te Reo 16.
Faine, Jules. 1936. Philologie créole. Port-au-Prince: Imp.
    de l'Etat.
_____. 1939. Le créole dans l'univers. Port-au-Prince: Imp.
    de l'Etat.

Ferguson, Charles A. 1971. Absence of copula and the notion
    of simplicity: a study of normal speech, baby talk,
    foreigner talk, and pidgins. Pidginization and creolization
    of languages, ed. by Dell Hymes, 141-50. Cambridge:
    Cambridge University Press.
_____. 1975. Toward a characterization of English foreigner
    talk. Anthropological Linguistics 17.1-14.
Givón, Talmy. 1975. Prolegomena to any creology. Paper
    presented at the International Conference on Pidgins and
    Creoles, University of Hawaii, January 6-11.
Goodman, Morris F. 1964. A comparative study of Creole French
    dialects. The Hague: Mouton.
_____. 1971. The strange case of Mbugu (Tanzania).
    Pidginization and creolization of languages, ed. by Dell
    Hymes. Cambridge: Cambridge University Press.
Gougenheim, Georges. 1971. Étude sur les périphrases verbales
    de la langue française. Paris: Nizet.
Grégoire, Antoine. 1947. L'apprentissage du langage,
    Vol. 2: La troisième année et les années suivantes,
    Fascicule CVI, Bibliothèque de la Faculté de Philosophie et
    Lettres de l'Université de Liège. Paris: Société des
    Belles Lettres.
Gumperz, John J. and Robert Wilson. 1971. Convergence and
    creolization: a case from the Indo-Aryan/Dravidian Border.
    Pidginization and creolization of language, ed. by Dell
    Hymes, 151-68. Cambridge: Cambridge University Press.
Hall, Robert A., Jr. 1950. Nasalization in Haitian Creole.
    Modern Language Notes 65.474-78.
_____ et al. 1953. Haitian Creole: grammar--texts--
    vocabulary. Memoirs of the American Folklore Society 43.
_____. 1966. Pidgin and Creole languages. Ithaca, N.Y.:
    Cornell University Press.
Heine, Bernd. 1975. Some generalizations on African-based
    pidgins. Paper presented at the International Conference on
    Pidgins and Creoles, University of Hawaii, January 6-11.
Hesseling, D. C. 1934. Gemeng de taal, mengentaal, Kreools en
    Kreolisering. De Nieuwe Taalgids 28.310-22.
Hjelmslev, Louis. 1939. Caractères grammaticaux des langues
    créoles. Congrès international des sciences anthropologiques
    et ethnologiques. C.R. de la 2e Session, 371-72.
    Copenhagen.
Hoenigswald, Henry M. 1971. Language history and Creole
    studies. Pidginization and creolization of language, ed.
    by Dell Hymes, 473-80. Cambridge: Cambridge University
    Press.
Hull, Alexander. 1974. Evidence for the original unity of
    North American French dialects. Revue de Louisiane 3:1.59-70.
_____. 1975. On the origin and chronology of the French-
    based Creoles. Paper presented at the International
    Conference on Pidgins and Creoles, University of Hawaii,
    January 6-11.
Jourdain, Élodie. 1956. Du français aux parlers créoles.
    Paris: Klincksieck.

Klausenburger, Jurgen. 1974. Historische französische
    Phonologie aus generativer Sicht. Romanistische Arbeitshefte
    12. Tübingen: Max Niemeyer.
Moorghen, P.-M. J. 1972. Étude structurale du créole de l'île
    Maurice. Nice: University of Nice dissertation.
Pope, Mildred K. 1934. From Latin to Modern French.
    Manchester: Manchester University Press.
Sankoff, Gillian and S. Laberge. 1973. On the acquisition of
    native speakers by a language. Kivung 6:1.32-47.
Sauvageot, A. 1962. Français écrit, français parlé. Paris.
Schane, S. A. 1968. French phonology and morphology.
    Cambridge, Mass.: MIT Press.
_____. 1973. There is no 'French truncation rule'. Linguistic
    studies in Romance languages, ed. by R. J. Campbell, M. G.
    Goldin, and M. Clayton Wang. Washington, D.C.: Georgetown
    University Press.
Sechehaye, C. Albert. 1926. Essai sur la structure logique de
    la phrase. Paris: Champion.
Stewart, William A. 1963. The functional distribution of
    Creole and French in Haiti. Thirteenth annual roundtable of
    languages and linguistics. Georgetown University Monograph
    Series 15.149-59.
Tinelli, Henri. 1974. Generative and creolization processes:
    nasality in Haitian Creole. Lingua 33.343-66.
Traugott, Elizabeth C. 1973. Le changement linguistique et
    sa relation à l'acquisition de la langue maternelle.
    Langages 32.39-52.
Valdman, Albert, et al. 1970. Basic course in Haitian Creole.
    Bloomington, Indiana: Indiana University Research Center
    for the Language Sciences.
Valkhoff, Marius F. 1966. Studies in Portuguese and Creole.
    Johannesburg: Witwatersrand University Press.
Wartburg, W. von. 1928. Französisches etymologisches
    Wörterbuch. Bonn.

ROMANCE LINGUISTICS: WHENCE AND WHITHER?

ROBERT A. HALL, JR.

Cornell University

Elsewhere,[1] I have distinguished three main uses of the term *linguistics:*

1. Speculations concerning language in general, from a primarily philosophical or theological[2] point of view.
2. The description of a language for practical purposes, chiefly those of teaching it to non-native speakers.
3. The application of scientific method to the study of a language or group of languages, and to language in general based on the examination of data from specific languages.

My concern here will be largely with the history of linguistics 3, as applied to the study of the Romance languages.

In the development of any science, a number of different factors are at work: practical needs, the available technology, the social situation, and--last of all--theoretical considerations In general, these last grow out of the first three, but stand in a reciprocal relationship with them, both opening the way for and conditioned by further developments. Abstract science does

not normally arise nor continue independently of real-life
situations.   This has been true in Romance linguistics ever
since its inception in Dante's *De vulgari Eloquentiâ*.

For a subject to be studied at all, it has to be recognized
as having an existence independently of other subjects.   In
the Romance languages, it is generally considered that this
point was reached with the mention of the *rustica Romana lingua*
in the Edict of Tours (813).   But for five more centuries,
people continued talking in the gradually differentiating
Romance dialects, and began to compose literary works and write
them down, without needing to develop anything resembling
linguistics 3.   True, practical grammars like the *Donatz
proensals* and the *Leys d'Amors* were written for contemporary
Provençal in the thirteenth century, to assist non-native
speakers in poetizing in that language.   But Dante's discussion
in the *De vulgari Eloquentiâ (De v. E.)* in the 1290's was the
first theoretical treatment of the Romance languages, growing
out of the particular problems facing the would-be user of an
Italian literary language--which, however, did not yet exist.[3]

The problems with which Dante dealt in the *De v. E.* were
restricted to a narrow circle of poets and intelligentsia, and
did not concern the general mass of people, who went on talking
(and, by this time, writing down their business-memoranda,
reports, and the like) in their everyday local speech.   Dante's
aim was basically literary: to describe--in abstract and, to
a considerable extent, negative terms--an ideal *vulgare illustre*
'illustrious vernacular' which should be suitable for the
highest level of literature and especially for lyric poetry.
It was to be derived from features common to all the Italian
dialects, but identical to none of them, a vernacular *quod in
quâlibet redolet civitate nec cubat in ullâ* 'which is
perceptible in every city but has its lair in none' (*De v. E.*
1.16.4).   Dante's model for this ideal was his conception of
Latin, which he thought to have been set up by a consensus of
learned men, as an abstraction embodying the features common to
the various Romance vernaculars.   His *vulgare illustre* would
have been a similar artificial koiné based on the Italian
dialects, like the one which was actually constructed nearly
six centuries later by Ivar Aasen in his Norwegian *Landsmål*.[4]

In actual fact, Dante's ideal of the *vulgare illustre* was--
as was pointed out in the sixteenth century by Machiavelli[5] and
also by many others since then--unrealistic, unattainable, and
based on an inaccurate perception of the relation of Latin to
the Romance languages.   In the first book of the *De v. E.*, most
of the first part is linguistics 1, based on abstract philosophical and theological scholastic speculation about the nature and
origin of language.   But in the second part of the first book,
Dante takes up specific considerations connected with the ideal
of the *vulgare illustre*:   how it is to be identified and where
it is to be found.   In the course of his discussion, Dante was
the first to recognize and treat several important themes of
concern to Romance linguistics: the psychological importance
of the mother tongue and of first-language learning; the
classification of the Romance languages;[6] and the identification

of the Italian dialects.[7] Dante's views on these matters have
long since been, to a certain extent, superseded; he was
nevertheless the first to have drawn attention to them.

The various Romance literary languages, from Provençal in the
eleventh century to Italian and Catalan in the fourteenth, were
in fact established by one dialect coming to occupy a position
of prestige superior to the others--a quite different process
from the one Dante envisaged. They simply 'growed', more or
less like Topsy, with very little discussion beyond the writing
of some practical grammars. Dante left the *De v. E.* unfinished,
and it remained unpublished until the early sixteenth century,
without exerting any influence on the course of events or
discussion. Had this state of affairs continued, it would have
been only a historical curiosity, like the treatise of Iceland's
First Grammarian.[8] But Gian Giorgio Trissino (1478-1550)
rediscovered and published it in 1529, after which it became
one of the important documents in the sixteenth-century debates
(the so-called *Questione della Lingua*) over the origin and
nature of standard Italian.

The slow growth of the literary languages was greatly accelerated in the Renaissance by the invention of printing with
movable type. Reading matter became much more widely available,
and the reading public more numerous and relatively skilled in
rapid perusal of printed texts. Accurate and standardized
editions of classical and modern literature were demanded, as
well as unified orthographies which would not delay immediate
(even if often superficial) comprehension. Strong pressure
therefore arose for the standardization of alphabets and of the
shapes of letters. But should literary composition be in Latin
or the vernacular? Which, of several competing varieties,
should be the vernacular standard in each country? What kind
of orthography should be used--etymologizing or consistent with
current pronunciation? Debates over these and related topics
were widespread all over western Europe in the sixteenth
century--first in Italy,[9] then in France, Spain, and Portugal.

As in Dante's case, despite their basically literary
orientation, and also despite their often superficial or even
frivolous nature, these debates gave off some valuable by-
products from the point of view of the development of
linguistics 3. Once the strangle-hold of scholastic logic on
linguistic theory had been broken, the debaters were able to
see language as a social, as well as an individual,
phenomenon.[10] The relation of the Romance languages to Latin
was at last definitively clarified: after the famous Bruno-
Biondi debate of 1435,[11] it was generally recognized that
Romance had developed out of spoken Latin over the centuries.
The greatest single advance, perhaps, was one which I have not
tired of calling attention to for the past forty years, namely
Claudio Tolomei's (1492-1555) clear perception of the principle
of regularity in phonetic change.[12] He realized, before anyone
else did, that this is the first aspect of structural development to be dealt with in studying the history of a language,
since it enables us to sort out and recognize other factors

such as learned borrowings--and, of course, other types of more
interesting but less easily identifiable variations due to such
influences as analogical change, dialectal and cultural
borrowings, slips of the tongue, etc. We should not be
surprised that this fundamental discovery in historical
linguistics was made first in the Romance field, since the
continuity of the Romance languages from Latin was the first to
be recognized in the course of the Renaissance debates.

To profit most by Tolomei's truly revolutionary discovery,
it would have been necessary to investigate, accurately and in
detail, the medieval attestations of the Romance languages and
to correlate them with what was known of both classical and
non-classical Latin. There were only two scholars--an Italian,
Celso Cittadini (1553-1627), at the end of the sixteenth
century,[13] and a Frenchman, Gilles Ménage (1613-1692), in the
middle of the seventeenth[14]--who made any extensive efforts in
this direction. But the temper of the times was such as to
give, not only no encouragement, but active discouragement, to
efforts along this line. The intellectual atmosphere of the
Renaissance and Baroque periods, from the sixteenth to the
eighteenth centuries, was primarily one of Neo-Classical
absolutism, with (at least theoretically) rigid standards of
'correct' usage and style in language. To this was added, from
the time of Richelieu and Louis XIV onwards, an equally rigid
absolutism in political matters. Especially in France, the
intellectual center of western Europe in these centuries,
cultural ethnocentrism prevented even serious scholars from
seeing any interest or merit in the literature or language of
earlier times.[15]

Still worse, theorists of language in the later seventeenth
and in the eighteenth centuries were obsessed--reflecting the
absolutism and authoritarianism of their time--with abstract
'reason' and its presumed expression in 'general grammar'.
Arnauld and Lancelot's *Grammaire générale et raisonnée* (often
called the *Grammaire de Port-Royal*) of 1660, which was
basically practical in its aims,[16] was elevated to the rank of
an authority on 'universal grammar', and became the first of a
series of works purporting to expound this topic.[17] These
works, based almost exclusively on the structure of Latin and
French, could hardly be counted among the achievements of
Romance linguistics.[18]

Such contributions as were made to Romance linguistics 3 in
this period were--from the lofty viewpoint of 'general grammar'
--decidedly modest and humble. Local dialectal speech was far
beneath the dignity of virtually all grammarians and
littérateurs for much notice to be taken of it, especially in
France. Some attention was paid to dialects in Italy, where
poetry written in the local speech--especially humour and
satire--served as a kind of protest against the pretentious,
convoluted effusions of Baroque literature. From the sixteenth,
seventeenth, and eighteenth centuries date the earliest Romance
dialect-dictionaries,[19] beginning a trend which did not
increase markedly until the nineteenth century. A major step
in the establishment of our view of the Romance family was the

recognition that Rumanian (which had previously been regarded
as Slavic, because of the use of the Cyrillic alphabet in
writing it) had developed out of Latin. The 'Transylvanian
School' (Școala Ardeleană) of the eighteenth century was
especially insistent on this relationship.[20] The origin of the
Romance languages was extensively discussed, by such Frenchmen
as Pierre-Nicolas Bonamy (1694-1700) and J.-B. La Curne de
Sainte-Palaye (1697-1781),[21] and by such Italians as Ludovico
Antonio Muratori (1672-1750),[22] but without going essentially
beyond the positions reached in the sixteenth-century Italian
debates, principally because they discussed the relationships
of words rather than of structural features.

The Middle Ages were not wholly forgotten, although, as
Gossman says (1968:257), 'There was no public for serious works
of medieval scholarship'. In the Académie des Inscriptions et
Belles-Lettres of Paris there was a thin trickle of scholarly
investigation, exemplified especially in the work of Sainte-
Palaye and a few of his fellow-Academicians.[23] However, the
royal government did not desire too detailed an investigation
into its own origins or other aspects of medieval times. Hence
little encouragement was given to the publication of works on
the Middle Ages, including Sainte-Palaye's Old French glossary,
of which only the first volume was published in the eighteenth
century and the whole work not until 1875-1882.[24] Only after
the end of the Ancien Régime and the upheavals of the Revolution
and the Napoleonic period did a freer atmosphere prevail, in
which more extensive investigations into the medieval period,
so essential to Romance philology, could be pursued. François
Raynouard (1761-1836) was able to carry through to completion,
for Old South French, a work of the type envisaged by Sainte-
Palaye, in his anthology Choix des poésies originales des
Troubadours[25] (1816-1821) and in his Lexique roman ou
Dictionnaire de la langue des Troubadours (1838-1844).
Raynouard's thorough philological investigations coincided with
the Romantic revival of interest in the Middle Ages in general.
His view of Old Provençal as a kind of Proto-Romance, from which
the other Romance languages had been differentiated, has not
stood the test of time; but his basic method of establishment of
texts and their philological analysis has remained valid down to
the present. He is therefore rightfully termed the 'father of
Romance philology'.

Up to the end of the eighteenth century, the curricula of
universities had been quite narrowly limited--in general, to
theology, law, and medicine.[26] Work outside these fields was
normally carried on by amateurs. These investigators were
often, indeed, highly able and gifted amateurs, but nevertheless
they were not professional philologists, because such a
profession did not exist. They might make their living in ways
ranging from humble trades (e.g. G. B. Gelli, the sixteenth-
century Florentine cobbler and philosopher of language) to
teaching (the Messieurs de Port-Royal), being librarians and
archivists (L. A. Muratori), or holding at least nominal
positions in the Church (such abbés as Ménage and Galiani), or

else they were members of the leisure-class with independent
incomes. Only in the early nineteenth century was the number
of universities greatly increased (to meet the increased demand
for secondary-school teachers) and their curricula expanded to
include Indo-European and modern philology. Hence the study of
language became, for the first time, institutionalized and
professionalized, with an accompanying expansion in the number
of its practitioners, and consequent extension of investigation
to previously untouched materials and fields of research.[27]
The resultant increase in knowledge also inevitably brought
greater awareness of methodological problems and needs, and
hence a more rapid development of technological resources.
In this, Romance and other philologies simply followed the
same course as did the rest of scientific investigation in
modern times.

The first chair of Romance philology and linguistics was at
Bonn, and its occupant was Friedrich Diez (1794-1876), who is
often considered the 'father of Romance linguistics'. Like
Raynouard, Diez drew his first inspiration from Old Provençal,
and his first work was on troubadour lyric. Later, however, he
extended his purview to cover the other Romance languages as
well, and was the author of the first comparative Romance
grammar on a valid basis (*Grammatik der romanischen Sprachen*,
1836-1838) and etymological dictionary (*Etymologisches
Wörterbuch der romanischen Sprachen*, 1853), which were the
standard works for the rest of the century. In these, he was
of course dependent to a certain extent on earlier attempts at
tracing the history of the Romance languages,[28] but his major
contribution lay in adapting the comparative method, as applied
to linguistic structure in contemporary work on Indo-European,
to the Romance field.

The first half of the nineteenth century, following the
examples set by Raynouard and Diez, was marked by far more
extensive work than had ever been done before in the establishment and publication of medieval Romance texts. The general
availability of this material (helped by major improvements in
the manufacture of paper and in printing, and resultant lowering
of their cost), and its study at many centers of learning, was
an indispensable condition for the further development of
Romance philology--and was, in its turn, dependent on the *Lern-
und Lehrfreiheit* which in those days characterized German
universities. Through detailed study of attested data, many of
the speculations of earlier theorists--e.g. concerning the role
of Celtic or Germanic in the development and differentiation of
the Romance languages--could be checked and their verisimilitude
assayed. There were dangers, too, in an excessively document-
oriented *Schreibtischphilologie*. It was all too easy to
overestimate the importance of ancient documentary evidence,
and to mistake data attested in writing for the totality of
human linguistic activity. Both social and technological
developments in the nineteenth century, however, aided in
guarding against this danger and in extending our knowledge of
Romance speech beyond the borders of philology proper.

Post-Napoleonic social changes contributed to a greater interest in and emphasis on the role of dialects. On the one hand, it was often thought--especially in France, with its tradition of centralization and pretensions to intellectual predominance-- that any variation from 'correct' usage was an evil, to be stamped out as soon as possible. The linguistic history of the past hundred and fifty years in France has been, to a large extent, the carrying out of this program. However, as is well known, the initial impetus to the study of French dialects came from a drive to extirpate them, at the time of the Revolution, leading to an investigation aimed at getting precise information on them.[29] Many nineteenth-century dialect- dictionaries were intended primarily to aid speakers of local nonstandard varieties to acquire the national standard. Others grew out of interest and pride in the characteristics of local speech, through a combination of inherited 'campanilismo' with Romantic belief in the superiority of humble, unpretentious folk-ways (including language) to the artificial conventions and 'correctness' of civilization. This was especially the case in Italy (e.g. in Venice, Piedmont, Sicily) and Catalonia, and to a lesser extent in Spain and southern France. It is to such regionalistic particularism that we owe the resurgence of Modern Provençal literature,[30] not only in the poetical output of the Félibres, but also in Mistral's great dictionary (*Trésor dou Félibrige*, 1878).

   Technological developments also opened new horizons. Advances in the study of human anatomy and of physics afforded a basis for the development of an objective, nonimpressionistic science of phonetics in the middle of the century, on an experimental basis. Phonetic alphabets, going far beyond any framework afforded by conventional orthography for recording often minute differences of sound, made it possible for the first time to go beyond conventional orthography in analyzing language, whether standard or nonstandard. The effects of this advance were felt both in practical language teaching (in the 'phonetic method' set forth towards the end of the century by Viëtor and followed by Otto, Passy, Palmer, Grandgent, and others[31]) and in dialectology. At the same time, with the growth in number and availability of dialect studies, it became evident that there were aspects of language which had a geographical distribution. Phonetic transcription afforded a means of recording linguistic data in a form that rendered cross-dialectal comparison possible, free from the vagaries of individual scholars' adaptations of traditional spelling. The earliest collections of regional dialect-material, whether in tabular or cartographic shape, date from the latter part of the nineteenth century, and were the precursors of the great atlas projects of the end of that century and of the twentieth.[32]

As is well known, the last third of the nineteenth century was marked by extensive debates over methodological stringency, particularly as formulated by August Leskien in 1876 in the aphorism *Die Lautgesetze kennen keine Ausnahmen* 'Sound laws admit of no exceptions'. This dictum was simply the extreme,

oversimplified form of the basic principle, embodied in the
practice of the group nicknamed *Junggrammatiker* or 'Neo-
Grammarians', that phonetic change would proceed regularly if
there were no interfering factors, and that every exception to
regularity in sound change must be explainable as due to
interference of one kind or another--which, if sufficient data
are available, can be identified.[33] Here, a principle first
set forth and exemplified in Romance (by Tolomei; cf. above)
had been forgotten. Rediscovered in the Indo-European field,
it was very soon followed in Romance (as in other branches of
linguistics). A proof of its validity was soon afforded by
the 'Vulgärlateinische Substrate romanischer Wörter' (1884-1890)
of Gustav Gröber (1844-1911), a series of articles in which
Gröber used sets of cognates to establish hypothetical 'Vulgar
Latin' ancestral forms, many of which were later confirmed by
newly discovered attestations.[34] Its major application,
however, was in the monumental achievement of Wilhelm Meyer-
Lübke (1861-1936), whose *Romanische Grammatik* (1890-1900) and
Romanisches etymologisches Wörterbuch (1911; 3rd ed., 1936) have
been basic research tools ever since their appearance. In
Romance, therefore, as in other fields of historical lingustics
near and far (e.g. Algonquian and Athapascan[35]), the regularist
hypothesis has proved its validity and necessity as a basis for
scientific investigation.

The opposition to the Neo-Grammarians, which arose
immediately on the formulation of their principle of the
regularity of sound change,[36] was unfortunately particularly
strong in the Romance field, so that confusion on this point
has prevailed for a whole century and shows little sign of
abating. One of their leading opponents was Hugo Schuchardt
(1842-1929), who, after publishing a major work on *Der
Vokalismus des Vulgärlateins* (1866-68), frittered away the rest
of his scholarly activity on small points of etymology (very
often in polemics against other investigators) and on fragmentary
attestations of pidgin and creole languages. Misunderstanding
the theoretical basis of the Neogrammarians' principle,
Schuchardt attached them (in his *Über die Lautgesetze: Gegen
die Junggrammatiker*, 1885) in a superficial way. He interpreted
(as did many) the dictum *Die Lautgesetze kennen keine Ausnahmen*
in its most literal and vulnerable sense, and promulgated the
doctrine that 'every word has its own history'--which, though
perfectly true, is irrelevant to the discussion of sound change,
since words are on a different level of linguistic structure
from that of sounds.

Out of the earlier studies on the geographical distribution of
words and other linguistic features grew the projects for great
atlases on a nation-wide scale--first of all the *Atlas
Linguistique de France* of Jules Gilliéron (1854-1916) and
Edmond Edmont (1848-1926), published in 1902-1910. In his
teaching, Gilliéron aroused the strong interest and enthusiasm
of a number of younger men, of whom several undertook similar
projects for their own countries. Of these, the only one to be
completed and published with minimum delay was the *Atlante*

linguistico-etnografico dell'Italia e della Svizzera meridionale
(1928-40) with supplementary volumes of photographs [1943,
1956] and index [1960]) of Karl Jaberg (1877-1958) and Jakob
Jud (1882-1952).   Others were badly delayed, e.g. Mossèn Antoni
Griera's Catalan atlas, that of T. Navarro Tomás for the
Iberian peninsula, that of Sextil Puşcariu for Rumania, and--
worst of all--the *Atlante linguistico italiano*, originally the
brainchild of Matteo Giulio Bàrtoli (1873-1946), which was
begun in the early 1920's and of which, over half a century
later, only two sample maps have appeared.   These very ambitious
projects were, it is evident in retrospect, possible in periods
of great prosperity, but not in less favored times such as the
troubled mid-twentieth century.   Later atlas projects have, for
obvious reasons of finance and personnel, been less ambitious,
and have been planned on a regional rather than a national
scale.
  Gilliéron's studies in linguistic geography led him to
emphasize the importance of the geographical spread of words
(and structural features) above all other factors in language
change.   He justifiably criticized etymologies founded too
narrowly on 'sound-laws' alone, but the title of one of his
best-known works, *La faillite de l'étymologie phonétique* (1919),
indicates the direction in which he and his followers tended to
exaggerate.   As Gilliéron and others recognized, the
geographical distribution of linguistic phenomena often gives
hints as to their probable origin and relative age.   These
hints were organized--but with full recognition of their
statistical character--by Bàrtoli into a system which he
baptized 'Neolinguistica' and set up in opposition to the
Neogrammarian doctrine of regular sound change.[37]   A disciple
of Bàrtoli's, Giuliano Bonfante (1904-   ), pushing
Neolinguistic doctrines to an extreme, converted them from
statistical probabilities into dogmas (cf. note 2).[38]   Other
linguistic geographers, however, especially Jaberg and Jud and
their Swiss trainees, did not fall into Bartolian excesses.
It is due primarily to Jaberg's and Jud's solid work, combining
the best of regularist historical linguistics with
Gilliéronian geography, that the development of dialectology
and particularly of atlas work stands out as the major original
contribution of the Romance field to linguistic methodology in
modern times.
  From a more theoretical angle, also, the regularist approach
was criticized, on philosophical grounds, by the 'idealistic'
school in the first third of the twentieth century.[39]   On the
basis of a Neo-Platonic type of dualism between spirit and
matter, the Italian philosopher Benedetto Croce (1866-1952),
although devoid of competence in linguistic analysis as
practiced in his time, preached the impossibility of studying
language from any except an esthetic angle, as a manifestation
of poetic creativity.   Croce's viewpoint was largely shared by
certain influential philologists in Germany, especially Karl
Vossler (1872-1949) and Leo Spitzer (1887-1960), and in Italy,
such as Giulio Bertoni (1878-1942).   This group emphasized the
presumed superiority of spirit over matter and hence of meaning

over linguistic form, of syntax over phonology, and of
'creativity' over regularity of sound change. In the works of
the above-mentioned scholars and their disciples these doctrines
became a theology, and idealism a religion (cf. note 2). The
movement lost momentum after the passing of its major exponents
in the mid-twentieth century, and is by now passé except in
Italy.[40] Nevertheless, intellectual and emotional attitudes
deriving from Crocean-Vosslerian idealism are still widespread,
in diluted but recognizable form, in much of current Romance
linguistics.

Not reflecting the approach of any particular 'school', but
growing during the first half of the twentieth century, was
interest in the influence of pre-Latin languages ('substrata')
and post-Latin languages ('superstrata') on the development and
differentiation of Romance speech. With extensive data available
by this time on medieval and modern Romance dialects, and with
relatively abundant (though often vague) indications of the
names of pre-Latin populations, there has been considerable
speculation on the nature and extent of substratum influence in
Romance.[41] In some instances, such as the development /nd/ >
/nn/ and /mb/ > /mm/ in central Italy, such influence seems
quite plausible;[42] in others, e.g. that of Celtic on the
representation of Proto-Romance /uˆ/ by /y/ in Gallo-Romance,
the best that can be said is 'non liquet';[43] and in still
others, e.g. the notorious 'gorgia toscana' as a case of
Etruscan substratum influence, the notion has been definitively
proven fallacious.[44] More far-reaching speculations, concerning
the relation of presumed 'Mediterranean' words to Caucasian and
other Asiatic language-families,[45] have met with some skepticism.
Perhaps because more material is available for presumed superstratum than for substratum languages, scholarship dealing with
Germanic, Arabic, and Slavic influence has been relatively
sober.[46]

In the third quarter of the twentieth century, Romance
linguistics appeared to some observers[47] to be particularly
rich along certain lines, with potentialities for detailed
investigation of etymology, dialect geography, early texts, and
the relation between standard languages (in their rise, spread,
and sometimes decline) and less favored dialects. To others,
however, it also seemed deficient in other respects--notably
the assimilation of currents which had entered general
linguistics since the time of Gilliéronian dialect geography.
In fact, a fairly strong resistance was opposed to both pre-
and post-Second World War structuralism in its various European
and American manifestations. Ordinary Romanists seemed to feel
quite happy to get along without Troubetskoian, Hjelmslevian,
or Sapirian-Bloomfieldian analyses.[48] They also seemed to care
little for a further development of comparative-reconstructive
studies, having in general been persuaded by Schuchardtian
opposition to the Neo-Grammarians, by Crocean-Vosslerian
idealism, and by Gilliéronian-Bartolian interpretations of
linguistic geography, that the regularist principle was invalid

and that comparativism in Romance was passé. This at a time
when, in a completely different field (that of American Indian
languages), the validity of the principle had been proven anew
(cf. note 35). Or is this so strange after all, in view of
some Romance scholars' belief that 'their' languages are
special hot-house flowers of high civilization,[49] as opposed to
the wild and uncultivated blossoms of mere 'primitive' speech?
Perhaps traceable to this kind of attitude, reinforced by still
widespread purism (especially in the French field), is the
impermeability of many Romanists to even slight doses of
linguistic relativism.[50]

The types of analysis we have been discussing can be carried
on with the kinds of visual communication that have been common
since the Renaissance--pencil, pen, printing press, and (in the
present century, as a substitute for these but not involving
any basic change in methods of symbolization) typewriter. A
markedly different technology was involved in the development
of electronic computers, requiring the advance preparation of
formulae designed to take a given input and produce a given
type of output. Often these formulae were very extensive and
complicated. Computers themselves could be used to relieve
scholars of burdensome mechanical tasks, such as the preparation
of concordances and indices of various kinds. Computer analysis
can also be extended to the frequency and distribution of
phenomena ranging from phonology to morpho-syntax and lexicon.
The largest project of this kind to date has been the analysis
of Old and Modern Italian texts directed by M. Alinei at the
University of Utrecht (Netherlands).

A less commendable development, at least influenced by
computer techniques, has been the widespread popularity of
formulaic statements of linguistic structure couched in terms
of 'rules' or instructions for proceeding from one combination
of elements to a following one, in a particular order, so as to
take an already known input and produce an already known output.
Since computers perform their operations at what--for humans--is
a tremendous speed, the number of intermediate steps is for
them irrelevant. This outlook has been carried over to the
'transformational-generative' approach to the description of
language, leading to the introduction of manifold intermediate
stages in formulation which often bear little or no relation
either to actual speech or to real grammatical relationships.
As Ernst Pulgram (1967:83) has said:
    ...there is no evidence at all for assuming that the
    speaker's brain, engaged in the marvellous task of
    generating speech, busily scampers and scuttles through
    the transformationalist's rules of creation.
In some instances a transformational statement can be useful in
formulating a complicated grammatical relationship, e.g. the
Spanish construction with *lo* (invariable) + adjective (variable)
+ *ser* or *estar* referring to a condition or characteristic, as in
lo húmeda que estaba la pista asfalteada 'the wet condition that
the asphalt-pavement was in' ←*la pista asfalteada estaba húmeda
+ lo estaba*. But in others, all it gives is a pseudo-
grammatical formulation of the semantics of morphological
classes, as when the Romance possessive adjectives are

interpreted[51] as not being 'really' adjectives at all, because
they are said to be transformations of pronouns in a 'deep
structure'. All that this tells us is that they indicate
possession and have pronominal reference--which we knew already.

Combined with this approach--which can, in some instances,
be helpful, but not necessarily in all--there has been a strong
recrudescence of a basically idealistic philosophy of language,
with a theology based on Neo-Platonic dualism, postulating
mental reality for an imaginary 'deep structure', and rejecting
objective study of data for subjective (and often incomplete or
inaccurate) intuitions dressed up in quasi- (but only quasi-)
mathematical sequences of formulas. The linguist's attention,
in this approach, is limited to 'well-formed sentences',
narrowly defined by absolutist logic and thinly disguised
Renaissance- and Baroque-type authoritarian purism. To master
the techniques of this kind of description, the neophyte needs
to know no language but his own, without going beyond
conventional spelling or traditional grammar, and without having
to divest himself of any of the academic or puristic folklore
that may be attached to his language.

The resultant flood of studies on the syntax of contemporary
Romance and other languages undoubtedly contains much valuable
data--which will, however, eventually have to be recovered and
restated, where necessary, in better terms. This is one of
the major tasks awaiting Romance linguists in the rest of this
century and in the next. What other directions are there for
Romance linguistics to take? None of the techniques that have
been developed in the past two hundred years should, it seems
to me, be wholly abandoned. There is still room for extensive
philological study of already edited texts, and for the editing
of many texts (nonliterary as well as literary) that are still
lying unpublished. The etymology of many individual words, in
every Romance language, has still not been explained, and
there are still a great many semantic fields to be analyzed.
The day of the great national linguistic atlases is probably
past, but the material collected in them, as well as in more
recent regional atlases, is still largely unexplored. The
dialectology of social, as opposed to regional, stratification
is only in its beginning,[52] and needs much further exploration.
Descriptive and historical syntax are still very fertile fields.
Stylistics, also, can be brought closer to the core of Romance
linguistics by the application of objective methods.[53]

Most important of all, however, is a degree of tolerance
which has unfortunately been absent from much of this century's
linguistics, with its harmful division into 'schools' and
mutual hostility between needlessly opposing camps. (Even
transformational grammar can have its merits, which stand a
better chance of recognition if its proponents can take the
chips off their shoulders and abandon their 'eclipsing
stance'.[54]) Some of the disagreements have been due to merely
terminological divergences, others to differences in underlying
assumptions. Most harmful of all have been extraneous
considerations such as those of politics, which have no place
at all in scientific endeavor. If these hindrances can be

removed, Romance linguistics can be brought closer to making
the contribution to our knowledge of both the Romance languages
and human language in general which has been claimed as its
peculiar potential.[55]

NOTES

[1]Hall 1974:227.

[2]I repeat from Hall 1974:245 (note 2) my definitions, based
on observation of actual usage, of *science* and *theology*:
A theology is a set of statements brooking no contradiction
(*dogmas*), concerning forces or beings (e.g. deities, spirits,
devils, souls) which are not accessible to human observation
in any controllable or verifiable fashion, but whose
existence, paramount importance, and supreme power is
assumed a priori and is considered an undeniable,
irrefutable factor which has to be taken into account as
determining everything else in the study or discussion
of the universe. A science is a method for arriving at
statements which brook contradiction, concerning only
phenomena which are accessible to human observation or are
deducible on the basis of observation; whose existence is
assumed only on the basis of hypotheses which can be tested,
checked, and confirmed (or disconfirmed) by procedures
accessible to all observers; and whose function in the study
or discussion of the universe is never considered permanently
undeniable or irrefutable.
I am further defining, for the purposes of this discussion, a
religion as an emotionally based adherence to a theology.

[3]The thesis of Ewert 1940, that Dante was, in the *De v. E.*,
describing an already existing koiné, has not been generally
accepted. For general discussions of the *De v. E.*, cf.
especially Francescato 1965, Bahner 1965, Grayson 1965, and
many other items listed in Hall 1958: §§6710-6734 and 1969:
§§9289-9309.

[4]This comparison was first made by Labande-Jeanroy 1925:21-
4, 42-9.

[5]Cf. Grayson 1960.

[6]Cf. Pabst 1952.

[7]Cf. von Richthofen 1954.

[8]Cf. Haugen 1950.

[9]Cf. Hall 1942; Migliorini 1949; Sozzi 1955; Vitale 1960.

[10]Cf. Hall 1939.

[11]Cf. Vitale 1953. For the concept of 'Vulgar Latin' in
sixteenth-century Italian and French speculations, cf. Strauss
1938.

[12]In his dialogue *Il Cesano* (ca. 1530). Cf. my discussion in Hall 1974:231-2, 237.

[13]Cf. Sensi 1892; Vannini 1920; Weiss 1946.

[14]Cf. Zehnder 1939.

[15]As is well known, Du Bellay (in his *Deffense et Illustration* of 1548) considered Villon, in the previous century, as having written in 'Old French'; and Boileau (in his *Art Poétique,* 1674) dismisses virtually all literature before Malherbe (*Enfin Malherbe vint* ...).

[16]As pointed out by Chevalier 1967.

[17]The excellent discussion of the Port-Royal grammar by Donzé (1967) has unfortunately been overshadowed by the distortions and misrepresentations of Chomsky (1966). Cf. Hall 1971b.

[18]Similarly, the great Academy-dictionaries of Italian (Accademia della Crusca, 1612), French (Académie Française, 1694), and Spanish (Real Academia Española 1726-1729) are, despite their undeniable merits, too narrowly puristic and literary in their orientation to count as belonging to anything but linguistics 2.

[19]Such as Valla's and Scobar's Sicilian dictionaries in the 1500's; Bumaldi's *Vocabulista bolognese* of 1660; and the Abbé Galiani's works on Neapolitan in the eighteenth century. Cf. Hall 1974:234.

[20]Cf. Macrea 1969; Nicolescu 1971.

[21]Cf. Gossman 1968:195-211.

[22]Cf. Monteverdi 1948.

[23]Cf. Gossman 1968, especially 175-95.

[24]Cf. Gossman 1968:187-8.

[25]The adjective *originales* in Raynouard's title is a reference to the pseudo-medieval productions of the previous century, especially the so-called 'genre troubadour'.

[26]It was only at Leyden that modern languages had been the subject of university-level instruction since the beginning of the seventeenth century (cf. d'Irsay 1933-35:2.14). The natural sciences gradually entered the university curriculum in the seventeenth and eighteenth centuries (cf. Aigrain 1949:70, 75), but the modern 'humanities' did not enter until after Napoleon's time, and first in Germany.

[27]Those who protest against the 'Verschulung' of knowledge and research (e.g. Malkiel 1972/73:14) lose sight of the manifold advantages brought by institutionalization and professionalization.

[28]Cf. Sykorra 1972; Malkiel 1974.

[29]Cf. Pop 1950:1.xxix, 12-3.

[30]Cf. Ripert 1917; Camproux 1953.

[31]Cf. Viëtor 1882; Palmer 1917, 1921; Otto 1921 (and, on Otto, Cochran 1950).

[32]Cf. Pop 1950:1.xxxvii-xxxix, with the remark concerning the period 1871-1880: 'C'est la période la plus importante du XIXe siècle: les travaux publiés pendant ces dix ans ont posé le fondement de la dialectologie'.

[33]Cf. my discussion of this point in Hall 1957 and 1964:2. 295-313; also Hoenigswald 1963.

[34]Unfortunately, the 'Vulgärlateinische Substrate' articles were never published in book forms, and Gröber's results were absorbed into Meyer-Lübke's *Romanisches etymologisches Wörterbuch,* so that the originality and importance of Gröber's work has been badly underestimated.

[35]Cf. Sapir 1931; Hockett 1948.

[36]Cf. the discussions in Pedersen 1931:277-310 and in Tagliavini 1963:164-208.

[37]Cf. Hall 1946.

[38]Bonfante's reply (1947) to Hall 1946 was remarkable for the large numbers of authorities cited in footnotes and for ignorance of the contents of the material cited. The Italian translation of Bonfante 1947, published a quarter of a century later, was virtually unchanged from the original.

[39]Cf. Hall 1963.

[40]Cf. Posner 1970. From one point of view, my criticisms of the idealistic school (in Hall 1963) were indeed (as they were once termed) 'anachronistic'; however, the persistence of idealistic philosophy in Romance linguistics, which still needed refutation in the 1960's, was also anachronistic.

[41]For general problems of substratum influence in Iberia, cf. Jungemann 1955; for Celtic substratum, cf. Tovar 1968; for Greek, cf. Rohlfs 1947 and 1964/65; for Oscan and Umbrian, Devoto 1974:146-7.

[42]Cf. Hall 1950b.

[43]Most scholars in the Gallo-Romance field seem to accept this and other hypotheses of Celtic substratum influence without much question; but cf. the skepticism expressed by Meyer-Lübke (1914-19).

[44]By Izzo 1972.

[45]Especially in the extensive work of J. Hubschmid; cf. the items by this author listed in Hall 1958 and 1969.

[46]Especially, for Germanic, in Gamillscheg 1934-36; for Arabic, in Pellegrini 1972; for Slavic, in Sandfeld-Jensen 1930, Niculescu 1965, and--for phonology--Petrovici 1956, 1957.

[47]E.g. Malkiel 1973/74.

[48]Significantly, the only structuralist approach to win much favor in the Romance field has been Martinet's, which combines a specifically European approach (Prague- and Copenhagen-style) with certain very French attitudes, particularly as regards elegance of patterning and teleology. My attempt (in Hall 1950a) to combine structuralism and comparativism can hardly be said to have won much approval.

[49]As suggested by Malkiel 1962/63.

[50]As shown, for instance, by the horror manifested by Baldelli (1958) at my having dared to compare certain Lombard constructions with similar phenomena in Melanesian languages.

[51]Cf. Zdrenghea 1967.

[52]As exemplified in such works as Badia i Margarit 1969; Pautasso 1969; Berruto 1970.

[53]Exemplified in theory by Riffaterre 1959 and 1960, and in practice by Colby 1965.

[54]Term suggested by Voegelin and Voegelin 1963.

[55]E.g. by Malkiel 1972/73.

REFERENCES

Aigrain, René. 1949. Histoire des universités. Paris: Presses Universitaires de France.

Badia i Margarit, Antoni. 1969. La llengua dels barcelonins: resultats d'una enquesta sociolinguística. Barcelona.

Bahner, Werner. 1965. Dantes theoretische Bemühungen um die Formung der italienischen Literatursprache und die 'Sprachenfrage'. BRPh. 4:2.29-35.

Baldelli, Ignazio. 1958. Notice of R. A. Hall Jr.'s review of F. Spiess: Die Verwendung des Subjekt-Personalpronomens in den lombardischen Mundarten (RPh. 11.395-98 [1957/58]). RLI 62.493.

Berruto, Gaetano. 1970. Dialetto e società industriale nella Valle d'Andorno. Torino: Istituto dell'Atlante Linguistico Italiano.

Bonfante, Giuliano. 1947. The neolinguistic position. Language 23.344-75. Italian translation: La dottrina neolinguística--teoria e pràtica. Torino: Giappichelli, 1970.

Camproux, Charles. 1953. Histoire de la littérature occitane. Paris: Payot. (2nd ed., 1971.)

Chevalier, Jean C. 1967. La Grammaire générale de Port-Royal et la critique moderne. Langages 7.16-33.

Chomsky, Avram Noam. 1966. Cartesian linguistics. New York: Harper and Row.

Cochran, Emory Ellsworth. 1950. The experimental didactics of
    Ernst Otto. Berlin: De Gruyter.
Colby, Alice M. 1965. The portrait in twelfth-century French
    literature. Genève: Droz.
Devoto, Giacomo. 1974. Il linguaggio d'Italia. Milano:
    Rizzoli.
d'Irsay, Stephen. 1933-35. Histoire des universités françaises
    et étrangères, des origines à nos jours. Paris: Picard.
Donzé, Roland. 1967. La grammaire générale et raisonnée de
    Port-Royal. Berne: Francke. (2nd ed., 1971.)
Ewert, Alfred. 1940. Dante's theory of language. MLR 35.
    355-66.
Francescato, Giuseppe. 1965. Teoria e realtà linguistica in
    Dante. Miscellanea Dantesca 128-37 (Utrecht).
Gamillscheg, Ernst. 1934-36. Romania Germanica. Sprach- und
    Siedlungsgeschichte der German auf dem Boden des alten
    Römerreichs. Berlin und Leipzig: De Gruyter.
Gossman, Lionel. 1968. Medievalism and the ideologies of the
    Enlightenment: the world and work of La Curne de
    Sainte-Palaye. Baltimore: The Johns Hopkins Press.
Grayson, Cecil. 1960. Lorenzo, Machiavelli, and the Italian
    language. Ady Memorial Volume 410-32.
_____. 1965. 'Nobilior est vulgaris': Latin and vernacular
    in Dante's thought. Centenary essays on Dante, 54-76.
    Oxford, England.
Hall, Robert A., Jr. 1939. Synchronic aspects of Renaissance
    linguistics. Italica 16.1-11.
_____. 1942. The Italian Questione della Lingua: an
    interpretative essay. Chapel Hill, N.C.: University of
    North Carolina Press. (UNCSRLL no. 4.)
_____. 1946. Bàrtoli's 'Neolinguistica'. Language 22.273-83.
_____. 1950a. The reconstruction of Proto-Romance.
    Language 26.6-27. (Reprinted in Readings in linguistics, ed.
    by M. Joos, 303-14. Washington, D.C.: American Council of
    Learned Societies, 1957.)
_____. 1950b. Nasal + homorganic plosive in Central and
    South Italian. ArL 1.151-56, with 1 map.
_____. 1957. Scopi et metodi della linguistica. AGI 42.
    57-69, 148-61.
_____. 1958. Bibliografia della linguistica italiana.
    Firenze: Sansoni.
_____. 1963. Idealism in Romance linguistics. Ithaca, N.Y.:
    Cornell University Press.
_____. 1969. Bibliografia della linguistica italiana: primo
    supplemento decennale. Firenze: Sansoni.
_____. 1971. Some recent studies on Port-Royal and Vaugelas.
    AcLHa. 12.207-33.
_____. 1974. Comparative Romance grammar: I. External
    history of the Romance languages. New York: American
    Elsevier.
Haugen, Einar. 1950. First grammatical treatise: the earliest
    Germanic phonology. Baltimore: Linguistic Society of
    America.

Hockett, Charles F. 1948. Implications of Bloomfield's
   Algonquian studies. Language 24.117-31. (Reprinted in
   Readings in Linguistics, ed. by M. Joos, 281-9, Washington:
   American Council of Learned Societies, 1957; and in A
   Leonard Bloomfield anthology, ed. by C. F. Hockett, 495-511,
   Bloomington, Ind.: Indiana University Press, 1970.)
Hoenigswald, Henry M. 1963. On the history of the comparative
   method. AnL 5.1-11.
Izzo, Herbert. 1972. Tuscan and Etruscan: the problem of
   substratum influence in central Italy. Toronto: University
   of Toronto Press.
Jungemann, Frederick Henry. 1955. La teoría del sustrato y
   los dialectos hispano-romances y gascones. Madrid: Gredos.
   (BRH no. 7.)
Labande-Jeanroy, Thérèse. 1925. La question de la langue en
   Italie. Strasbourg: Istra.
Macrea, Dimitriu. 1969. Şcoala ardeleană şi probleme de
   lingvistică romanică. CL 14.7-13.
Malkiel, Yakov. 1962/63. Review of L. Bloomfield and
   C. L. Barnhart: Let's Read. RPh. 16.83-91.
_____. 1972/73. The first quarter-century (and some
   antecedents). RPh. 26.3-13.
_____. 1973/74. Jakob Grimm and Friedrich Diez. RPh.
   27.448-50.
_____. 1974. Friedrich Diez's debt to pre-1800 linguistics.
   Studies in the history of linguistics, ed. by Dell B. Hymes,
   315-30. Bloomington, Ind.: Indiana University Press.
Meyer-Lübke, Wilhelm. 1914-19. Zur u--ü Frage. ZFSL 41.1-7
   (1914/15); 44.75-84 (1916/17); 45.350-57 (1917/19).
Migliorini, Bruno. 1949. La questione della lingua. Questioni
   e correnti di storia letteraria, ed. by Attilio Momigliano.
   Milano: Marzorati.
Monteverdi, Angelo. 1948. L. A. Muratori e gli studi intorno
   alle origini della lingua italiana. AMArcadia III.1.81-93.
   (Reprinted in Cento e Duecento, ed. by Monteverdi, 97-116,
   1971.)
Nicolescu, Aurel. 1971. Scoala ardeleană şi limba română.
   Bucureşti: Editura Ştiinţifică.
Niculescu, Alexandru. 1965. Individualitatea limbii romîne
   între limbile romanice. Bucureşti: Editura Ştiinţifică.
Otto, Ernst. 1921. Methodik und Didaktik des neusprachlichen
   Unterrichts. Leipzig: Velhagen und Klasing.
Pabst, Walter. 1952. Dante und die literarische Vielsprachigkeit
   der Romania. RJb. 5.161-81.
Palmer, Harold E. 1917. The scientific study and teaching of
   languages. London: Harrap. (Reprint, London: Oxford
   University Press, 1968.)
_____. 1921. The oral method of teaching languages.
   Cambridge, England: Heffer. (Reprint, 1965.)
Pautasso, Mariella. 1969. Dialetto, lingua e integrazione
   linguistica a Pettinengo. Torino: Giappichelli.

Pedersen, Holger. 1931. Linguistic science in the nineteenth
    century: methods and results. Cambridge, Mass.: Harvard
    University Press. (Reprinted under title 'The Discovery of
    Language'. Bloomington, Ind.: Indiana University Press,
    1962.)
Pellegrini, Giovanni Battista. 1972. Gli arabismi nelle
    lingue neolatine, con speciale riguardo all'Italia. Brescia:
    Paideia Editrice.
Petrovici, Emil. 1956. Influenţa slavă asupra sistemului
    fonemelor limbii române. Bucureşti: Societate de stiinţe
    istorice şi filologice.
_____. 1957. Kann das Phonemsystem einer Sprache durch
    fremden Einfluss umgestaltet werden? The Hague: Mouton.
    (JL no. 5.)
Posner, Rebecca R. 1970. Thirty years on. Supplement to
    revised ed. of Iorgu Iordan and John Orr.: An introduction
    to Romance linguistics, its schools and scholars (London:
    Methuen, 1970).
Pulgram, Ernst. 1967. Sciences, humanities, and the place of
    linguistics. Research: definitions and reflections, 67-95.
    Ann Arbor: University of Michigan Press.
Riffaterre, Michael. 1959. Criteria for style analysis. Word
    15.154-74.
_____. 1960. Stylistic context. Word 16.207-18.
Ripert, Emile. 1917. La Renaissance provençale (1800-1860).
    Paris: Champion.
Rohlfs, Gerhard. 1947. Griechischer Sprachgeist in
    Unteritalien. München. (SbBayr. 1944/46:8.)
_____. 1964/65. Ellenismo e latinità nella Sicilia d'oggi.
    Kōkalos 10/11.565-78.
Sandfeld-Jensen, Kristian. 1930. Linguistique balkanique:
    problèmes et résultats. Paris: Champion.
Sapir, Edward. 1931. The concept of phonetic law as tested in
    primitive languages by Leonard Bloomfield. Methods in social
    science: a case book, ed. by S. Rice, 197-306. Chicago:
    University of Chicago Press. (Reprinted in Selected writings
    of Edward Sapir in language, culture, and personality, ed.
    D. Mandelbaum, 73-82. Berkeley and Los Angeles: University
    of California Press, 1949.)
Sensi, Filippo. 1892. Per la storia della filologia neo-latina
    in Italia. AGI 12.441-60.
Sozzi, Bortolo Tommaso. 1955. Aspetti e momenti della
    questione linguistica. Padova: Liviana Editrice.
Strauss, Franz. 1938. Vulgärlatein und Vulgärsprache im
    Zusammenhang der Sprachenfrage im 16. Jahrhundert
    (Frankreich und Italien). Marburg: Elwert. (MBRP no. 21.)
Sykorra, Wolfgang. 1972. Friedrich Diez' Etymologisches
    Wörterbuch der romanischen Sprachen und seine Quellen.
    Bonn: Romanisches Seminar der Universität. (RVV no. 47.)
Tagliavini, Carlo. 1963. Panorama di storia della linguistica.
    Bologna: Pàtron.
Tovar, Antonio. 1968. Lo que sabemos de la lucha de lenguas
    en la Península Ibérica. Madrid: Gregorio del Toro.

Vannini, A. 1920. Notizie intorno alla vita e all'opera di
    Celso Cittadini, scrittore senese del secolo XVI. Siena.
Viëtor, Wilhelm. 1882. Der Sprachunterricht muss umkehren.
    Heilbronn. (3rd ed., Leipzig: Reisland, 1905.)
Vitale, Maurizio. 1953. Le origini del volgare nelle
    discussioni dei filologi del '400. LN 14.64-9.
_____. 1960. La questione della lingua. Milano e Palermo:
    Palumbo.
Voegelin, Charles F., and Florence M. Voegelin. 1963. On the
    history of structuralizing in 20th-century America.
    AnL 5.12-37.
von Richthofen, E. 1954. Il trattao di Dante alla luce della
    geografia linguistica moderna. Homenaje a Fritz Krüger
    2.71-84.
Weiss, Roberto. 1946. The Sienese philologists of the
    Cinquecento: a bibliographical introduction. IS 3.34-49.
Zdrenghea, Mircea. 1967. Există adjective posesive în limbile
    romanice? CL 12.81-8.
Zehnder, Joseph. 1939. Les 'Origini della lingua italiana'
    de Gilles Ménage: étude historique et critique. Paris:
    Flory.

THE ROLE OF APPLIED LINGUISTICS IN THE TEACHING OF
ROMANCE LANGUAGES: PANEL DISCUSSION

INTRODUCTION

MICHIO PETER HAGIWARA

The University of Michigan

Several years ago, in preparation for an ACTFL seminar, I
conducted a survey of graduate language departments that had a
required course in methods or applied linguistics for their
teaching assistants. I requested a copy of the syllabus, and
the result showed that a little over 60% offered courses in
applied linguistics, and the remainder in methods. What
interested me most was the wide range of course content in the
former: they seemed to range from a detailed, non-contrastive
linguistic analysis of the target language to a strong
orientation toward methodology with a faint echo of contrastive
phonetics. Many of us present here have probably taught--or
taken--a course in applied linguistics. There no longer seems
to be a consensus on just what such a course is supposed to be.
I would like to summarize what role it has played in language
instruction, and ask each panel member to discuss what place it
ought to have in the teaching of Romance languages.

It was in the early fifties that some linguists began advocating the inclusion of linguistics in the preparation of college-level instructors (e.g. Politzer 1953, Pulgram 1954). Lado's *Linguistics Across Cultures* (1957) discussed the importance of linguistics, especially contrastive analysis, and contributed more than any other to the development of applied linguistics. The new field grew rapidly in the early sixties. Texts intended for language teachers such as Politzer 1960, Politzer and Staubach 1961, Belasco and Valdman 1961, and Belasco and Cárdenas 1961 were widely used in NDEA Institutes, whose participants received training not only in language skills but also in methods, civilization, and applied linguistics. The growth of the discipline culminated in the 'Contrastive Analysis Series' under the direction of Charles Ferguson (Moulton 1962, Kufner 1962, Agard and Di Pietro 1965ab, Stockwell and Bowen 1965, Stockwell, Bowen, and Martin 1965). Foreign Language teaching was firmly associated with the 'New Key' method, also erroneously called the 'linguistic' method. Applied linguistics was hailed as a must for language teachers and, overnight, the country saw a profusion of applied linguists (rather than 'linguists applied', as one of the prominent scholars once remarked) engaged in curriculum design, methodology, and material preparation.

What was supposed to be the contribution of applied linguistics? The emphasis on 'primary communication skills' was said to be one. The structural linguist, especially when engaged in field work, always begins by gathering a corpus based on spoken language. His first task is a phonological analysis--he being careful not to 'mix levels'--and the primacy of spoken language in teaching was at least partly due to the influence of structural linguistics. But a linguistic analysis of the target language was also supposed to result in a determination of 'linguistic units' and a more efficient explanation of structures. A contrastive analysis would predict areas of interference and potential learner errors, and would lead to more effective teaching devices. Pattern drills were said to be modeled after certain methods of linguistic analysis, and the description of language structures based on its spoken form was to result in a clearer presentation of grammar points.

Of course, the leading linguists engaged in applied linguistics were quick to point out that linguistic analysis as such should not be applied directly to the teaching of foreign languages. Politzer warned: 'Contrastive analysis will not design *the* teaching method or solve psychological factors or problems of language teaching' (1960:5). Likewise, Belasco cautioned the language teachers: 'Of course, the responsibility of the structural linguist ends when he uncovers the patterns... Some of the structuralist's findings are bound to undergo modifications when they reach the classroom. Simplicity and completeness of presentation must be dictated by pedagogical situations' (1961:ii-iii). Yet it is no exaggeration to say that little, if any, of the linguistic grammar was ever adopted by those who prepared pedagogical materials. Where linguistics could provide insights into language structures, as pointed out

by Bull and Lamadrid 1971, most writers of pedagogical grammars
clung tenaciously to traditional approaches. Attempts to apply
linguistic principles such as Desberg and Kenan 1964 and
Belasco and Valdman 1965 appeared to result in unnecessary
complication rather than simplification. Instead of intensive
work in sound-symbol association, they brought in the concepts
of morphemes and allomorphs with hundreds of phonetic
transcriptions. Perfectly usable traditional terms were
replaced by new ones such as P-slot and N-slot. Indeed, aside
from matters related to phonetics, most teachers, even after
course work and workshops, found the subject of linguistics too
abstract to be of use in normal classroom situations.

   There is little doubt that linguistics contributed to a more
accurate comparison and description of the phonemic systems of
English and the target language. Yet, despite admonition by
Stockwell and Bowen that contrastive analysis of phonology
should be only for the teacher and their practical suggestion
that 'the best pronunciation is the one that attracts least
attention to itself' (1965:121), most texts stressed not only
spoken language but also the acquisition of native-like fluency
and pronunciation. Speaking tests, considered one of the
contributions of the audio-lingual method, gave undue attention
to pronunciation rather than to the ability to communicate in
the target language. On the whole, applied linguistics in the
early sixties contributed much to the presentation of phonology
but very little to that of syntax. This is perhaps indicative
of the predilection of structural linguists in the preceding
decades: *Outline of Linguistic Analysis* by Bloch and Trager
(1942) devotes 53% of its content to phonology, 19% to
morphology, and a scant 8% to syntax; *Structural Sketches: I*
of Robert A. Hall, Jr. (1949) has less than 20% of its space
devoted to syntax. As Bolinger 1968 suggests, it is disputable
that pattern drills were invented by linguists. We all
remember the enthusiasm with which they were received: Brooks
1960 admitted that they made no pretense of being communication,
and Lado 1963 proclaimed their superiority, pointing out that
they enabled the instructor and students to handle up to 1500
utterances in a single class period. We all know that those
unending cycles of stimulus-response drills, heavily imbued
with behaviorist psychology, that filled many a textbook did
not result in better language acquisition.

Already by the mid-sixties, there was general disenchantment
with linguistics--inescapably associated with the 'New Key'
method--among language teachers, especially as the discipline
became more abstract with the advent of transformational-
generative grammar and the subsequent polemics among some
linguists in the United States. After the audio-lingual and
audio-visual methods, language teaching began to drift away
from anything related to linguistics. There have been many
bandwagons ever since--programmed instruction, cultural
approach, performance-oriented objectives, multiple-tracking,
interaction analysis, and individualized instruction. On the
whole, applied linguistics as developed in the early sixties
seems to occupy only an insignificant role in teacher training

and production of instructional materials.

The state of linguistics was so confusing that Hanzeli virtually admitted the impracticality of applying linguistics to language instruction and reverted to the earlier nebulous opinions of some linguists at the inception of applied linguistics: '...individual teachers owe it to themselves to study current developments in linguistics, not in the hope of finding in them immediate answers to specific teaching questions, but because it will further their understanding of the subject matter they teach' (1968:48). The possibility of applying the principles of TG grammar to language teaching was suggested by Saporta, who pointed out that linguistics had been totally misapplied: 'The influence of linguists was more on the goals and methods of language instruction than on the elucidation of the pertinent linguistic facts' (1966:82). The papers presented at the 19th Georgetown Round Table on contrastive linguistics and its pedagogical implications (Alatis 1968) were generally reflective in mood, although affirming the validity of applied linguistics. Those presented at the 1971 Pacific Conference on Contrastive Linguistics and Language Universals (Jackson and Whitman 1971) were frankly more critical of the past work and sought new directions in contrastive analysis. A particularly vulnerable aspect of applied linguistics was the excessive claim by some linguists that contrastive analysis predicts areas of interference and potential errors. Wardhaugh 1970 and Oller 1972 attacked this alleged predictive power (though not its explanatory role), and Whitman and Jackson 1972 not only questioned the contrastive analysis hypothesis but also claimed that interference had only a minor role in the process of language learning.

All the general assessment and the search for new directions have not resulted in a clearer definition of applied linguistics. Pattern drills have been denounced as being useless (e.g. Saporta 1966); it has been claimed that written language is a better representation of underlying forms, even for teaching languages (e.g. Ritchie 1967); only fragmentary samples of contrastive analysis utilizing new linguistic concepts have been made available (e.g. Dingwall 1964, Brown 1971, Di Pietro 1971). Some people began to regard psycholinguistics as the proper domain of applied linguistics, rejecting any notion that linguistic analysis itself has any direct influence on language teaching (e.g. Jakobovits 1970, Pimsleur and Quinn 1971, Politzer 1972). Error analysis, deemed effective but nonlinguistic by many, received encouragement and a more systematic treatment by Corder 1967 and gained wide attention at the third congress of the International Association of Applied Linguistics (Nickel 1974).

In the meantime, as compared to the heyday of applied linguistics, the majority of linguists appear convinced that linguists should talk only about linguistics. We all recall the upheaval Chomsky caused when, invited to address the 1966 Northeast Conference, he proferred these words: 'Furthermore, I am, frankly, rather skeptical about the significance, for the teaching of languages, of such insights and understandings as

have been attained in linguistics' (1966:43). The TG linguistics
since the mid-sixties has seen further development and a
profusion of theories including case grammar, generative
phonology, and generative semantics. The concept of kernel
sentences, considered useful by some language teachers, quickly
became obsolete, and that of deep structure has become even
deeper and more abstract. Indeed, as aptly summarized by
Quinn, 'current linguistics is preoccupied with theory building,
and the concepts being elaborated are not likely to be of
immediate relevance to language teaching' (1974:340).

There are two general questions I would like to address to the
panel members. The first concerns the applicability of the many
linguistic concepts and theories advanced since the late sixties:
language universals, distinction between competence and
performance, generative phonology, generative semantics, case
grammar--can any of these be applied to the teaching of Romance
languages? The second question is in the specific areas of
application. Language instruction may be considered in terms
of several phases such as the production of instructional
materials, the training of instructors, and the learner; the
explanation of structures, the learning exercises and activities,
and testing; the target language itself such as its phonological,
morphological, and syntactic components. Given such diverse
aspects, in what areas can we consider the role of applied
linguistics to be most crucial?

APPLIED LINGUISTICS AND LANGUAGE TEACHING

H. DOUGLAS BROWN

The University of Michigan

The term *applied linguistics* is difficult to define. In a
general sense of the term, applied linguistics involves the
applications of linguistic principles or theories to certain
more 'practical' matters. Language teaching seems to be a
major concern for many applied linguists; in British tradition,
applied linguistics is often actually synonymous with language
teaching. While that has indeed claimed the interest of many
applied linguists, the applications certainly extend well
beyond language teaching. But the term remains disturbingly
vague.

One potentially constructive approach to an understanding
of what applied linguistics is or is not, is to examine the
term 'linguistics'. Linguistics is the study of language, a
scientific discipline the goal of which is the construction of
a theory of language. Consider the following definition of

language (Finocchiaro 1964): 'a system of arbitrary, vocal symbols which permit all people in a given culture, or other people who have learned the system of that culture, to communicate or interact'. The following topics emerge from such a definition:

(1) Language is systematic--possibly a generative system.
(2) Language is a set of arbitrary symbols.
(3) Those symbols may be primarily vocal, but also visual.
(4) The symbols have conventionalized meanings to which they refer.
(5) The goal of language is communication.
(6) Language operates in a speech community or culture.
(7) Language is essentially human, though possibly not limited to humans.
(8) Language is universally acquired by all people in a speech community.

Among these topics are a number of areas which are typically thought of as 'applied' areas; is it possible to draw a line of demarcation which separate such applied areas from the theoretical? Items 3, 4, 5, 6, 7, and 8 are all 'applied' in some sense, and yet there is much in all six items that is theoretical in the sense of seeking an extended definition, or, a theory, of language.

Must we conclude, therefore, that there is really no such thing as applied linguistics? This is indeed too simplistic and too easy a solution. Every discipline has its theoretical and its applied aspects. The theoretical and the applied areas simply must not be thought of as necessarily *mutually exclusive*. An area of inquiry may be more or less applied, sharing certain attributes of applications *of* something *to* something, but also sharing a contribution to the understanding of a theory of language. Thus items 1 through 8 may all share applied *and* theoretical aspects.

Politzer 1972 noted that applied linguistics, with respect to foreign language teaching, is a stage in which, using linguistics as a base, one formulates assumptions about foreign language teaching and learning and also devises teaching procedures based on these assumptions. Pap 1972, admitting both an inherent ambiguity in the term as well as its rather vague reference to 'practical applications', concluded that applied linguistics 'may in effect be considered a crossroads, an interdisciplinary area, a combination of linguistics with psychology, pedagogy, mathematics, electronics, political science, and so forth' (p.111-112). Corder 1973 pointed out that:

The application of linguistic knowledge to some object--or applied linguistics, as the name implies--is an activity.
It is not a theoretical study. It makes use of findings of theoretical studies. The applied linguist is a consumer, or user, not a producer, of theories. (p.10)

The term *applied linguistics* is a very misunderstood term. But

as language teachers we are all *linguists* and we all are
committed to the goal of discovering what language is and how
people learn a language. To achieve that goal we must draw
upon whatever insights we can in 'linguistics', psychology,
sociology, and many other disciplines. We should not quibble
over terminology; we should rather pursue vigorously our major
goals as language teachers.

APPLIED LINGUISTICS AND THE TEACHING OF FRENCH

E. DEAN DETRICH

Michigan State University

At the outset I should explain that I personally do not consider
applied linguistics to be an autonomous formal discipline.
However, this is primarily a question of terminology. I do not
mean to imply that people currently working in the field are
doing nothing of merit. I do believe that we are talking about
foreign language pedagogy and that a name such as applied
linguistics is too restrictive and, to some people, too awesome.
All of us who are concerned with teaching basic second-language
skills are aware that we must continue to struggle against those
who affirm that anyone who is master of a given language can
successfully teach that language. This problem does not justify
the creation of a separate discipline bearing the name *applied
linguistics*. The insight of linguists can be of enormous help
to foreign language teachers, but so can insights into the
literature and culture of the foreign language being studied.
    The term *applied linguistics* has been used largely thanks to
the fact that it was linguists who reminded foreign language
teachers that language is first and foremost a spoken medium,
that it did not suffice simply to have students learn to read
a language and memorize a few paradigms. In an attempt to
attack the problem of teaching the spoken language, linguists
suggested what eventually became known as the audio-lingual
method of teaching. Though this was a laudable effort to
provide students with a mastery of the spoken language, it
suffers from several serious drawbacks.
    The most obvious drawback is that by their very nature the
pattern-practice drills, which are the backbone of this method,
can be excruciatingly boring. Only the most highly motivated
students can profit by such drills in the language laboratory
or in the classroom for more than fifteen minutes at a time.
Another real problem is that often the students who are most
successful in doing the drills have learned only to perform

a given task. They have no idea what they are saying. They may
be restating a sentence with the verb in a past tense, but they
have attached no semantic interpretation to what they have said.

I do not mean to imply in this brief critique that pattern-
practice drills have no place in language teaching, but they
should certainly not be the heart of a course, unless our goal
is to dissuade students from taking foreign languages. To my
mind such procedures are most useful when used to assist
students who are taking classes in a target language while
living in the cultural setting of that language, as is the case
with foreign students learning English at the English Language
Institute at The University of Michigan or with American
students studying French at the *Alliance Française* in Paris
using the CREDIF materials. In these cases pattern practice
serves to organize and clarify what the student hears constantly
around him.

A program based solely on an audio-lingual approach is not
appropriate for students learning a second language while
isolated from the culture in which that language is spoken.
This is generally the case with the American university student.
When determining how best to teach foreign languages at the
university level we should first establish our goals. If our
primary goal is the teaching of speaking and listening skills,
I personally cannot justify instruction in a foreign language,
for the simple reason that the vast majority of the students
will never have occasion to express themselves extensively in
the language they have studied. They may from time to time
travel overseas, but this is hardly justification for the
expenditure necessary to defray the costs of two years' worth of
university courses. I strongly feel that the main emphasis in
the university foreign-language courses should be placed on
reading skills, certainly not to the exclusion of other skills,
but reading should be pre-eminent.

I have several reasons for expressing this view, which may
to some seem almost reactionary. The most obvious reason
favoring this approach is that it is a feasible goal. We know
that we can teach people to read foreign languages, especially
western European ones, relatively quickly, thanks mostly to
orthographic similarities and common etymologies. Of the four
language skills, reading is the easiest to master and the most
profitable since the same individual who will almost never need
to speak a foreign language may very well make use of his
reading ability during his professional life. There is, however,
an even stronger argument for teaching students at the
university level first to read a language, and that is that the
students will be better able to learn to understand the spoken
language and subsequently to speak it.

One of the theoretical underpinnings of the audio-lingual
method is that small children can speak a language before they
learn to write it, and it was thought that the same should be
true in the learning of a second language. What was overlooked
was that small children learn to understand spoken language
long before they speak. I suggest that the appropriate ideal
order of teaching the four skills would be: listening,

330 E. DEAN DETRICH

speaking, reading and writing. However, given the university
student's knowledge of his own language combined with his
minimum twelve years of experience in developing learning
strategies and our proven ability to teach reading of foreign
languages, the natural progression of skill acquisition would
be reading, listening, speaking and writing. The ordering of
reading and listening before speaking and writing also reflects
the fact that in our native tongue all of us have a passive
competence which far exceeds our active performance. It seems
to me that this is doubly the case in a foreign language.
Therefore, we should not be surprised if students do not
manipulate well a language of which they have learned the
limited vocabulary provided in practice drills. We should first
provide the student with a vast passive vocabulary through
reading, and then proceed to listening comprehension, using some
of the same reading texts and explaining the relationship
between orthography and pronunciation (that is, teach the
student how to pronounce the orthography, not how to spell the
pronunciation). Then, building on the passive competence, we
can train the student to speak the language using pattern-
practice drills as one of the techniques. This way we will at
least know that the student doing the drills knows what he is
saying and is not simply a rat in a maze. Last and definitely
least comes training in writing. This is the skill that most
foreign language students will virtually never need. It can
only be taught after the student has a firm command of the
language.

These are the observations of a person trained in linguistics
who is concerned about foreign-language pedagogy, that is,
someone who applies linguistics. I do not expect that they
will cause any kind of massive change in teaching methods, and
I think we should all remind ourselves that, at most, linguistics
will change foreign language teaching only slightly. In the
post-sputnik era too much was expected of linguistics in the
area of language teaching. For some years we will pay the
price of having been too confident about our ability to improve
language teaching. One thing we must always avoid is the
implication that we have the only way to salvation. Most of
the language teachers in this country, many of whom are
extremely successful, know little about linguistics and resent
what they consider to be the haughty attitude of 'specialists'.
In suggesting improvements in teaching methods we must be
careful to avoid implying that our way is best and that all
which has gone before must be discarded. In example, if we
prepare a new textbook, we are obliged in my opinion to adopt
traditional terminology insofar as possible. We must also
remind ourselves that superb methods cannot replace student
motivation. Learning a second language is a massive task and
the student must be highly motivated to do so. Unfortunately
we cannot provide this motivation in most cases, and we should
not blame ourselves if our students are not motivated. A
general lack of motivation for the learning of foreign languages
is our greatest problem today. We must constantly justify what

we are doing. This is part of the work of a foreign language
pedagogue, not a linguist.

THE ROLE OF LINGUISTICS IN DESIGNING REQUIRED LANGUAGE COURSES

MARK G. GOLDIN

Indiana University

Most of the discussion of linguistics applied to language
teaching and learning assumes a situation where the learner's
objective is to approximate the skills of a native speaker of
the target language. I want to consider a different but
extremely common situation: language courses offered at the
college level in connection with some version of the 'foreign
language requirement'. Many Romance linguists are involved in
planning or teaching language courses on campuses where a foreign
language requirement exists. They can use their linguistic
training creatively to design nontraditional language courses
whose objectives are in accord with those of students enrolled
primarily to fulfill the requirement.
    It is difficult to know why college faculties charge
language departments with providing a one- or two-year program
of required studies. Many of the humanistic benefits attributed
to foreign language study (for examples see the references
abstracted in Svobodny, 1971) can be acquired only through a
much longer exposure to the language than is available in
required courses; others can be obtained without necessarily
learning the second language at all. At any rate, humanistic
arguments in favor of language study support only the case that
foreign languages are beneficial; they do not demonstrate that
foreign languages should be for everyone in a particular degree
program, nor do they relate languages to the liberal arts degree.
    The way I, as a linguist, reconcile my doubts about the
language requirement is by observing that foreign language
learning is different from other kinds of academic experience
that typically form part of a Bachelor of Arts degree.
Languages involve a peculiar combination of skill acquisition,
analysis, and memorization which is not experienced in other
academic fields. The foreign language requirement assumes that
this combination of mental activities is indispensable for the
liberal arts student.
    The language teacher's task, then, is to decide in what
proportion to provide each of the types of activities that
together make up language learning--remembering that the
approximation of a native speaker's behavior in speaking,
understanding, reading, and writing is neither a reasonable

objective for required courses, nor is it the motivation for students when they enroll. I will try to suggest how linguistic analysis can aid in establishing some objectives for a required course.

The following diagram labels some of the kinds of knowledge acquired in learning a language:

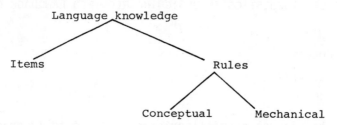

Many language items are learned one by one, so that whatever effort is expended in learning a single vocabulary item, irregular form, preposition governed by a particular verb, etc. yields knowledge of that form only, with no application to anything else in the language. Other language structures are learned by rule, so that once someone has learned how to form the plural of a noun, or how to use the subjunctive, the knowledge applies in new cases regardless of the lexical items used. This is the distinction between productive and nonproductive knowledge.

   Looking further at the nature of linguistic rules, we observe that some of them depend for their operation on conceptual information; that is, information about the real world of people, things, ideas, and events. Experienced teachers usually cite the learning of conceptual rules as the greatest difficulty in second language learning; Romance examples are the distinction between preterit and imperfect; the use of the subjunctive; the distinction between *ser* and *estar*. Mechanical rules, on the other hand, need information of a grammatical rather than conceptual nature for their operation; examples are the rules for producing verb forms and the rules for clitic pronoun placement. You learn that the object pronouns go before the verb unless it is a command or infinitive or whatever, and that is that. No information about people or events is needed to arrange pronouns.

   A learner attempting to approximate a native speaker's skills needs to acquire all these kinds of knowledge, and there may not be a great deal that linguistics can add to help with the task. However, when the student's objectives are more modest, some linguistic analytical ability on the part of the teacher can point to priorities that will help make the required language course a more rewarding experience. My personal preference is to give priority to productive learning over item learning, since the immediate reward for effort expended is greater. I further prefer to give priority to conceptual rather than mechanical learning, obliging students to consider language as a vehicle for communication, dealing with the world of people and events, and not as a form of puzzle solving. The humanistic basis of the language requirement is also reinforced in this way.

In connection with my preferences, I supervised an experiment (Lotito 1975) in which the experimenter devised conceptual and mechanical presentations of a single grammar problem, the mood of the verb in conditional clauses in Spanish. Both presentations were clearer and more complete than those usually found in elementary textbooks. The two approaches were presented to separate groups of second-semester students in a required Spanish course. On a test asking the subjects, given a real-life situation, to choose the correct verb form for a conditional sentence about that situation, the good students in both groups did equally well, and the poor students did equally poorly; but the average students in the group that had studied the conceptual approach performed significantly better than the average students in the group studying the structures mechanically. The experiment confirmed my supposition that typical students in required courses acquire meaningful knowledge when priority is given to the conceptual aspects of language.

There are other possibilities, of course. Many students learn better when new concepts are presented in a mechanical way, and many have an easier time memorizing 50 vocabulary words than learning a single grammatical rule applicable to thousands of cases. As we know, learners' strategies are different. So a teacher wishing to individualize a required language course could be prepared to present the same material in both conceptual and mechanical ways, and allow individual students to learn and be evaluated according to the process most meaningful to them. Valid, although different, insights about language can be gained through both approaches. The main point is that required language courses ought to have carefully limited objectives and priorities, and that a knowledge of linguistic analysis-- specifically the ability to identify productive and nonproductive knowledge, and conceptual and mechanical rules--is of even greater benefit in designing a required course than a conventional one.

LANGUAGE TEACHING IS NOT LINGUISTICS

GLADYS E. SAUNDERS

The University of Michigan

Before attempting to answer the questions raised by the moderator, I would like to make a few additional comments. First, foreign language teaching is not linguistics, and there

is no reason why it should be. Second, in spite of all the
dissension among linguists and language teachers, people still
learn languages--some better, and more proficiently than others,
doubtlessly. And third, shifts in linguistic, psychological,
and pedagogical concepts affect the popularity of a successful
method.

Considering the last issue first--Anthony and Norris 1969
discuss this in detail--one might say that as our basic feelings
about language shift, i.e. as our own belief about the nature
of language changes, so does our notion about what it means to
acquire, or to teach a language; and our faith in a particular
method is altered accordingly. If, for example, we view
language as a skill like typing or swimming, then our feelings
about how a language is learned or taught will differ from those
who regard language as an ability like walking or standing.
Thus, our attitude toward language plays a considerable role in
the success of pedagogical methods.

In reference to my first comment--foreign language teaching is
not linguistics, and there is no reason why it should be--I
would like to call forth three ways in which a language (foreign
or native) may be studied. These are not new, and are familiar
to all of us (see Anthony and Norris 1969, and references
therein). First, there is the 'training' approach. The person
who desires to gain native competence in a language because his
means of survival in a particular society depends on his speaking
and understanding the language of the society, would study
language in this way. Second, there is the 'literature'
approach. The person who is interested in the poetic or literary
value of language, who, by creating or criticizing artistic
works, hopes to arrive at a wider understanding of the meaning
of life, would study language in this way. Third, there is the
'linguistics' approach. The person who is interested in gaining
insights into the way language works, who is curious about its
peculiarities, who wants to know more about its geographical,
temporal or social spread, would study language in this way.

Obviously, these three ways of approaching language study
are not mutually exclusive, and the attempt to draw distinct
lines between them has led to confusion among language teachers
and linguists. After all, the language teacher and the linguist
are both interested in some of the same questions, for example,
language structures. We must identify our goals, and pursue
the direction or approach that allows us to meet the established
goals. If our goal is to train students to become proficient
in a foreign language, then the best method is the one that will
allow us to present the material to the students in the most
appropriate way so that they will be able to communicate in the
target language. Ideally, the linguist concerned with
describing how languages work can give the language teacher
(who should be informed to some degree on current linguistic
theories) insights into particular language structures. But it
is up to the language teacher (presumably well versed in
pedagogical and psychological matters, and fully competent in
the target language) to evaluate the pronouncements of the
linguist, to reject that which has little applicable value. In

short, some of the research currently underway in theoretical
linguistics may be useful to the foreign language teacher.
Whether it is useful in the classroom is of course another
matter, to be determined by the sound judgment of the language
teacher (not the linguist).

To return to the questions asked by the moderator, I would say
that the field of generative semantics appears to be a promising
one for the language teacher. Some of the current notions and
concepts concerning 'meaningful learning', 'situational contexts',
etc. will probably prove to have very positive effects on
language pedagogy. The work of John Oller, under the label of
pragmatics, seems particularly promising. Stress on languages
as a social phenomenon, and the contributions of the socio-
linguists and bilingual specialists also promise to be helpful
to the language teacher and to the materials-development
specialist.

   I find little applicability for most of the other relatively
recent linguistic theories, especially generative phonology. I
recently read two opposing views on the application of generative
phonology to the teaching of pronunciation. On the one hand,
Hammerly 1973 presents a case against the application of
generative phonology, on theoretical grounds. Generative
phonology, according to him, is 'complex, anti-behavioristic,
computer-like, and abstract'. His conclusion is that it can be
practically applied in only a very limited way. On the other
hand, Schnitzer 1974 presents a favorable case for the
applicability of generative phonology to the teaching of English
pronunciation. By taking the abstract model described by
Chomsky & Halle 1968, Schnitzer devised a set of rules which
would allow a person to correct his pronunciation. He first
worked with an aphasiac--a biology teacher, who had developed
phonemic paraphasia as a result of other illnesses. He assumed
that her mispronunciations were due to faulty underlying
representations and incorrect rule applications. The patient
with whom Schnitzer was working died before he was able to
complete his work; but he continued his research in a pilot
project. In the pilot project, he attempted to teach English
pronunciation to native speakers of French by rule, rather than
by rote. (Their mispronunciations were similar to those of the
aphasiac.) His results, which I find unconvincing, claim to
indicate an improvement in the pronunciation of the French
speakers who participated in the pilot project. Rather than
have his subjects memorize pronunciations of words, he required
them to memorize abstract phonological rules!

WRITTEN COMMENTS SUBMITTED BY PARTICIPANTS

EUGENE FONG

The University of Michigan

After some two decades of activity, the era of linguistics
applied to language teaching has come to rest. The halt in
activity on this tack is due to several reasons. Probably the
most important is the particular situation of 'applied
linguistics'. It is an *enfant naturel* claimed by neither
linguist nor pedagogue. Moreover, there are even linguists who
do not believe in it. For example, Selinker and Wardhaugh admit
that the concerns of the theoretical linguist are not relative
to language teaching, and hence, that linguistics is not
applicable in the classroom. Many pedagogues would agree, for
linguistics in itself does not constitute a methodology of
language teaching. They would believe that linguists who delve
into this domain have encroached upon a territory about which
they know little. Witness the failure of the audio-lingual
method--the creation of the linguist--and the reservations and
the criticisms which contrastive analysis has encountered. A
further attestation to the failure of applied linguistics is
the startling paucity of linguistically oriented textbooks which
incorporate the results of linguistic research. Some of the few
extant linguistically oriented textbooks are either so
complicated in notation that it would require a linguist to
teach or to learn from them, or they confuse levels of language
and teach both the standard and the colloquial dialects as
though they were one and the same. The remaining texts, the
truly good ones, are small in number.
    To resurrect the issue of linguistics applied to language
teaching is short of beating a dead horse. I do not, however,
wish to denigrate or to deny the importance of linguistics as
part of the baggage of the teacher. Although it has not resulted
in a new methodology, linguistics has contributed significantly
to the selection and organization of the units of the language
and to the manner in which they are taught and tested. A
linguistic orientation has succeeded in establishing a hierarchy
of goals which the language learner should attain, the most
important being to speak and understand the language (to learn
to master the language per se), and less importantly, to read
and to write it (to master the system of symbols used to
represent the noises of that language).
    Through the study of phonetics, we have arrived at an accurate
description of the segmentals and suprasegmentals of language.
Phonetic descriptions are made in concrete terms, i.e.
according to point and manner of articulation, as opposed to
impressionistic ones which abound in textbooks of traditional
orientations. Indeed, in non-linguistic texts, the phonetics
of a language is treated, if at all, only in cursory fashion.

The recognition of the primacy of the spoken language has resulted in the treatment of phonetics at the elementary levels. The field of linguistics has created teaching materials which present a language systematically and which give due attention to points of real difficulty. It has also made available a variety of drills which facilitate the task of the learner. Other methods, in particular, the direct method, require spending valuable classroom time in order to allow the student first to formulate a rule and then to internalize it. Moreover, the teacher is obliged to utilize much of the time providing the students with examples. The time is much better spent having the students practice the language. After all, the student, and not the teacher, is the one who needs the practice.

Although applied linguistics has not enjoyed the success which it perhaps has deserved, no one can deny the impact and the contributions which it has made to foreign language teaching. The instructor whose training includes the study of linguistics surely has an advantage over the one who lacks it and is surely better equipped to teach. Let me conclude by saying that I would rather have a linguistically trained non-native speaker than a linguistically naive native speaker teach me a foreign language.

MARTHA KRIEG

The University of Michigan

I may be prejudiced by having recently taught two poor sections of elementary Spanish, but it seems to me that we as teachers are reaping the results of mis-applied linguistics in the high school teaching of English grammar as well as of foreign languages. Many of my students are not only disinterested in learning a foreign language, but are severely handicapped in doing so by an absolute lack of even elementary understanding of basic standard grammatical terms as they refer to English or to any other language. This is partly due to secondary school teaching of Chomsky-ite trees which do not lead to command of a practical vocabulary and comprehension of surface structure. We are faced with people who do not know what pronouns or direct and indirect objects are, and who are thus unequipped to learn any language taught analytically. I have my own doubts about whether they are equipped efficiently to derive their own analysis of language presented in a non-analytical manner.

MARIO PARREAGUIRRE

World Bank, Washington, D.C.

First, a practical knowledge of phonology of the language being taught is certainly helpful. For example, demonstrating by articulatory procedures how to *produce* an /i/ and then go to /ü/ in French without resorting to the explanation 'high rounded front vowel' is indeed helpful to the student. The same is true of grammar. Second, we should be careful in stressing the fact that linguistics is not about language teaching. Third, a *practical* knowledge of the application of linguistics to language teaching may be helpful to teachers. But linguistic terminology should be out of the field of language teaching.

DOROTHY A. RISSEL

Indiana University

Rather than use the term 'applied linguistics', I will address myself to the question of the place of linguistics in the language classroom. In my crew, the teacher is the one who should know something about linguistic theory for the purpose of giving students a good explanation of the grammar. It is the task of the teacher however to simplify his knowledge of the structures of the language so that the students can learn what they need to know to function properly within the language. The teacher also needs to know something about the student's native language to draw parallels that will facilitate learning. The error in the past has often been to try to teach linguistic theory along with the language, rather than use the insights from linguistics to aid the learner and to structure the learning situation.

JUDITH SCARPELLA-WALLS

Western Kentucky University

I suppose that my sustained enthusiasm even at the eve of the last day of the Symposium may be due in part to the fact that

since the fall of 1972 I have been teaching part-time at a
university which was once a teacher-training institution and is
still dominated by a large group of education professors. The
person who teaches 'applied linguistics' is first and foremost
an education professor and incidentally a Spanish professor.
He teaches methodology to all our student teachers (French,
German, Russian, Spanish) but does not know the languages
except some Spanish and is not a linguist. Therefore, aside
from my husband who is a trained Romance linguist (Ph.D.
Cornell), I don't have anyone with whom to discuss theories of
acquisition, application of TG to language analyses, etc.

I am also still quite excited about just being here, and I'm
not quite sure why I read the only paper dealing primarily with
pedagogical problems. I had to pay my own way here (or I
should say my husband earns extra money testing Rumanian at Kent
State so I can have a career) or I would not have come.

About the panel discussion: As I said to Ms. Saunders, most
of us in the room have had linguistic training and whether or
not we teach language courses, I think it is clear that we
would prefer to continue to assume that the study of language in
general is an important part of a foreign language teacher's
preparation and that this same teacher should be familiar with
linguistic developments in his or her particular language and
language family and also possess a high degree of competence in
the language taught.

Someone said I was courageous to give a pedagogical paper at
this kind of symposium, but I feel comfortable with this group
of linguists and the panel made me feel even more at ease. I
think we need to continue to include forums for discussions of
the question of language acquisition at future symposia. I
want to know how the theoretical linguists feel and I hope they
are interested enough in the teaching of languages to come.
They seemed to be tonight.

I want to express my gratitude at having had the opportunity
to attend the symposium. It took me five years to muster up
the courage to talk to a lot of the people who are here who up
until now have only been names in lecture notes or authors of
journal articles and books. I don't think it will be hard from
now on. Thank you.

REFERENCES

Agard, F. B. and R. Di Pietro. 1965a. The grammatical
  structures of English and Italian. Chicago: University of
  Chicago Press.
_____. 1965b. The sounds of English and Italian. Chicago:
  University of Chicago Press.
Alatis, J. E. (ed.) 1968. Report of the nineteenth annual
  round table meeting on linguistics and language studies:
  contrastive linguistics and its pedagogical implications.
  Washington, D.C.: Georgetown University Press.

Anthony, E. M. and W. E. Norris. 1969. Method in language teaching. ERIC Focus Report No.8. (Reprinted in Readings on English as a second language, ed. by K. Croft [1972], 39-48).

Belasco, S. and A. Valdman. 1961. Applied linguistics: French; a guide for teachers. Boston: D. C. Heath.
_____ and S. Cárdenas. 1961. Applied linguistics: Spanish; a guide for teachers. Boston: D. C. Heath.
_____ and A. Valdman. 1965. College French in the new key. Boston: D. C. Heath.

Bloch, B. and G. L. Trager. 1942. Outline of linguistic analysis. Baltimore, Md.: Linguistic Society of America.

Bolinger, D. 1968. The theorist and the language teacher. Foreign Language Annals 2.30-41.

Brooks, N. 1960. Language and language learning: theory and practice. New York: Harcourt, Brace and World.

Brown, T. G. 1971. Pedagogical implication of a case grammar of French. IRAL 9.229-44.

Bull, W. and E. E. Lamadrid. 1971. Our grammar rules are hurting us. Modern Language Journal 55.449-54.

Chomsky, N. 1966. Linguistic theory. Northeast Conference on the teaching of foreign languages: language teaching; broader context, ed. by R. G. Mead, Jr., 43-9. Menasha, Wis.: G. Banta Co.

Chomsky, N. and M. Halle. 1968. The sound pattern of English. N.Y.: Harper and Row.

Corder, S. P. 1967. The significance of learner's errors. IRAL 5.161-70.
_____. 1973. Introducing applied linguistics. Baltimore, Md.: Penguin Books.

Desberg, D. and L. Kenan. 1964. Modern French. N.Y.: Harcourt, Brace and World.

Di Pietro, R. 1971. Language structures in contrast. Rowley, Mass.: Newbury House.

Dingwall, W. O. 1964. Transformational-generative grammar and contrastive analysis. Language Learning 14.147-60.

Finocchiaro, M. 1964. English as a second language: theory and practice. N.Y.: Regents.

Hall, R. A., Jr. 1949. Structural sketches: I; French. Language Monograph 24, Language 24:3.

Hammerly, H. 1973. Teaching pronunciation and generative phonology. Foreign Language Annals 6.487-9.

Hanzeli, V.E. 1968. Linguistics and the language teacher. Foreign Language Annals 2.42-50.

Jackson, K. and R. Whitman. (ed.) 1971. The PCCLLU [Pacific Conference on Contrastive Linguistics and Language Universals] papers. Honolulu: University of Hawaii Press.

Jakobovits, L. A. 1970. Foreign language learning: a psycholinguistic analysis of the issues. Rowley, Mass.: Newbury House.

Kufner, H. L. 1962. The grammatical structures of English and German. Chicago: University of Chicago Press.

Lado, R. 1957. Linguistics across cultures. Ann Arbor, Mich.: University of Michigan Press.

_____. 1964. Language teaching: a scientific approach.
    N.Y.: McGraw-Hill.
Lotito, B. A. 1975. Theory and practice: presuppositions in
    Spanish *si*-clauses and related constructions. Bloomington:
    Indiana University dissertation.
Moulton, W. 1962. The sounds of English and German. Chicago:
    University of Chicago Press.
Nickel, G. (ed.) 1974. Proceedings: third congress,
    Association internationale de linguistique appliquée. Vol.
    1: applied contrastive linguistics. Heidelberg: Julius
    Groos.
Oller, J. W., Jr. 1972. Contrastive analysis, difficulty, and
    predictability. Foreign Language Annals 6.95-106.
Pap, L. 1972. What do we mean by applied linguistics?
    Studies in language and linguistics, ed. by Ewton and
    Ornstein. Austin: University of Texas Press.
Politzer, R. L. 1953. Pedagogical training for our Ph.D.'s.
    French Review 27.;36-8.
_____. 1960. Teaching French: an introduction to applied
    linguistics. Waltham, Mass.: Blaisdell.
_____ and C. Staubach. 1961. Teaching Spanish: a linguistic
    orientation. Waltham, Mass.: Blaisdell.
_____. 1972. Linguistics and applied linguistics: aims and
    methods. Philadelphia: Center for Curriculum Development.
Pulgram, E. 1954. Preparation for language teaching. Applied
    linguistics in language teaching: Georgetown University
    Monograph series on language and linguistics, 6, ed. by
    E. Pulgram, 75-85. Georgetown: Georgetown University Press.
Quinn, T. J. 1974. Theoretical foundations in linguistics and
    related areas. Responding to new realities, ed. by
    G. A. Jarvis, 329-53. Skokie, Ill.: National Textbook
    Co.
Ritchie, W. 1967. Some implications of generative grammar
    for the construction of courses in English as a foreign
    language. Language Learning 17.
Saporta, S. 1966. Applied linguistics and generative grammar.
    Trends in language teaching, ed. by A. Valdman, 81-92.
    N.Y.: McGraw-Hill.
Schnitzer, M. L. 1974. Applied generative phonology: a
    methodology for teaching pronunciation. IRAL 12.289-306.
Svobodny, D. D. 1971. The foreign language requirement in
    colleges and universities: a bibliography with abstracts.
    New York: Modern Language Association.
Stockwell, R. and J. Bowen. 1965. The sounds of English and
    Spanish. Chicago: University of Chicago Press.
_____, J. Bowen and J. Martin. 1965. The grammatical
    structures of English and Spanish. Chicago: University of
    Chicago Press.
Wardhaugh, R. 1970. The contrastive analysis hypothesis.
    TESOL Quarterly 4.123-30.
Whitman, R. L. and K. L. Jackson. 1972. The unpredictability
    of contrastive analysis. Language Learning 22.29-42.

PROGRAM

THURDSAY, MARCH 20

MORNING

8:15	Registration
9:00	Opening Remarks

Billy E. Frye, Acting Dean, College of
  Literature, Arts and Science
Peter Hagiwara, Chairman, LSRL-V

9:20-10:30   Chairman: Servio T. Becerra

THE HEURISTICS OF SUBSTRATUM. Dieter Wanner,
  University of Illinois
THE 'AUX' IN ROMANCE. Frederick B. Agard,
  Cornell University

10:45-12:30   Chairman: Larry L. Dishman

LUSITANIAN PORTUGUESE [ɐ] IS [+ATR] AND [+CP].
  Wayne J. Redenbarger, *Boston University*
PARADIGMATIC EVOLUTION OF DIPHTHONGS: MARSIAN
  ITALIAN AND CHICANO SPANISH. Mario
  Saltarelli, *University of Illinois*

ASPECTS OF SPANISH VERB MORPHOLOGY. James W.
Harris, *Massachusetts Institute of Technology*

AFTERNOON

2:00-3:00   PRE-LATIN LANGUAGES AND SOUND CHANGES IN
ROMANCE: THE CASE OF OLD SPANISH /h-/.
Herbert J. Izzo, *University of Calgary.*
Introduced by Lawrence B. Kiddle

3:20-4:20   GENDER, SEX, AND SIZE, AS REFLECTED IN THE
ROMANCE LANGUAGES. Yakov Malkiel, *University
of California at Berkeley.* Introduced by
Ernst Pulgram

EVENING

7:30-9:30   Reception

Frank P. Casa, Chairman, Department of Romance
Languages

FRIDAY, MARCH 21

MORNING

8:45-10:30   Chairman: Eugene A. Fong

SUPERFICIALLY ILLOGICAL 'NON'. Donna Jo
Napoli and Marina Nespor, *University of
North Carolina*
THE EVOLUTION OF VARIABLE RULES: A CASE OF
LEXICAL CONSTRAINTS. John Reighard,
Université de Montréal
OBLIGATORY VERSUS OPTIONAL RULES IN PEDAGOGICAL
TEXTS: THE PARTITIVE CONSTRUCTION IN
ITALIAN. Judith Scarpella-Walls, *Western
Kentucky University*

10:45-12:30   Chairman: Jean-Jacques Thomas

TRUNCATION AND NASALIZATION IN MARAIS VENDÉEN
FRENCH. Yves Charles Morin, *Université de
Montréal*
VOCALIC ALTERNATION IN THE SPANISH VERB: A
REANALYSIS. David Nasjleti, *Harvard
University*
QUANTIFIERS AND AMBIGUITY: LOOKING ACROSS
DERIVATIONS. Jean Casagrande and Linda
Jackson, *University of Florida*

AFTERNOON

2:00-3:00   ON THE STRUCTURE AND DEVELOPMENT OF CREOLE
                FRENCH DIALECTS. Albert Valdman, *Indiana
                University*. Introduced by Raleigh Morgan,
                Jr.

3:20-4:20   ROMANCE LINGUISTICS: WHENCE AND WHITHER?
                Robert A. Hall, Jr., *Cornell University*.
                Introduced by Clifford S. Leonard

EVENING

7:30-9:30   PANEL DISCUSSION: THE ROLE OF APPLIED
                LINGUISTICS IN THE TEACHING OF ROMANCE
                LANGUAGES. Moderator: Peter Hagiwara.
                Panel Members: H. Douglas Brown, *The
                University of Michigan*, E. Dean Detrich,
                Michigan State University, Mark Goldin,
                Indiana University, and Gladys Saunders,
                The University of Michigan

SATURDAY, MARCH 22

MORNING

8:45-10:30   Chairman, Gladys E. Saunders

                COMPLICATION IN OLD FRENCH PHONOLOGY.
                Douglas C. Walker, *University of Ottawa*
                ON COMPLEXITY AND EXPLANATIONS IN LINGUISTIC
                CHANGE. Beban Chumbow, *Indiana University*
                RHOTACISM IN LATIN: PHONOLOGICAL OR
                MORPHOLOGICAL RULE? Jurgen Klausenburger,
                University of Washington

10:45-11:20   Chairman: Yves M. Verret

                IS THE USE OF MOOD IN SPANISH SUBJECT TO
                VARIABLE CONSTRAINTS? Tracy D. Terrell,
                University of California at Irvine and
                Mary Ellen García, *Georgetown University*

ORGANIZING COMMITTEE

Michio Peter Hagiwara, Chairman
Servio T. Becerra
Lawrence B. Kiddle
Clifford S. Leonard
Raleigh Morgan, Jr.
Ernst Pulgram
Jean-Jacques Thomas
David L. Wolfe

SELECTION COMMITTEE

Michio Peter Hagiwara, Chairman
Jean Casagrande, *University of Florida*
William Cressey, *Georgetown University*
Mark Goldin, *Indiana University*
Lawrence B. Kiddle, *The University of Michigan*
Clifford S. Leonard, *The University of Michigan*
David L. Wolfe, *The University of Michigan*